D1617138

Other titles in Modern Intellectual and Political History of the Middle East

*Algeria and France, 1800–2000: Identity, Memory, Nostalgia*
    Patricia M. E. Lorcin
*Britain and the Iranian Constitutional Revolution of 1906–1911: Foreign Policy,*
*Imperialism, and Dissent*
    Mansour Bonakdarian
*Class and Labor in Iran: Did the Revolution Matter?*
    •Farhad Nomani and Sohrab Behdad
*Democracy and Civil Society in Arab Political Thought: Transcultural Possibilities*
    Michaelle L. Browers
*Globalization and the Muslim World: Culture, Religion, and Modernity*
    Birgit Schaebler and Leif Stenberg, eds.
*In the Path of Hizbullah*
    A. Nizar Hamzeh
*The Kurds and the State: Evolving National Identity in Iraq, Turkey, and Iran*
    Denise Natali
*The Politics of Public Memory in Turkey*
    Esra Özyürek, ed.
*Quest for Divinity: A Critical Examination of the Thought of Mahmud Muhammad Taha*
    Mohamed A. Mahmoud
*Religion, Society, and Modernity in Turkey*
    Şerif Mardin

# The Urban Social History of the

# Middle East, 1750-1950

*Edited by*

# PETER SLUGLETT

SYRACUSE UNIVERSITY PRESS

Copyright © 2008 by Syracuse University Press
Syracuse, New York 13244-5160
All Rights Reserved

First Edition 2008
08  09  10  11  12  13        6  5  4  3  2  1

Mohamad El-Hindi Books on Arab Culture and Islamic Civilization are published
with the assistance of a grant from the M.E.H. Foundation.

The paper used in this publication meets the minimum requirements of
American National Standard for Information Sciences—Permanence of Paper
for Printed Library Materials, ANSI Z39.48–1984.∞™

For a listing of books published and distributed by Syracuse University Press,
visit our Web site at SyracuseUniversityPress.syr.edu.

ISBN-13: 978-0-8156-3194-1 (cloth)
ISBN-10: 0-8156-3194-4 (cloth)

**Library of Congress Cataloging-in-Publication Data**
The urban social history of the Middle East, 1750–1950 / edited
by Peter Sluglett. — 1st ed.
p. cm. — (Modern intellectual and political history of the Middle East)
Includes bibliographical references and index.
ISBN 978-0-8156-3194-1 (cloth : alk. paper)
1. Cities and towns—Middle East—History.   2. Urbanization—Middle
East—History.   3. Middle East—History.   I. Sluglett, Peter.
HT147.M53U73 2008
307.760956—dc22
2008034043

*Manufactured in the United States of America*

# Contents

# Tables

# *Preface*

❧ I AM DELIGHTED, and somewhat amazed, that this book at last seems inexorably bound to reach the reading public. There were dark days, dark months, even dark years, when its appearance seemed to hang in the balance, and I am more than grateful to all the contributors, who greeted each further delay with a combination of equanimity and resignation, as well as with a measure of kindly sympathy.

My own interest in Middle Eastern cities dates back to my first visit to the region, at the end of my first year as an undergraduate in the summer of 1963. I took a train from London to Istanbul and then went on by bus and train to Syria, which I entered from Bab al-Hawwa, arriving in Aleppo late in the evening. Sitting in one of the open-air cafés under the citadel a few days later—and with a few weeks in Turkey already behind me—I realized I had found something I had not quite known that I was looking for: I had always wanted to be a historian, and I had toyed with working on Italy (which I had visited) and on Central America (which I had not). After Aleppo, I knew that I would work on the Middle East. Whether this decision was wise, or brave, or foolhardy is difficult to say: it is a choice that I have never regretted and one that has brought extraordinary richness to my life.

When I first came to Aleppo and, to a greater extent, when I returned to the city with a more informed understanding of what I was looking at, I was profoundly excited by the suqs, the mosques, the citadel, the streets of the *medina,* and the magnificent mansions of the wealthy, both in the historic center and in the outer quarters. I had the great good fortune to get to know many families in the city, to visit them in their homes, and to understand the history of Syria and the complexities of its present politics through long conversations with them. I also remember wonderful excursions to the countryside, to Kurd Dagh, and to Qala'at Sam'an.

I had taught Middle Eastern history for several years before starting to think thematically about the social history of cities. In the late 1980s, I began to work on the history of Aleppo in the late nineteenth and early twentieth centuries, but other preoccupations have meant that the monograph that I still intend to write has so far eluded me. Like most of my contemporaries, I was profoundly influenced by the work of the two great pioneers of the study of the Islamic court records, André Raymond and Abdul-Karim Rafeq, the latter one of the loyal and patient contributors to this volume. Over the last twenty-odd years, I have attended a number of conferences with Raymond and Rafeq, and have had the great good fortune to get to know them in both academic and social contexts.

I am enormously grateful to those who have made this book possible. First and foremost, obviously, I must thank the contributors, who have stayed the course, updated their texts and bibliographies, endured different bibliographical regimes, and in some cases rewritten their chapters completely. I would like to thank Edmund Burke III, who suggested the project in the first place and kindly agreed to write part of the introduction.

Second, it is a great pleasure to thank Mary Selden Evans of Syracuse University Press, and Mehrzad Boroujerdi, the editor of SUP's series on the Modern Intellectual and Political History of the Middle East. Both were enthusiastic about the project when it was first submitted to them and encouraged me to bring it to fruition. I am especially grateful to Julie DuSablon, whose editorial skills and attention to matters of detail and consistency are truly extraordinary.

Third, I should like to thank the Warden and Fellows of All Souls' College, Oxford, for awarding me a Visiting Fellowship for the Hilary and Trinity terms in 2003, during which I was able to write most of the introduction in extremely congenial surroundings.

Fourth, I would like to thank my colleagues Harris Lenowitz and Peter von Sivers at the University of Utah for their careful reading of the introduction and their many valuable comments, most of which I have incorporated. I am also extremely grateful to Stefan Weber for his speedy assistance in devising a memorable cover for the book and for his friendship in many other ways.

Finally, I would like to thank my family. My stepchildren on both sides of the Atlantic have been more or less aware of this project for a long time, and have expressed only occasional skepticism about my capacity to "produce it in the end." It is difficult for me to express sufficient gratitude to Shohreh, who has indirectly absorbed more about the travails of editing a book than she could ever have imagined. More important, she has brought both excitement and contentment into my life with her unique amalgam of volatility, serenity, and solicitude. *Merci, azizam.*

# Contributors

EDMUND BURKE III is director of the Center for World History at the University of California at Santa Cruz, where he teaches Middle East and North African history, Mediterranean history and world history. He is the co-editor of *Genealogies of Orientalism: History, Politics, Theory* and *The Environment and World History, 1750–2000*.

LEILA FAWAZ is founding director of the Fares Center for Eastern Mediterranean Studies and Issam M. Fares Professor of Lebanese and Eastern Mediterranean Studies at Tufts University. She has published *Modernity and Culture from the Mediterranean to the Indian Ocean, An Occasion for War: Mount Lebanon and Damascus in 1860, State and Society in Lebanon*, and *Merchants and Migrants in Nineteenth Century Beirut*. Dr. Fawaz is currently working on the social history of the Levant in the late Ottoman period.

BERNARD HOURCADE is a geographer, formerly director of the French Institute of Iranian Studies in Tehran (1978–1993) and of the groupe de recherche "Monde Iranien." He is currently senior research fellow at Centre National de la Recherce Scientifique (Paris). He works on the political and cultural geography of Iran and on the city of Tehran. His most recent work (with Seyyed-Mohsen Habibi) is an *Atlas of Tehran Metropolis*.

ROBERT ILBERT is professor of history and director of the Maison Méditerranéenne des Sciences de l'Homme at the Université de Provence at Aix-en-Provence. His publications include *Héliopolis: Le Caire 1905–1922—genèse d'une ville* and *Alexandrie 1830–1930: Histoire d'une communauté citadine*.

DINA RIZK KHOURY is associate professor of history and international affairs at George Washington University. She is author of *State and Provincial Society in the*

*Ottoman Empire: Mosul 1540–1834* as well as several articles on Ottoman Iraq. She is currently working on a book on war and remembrance in modern Iraq.

GUDRUN KRÄMER is professor of Islamic studies at Freie Universität Berlin, a member of the Berlin-Brandenburg Academy of Sciences, and one of the executive editors of the third edition of the *Encyclopaedia of Islam*. She has published extensively on Middle Eastern history, Islamic movements, and Islamic political thought.

ABDUL-KARIM RAFEQ holds the William and Annie Bickers Professorship in Arab Middle Eastern Studies at the College of William and Mary in Virginia. He was formerly professor of Modern Arab History and chairman of the Department of History in the University of Damascus. His most recent book is *The History of the Syrian University, 1901–1946* (in Arabic).

SARAH D. SHIELDS is associate professor of history at the University of North Carolina, Chapel Hill. She has worked on the Arab provinces of the Ottoman Empire in the last century of the Ottoman Empire and has published *Mosul before Iraq, Like Bees Making Five-Sided Cells*. Her current research explores the creation of national identities in the Middle East in the decades between the two world wars.

PETER SLUGLETT is professor of Middle Eastern History at the University of Utah, Salt Lake City. He taught at Durham University for nineteen years before moving permanently to the United States in 1994. He is co-author of *Iraq since 1958: From Revolution to Dictatorship* and author of *Britain in Iraq: Contriving King and Country*, about the British occupation and mandate. He has co-edited (with Nadine Méouchy) a volume on the British and French mandates in the Middle East.

SAMI ZUBAIDA is emeritus professor of politics and sociology, Birkbeck College, London University, and has held visiting positions in Cairo, Istanbul, Berkeley, Paris, and New York. He has written and lectured widely on religion, culture, law, and politics in the Middle East and on food and culture. His works include *Islam, the People and the State, A Taste of Thyme: Culinary Cultures of the Middle East* (co-edited with Richard Tapper), and *Law and Power in the Islamic World*.

# The Urban Social History
## of the Middle East,
### 1750–1950

# *1*

# *Introduction*

## PETER SLUGLETT WITH EDMUND BURKE III

 URBAN SOCIAL HISTORY is one of the most fruitful and exciting areas of enquiry in the contemporary historiography of the Middle East. The opening up and utilization of Islamic court records and Ottoman administrative documents over the past few decades has greatly changed the parameters of our knowledge of the cities of the Middle East and North Africa between the seventeenth and early twentieth centuries, and in particular of the major cities of the region. The present work attempts to review the state of the art in this field in a number of different areas and is directed primarily toward an audience of historians and other social scientists seeking a background on the state of the literature on urbanism in the Arab Middle East.[1]

The statement that Islam is an "urban religion" may raise as many questions as it answers, but it is certainly the case that, with its institutionalization over the early centuries, it became a commonplace that "the good Islamic life" could be lived more to the full within cities than outside them.[2] The "other-

---

Pages 1–15 and 25–42 are by Peter Sluglett, pages 15–25 by Edmund Burke. Peter Sluglett would like to thank Harris Lenowitz and Peter von Sivers for their comments.

1. The most recent bibliography of the field is Bonine et al. 1994.

2. In the context of a discussion comparing rural and urban Islam in the Ottoman period, Bruce Masters states that "it was perhaps only in the Ottoman cities that Islam was practiced in its more recognizable, contemporary form. There the Ottoman sultans sought to promote a state-sponsored version of Islam, preached by men who were graduates of state-supervised

1

worldly" ethos generally characteristic of Christian monasticism, in both its anchoritic Near Eastern and its communal or "Benedictine" versions,[3] had no widespread echoes or equivalents in Islam. Like the yeshiva, the madrasa, when it appeared in Islamic cities in the eleventh century, functioned more as an academic than as a contemplative institution, whose members either had, or would have when they graduated, family and social lives very similar to those of the rest of the urban community around them.[4] Again, cities contain two of the major normative establishments of Islamic society, the Friday mosque and the law court. Prayer is a corporate, social act, not invalidated, certainly, if performed in private or in isolation, but somehow more "pleasing to God" if performed in public. The title of an article by Baber Johansen, "The All-Embracing Town and Its Mosques" (1981a), conveys this sense particularly well. As far as the law courts are concerned, a very large numbers of the studies examined in the following pages are based on the mass of records that they generated after the Ottoman conquest in the early sixteenth century.

The two hundred years between 1750 and 1950 have been selected as the beginning and end points of this book largely for pragmatic reasons. First, for much of the eighteenth century, as Abraham Marcus says, we are "on the eve of modernity" (Marcus 1989), and thus in many important ways, "still" able to examine societies which, though by no means functioning in isolation, had yet to experience the cataclysmic changes they would undergo in the nineteenth. Second, at the other end of the time period, the revolutions in the Middle East in the 1950s, and the general lack of access to contemporary documentary materials that followed them, has made it difficult to carry out *historical* studies on cities after that time.[5]

In general, then, cities in the Arab Middle East and North Africa have long attracted the attention and interest of historians, although a good deal of earlier

---

seminaries and paid salaries from the sultans' coffers *as urban Islam became institutionalized to a degree unknown before.*" Masters 2001, 27; italics added.

3. Christian monasteries in both East and West were often located in remote, sometimes barely accessible, rural areas.

4. In this connection, what were regarded as the "private" or "secret" aspects of Sufism attracted considerable suspicion for much of the classical period.

5. For studies of urban political anthropology, see Wikan 1980 and Singerman 1995.

writing on the topic tended to concentrate either on architecture and the built environment or on attempts to track down and identify the elusive notion of the "Islamic city." Although the first of these categories remains significant (Gaube and Wirth 1984; Escher and Wirth 1992; Marino 1997) the second has become somewhat passé, indicating as it does a quest for an essentialism that has ever diminishing relevance in a post-Orientalism world. "Middle Eastern cities," then, as far as this collection is concerned, are simply cities in the Middle East. Some of the cities discussed in this volume are of great antiquity, founded and flourishing as major centers of exchange long before the mid–eighteenth century; others may be able to date their foundation to a remote past, but owed their nineteenth- or twentieth-century prosperity to a combination of their geographical location and sets of specific socioeconomic conjunctures.

As far as the geographical and scholarly coverage of the volume is concerned, it has been decided to concentrate mainly on the Arab Middle East, that is, Egypt and the Fertile Crescent, and because it is intended primarily as an introduction to the field for nonspecialists, on publications in English, French, and German. Some of the contributors have special interests outside the core area and have thus been able to introduce a broader perspective. Readers may wonder why Anatolia/"Turkey" has not been covered more thoroughly; although a good deal of interesting work has been done for earlier centuries,[6] there do not appear to be any substantial studies of Turkish cities for the period on which this volume is focused.[7]

Thus, the principal concern of this volume is urban social history, the dynamics, sometimes apparently static, sometimes obviously changing, of urban life. The period under study forms an intersection or transition between the last century and a half of the Ottoman Empire and the beginnings, here

6. The list is impressive: see Çanbakal 2006 on seventeenth-century 'Aintab, Ergene 2003 on Çankırı and Kastamonu in the seventeenth and early eighteenth centuries, Faroqhi 1984 and 1987 on seventeenth- and eighteenth-century Ankara and Kayseri, Gerber 1988 on seventeenth-century Bursa, Greene 2000 on late seventeenth- and early eighteenth-century Crete, and the many important articles on Anatolia and Cyprus by Jennings, especially those collected in Jennings 1999.

7. A possible exception here is Çelik's study of nineteenth-century Istanbul (Çelik 1993), although the author, an architectural historian, is more interested in the development of the built environment than in urban social history.

earlier, there later, of sustained European economic and political influence and, in some places, control. The principal focus is the nineteenth century, a time of far-reaching change at all levels in the Ottoman Empire. It was also the period when many Western European nations began to focus increasing attention on their near neighbors in the Mediterranean and the Middle East, assessing the potential of these areas both as sources of agricultural and other raw materials and as markets for European manufactured goods.

In the same way that the notion of an "Islamic city" has largely ceased to occupy the attention, or interest, of scholars over the past few decades,[8] attitudes toward the Ottoman period have also changed. In the introduction to his monograph on Aleppo, published in 1941, Jean Sauvaget has little time for the Ottoman period; he sees a thrusting, vigorous Europe overtaking an "Islam" that has ceased to flourish "comme frappé de sclérose."[9] In contrast, in *Les grandes villes arabes à l'époque ottomane*, published in 1985,[10] and in other books and articles, André Raymond has drawn attention to the dramatic growth experienced by most of the major Arab cities in the Ottoman Empire between the sixteenth and eighteenth centuries, both in terms of spatial extent and of population. It is clear from evidence both of commercial and manufacturing activity, and of the scale and number of religious endowments initiated under the Ottomans, that these centuries can no longer be regarded, or accurately described, as a period of unremitting economic decline.[11] It also

8. For a summary of recent writing, see Eickelman 1974; al-Azmeh 1976; K. Brown 1986; Chevallier 1986; Abu-Lughod 1987; Ellis Goldberg 1991; Raymond 1994a. See also chapter 6 by Hourcade.

9. Sauvaget 1941, 191: "En face d'une Europe toujours mieux outillé, toujours plus entreprenante et plus audacieuse, l'Empire ottoman se présente ainsi comme un État moralement divisé, affaibli dans sa structure économique comme dans son organisation administrative, amoindri dans sa force de résistance et à l'ingérence de l'étranger." For a similar mindset, see Longrigg 1925.

10. Parts of the book appeared a year earlier in English (Raymond 1984). For a summary of Raymond's notions of urban expansion under the Ottomans, see Raymond 1974 and 1979–80. He takes the increase in the numbers of public baths and fountains as indicators of spatial and population growth.

11. See, for example, Doumani 1995; D. Khoury 1997a; van Leeuwen 1999. For a convincing critique of the decline theory, see Quataert 2003.

emerges, again in contradiction to much of the received wisdom, that the bulk of the trade of, say, late eighteenth-century Ottoman Egypt, was with areas farther East—mostly Iran and India—(36 percent) and with other Ottoman provinces (50 percent), rather than with Europe (14 percent) (Raymond 1985, 44).

Another major topic of inquiry in the study of Middle Eastern and North African cities is the question of the changing nature and extent of the control exercised over the city by the central state.[12] In "Urban Life in Pre-Colonial North Africa," the Tunisian sociologists Stambouli and Zghal (1976) situated state/city relations on a continuum running between the more or less autonomous medieval Italian commune on the one hand, and on the other, the Chinese imperial city, which was completely controlled by the crown. Arab cities, or more accurately, the cities in early modern North Africa that feature in the article, are evidently somewhere near the Chinese end. As in early modern France, Portugal, and Spain, all senior appointments (such as, for example, governorships of provinces) were made by the central state, and appointees were constantly rotated, often with bewildering frequency.[13] In addition, the officials from Istanbul were often set apart from the local population during the Ottoman period by the fact that they spoke a different language. Thus in any given city most of the military and the upper bureaucracy tended to be outsiders, originating from other parts of the Empire, with no local roots, reflecting an attempt on the part of the state to prevent the officials making common cause with the people they had been appointed to rule.

Of course, it was not necessarily (if ever) the case that the local elites were any more solicitous of the welfare of their fellow townsmen simply because they were locals. During the long period of great disorder between the mid-1770s and the beginning of the nineteenth century,[14] when the central government lost control of Aleppo and several other provincial cities to members of

---

12. Dina Khoury discusses this topic in greater detail; see chapter 3.

13. For provincial administration in the Ottoman classical age, see Kunt 1983. Kamil al-Ghazzi (1926) lists the thirty-two governors appointed to Aleppo between 1850 and 1900—that is, at the height of the Tanzimat reforms.

14. At a time when the empire was also involved in a series of disastrous wars with Austria and Russia; see Thieck 1985.

the provincial elites, the seizure of power by local strongmen does not seem to have brought about any obvious improvements:

> The increase in the power of [the Janissaries and *ashraf*] was actually disad-
> vantageous to most of their fellow Aleppines, who in some respects suffered
> greater abuse than in the preceding period of effective Ottoman control.
> Unlike government officials, the local power figures worked from a perma-
> nent base in the community and an intimate knowledge of its inner working.
> They saw in their increased power a license to exploit the public rather than
> a civic responsibility to serve it. (Marcus 1989, 94)[15]

Stambouli and Zghal tried to calculate how much autonomy the urban population had in the politics and administration of the city, and in the organization of its economic, cultural, and religious activities. In terms of politics and
administration, while the urban notables may have played an important, often
crucial, role in the economy, they certainly did not enjoy "autonomy." In addition, they frequently became divided into factions who fought one another
for control over local resources; they only rarely challenged the state directly,
since they were dependent upon it for confirmation in their official positions.
On the other hand, as far as economic autonomy was concerned, local control
over the agricultural surplus[16] and over the day-to-day functioning of trade,
crafts, and manufacture through the guilds generally ensured that provided
the city or region paid something approximating to its prescribed tax liabilities
to the central state, the state would rarely interfere in the details of the city's
economic activities.

The same can also be said of cultural and religious activities, because these
generally conformed to the norms and ideological premises that the state itself
upheld and only rarely featured as matters of dispute between center and periphery. The state would nominate members of the local religious notability to the

---

15. Some provincial warlords of the late eighteenth and early nineteenth centuries such
as Zahir ʿUmar in Galilee and Ahmad Jazzar Pasha in Acre have been represented as proto-
nationalists, seeking freedom from Ottoman imperialism, but it is difficult to interpret their
motivation as other than personal gain.

16. For examples of partnerships between Ottoman officials and local merchants and
landowners in Mosul and Baghdad see D. Khoury 1997a and Fattah 1997.

posts of *mufti* and *naqib al-ashraf,* and lesser figures as imams in neighborhood
mosques or teachers in madrasas, and after the Ottoman state's takeover of
(Sunni) endowments in 1826 the salaries of religious officials were paid from the
central treasury.[17] For this and other reasons, the Sunni ulama generally tended
to act as legitimators of political power and the social order. In all spheres save
the narrowly political, therefore, the notables themselves were involved in the
reproduction of the system, so that the whole question of their relationship to
the state, and, even more broadly, the nature of the state itself, needs to be more
carefully conceptualized and defined.[18] Hourani's article on the notables of the
Arab Middle East in the nineteenth century (Hourani 1968), written forty years
ago, still serves as a starting point for studies concerned with relations between
Ottoman state and its provinces (P. Khoury 1990; Provence 2005, 6–8).

## European Urban Social History:
## A Note on the Literature

What follows is an attempt to examine some of the topics that have attracted
the attention of colleagues working on the postmedieval history of cities in
Europe (and in some European colonies) over the past few decades, because
this was the original focus of urban social history as a discrete field of study.
To aim at anything like comprehensiveness would be unrealistic, but it seems
worth trying to place the urban social history of the Middle East in the context
of at least part of the rest of the field.[19]

If we discount traditional histories of cities, written sometimes well, sometimes badly, by local antiquarians from the late eighteenth century onward,
what might be called the serious study of European (perhaps more specifically,
British) cities and their societies as discrete entities is generally agreed to have
been initiated by H. J. Dyos (1921–1978) at the University of Leicester in the

17. The Ottoman state organized the department of religious endowments (*evkaf*) into a
Ministry in 1837.

18. See chapter 3 by Dina Khoury.

19. A useful, if inevitably rather dated, bibliography of European urban social history is
Engeli and Matzerath 1989. For a variety of reasons, including the fact that most North American cities can best be described as postindustrial, it did not seem reasonable to include them
in this brief survey.

1950s and 1960s. Dyos was the first British historian to have a chair in urban history; he came to Leicester in 1952 and remained there for the rest of his life. His particular interest was the history of Victorian London; his major work was *Victorian Suburb: A Study of the Growth of Camberwell* (1961). To quote an appreciation written by a close colleague, he was "the chief inspiration, proselytiser and ambassador of urban history in Britain."[20] In addition to supervising a large number of postgraduates (and thus ensuring the future of the field), Dyos understood the importance both of bringing the subject to the attention of a wider audience and of disseminating news of developments in the field to a widely scattered body of practitioners. He produced the *Urban History Newsletter* between 1963 and 1973, followed by the *Urban History Yearbook* (1974–91), itself superseded by a quarterly journal, *Urban History*, in 1992.[21]

Broadly speaking, Dyos and his students were and to some extent still are interested in various aspects of urban growth and urban change, especially, but not exclusively, since the early nineteenth century.[22] Those working on the history of European cities in the modern period are fortunate to have at their disposal a variety of voluminous and generally accessible collections of local materials, including censuses, parish registers, court proceedings, assessments of rateable value, title deeds, charity records, the minutes of town councils, the records of municipal planning commissions (especially in Britain) and so on,

20. See Reeder 1979, which contains a bibliography of Dyos's writings. Both Reeder and the present professor of urban history at the University of Leicester, Richard Rodger, were colleagues of Dyos.

21. All three publications have surveyed and continue to survey the field through a running bibliography, reviews of recent theses, and reports on the subject from the front line. For instance, the 1979 *Yearbook* has an article entitled "Australian Urban History: A Progress Report"; the 1980 *Yearbook* has a twelve-page article entitled "Urban History in France"; the 1981 *Yearbook* has an article on urban history in India; and the fourth volume of *Urban History* in 2001 has an essay entitled "Urban History in Latin America." Hence, albeit in a somewhat ad hoc manner, the yearbooks and the journal have enabled interested readers to keep abreast of major developments in the field.

22. "From the later 1970s urban history went into abeyance, tainted with antiquarianism in some quarters and overtaken by social history, but it has undergone something of a renaissance since the mid-1990s. The reasons for this are various, but it is undoubtedly linked to the resurgence of interest in the city, urban cultures and the experience of urban life evident in wide areas of the humanities and social sciences." Gunn 2002, 59.

as well as such invaluable secondary sources as novels, contemporary diaries, newspapers, popular literature, and broadsheets. It is difficult for those of us working on Middle Eastern and North African cities in this period to avoid at least some pangs of jealousy at our colleagues' enjoyment of such extraordinary abundance, although it has become clear, over the past three decades, that Middle Eastern and North African urban societies in which a substantial corpus of Islamic court records has been preserved can also be studied in very considerable detail.[23]

Although Dyos's pioneering role is widely acknowledged, there have been a number of more recent works of synthesis discussing the rise of the city in Europe. I will look briefly at *The European City*, by Leonardo Benevolo (1993), and *The Making of Urban Europe 1000–1994*, by Paul M. Hohenberg and Lynn Hollen Lees (1995). Benevolo is primarily an architectural historian, interested in spatial growth and experimentation in construction, but he also pays attention to political structures, especially in Italy: "A good proportion of the medieval centres survive today as local administrative units . . . characterized by limited but not artificial autonomy and a real and living role in popular customs and imagination."[24] He also emphasizes the fact, so obvious in Mexico today, that the Spanish and Portuguese exported late Gothic architecture to the New World and replicated what gradually became almost standardized models of their own cities at the time in their new settlements in Nueva España such as Cholula, Huejotzingo, Oaxaca, Puebla, Querétaro, and Veracruz, generally building on top of previous urban settlements (Crouch, Garr, and Mundigo 1982)—Tenochtitlan, on which Mexico City was constructed, is probably the best known example. This is an interesting contrast to the *villes nouvelles* of North Africa, like Fez Jadid or the new city of Meknès, which were constructed alongside the older urban structures.

Hohenberg and Lees extend themselves over a wide canvass, concentrating on three main issues. How and why did cities originate, and what

23. See the discussion of the work of Abdul-Karim Rafeq and André Raymond later in this chapter; for some recent studies involving extensive use of sharia court records, see Hanna and Abbas 2005; Agmon 2006; Hudson 2008.

24. Benevolo 1993, 73, and 76, 102–3 below.

characterized their early development? What economic and demographic processes are particularly characteristic of urban populations? What are the social consequences of urban life, that is, the psychological and cultural differences between urban life on the one hand and rural life on the other? The second and third of these questions (the first precedes the chronological framework of this book) have not, on the whole, been asked about Middle Eastern cities in the same way. European cities experienced highly uneven processes of growth, relatively rapid between 1000 and 1350, much less sharply between the fifteenth and eighteenth centuries, and then more or less explosively after 1750. Until the eighteenth century, Hohenberg and Lees suggest, "cities retarded the development of nation-states,"[25] since, as is clear from their foundation charters, they often enjoyed a wide measure of autonomy. By 1700, European urbanization was no longer concentrated in the Mediterranean basin; by 1900, northern and western European cities were growing exceedingly rapidly, with relatively new towns such as Birmingham, Glasgow, Manchester, Berlin, and St. Étienne experiencing enormous growth.[26] As Bernard Hourcade's chapter indicates, many Middle Eastern cities, especially the Mediterranean ports engaged in trade with Europe, experienced comparable growth, beginning in the second quarter of the nineteenth century and continuing exponentially into the twentieth. One major contrast between cities in Europe and cities in the Middle East (and in much of the rest of the developing world) has been the emergence of huge capital cities, often two or three times the size of the second and third cities in their countries,

25. "To the west and east of the [old European urban core on the north/south trade routes to the Mediterranean], where post-feudal monarchs and their armies could dominate them, cities were turned into agents of centralization by princes intent on binding the territories of the realm even more tightly to the crown. By borrowing their money and selling them royal offices with perquisites of status attached, French kings co-opted the urban middle classes almost as effectively as they did the courtiers at Versailles.... Cities therefore helped to provide the cultural cement that molded urban residents into citizens and that lifted regional notables into a national aristocracy." Hohenberg and Lees 1995, 170–71.

26. Berlin owed its growth partly to industrialization and partly to its emergence as the capital of (a unified) Germany in 1871. It had 30,000 inhabitants in 1701, 170,000 in 1800, 400,000 in 1850, and 1.6 million in 1890. By 1925, 4 million Berliners lived in a city that extended over 325 square miles.

largely because of the extreme centralization of political and administrative functions in the developing world.

Apart from the emergence of nation-states after 1648, the most important event affecting the growth and changing the nature of European cities was the Industrial Revolution.[27] The qualitative changes that took place in the century between c. 1760 and c. 1860 were fueled by a combination of the breakdown of previously institutionalized socioeconomic barriers, the spread of technological innovation, and major new investments in agriculture that gradually increased productivity. Many cities in Europe grew to such an extent that they could not easily be supplied with food from their immediate hinterlands, and a long distance grain trade grew up that eventually extended to the eastern Mediterranean in the middle and later nineteenth century. More generally, the countryside became (permanently) subjected to the rule of the cities. For the Middle East and Ottoman Europe, Owen (1981a), Quataert (1996), and Todorov (1983) have shown that there was a fair degree of innovation, especially in textile manufacture, but in most other ways the domination of the advanced capitalist countries meant that the region remained largely confined to the periphery of the global economy (Rafeq 1983, 1991).

In Western Europe, industrialization was qualitatively novel in a number of important ways. It required major investment in social overhead (housing, sewage, transport systems) as well as a degree of more or less rapidly introduced government regulation (factory acts, public health acts, and so on). Hollenberg and Lees chart three phases: proto-industrialization followed by early coal-based industrialization, and then the second industrial revolution, during which the discovery or utilization of new sources of mechanical power meant that location (for example, near coalfields) became less important. Especially in northern England (Barnsley, Dewsbury, Halifax, Leeds, and subsequently Bolton, Bury, Preston, and Stockport) and in the Ruhr Valley (Bochum, Essen), manufacturing villages gradually developed into industrial towns, a process that sometimes produced large conurbations, some planned, some not.

It took some time for factory industry to dominate the urban landscape, probably not until well into the latter half of the nineteenth century. In Milan

27. Some of the growth had evidently taken place rather earlier; Madrid had grown from 6,000 in 1520 to 150,000 in 1780, and Moscow from 36,000 to 238,000 over the same period.

in the 1890s, for example, only half the working population was in industry; others were involved in transporting, packing, cooking, and moving food, all of which came from the city's immediate hinterland. The interdependence of town and country was a vital part in these processes of growth. These changes have proved both cataclysmic and durable.[28] In addition, the expansion of shops, offices, banks, and other services introduced new occupations for both men and women. Although the total population of Europe doubled between 1800 and 1910, the urban population grew sixfold. The process followed different patterns in different European countries; Britain urbanized very fast, France much more slowly. In spite of this, the population of Europe was still more rural than urban in 1918, and, if the USSR is included, remained so in 1945. In the Middle East, extremely rapid urban growth was a marked feature of the latter part of the twentieth century. By 1977, for example, 64 percent of the population of Iraq lived in cities and only 36 percent in the countryside, the exact opposite of the situation in the census of 1947 (Farouk-Sluglett and Sluglett 2001, 246). This was the result of three tendencies: the extreme centralization already mentioned, the greater availability of services in the cities, and finally, social and economic conditions in the countryside that made agriculture increasingly unprofitable and unattractive.[29]

Let us briefly consider two case studies of France and one of Germany. Robert A. Schneider, *The Ceremonial City: Toulouse Observed, 1738–1780* (1995); John Merriman, *The Margins of City Life: Explorations of the French Urban Frontier, 1815–1851* (1991); and Jan Palmowski, *Urban Liberalism in Imperial Germany: Frankfurt am Main, 1866–1914* (1999). Like many historians of urban Europe, Schneider is concerned with the changing function of public

28. "It was also imperative to prod and guide the transformation of the countryside, without whose food, labor and increasing custom the whole enterprise must grind to a halt. This became the quintessentially urban role, the truly 'basic' productive function of the urban system, which extended from quiet market centers and manufacturing towns like Bochum to great nerve centers like London and Milan, whose administrators, financiers and entrepreneurs masterminded the flow of information and goods." Hohenberg and Lees 1995, 213–14. See also Tilly 1992.

29. To which should be added the extreme concentration of private landholding that had increased exponentially in most of the Arab Middle East since the end of the First World War. See chapter 2 by Sarah Shields.

space. Increasingly, it seems, in the decades before the French Revolution, a number of large public squares were cleared and opened up in several parts of Toulouse, which provided "new and vastly expanded arenas for urban ceremony," including "gigantic festivities [such as firework displays, which] would have been inconceivable without the new public space that now accommodated them" (185). Executions and other forms of punishment for criminals had of course long been carried out in public (as in the rest of Europe and in the Muslim world at the time), but while this continued, more generally festive large-scale public events, where "the state" or "the crown" was "represented" or celebrated, became increasingly common. Of course, the newly created spaces could be used for demonstrations as well as for military parades, whether in eighteenth- and nineteenth-century France or in the anticolonial world of the Middle East in the middle decades of the twentieth century.

In *The Margins of City Life*, Merriman studies the phenomenon of the growth, and the perceived menace, of the urban margin or urban periphery, the new areas on the outskirts of French cities where the "dangerous classes" lived, hard by the new factories. The newly inhabited areas were feared by wealthier and longer established city-dwellers because of the presence of "marginal people," or rootless "new barbarians," associated with various forms of dissoluteness and criminality (Merriman 1991, 5, 12, 224).[30] Here again, large open spaces enabled people to gather together to vent their grievances and to press their demands on employers or the state. French cities grew at the edges because land was cheaper there, but also because the new inhabitants could avoid paying the *octroi,* which was levied at the official limits of the city. City walls were no longer needed for defensive purposes by the 1840s, and the ramparts were allowed to fall into disrepair, permitting and facilitating growth *extra muros.* This process had begun much earlier in, for instance, Aleppo, where new quarters had grown up outside the city walls as early as the fifteenth century (Gaube and Wirth 1984, 88). Links binding townspeople to the rural hinterland remained strong: 37 percent of the population of Narbonne and 23 percent of the population of Angoulême worked in

30. Nevertheless, the forbearance, suffering, and often the nobility of individuals living in dreadful conditions are major themes of *Germinal, Our Mutual Friend,* and numerous other novels of the period. See also 231 below.

agriculture in 1851.[31] By the end of the century, however, many of the new sub-urbs had developed into "forts of socialism" (Merriman 1991, 82)—around Paris (Belleville, Bobigny, and Ivry) and the Rotgürtel around Vienna. Urban elites considered the "conquest" and policing of the suburbs as vital objectives of city governments and also encouraged the building of churches on city peripheries to bring about the socialization of these areas. Merriman also points to an interesting contrast between French and North American cities; in the nineteenth- and twentieth-century United States, elites generally lived in the suburbs and the working class in the center, whereas the situation in France was the reverse.[32]

The subject matter of the German case study highlights another important contrast between a city in the industrialized heart of late nineteenth-century Europe and the cities of the Ottoman Middle East. Palmowski's *Urban Liberalism in Imperial Germany* (1999) is concerned with local government and urban politics, contrasting the frailty of the national democratic tradition in Germany with the far more lively and vigorous participation of German towns-people in local affairs, especially matters concerning education and municipal taxation. Thus "with reference to Benedict Anderson, the nation was clearly an imagined, if not artificial community, whereas this was less clear about a local community with which people readily and naturally identified" (312). In the Ottoman Empire in these years, there was only a very limited notion of

---

31. "Rural life remained . . . an integral part of cities and towns well beyond the middle of the nineteenth century." Merriman 1991, 113. Like many *barrios* in South American cities, some more recent settlements on the edges of Middle Eastern cities are named after the villages or rural areas from which the majority of their inhabitants originated. However, in contrast to the situation in the *barrios*, whose inhabitants often form associations to pay for wells to be dug or schools to be built in the villages they have left behind, such attachment to "home" on the part of the new urban dwellers of the Middle East and North Africa is largely confined to migrants from the mountainous regions, where living conditions were generally less oppressive.

32. For a study of changing elite habitat in Aleppo in the nineteenth and twentieth centuries, see David 1990. Sadly, the departure of the elite families to the suburbs (generally in the late 1940s and 1950s) was often accompanied by the destruction of family records, deemed too dirty (or too voluminous) for storage even in the most spacious urban apartment. Personal observation, Aleppo 1987–90.

identification with the local community in the sense of the-city-as-a-totality, partly because of the lack of local autonomy and partly because of a general tendency to identify first and foremost with the *religious* community into which one was born.[33] (For similar reasons, the notion of Ottoman citizenship was equally elusive, although it had been introduced in the two main reforming edicts of the Tanzimat, the *Hatt-i Şerif* of Gülhane of 1839 and the *Hatt-i Hümayün* of 1856.) For a variety of reasons, the institution of the municipality only made a fairly late and sporadic appearance in the Middle East, where its most significant manifestations were in cities or suburbs with large European populations, such as Alexandria or the more cosmopolitan parts of Istanbul (Rosenthal 1980a; Çelik 1993; Reimer 1993; Seni 1994; Lafi 2005).

Let us now turn to the history of scholarship on Middle Eastern cities, beginning with its origins in late eighteenth- and early nineteenth-century France.

## French Scholarship on Middle Eastern and North African Cities

The study of Middle Eastern cities has a long history in French scholarship. The modern tradition began with the late eighteenth-century French travelers in the Middle East, most notably with Volney, whose *Voyage en Egypte et en Syrie* (1787) paid special attention to Middle Eastern cities. Volney sought to develop a scientific methodology for the study of other societies that would provide an alternative to orientalist representations. His self-consciously scientific approach to Middle Eastern society later found fulfillment in the *Description de l'Égypte,* a twenty-four volume monument to contemporary French orientalist scholarship. Despite the manifest insufficiencies of many of the essays in the *Description* and the imperial auspices under which the project was conceived, the *État Moderne* section contains three important essays by Chabrol de Volvic (1822), Girard (1812) and Jomard (1822) on Cairo and Cairene society. Taken together, they constitute a source of documentation on the city at the end of the eighteenth century that has been much utilized by later scholars. Thus André Raymond drew heavily upon their work in his magisterial *Artisans et commerçants au Caire* (1973–74).

---

33. Although it cannot be emphasized too often that there was no necessary connection between inherited religious identity and religious belief.

It is important to emphasize that the work of Volney and the *Description* stand in sharp contrast to much subsequent French scholarship on Middle Eastern and North African cities over the period 1830–1950. Nothing in French colonial ethnography on Algeria and Morocco comes close to the effort of careful statistical documentation of standards of living and precise attempts to chart the ways of life of ordinary Egyptians that can be found in the early essays of Chabrol de Volvic, Girard, and Jomard. Nowhere else does one find a major effort to map a particular city street by street, including its workshops, mosques, baths, and other public buildings. It was only after 1960 that this tradition reemerged as a major characteristic of French urban historiography of the Middle East and North Africa.

Why were these early studies so successful in developing a statistical documentation of the social and economic characteristics of the Cairene population? Why did they refuse to utilize orientalist categories? To be schematic, Volney and the authors of the *Description* were imbued with the universalist values of the Enlightenment and the French Revolution. Men like Chabrol de Volvic were strong believers in the importance of placing science at the service of the state. Some years later, when he was Prefect of the Département de la Seine, Chabrol de Volvic developed a statistical study of the population of the Paris basin that drew upon the methods first employed to make a statistical map of the urban population of Cairo (Bourguet 1995). Later French orientalist scholarship on Middle Eastern cities would move away from the universalistic concern with the lives of ordinary people and public health, operating in terms of a set of categories based upon the supposedly primary formative influence of Islam.[34]

After the conquest of Algeria in 1830, French interest in the Middle East shifted to the Maghrib. However, since Algerian cities were for the most part easily conquered and quickly remolded according to French tastes and desires, the subject of cities did not figure large in the orientalist imaginary. (Given the protracted difficulties encountered in the course of the attempted conquest

34. See the work of the brothers William (1872–1957) and Georges (1876–1962) Marçais, and their younger colleague Gaston Deverdun. William Marçais was a linguist and philologist; Georges Marçais was an architectural historian of the Maghrib and Muslim Spain. Deverdun is best known for his two-volume study of Marrakesh: Deverdun 1959.

of Constantine, which might have provided a degree of motivation for urban studies, this is not entirely self-evident; Grangaud 2002.) Instead, resistance was based primarily in the North African countryside, rather than in the cities, and French ethnographers were more focused on matters concerning the tribes and rural religion. As a result, French nineteenth-century ethnographic studies of Algeria seem preoccupied with rural religion, including the Sufi orders and maraboutism, as well as with the political organization of the tribes.

In the era of *colon* dominance that followed the defeat of the last major rural uprising, the Mokrani rebellion (1871–72), the North African field was also being transformed by metropolitan intellectual and institutional currents. Numa Denis Fustel de Coulanges's *La cité antique* (1864) proved widely influential among urban historians. It proposed a radical reading of the Greek *polis* based upon the apparently formative role of its ancestral religious cults. It played a particularly important part in shifting the scholarly agenda back to cities in France and was taken up by Émile Durkheim and his followers, thereby influencing the newly emerging discipline of sociology. It also inspired Émile Masqueray (1843–1894), a graduate of the prestigious École normale supérieure, who was appointed Rector of the University of Algiers in 1878. His doctoral thesis, *La Formation des cités chez les populations sédentaires de l'Algérie*, was intended as a critique. Utilizing Fustel de Coulanges's criteria, Masqueray examined different Algerian Berber polities (Kabylia, Awras, Mzab) as forms of tribal republic (Masqueray 1886). By audaciously finding the roots of urban polity in North Africa, his dissertation sought to correct Fustel de Coulanges's eurocentrism. Although little understood in its day, Masqueray's work showed the way toward refashioning the study of North African society into a topic of interest to those working on the history of metropolitan France. However, it was not until after World War I that his example began to bear fruit in a series of important studies of North African cities.

The conquest of Morocco in 1912 provided the impetus that led to the renewal of the study of Middle Eastern urban history in France. The diplomatic context of the Moroccan Question dictated that a French takeover could occur only if approved by the Moroccan ulama and urban notables, but the French were largely ignorant of North African cities, since the resistance in Algeria had been based in the countryside and the cities had been little studied. French policy makers were convinced that mastery of the cities was a key to the eventual establishment of a protectorate, with the result that a crash program in studying Moroccan cities was in order. After 1912, this interest was carried forward by a series of volumes under the collective title of *Villes et Tribus du Maroc*, prepared by the members of the native affairs section of the protectorate administration. Because of its religious and commercial importance, Fez in particular attracted a great deal of attention. Urban studies constituted the core around which the early French studies of Moroccan society tended to gravitate.

Given these concerns, it is not surprising that the French should have been vitally interested in obtaining precise information about the city of Fez, long regarded as one of the essential keys to Morocco. Fez was the political and religious capital of the country as well as a national and international center of trade and commerce. Prior to 1904, French studies on Fez were limited, but with the publication of Eugène Aubin's *Le Maroc d'aujourd'hui* in 1904 and Henri Gaillard's *Une ville d'Islam: Fès* in 1905, things began to change. This was followed by a series of articles by Charles René-Leclerc on the economy of Fez and another series of articles in *Archives Marocaines* devoted primarily to the role of Islam in the city. By 1912, the picture was all but complete; thereafter the literature largely fills in the blanks, adding detail and color, rather than developing new categories of analysis. The relatively short time required for the elaboration of an ethnography of Fez (the same is true of Morocco more generally) is quite striking. So too was the development of certain research topics and the neglect of others. The only significant opening of a new topic was the emergence of a literature on the artisan craft guilds of Fez, beginning with the work of Louis Massignon (1920, 1924).

## 1919–56

French studies of Middle Eastern cities underwent important changes after World War I. The chief center of French urban studies in the interwar period, and indeed until the Suez expedition of 1956, was Cairo. The *Institut Français d'Archéologie Orientale* (whose origins can be traced back to Napoleon's *Institut d'Égypte*) provided the institutional context in which generations of scholars were introduced to the study of the city. It was first directed by Gaston Wiet (1887–1971), an orientalist who was broadly interested in the urban history and culture of Mamluk Cairo, including epigraphy, the history of architecture and Islamic art, and Arabic manuscripts. Wiet produced over fifty works over the course of a long and distinguished career, including a major translation of the classical author al-Maqrizi's study of the markets of Cairo (Raymond and Wiet 1979; Rosen-Ayalon 1977).

A second major center for the study of cities was Damascus, where the *Institut Français d'Archéologie de Damas* (later the *Institut Français d'Études Arabes de Damas*) provided a context for the study of the Levant comparable to that provided by Cairo for Egypt (Avez 1993). Here the central figure was Jean Sauvaget, who helped train a generation of French and Syrian urban historians until his early death in 1950. Sauvaget is best known for his history of Aleppo (Sauvaget 1941) and for his editions of Arabic historical manuscripts, many of which relate to the life of Syrian cities.[35] Now thought of primarily as an orientalist, Sauvaget in fact had broader interests that included medieval Syrian art history as well as material life (including a book on the postal service and horses). A third major figure in the study of Middle Eastern cities was Robert Mantran (1917–1992), whose *Istanbul dans la seconde moitié du XVIIe siècle* (1962) is still a basic text on Ottoman Istanbul.

Against this background, Roger Le Tourneau's *Fès avant le Protectorat* (1949) stands as a fitting capstone to a tradition of urban ethnography and social history. With Le Tourneau (1907–1971) one also begins to see a different approach to the history of Middle Eastern cities on the part of French scholars. In its time, *Fès avant le Protectorat* was a major innovation; it was one of the first books by a European scholar to take the social history of a Middle Eastern city as a discrete object of study. Although it drew heavily on the existing Arabic and European written sources (published and unpublished), it was also the product of intensive ethno-historical field studies of the artisan guilds—their specific histories, technologies, and economic basis—many of which were published separately. As such it was an innovative blending of the genres of history and sociology. Not since the authors of the *Description de l'Égypte* sought to make an inventory of the classes of Cairene society had the urban working classes of Islamic societies appeared on the French scholarly agenda. Le Tourneau's *Fès*

35. For his career, see Sourdel-Thomine 1954. For a critical account of the activities of the French Institute in Damascus in the context of *le savoir colonial*, see Métral 2004 and Trégan 2004.

was therefore not just a work of social history, it was also marked by the sign of power: how best to manage the city so as to avoid provoking hostilities. In this context, Fez was viewed at the time as one of a number of Arab cities in which a volatile new political chemistry was brewing.

Thus, French interest in the cities of the Middle East and North Africa increased further after World War II. In part, this new interest derived from the centrality of urban spaces in the challenges to French colonial rule posed by national liberation movements throughout the region. In this there is much to remind us of the historic role of French urban political upheavals in stimulating the emergence of sociology in France in the nineteenth century, as portrayed by countless studies of the role of the working classes in the French revolution and its nineteenth-century aftershocks.[36] It is hard not to see the influence of Louis Chevalier's study of the Paris working class on French authors writing about Middle Eastern and North African cities in the 1950s and 1960s (Chevalier 1958; Merriman 1991). One can also trace this influence in studies of urban shanty towns by Robert Montagne (1952) and André Adam (1972) as well as Adam's political history of Casablanca before 1914 (1968). Roger Le Tourneau's *Les villes musulmanes de l'Afrique du Nord* (1957) was an attempt to provide an historical overview of the changes affecting the post-1945 cities of North Africa. Thus, the struggles over decolonization had a significant impact on the way French authors interested in Middle Eastern and North African cities approached their subject. The new urban history, however, was to come from a different quarter.

### André Raymond and His Students

The work of André Raymond is central to any appreciation of the study Middle Eastern cities in the Ottoman period.[37] Trained during the era of decolonization, Raymond was an early critic of French colonialism as well as an advocate of modern methods of research and training that were at variance with the shibboleths of French Orientalism, which remained resolutely focused upon

---

36. Karl Marx's *Eighteenth Brumaire of Louis Napoleon* is the classic instance.

37. For an overview of Raymond's career see Hourani 1990. Between 1951 and 1953, Raymond completed his D.Phil. at Oxford (1953) under Hourani's supervision. See also Rafeq 1998 and Hanna and Abbas 2005:1–6.

the study of Arabic classical texts largely to the exclusion of other sources. Three things distinguish Raymond's approach from earlier French studies. *Artisans et commerçants au Caire au XVIIIe siècle* (1973–74) was the first full-length work to exploit the sharia court records as a source for the social and economic history of Middle Eastern cities. Through the study of Islamic wills, Raymond was able to add a quantitative dimension to an evaluation of economic change in the period. Second, Raymond and his team of graduate students and others also innovated in developing an archeological survey map of the buildings of old Cairo, and the history of their construction and of the development of the urban space of Cairo (see Maury et al. 1982–83). Here Raymond built upon the work of his mentor Gaston Wiet, who had pioneered the epigraphy of Cairene monuments, and sought to produce a reliable edition of al-Maqrizi's description of the markets of Cairo, a task that Raymond completed after Wiet's death (Raymond and Wiet 1979). A third feature of Raymond's work on Cairo was his use of the archives and publications of the French Expedition to Egypt in 1798, notably the twenty-four-volume *Description de l'Égypte*, previously little used by historians. Another aspect of Raymond's work was equally innovative: his early conviction that the eighteenth century, long neglected by historians of the Middle East as a period of stagnation, was in fact crucial to any understanding of how the region came to modernity (cf. D. Khoury 1997a, 3–16).

Raymond's influence on the development of the urban history of the Middle East and North Africa is incalculable, both because of the number of graduate students, both French and Middle Eastern, who were trained under him as well as his enormous energy and productivity and his broad vision of the place of urban history in the larger history of Middle Eastern societies. A partial survey of his publications lists more than a dozen books and some sixty articles, several of which are in English. Perhaps his best known book is *Les grandes villes arabes à l'époque ottomane* (1985), part of which has appeared in English as *The Great Arab Cities in the 16th–18th Centuries* (1984), and *Le Caire* (1993). Two important retrospective collections of his major essays appeared in 1998 and 2002.[38]

---

38. *La Ville Arabe, Alep, à l'époque Ottomane (XVIe–XVIIIe siècles)* (1998); *Arab Cities in the Ottoman Period: Cairo, Syria, and the Maghreb* (2002).

Middle Eastern urban history in France is thus is largely the fruit of what might be called the Raymond school, which also includes several distinguished scholars working on periods before the eighteenth century. Robert Ilbert has focused upon the impact of the incorporation of the Middle East into the world market and on the political struggles over colonialism as viewed in two rather different Egyptian cities. Ilbert's two major studies, *Héliopolis* (1981) and *Alexandrie 1830–1930* (1996) explore the inner workings of two Egyptian colonial cities. His central concern is the way in which the urban fabric was successively remolded in the century following 1830 as a result of the decline of the old social classes and the rise of new ones, the imposition of colonial rule, and major cultural and social changes. Other scholars associated with or students of Raymond writing in French about the history of Middle Eastern cities include Jean-Claude David, Colette Establet, Nelly Hanna, Farouk Mardam-Bey, Brigitte Marino, Jean-Paul Pascual, and Tal Shuval. There are numerous edited volumes on aspects of Middle Eastern cities by Francophone scholars, including *La ville arabe dans l'Islam* (Bouhdiba and Chevallier 1982); *Etat, Ville et Mouvements Sociaux au Maghreb et au Moyen Orient* (K. Brown et al. 1989); *Villes et territoires au Maghreb* (Hénia 2000); *Society and Economy in Egypt and the Eastern Mediterranean 1600–1900* (Hanna and Abbas 2005). The urban history of the Middle East and North Africa long remained a French quasi-monopoly, and Anglophone authors have only begun to challenge this state of affairs since the 1960s.

### American Studies of North African Cities

Until the mid-1960s, there was a general tendency in the Middle Eastern field for scholarship to follow the flag, with British scholars studying "their" Middle East, while the French studied theirs. As the colonial boundaries receded, however, important changes occurred. Modern-trained scholars from the former colonial dependencies became increasingly involved in scholarship on the region, while indigenous sources, especially in Arabic, gradually became more central to the scholarly enterprise. At the same time, scholars began to develop interests that no longer reflected the old colonial division of scholarly labor. The end of empire and the rise of the United States as a leading player in the politics of the region did not immediately change this division of labor, at least at first. American scholars were primarily interested in those parts of the

Middle East that had been under British rule (Egypt, Palestine/Israel, Jordan, Iraq, and Iran), while the former French, Spanish, and Italian domains were primarily studied by metropolitan and indigenous scholars trained in those contexts. The result of these changes was a deepening of historical scholarship. As we have seen, scholarship on the Maghrib remained predominantly in French until the early 1960s. This soon began to change as a new generation of American scholars began to devote their attention to North Africa. The result was the rise of the history of North African cities as an important American subject of research. A number of notable contributions can be mentioned.

Among the first American historians of North African cities was Kenneth Brown, whose *People of Salé* was published in 1976. Brown combined extended ethnographic fieldwork among the urban populations of Salé with a comprehensive study of Arabic source materials relating to the subject. Brown's Salé is not the timeless city of the orientalists; rather, it is historically situated in the context of the transformation of Morocco in the period. Brown analyzes the differential impacts of successive changes as they affected Slawis of different classes and occupations. Deeply immersed in the details of the life of the guild and merchant communities, it is informed by a generous and humanistic vision of Moroccan society. In some respects, notably its effort to document already fading guild and other urban structures and practices, Brown's *People of Salé* is clearly inspired by Le Tourneau's *Fès avant le Protectorat* (1949), with which it merits comparison.

Very different in focus is Janet Abu-Lughod's *Rabat*, a sociological study of postcolonial Rabat (1980). Abu-Lughod is an urban demographer and sociologist of rural to urban migration, best known in this context for her *Cairo: 1001 Years of the City Victorious* (1971).[39] Unlike Brown (and Le Tourneau before him) her book shows little interest in the social and cultural life of the inhabitants. Instead it focuses upon the historical origins and political consequences of urban settlement patterns, or what she describes as "urban apartheid." She traces the long-term political consequences of the settlement patterns of successive generations of rural migrants, largely against the wishes of the authorities, whether French or Moroccan. In retrospect, Abu-Lughod's research seems inspired by contemporary ghetto riots in American cities and

39. A projected third volume on Tunis never appeared.

the report of the Kerner Commission on their causes. Her research on rural migration and urban social tensions thus reflects an opportunity to develop a set of comparative cases to test against American data.

Daniel Schroeter's *Merchants of Essaouira* (1988) is a third major American study of a Moroccan city, which reflects the changing research context in Morocco as well as the maturing of urban history itself.[40] It was one of the first books to have been based on Moroccan state archives as well as on Arabic, Hebrew, and European sources. Unlike Fez, Rabat, and Salé, Essaouira was of relatively recent origin, founded by royal fiat in 1764 as the principal Atlantic port for the trade of southern Morocco. Essaouira thus serves as a convenient window through which to observe the incorporation of Morocco into the world market in the nineteenth century. Basing himself upon a wealth of documentation, Schroeter paints a complex and nuanced portrait of the life of the city. Of special interest is his study of the city's commercial relations with the Moroccan interior and with Europe, in which he is able to follow the fortunes of individual merchant families as well as to develop aggregate figures for the overall trade. The book provides an important corrective to French colonial speculations about the evolution of Moroccan foreign trade in the nineteenth century and the onset of economic dependence. Indeed, it merits comparison with Raymond's more comprehensive study of Cairo, discussed elsewhere in this introduction.

Another American study of a Moroccan city that may be mentioned here is *Meaning and Order in Moroccan Society,* by Clifford Geertz, Hildred Geertz, and Lawrence Rosen (1979). Primarily an anthropological investigation, the book provides a kind of model study of the bazaar economy, social relations, and kinship in Sefrou, a small city 90 kilometers south of Fez on the edge of the Middle Atlas mountain range. The three essays in the book deploy historical evidence as well as data from oral fieldwork in an effort to explore the complexities of the Sefrou marketplace. The book's careful and detailed attempts to reconstruct the workings of the bazaar economy of Sefrou, a major rural and urban market, make it relevant to historians of Middle Eastern cities. *Meaning and Order in Moroccan Society* also includes an important photographic

---

40. The book is based on his doctoral dissertation at Manchester University, where he was supervised by Kenneth Brown.

documentation of the life of Sefrou, which can be compared with the abundant photographic images in Le Tourneau's *Fès avant le Protectorat*. Although North African cities were the subject of other U.S. dissertations in the 1970s and 1980s, they seem gradually to have lost their attraction for American scholars, perhaps temporarily. Since the 1980s, American academic interest in the social cities of cities has tended to shift to the Arab East, notably Aleppo and Mosul.[41]

## Abdul-Karim Rafeq and André Raymond: Pioneers in the Use of the Islamic Court Records

In recent decades, the urban social history of the postmedieval Middle East (between the sixteenth and nineteenth centuries) has been given new direction by the work of two major figures, Abdul-Karim Rafeq of the University of Damascus and the College of William and Mary (Richmond, Virginia) and André Raymond of the University of Aix-en-Provence, whose contribution has already been discussed, and the work of their students, colleagues, and those influenced by them in Europe, the Middle East and the United States. Rafeq, one of the contributors to this volume, studied under Peter Holt and Bernard Lewis at the School of Oriental and African Studies at the University of London in the late 1950s and early 1960s[42] and has worked almost entirely on the area which is now the state of Syria. Raymond has written on Egypt, Greater Syria, and to a lesser extent Ottoman North Africa. Both Rafeq and Raymond would recognize the crucial role played in this field by Albert Hourani, whose extraordinarily influential article on the politics of the notables (Hourani 1968; P. Khoury 1990) drew many of his students and colleagues into the study of the urban history of the Middle East.[43]

The major contribution of both Rafeq and Raymond, based on their intensive use of court records, has been to shift the focus of the study of Middle

41. For Aleppo, see Masters 1988, 1990; Marcus 1983, 1989; Meriwether 1999; and Watenpaugh 2006. For Mosul, see D. Khoury 1997a and Shields 2000.

42. See Rafeq 1962–63 and 1970. See also Sluglett forthcoming.

43. Ira Lapidus's influential *Muslim Cities in the Later Middle Ages* (1967) focuses on Mamluk Egypt and Syria, that is, on a period very much earlier than any of the works discussed here.

Eastern cities from the perspective of the outside to the inside. In contrast to earlier socioeconomic historians, who made little or no use of locally generated materials and based their work mostly on consular reports and travel accounts, Rafeq and Raymond and their students have written their histories principally from the documents generated by the Islamic courts, which are abundant for the period from the Ottoman conquest until the early twentieth century.[44] These hitherto unexploited materials have opened up a treasure trove of contemporary information for Christian and Jewish as well as for Muslim communities. In addition, given the nature and scope of Islamic law, the procedures of the court system covered, and were applied to, very broad areas of economic and social life.

As well as being the place of resort for the resolution of disputes, courts were used for notarial purposes, recording transactions such as debts and house and land sales, as well as some, though not all, marriages and divorces, and the financial transactions that accompanied them. As Raymond shows extensively in *Artisans et commerçants au Caire,* a court official (the *qassam shar'i*) made inventories of the possessions of the deceased, in order to arrive at the canonically correct proportions to be distributed amongst the heirs.[45] A comparison of sets of inheritance documents over a particular time span

44. After the promulgation of the Ottoman Civil Code (the *mecelle*) in 1876, large areas of jurisdiction were transferred to the purview of the new civil courts. The records (*sijillat*) of the Islamic courts (*mahkama/mahakim shar'iyya*) of Ottoman Syria have survived largely intact (and are preserved at the Centre for Historical Documents in Damascus). Unfortunately, less attention was given to the preservation of the records of the "new" civil courts during the last forty or fifty years of Ottoman rule (and indeed for much of the mandate), which seem to have disappeared. The court records of what is now Jordan have been preserved at the Centre for Archives and Manuscripts at the University of Jordan, Amman; see the handlist by Muhammad 'Adnan al-Bakhit (1984). In Egypt, some of the court records have remained in the provincial centers, and others are in Dar al-Watha'iq in Cairo. Najwa Al-Qattan (2003) has surveyed (and partially catalogued) the surviving sharia records of Beirut between 1843 and World War I. It is possible that many of Iraq's *mahkama* documents were destroyed or looted after the fall of Baghdad in April 2003. Dina Khoury made extensive use of the Mosul court records in *State and Provincial Society in the Ottoman Empire* (1997a).

45. Pascual and Establet (1994, 1998) used the succession registers for early eighteenth-century Damascus; Hudson (forthcoming) used them for the late nineteenth and early twentieth centuries.

shows how the fortunes of families rose and fell. One important conclusion for the period in question is that it was only ulama families who maintained significant fortunes through their control of *awqaf* for any length of time.

The *qadis* (judges in the Islamic courts) adjudicated in all kinds of family matters and ordered debtors to deceased individuals to discharge their debts to the family of the deceased. They drew up the foundation documents of *awqaf* (Roded 1988, 1990), and were frequently called to adjudicate on matters arising from them. As well as acting as notaries, judges pronounced (inter alia) on matters affecting guilds and markets, prescribed the width of streets, and gave or withheld permission for extensions to houses. Of course, since legal procedures were not provided free of charge, it must be assumed that many less-well-off people did not avail themselves of the courts, and to that extent the historical record is incomplete. On the other hand, as Abraham Marcus observes for mid-eighteenth-century Aleppo, "Women and ordinary people, who barely figure in most other sources, appear on virtually every page of the records."[46] Focusing on the court records, or *sijillat,* often gives us the opportunity to study social history in minute detail; changes in bride-price, urban house prices, changes in the nature of pious foundations, the activities of the guilds—the list is extremely comprehensive. Of course, the documents do not by themselves constitute "unproblematic reflections of social reality," as James A. Reilly has remarked (2007); in addition, although this may seem a somewhat subjective observation, the major disadvantage of this material is that the absence of what might be called surnames (or other forms of identification) means that the information obtained is often generic rather than personal. Thus, there may be a long case involving an individual, but short of reading through every document (and even that is not foolproof) it is difficult to see where, or if, he or she figures in the records again, whether the sentence was carried out, or if the defendant or the plaintiff appeared in court again. So it is difficult, for instance, to piece together the details of an individual's life or to write wonderful micro-histories like those of Le Roy Ladurie or Carlo Ginzburg.[47] It

46. "It bears remembering that the source material on eighteenth century Aleppo recounts in its totality no more than a tiny fraction of what took place. As in other past societies, most of the historical information was never recorded at all." Marcus 1989, 11.

47. This has been attempted occasionally; see Toledano 1993.

is conceivable that all these legal registers—between five and seven for Aleppo every year between 1540 and 1918, for example— might one day be computerized and indexed, but that is probably quite a long way off. Another source of considerable potential value that has been little utilized so far is the collection of what are called in Arabic *awamir sultaniyya,* the general administrative decrees and specific orders sent out by Istanbul to the provinces, which are available for most of the Ottoman period.[48]

### The Contributions to the Volume

In "Interdependent Spaces: Relations between the City and the Countryside in the Nineteenth Century," Sarah Shields emphasizes the linkages between cities and their hinterlands. Rural dwellers depended on city merchants to sell their crops or their sheep for them, to lend them money in hard times, and to put out materials for rural textile manufacture. They depended on the government to maintain, or to attempt to maintain, security in the countryside, so that crops and flocks would not be damaged or stolen. The state depended on rural producers to provide foodstuffs to feed the cities and to generate agricultural surpluses, which could either be remitted to Istanbul in cash or be used locally to feed, clothe, or pay the state's soldiers and bureaucrats. Merchants and "landowners" were dependent on peasant labor for their own fortunes; the rest of the urban population depended on rural production for its own sustenance.

Although an obvious symbiosis characterized these relations for most of the Ottoman period, major changes took place after the early nineteenth century as the world-system penetrated more thoroughly into areas such as rural Egypt, Iraq, and Syria. These changes gradually tilted the economic balance of power firmly in favor of wealthy city dwellers and gradually disempowered the cultivators and herders, or at least put them in positions of increasing dependence. A particularly crucial instrument in this process, as a signifier of these developments and as a major accelerant, was the Ottoman Land Code of 1858 (Farouk-Sluglett and Sluglett 1983a; Sluglett and Farouk-Sluglett 1984), which effectively instituted a regime of private property on grain-growing land. This facilitated the wider spread of hierarchical social relations

---

48. Masters (2001) has made extensive use of these documents.

in the countryside and caused many peasants who could not prove their title, or who believed that land registration was simply a prelude to conscription, to lose their lands. Merchants often created famines or artificial shortages, either to keep out foreign competition or to increase their own short-term profit, and the local representatives of the Ottoman state regularly connived in these activities (Fattah 1997, 139–57). Hence the nineteenth century saw the beginnings of the increasing impoverishment of the peasantry, a process whose many ramifications would bring widespread social unrest to the whole region in the 1950s and 1960s.[49]

In "The Economic Organization of Cities in Ottoman Syria," Abdul-Karim Rafeq shows how a synthesis was made in the premodern period between different contemporary legal systems to produce pragmatic means of regulating the economy. Over time, especially in the nineteenth century, legal codes would be imported from Europe to regulate the growing volume of European and Ottoman trade. One of the principal urban economic institutions was the guild, a form of organization that seems to have survived more or less intact at least from the sixteenth to the mid–nineteenth century. The guilds grouped together craftsmen engaged in the same fields of production, sale, and services, and members of the various guilds would appear as a group for a variety of purposes before the *qadi* in his court. Some guilds (butchers, builders) were closely controlled by the Ottoman government, but most were not. New guilds were developed as new tastes and activities arrived in the Syrian cities; associations of those who sold coffee or ran coffee houses, of those who sold tobacco or provided spaces where pipes could be smoked. Many guilds were linked with the Sufi orders, and progression from one rank to another (apprentice/journeyman/master) was often marked by religious ceremonies. The guilds tended to practice a closed shop in the sense that only guild members were permitted to practice a certain occupation within a defined geographical area (normally a city), and they also maintained (or specified) quality and price control. Some occupational guilds were mixed, containing Christians, Jews, and Muslims (or any two of the three), while some only contained members of a single religious community. There are examples of Muslim guild members electing a Christian guild master or shaykh; we know about guild members' religious

49. See Batatu's studies of Iraq (1978) and Syria (1999); for Egypt, see Abdel-Fadil 1975.

affiliations because these are mentioned in the records on the occasions when they appeared together before the *qadi*.

Rafeq also discuses aspects of business practice, especially the complex question of credit and interest, both forbidden in Islamic legal theory, but evidently practiced widely and recorded regularly before the *qadi*.[50] The records enable us to identify the lenders and the borrowers, and show, for instance, in sixteenth-century Hama, that peasants were the most indebted social group and the military the most frequent and the wealthiest lenders. In cases coming to court between the 1730s and 1850s, interest rates ranged from 15 to 25 percent, often for periods as brief as six months.

There were radical changes in Syria after the French and Industrial Revolutions. Trans-desert overland trade gradually declined, especially after the opening of the Suez Canal in 1869; pilgrims going on the hajj could make the journey much less strenuously by sea. Raw materials, especially cotton, silk, wheat, and wool, were exported cheaply to Europe. Although the story is complex (in that there are examples of positive or innovative adaptation to changing economic circumstances), most Syrian textile manufacturers suffered to a greater or lesser extent in the late nineteenth century (Issawi 1986, 374–75; Quataert 1993b; Sluglett 2002). Commercial courts, with a mixed composition of foreign consuls and their protégés and local Ottoman subjects, were introduced in Aleppo in 1850 and Damascus in 1855. These changes, accompanied by novel and psychologically unsettling declarations of the equality of all Ottoman citizens on the part of the sultan and his representatives, brought about the sense of a world turned upside down, which seems to have been at the heart of the sectarian clashes of the 1850s and 1860s in Syria, Lebanon, and elsewhere. By the early twentieth century, economy and society had existed in a confusing state of transition for many decades, and many familiar social institutions had been transformed beyond recognition (Fawaz 1994; Harel 1998; Masters 1990, 2001; Rafeq 1988a; Rogan 2004).

In "Political Relations between City and State in the Middle East, 1750–1850," Dina Rizk Khoury begins with a brief discussion of the recent

---

50. Compare: "Despite Islam's well-known ban on usury, a dependence on credit in various forms permeated the entire fabric of Aleppo's commercial life." Masters 1988, 153. See also Jennings 1973.

historiography of the Ottoman Empire, commending recent trends in history writing that stress the importance of looking at the sources from both the imperial (Ottoman) and provincial-urban (Arab) perspective. However, as she remarks in chapter 3, historians are laboring at a considerable disadvantage because "with some notable exceptions, there have been very few monographs based on the use of a combination of local and imperial records that have explored the ways that the power of the state impinged on the lives of ordinary subjects."

After the Ottoman conquest, the cities of Anatolia and the Fertile Crescent became the inheritors of the legacies of the Byzantines and the Seljuks. From the Byzantines came the notion that provisioning cities and armies would guarantee social order and facilitate the expansion of the empire;[51] from the Byzantines and the Seljuks (and the Mamluks in the Fertile Crescent) came the belief in the state's obligation to control the price and quality of goods. Judges and governors were appointed to each province or city directly from the center, so a model of the society resembled the spokes of a wheel with (at least in theory) a highly centralized state at the hub. The legal system was based on a combination of Islamic law (sharia) and imperial edicts or statutes (*qanun*).

However well or badly the traditional system may have worked in earlier periods, the capacity of the Ottoman state to enforce its will over many of the provinces had largely broken down by the late eighteenth century. In Egypt and Iraq, a succession of Mamluk rulers took power, while in Syria and Palestine various condottieri took advantage of the vacuum to impose their will on the local population.[52] However, Khoury cautions against an unquestioning acceptance of the standard interpretations of late seventeenth- and eighteenth-century Ottoman history. She considers that the institution of tax farming, rather than being symptomatic of the disintegration of state control, gave some members of the local gentry a stake in the system (and thus had a certain integrative function, although it is not clear whether this was the *intention*

---

51. Hence the frequent attempts by the Ottoman state to ban wheat exports. See Braudel 1975, 1:592–94, and Masters 1988, 186–215.

52. See note 14 above. For eighteenth-century Egypt, see Hathaway 1997. For eighteenth- and nineteenth-century Iraq, see Lier 2004.

of the Ottoman government). Also, state and city relations varied considerably throughout the empire, according to the nature and economic power of the urban elites, even within a given geographical area (such as "Egypt" or "Syria"). Khoury suggests a categorization of urban centers in ways that may make meaningful generalizations possible: major administrative and commercial centers, port cities, small interior towns, and urban pilgrimage centers. The rest of the chapter concerns the first two categories.

In theory, Ottoman provincial governance was divided into three spheres—administrative, military, and judicial—although by the early eighteenth century this compartmentalization had largely ceased to function. In the larger cities, the state negotiated agreements over military mobilization and taxation, under which powerful local elites and their families became provincial governors and bureaucrats while individuals outside these elites were given long-term or lifetime tax farms(*malikanes*), thus creating a degree of tension between the two groups. Thus, for example, the 'Azms of Damascus and the Jalilis of Mosul set up households that were able to maintain power locally with the tacit acquiescence of Istanbul. Gradually, the judges lost their power to the governors; they were no longer in charge of military provisioning, as this function had devolved to local elites or to the governors themselves, who would buy the provisions that the military consumed on the open market or produce them on the lands that they owned themselves. They had also lost charge of the recruitment of mercenaries and of the policing of the cities, in both cases to the governor or to members of his household.

For a variety of reasons, the military functions of the janissaries gradually declined in the course of the eighteenth century, and most of the former soldiers became absorbed into the urban social fabric as artisans or small merchants. The relationship between the provincial notables, or *a'yan* (that is, those on lower rungs of the socioeconomic ladder than, say, the 'Azms or the Jalilis) and the state also changed in the late eighteenth century. The state became increasingly reliant upon the *a'yan* for the collection of taxes, and those with *malikanes* had little incentive to forward more than a bare minimum to the center and thus became increasingly independent of it.

The fortunes of the port cities were much more varied, depending on their location and the political situation in their hinterlands. By the eighteenth and nineteenth centuries the ports had become heavily involved in trade with

Europe, and the Ottoman state had far less control over them than it had over other cities in the empire. Khoury concludes by setting out several items on a future research agenda. In the first place, the Ottoman Empire was clearly not a monolith, and it is important to assess its impact, and the extent of its power, from city to city. How did the interaction between state and society shape power at a local level? Did the trajectories of urban elites vary from place to place? Did the Tanzimat really represent such a sharp break with the past as the received wisdom suggests? Finally, what can an examination of state and city relations between the eighteenth and mid–nineteenth centuries tell us about Middle Eastern urban society?

In "Political Relations between City and State in the Colonial Period," Leila Fawaz and Robert Ilbert discuss the transition from Ottoman to European rule at various times in the nineteenth and twentieth centuries. They point out that the role played by the Ottomans in the urban administration of their Arab provinces has sometimes been presented in a rather negative fashion by British, French, and Arab writers, the British and French seeking to draw favorable conclusions from comparisons of their own administration of the cities with that of the Ottomans (Sauvaget 1941; Longrigg 1925); in later times the Arabs tended to paint the Ottomans as proto-colonialists. The principal beneficiaries of the major shift of the region's trade toward Europe were the entrepreneurs of the port cities, especially those of Alexandria, Izmir, and Beirut. As has been noted, these cities increased greatly in size throughout the nineteenth century, attracting a mass of migrants from their rural hinterlands, who often brought their sectarian fears and prejudices with them.

Well into the semicolonial and colonial periods, cities and their elites continued to play the pivotal roles they had played under the Ottomans. With the arrival of the mandatory regimes, for instance, the notables developed new contacts both with the colonial administrations and with a new generation of "national" politicians. In addition, with the fall of the Ottoman Empire, the political and socioeconomic elites of Aleppo, Basra, or Mosul no longer had direct access to the center of power and thus were obliged to redefine their identities within the parameters of the newly constructed nation-state. In the process, some of the old notables lost what remained of the mediating role they had played under the Ottomans, since they were considered to have thrown in their lot too wholeheartedly with the colonial (or occupying) power. This was particularly true of Iraq, but less so of Syria, where popular disenchantment with French rule made collaboration a much less easy option. However, although the colonial powers profoundly influenced the histories of the Arab states of the Middle East, they made less impression on the physical environment,[53] in striking contrast to French North Africa, with its many *villes nouvelles*.

The authors stress the continuing importance of connections, *wasta* in Arabic, of go-betweens mediating between individuals or groups and the state (and its various bureaucracies), in spite of the widespread adoption of modern technologies. In the modern period, cities have also served increasingly as communications and media hubs, and it has unfortunately been the case, at least until the comparatively recent arrival of the Internet, that the media has played a crucial role in the maintenance in power of highly centralized and controlled dictatorial regimes throughout the region.

The military coups of the 1950s and 1960s largely broke the power of the urban notables who had played a crucial role under the Ottomans, under the various colonial regimes and, for a while, after independence in most of the states. Of course, especially in the twentieth century, it is not always easy to arrive at an accurate definition of "notable." Should that definition have been applied to Nuri al-Saʻid, fourteen times Prime Minister of "Independent Iraq," a military officer originally from a lower middle class background, like many of his closest associates, but who became a tenacious defender of the privileges of the class to which British assistance had elevated him? After the overthrow of the various anciens régimes, the Middle East has experienced a new phenomenon, the seizure of power by military men, most of whom have originated from small country towns. This is not, it can be confidently asserted, a modern instance of Ibn Khaldun's cycles of urban brilliance, followed by urban corruption and decline, followed by renewal and reinvigoration from the desert or remote rural areas. Although it may not have been immediately obvious, it soon became clear that the middle ranking officers who replaced the notables turned out to be far more dangerous, and single-mindedly ruthless, than their predecessors.

53. Shepherd (1999, 1–2) notes how little of British mandatory Jerusalem remains visible today. However, see chapter 5, note 13, on the influence of Michel Écochard on the urban landscape of contemporary Damascus.

In "The Demography of Middle Eastern Cities and the Expansion of Urban Space," Bernard Hourcade presents a survey of the principal population trends in the region during the period. He draws attention to the dominant role played by the two great cities of Istanbul and Cairo, the heterogeneity of Middle Eastern and North African cultural contexts and the existence of several different types of city, varying in age and economic activity. In 1950, the Middle East was 24 percent urban, occupying an intermediate position between Europe and North America (around 54 percent) and the major rural subcontinental regions such as China and West Africa (around 10 percent). Of course, precise statistics for most of the period before the late nineteenth century are hard to find, and Hourcade has made extensive use of recent monographs on the history of the region, using a sample of fifty cities. In general, the population of the region probably quadrupled between 1800 and 1950, from about 27 million to about 111 million.

At the beginning of the period, there were only "traditional" or "oriental" cities (although Hourcade's categorization is extremely broad). By the end of the period "dual cities" had emerged, with suburbs inhabited by Europeans or the new local elites, alongside the older city. It is interesting to see how the list of the ten largest cities in the region has fluctuated over the centuries; only Cairo, Istanbul, and Damascus remained on the list between 1800 and 1970. In more recent times, two of the main demographic trends in the region have been substantial rural to urban migration beginning in the 1950s and the disproportionate growth of capitals in comparison with the sizes of the next largest cities.[54] For most of the nineteenth century, however, demographic growth was as little as 1 percent per annum, rising to 1.5 percent per annum between 1870 and 1930, followed by a spurt of rapid growth that has continued to increase exponentially ever since. Slow growth in the nineteenth century was due partly to cholera and other epidemics, together with high mortality and fertility rates, but also by a degree of rural and urban integration. Thus, much craft industry was carried out on a subcontracting basis, with urban entrepreneurs providing, say, rural weavers, with piecework or work at a particular stage in the production process. Improvements in sanitation and advances in

54. Thus, according to U.N. figures for 2002, Greater Baghdad had a population of 6.7 million, followed by Mosul (1.79 million), Basra (1.4 million).

medicine brought about declining mortality rates, and, as noted above, rural people began to migrate to the cities in large numbers by the 1950s.

Hourcade uses a number of examples to illustrate different factors promoting population growth or decline: the emergence of new capitals under the mandates, the relative integration of subregions into the world economy, and in the case of Istanbul a massive out-migration of Greeks, Armenians, and Jews by 1923, resulting in a declining population, and in the case of Tel Aviv, mushrooming growth due to Jewish immigration.

In the nineteenth century, even under conditions of fairly slow demographic growth, Middle Eastern and North African cities became overcrowded, largely because of their confinement within their city walls. The streets were narrow and crowded and there were few open public spaces. At least as long as the original foundations remained in existence, *waqf* properties were maintained and kept in order; of course they could not be sold, which meant that a significant proportion of urban real estate was frozen. This partly explains the fairly long survival of traditional inner cities, at least until the appearance of the revolutionary regimes of the 1960s and 1970s.[55]

At the end of the nineteenth century, rulers who had visited Europe or had European advisors began to reconstruct their capitals; this took place in Teheran, Cairo, and Istanbul. Major transformations took place after 1870, with new European cities being built alongside the medinas of Algiers, Meknès, Marrakech, and Rabat; the North African cities generally lacked an indigenous modern bourgeoisie. New "Western" suburbs were built in Aleppo and Cairo, and, rather later, in Tehran, which was extensively redesigned under Reza Shah. Thus, between 1800 and 1950 many Middle Eastern and North African cities found new identities, largely as a result of the recasting of the relationship between their traditional cores and their modern peripheries.

In "Moving Out of Place: Minorities in Middle Eastern Urban Societies, 1800–1914," Gudrun Krämer discusses the changing role of the minorities in the twin contexts of nation-formation and modernization, suggesting that non-Muslims were the most visible consumers and agents of modernity. She is concerned with three sets of questions: first, what was the extent to which

---

55. For a discussion of the "problem" of urban waqf in mid-twentieth-century Aleppo and the state's attempts to tackle it, see David and Hreitani 1984.

social and physical boundaries were modified or redrawn in the course of modernization? Second, how far did the effects of modernization involve a break with traditional patterns of interaction between Muslims and non-Muslims? Third, how general was the phenomenon, and how far was it characteristic of nineteenth-century Middle Eastern urban society?

Of course there were and are many kinds of minority in the Middle East: ethnic, religious, heterodox Muslims, and so on. Much of the literature on minority communities focuses on the larger cities, and it is the case that Jewish communities have been studied more widely than Christian ones. Again, the diverse functions of the minorities in different cities, and the very varying state of knowledge about them, means that it is often difficult to generalize.

Clearly, religious affiliation was and, although not always in the same ways, still is an important marker of group identity in the Muslim world. "Built-in" Muslim privilege was not necessarily a cause of tension, since those involved knew the rules well enough. Historically, Muslim/*dhimmi* relations were regulated by placing clear and visible boundaries between the two. Most obviously, all able-bodied adult male *dhimmi*s paid an additional tax, the *jizya*, until its abolition by the Ottomans in 1856. The situation of the non-Muslims varied according to historical circumstances; thus the Crusades ushered in a period where the lot of the Christians became noticeably harsher, and at other times conversion to Islam (especially among Christians) caused the communities to diminish in number over time. By the early nineteenth century the millet system in the Ottoman Empire gave the communities so designated (and more were added in the course of the century) a degree of communal autonomy under the authority of their bishops, patriarchs, rabbis, etc. Of course, as has already been noted, this kind of autonomy did not prevent the minority communities from pursuing, for example, cases against one another in the Islamic courts.

Except in Morocco and Iran at various times, there was no enforced social segregation of the communities, although there was a tendency for communities to concentrate in specific neighborhoods. Jews tended to live in largely Jewish quarters grouped round the synagogue (Judaism has a series of regulations on the subject of how far one can walk on the Sabbath), and there were some city quarters, in Aleppo, for instance, which were entirely Christian, grouped round the city's churches. Gaube and Wirth's tables show that out of the ninety-nine quarters of the old city, fifty were entirely Muslim, one was 91 percent Jewish, eighteen were more than 80 percent Christian, and the rest more thoroughly mixed.[56] In any case, "quarters" were far less static in some cities than in others; some were enclosed by walls and gates which were shut at night, while others were not.

The only major instance of labor segregation was in the military, where non-Muslims did not serve. Otherwise, Muslims and non-Muslims worked alongside each other in most occupations (see chapter 4). Non-Muslims were disproportionately represented in long-distance trade, often supported in these endeavors by, for instance, the Safavid state in the case of the Armenians of New Julfa and the sultans of Morocco in the case of the Jews of Mogador. Jews and Christians often held sizeable tax farms and acted as bankers to Ottoman provincial governors.

In the course of the Tanzimat reforms, various Islamic legal provisions relating to the minorities were relaxed, culminating in the formal ending of legal inequality between Muslims and non-Muslims and the creation of a form of universal Ottoman citizenship. Non-Muslims could now serve in the army (or, as most did, pay an exemption fee). Christians and Jews could now build churches and synagogues, if they could obtain the necessary building permits from the Ottoman authorities. The capitulations (in Arabic *imtiyazat* [*ajnabiyya*]), which had benefitted foreigners and their local protégés since the sixteenth century, were greatly extended in the nineteenth century, so that many thousands of locals and their descendants acquired either foreign protection or (more rarely) foreign citizenship. More generally, the powers acted "officially" as the protectors of the various minority communities, although the benefits of this connection did not always flow very far down the social scale. On the other hand, less respectable foreigners often lived beyond the reach of the law in many Middle Eastern cities (Alexandria, Cairo, Istanbul, Izmir), because it was extremely difficult for the local authorities to arrest or try them.

The nineteenth century also saw considerable growth in the urban non-Muslim population, composed partly of foreigners (in Alexandria, Istanbul, and Izmir), and partly of rural immigrants. One of the reasons for this was

56. Gaube and Wirth 1984, 427–33. The tables are derived from volume 3 of al-Ghazzi 1926.

the considerable liberalization in trade with Europe after the signature of the Treaty of Balta Liman (the Anglo-Ottoman Commercial Treaty) in 1838, which was followed by similar agreements with other European powers. Once more, non-Muslims played a disproportionately large role, although Muslims still dominated the grain trade and much of the trade with the hinterlands of the inland cities.[57] Local non-Muslims, educated in schools run by foreign missionaries or by the Alliance Israélite Universelle (founded in 1860), could be extremely useful to European businessmen, in that the non-Muslims could communicate with them and generally knew both Arabic and Ottoman Turkish. In spite of all this it must be remembered that most Middle Eastern Christians and Jews remained as poor, illiterate, and cut off from the benefits that modernity was showering as much upon their richer co-religionists as their Muslim counterparts.

With the Tanzimat reforms came various declarations of equality for the non-Muslims, accompanied by the abolition both of barriers to social mobility and of the distinctive markers that had enabled members of the various communities to recognize each other in public. Wealthy Christians and Jews could now build houses as opulent as those of wealthy Muslims and increasingly shared the fashionable suburbs with them.[58] Of course, centuries of legally superior and inferior status could not be made to disappear overnight with the stroke of a pen, and "the 'vertical' element of religious and ethnic identification was never fully supplanted by the 'horizontal' element of class." Other chapters in this volume mention the violent incidents that wrought havoc in Aleppo in 1850, Damascus in 1860, and elsewhere, explaining them less as the result of sectarian antagonism than as stemming from a general sense, especially on the part of the Muslim *Lumpenproletariat*, that a familiar world order was crumbling about their ears, which made them lash out in panic against those whom they saw as the source of their misfortunes. But, as Krämer emphasizes, these were not religious wars against non-Muslims. Poor Christians and Jews, especially those living in the quarters of

57. For an analysis of a list of merchants trading in various commodities in Aleppo in 1908, see Sluglett 2002.

58. Non-Muslims formed 91 percent of the population of the six new suburbs built outside Aleppo between 1868 and 1895; see Gaube and Wirth 1984, 434.

Damascus with Muslim majorities, were rarely attacked and indeed in many instances were protected by their Muslim neighbors. On the other hand, the better-off non-Muslims were regarded as associates and agents of the European powers, a sort of local economic fifth column, helping outsiders to weaken the infrastructures of the state. They became objects of suspicion on the part of their contemporaries, their loyalty to the Ottoman state increasingly open to question.

In "Urban Social Movements, 1750–1970," Sami Zubaida describes the gradual emergence of modern politics from old patterns of urban popular mobilization in the eighteenth and early nineteenth centuries. In traditional urban politics, the principal actors were, first, the 'askaris, the Ottoman military rulers, the pasha with his retinue of soldiers and administrators. Ottoman cities also had janissary regiments, but, as has been noted already, the janissaries' functions as soldiers of the crown had gradually declined over time, and they had become increasingly absorbed into the local population. Apart from the military, the urban power elite consisted of the notables, both religious and civil (merchants and landowners), whose fortunes and families were often intertwined.

Below the power elites were the ra'ya, or subjects, who (together with their peasant contemporaries) paid the taxes exacted by the state, often set quite arbitrarily by governors bent on making profits as quickly as possible. Ordinary taxes were supplemented by extraordinary ones (such as those to finance military campaigns to subdue local tribes). The Christian and Jewish communities were frequently subjected to Draconian demands that would be rescinded in return for cash payments.

Much urban conflict in the premodern period concerned taxation and the provision (or the shortage) of food. Often with the connivance of the authorities, merchants hoarded food to force prices up, and the poor would riot in protest. Although the exactions of the Ottoman state were often extremely harsh, local notables behaved no less brutally during the periods when the state temporarily lost control, as in much of Syria and Egypt in the late eighteenth century. In "Urban Social Movements, 1750–1950," Sami Zubaida gives vivid examples of popular activity in the poor quarters of Cairo in the seventeenth and eighteenth centuries and then again in the early nineteenth centuries (particularly during the events between the Napoleonic invasion and the installation of Muhammad

'Ali as viceroy). In the earlier period, food shortages, price fluctuations, and currency debasements would cause crowds to assemble at the citadel; stones would be thrown and stores looted. Reactions would vary; sometimes severe repression would follow, sometimes edicts regulating prices and supplies would be issued. Such incidents were relatively rare at times of stable prices.

Such instances of popular protest were generally tied to purely material demands, although there would often be calls for a "just prince" to settle matters justly by applying sharia law in an equitable manner. (There was also an element—however tongue in cheek—of "If only our ruler knew what crimes his servants were committing in his name.") Notions of right and wrong were invariably tied to religious concepts, although the ulama, especially the higher ulama of, say, al-Azhar, rarely protested against the imposition of noncanonical taxes, and their interests were seldom close to those of the masses.

With the advent of Muhammad 'Ali and the fairly universal application of the Tanzimat reforms in Greater Syria by the 1840s, and in Iraq by the 1870s, the foundations of what became, or were to become, centralized nation-states were laid throughout the region.[59] New classes emerged: the secular (that is, modern educated rather than religious educated) intelligentsia, and the industrial workers. However, the mass of the urban population, swollen in the twentieth century by increasing rural to urban migration, was only casually or occasionally employed, and then mostly in "the informal economy" (Santos 1979). Sometimes the urban poor could be mobilized by the Communists, as in mid-twentieth-century Iraq and Iran, sometimes by the Nasserists, and perhaps most obviously by the Islamists in Iran in the late 1970s.

In Egypt in the 1940s there was a struggle for control of the labor movement between the Wafd, the Communists, and the Muslim Brothers; in Iraq the Communists were more firmly in control. The main actors in all these movements were from the modern secular intelligentsia: teachers, junior military officers, bureaucrats, students, and organized workers. Iran centralized much later, so elites retained power in provincial cities for much longer. In the late nineteenth and early twentieth centuries there were protests against the Qajar shahs' grants of concessions to foreigners, and of course the Constitutional Revolution of 1905–11, which contained a complex mix of traditional

59. This did not take place in Iran until the reign of Reza Shah (1925–41).

and modern elements, led to a long civil war between royalists and constitutionalists. As in other comparable situations, the poor were on both sides of the divide, according to their view of which faction best supported their own material interests.[60] The struggles of the 1940s and 1950s, and in a sense the Iranian Revolution, all represent an extension of this conflict. By the beginning of the twenty-first century "the newly urbanized poor [had] been largely cut off from any source of political organization or mobilization, except, that is, for 'Islam,' which was generally able to escape repression through the mosque, communal networks, and welfare services."

The chapters in this book represent a variety of approaches to urban social history and range over a number of different topics in economic and social history. The contributors are generally agreed on a number of points: the interconnectedness of city and countryside until the region's more thoroughgoing exposure to the forces of the world market; the often cataclysmic effects of that exposure in the nineteenth century; the importance (and freedom of maneuver) of local political actors in what is often characterized as the apparently despotic and highly centralized Ottoman Empire); the general absence of deep-rooted sectarian hatreds; and the explanation of sectarian violence as having economic rather than religious roots. As the Middle East and North Africa begin the long and fitful march toward democracy and civil society, it is essential that urban organizations and institutions, however battered they may have been by the events of the last half century, will be able to play their part in the political revitalization of the region, and in particular in implementing visions of a better future for its long-suffering inhabitants.

60. Cf. the following salutary warning, here in the context of the Peruvian "middle class" in the first half of the twentieth century: "At the very least, we must reject the idea that social classes speak with a single voice, act as a single individual or play a single role in the shaping of historical destiny." Parker 1998, 6.

# 2

# *Interdependent Spaces*

## Relations Between the City and the Countryside in the Nineteenth Century

### SARAH D. SHIELDS

☙ IN THE COURSE of the nineteenth century, cities and their hinterlands throughout the world became more intricately linked together as increasing demand for raw materials both on the part of growing local populations and of expanding European industries made agricultural production more valuable. City people with money to invest in the countryside found lucrative opportunities, but at the same time the consolidation of their control over rural production left both peasants and urban dwellers vulnerable, especially the former.[1] The rural Middle East was a diverse world, with a variety of languages, architectural styles, clothing, and terrain. Peasant customs, land tenure, and methods of cultivation varied substantially between the highlands of Iran

---

1. As perceptively summarized for rural Syria more than seventy years ago: "The dependence of the rural areas on the city is an essential feature [of the relationship].... The relative situation of the parties is inherently unequal. On the one hand, the city has the monopoly of all power: wealth, education, political and administrative capacity, even religious pre-eminence, since Islam is an urban religion. On the other, the peasant, the 'fellah,' without resources, is permanently at the mercy of a bad harvest; without education, he is at the mercy of administrative or private exactions; without both political power and religious knowledge, he can only obey the wishes, or the whims, of the city dwellers." Weulersse 1934, 30 (translated from the original French).

and the Syrian desert. What rural inhabitants did have in common was their importance as laborers, consumers, and producers of food and raw materials. Peasants grew wheat, barley, and legumes, the basic food crops of the region. In addition, they harvested fruits, vegetables, tobacco, and nuts; collected dyestuffs; and raised animals.

Even as the nineteenth century opened, the city and the countryside lived not in separate impermeable spaces, but in a mutual space, sharing people, the things they made, and the things they used. Labor was exchanged between the urban and rural populations, and regular movements of people were common. In Mount Lebanon, for example, silk production tied the city and the hinterlands together, as peasants from Mount Lebanon traveled to the suburbs of Beirut to help with the silk harvest, and merchants from the mountain came to conduct business (Fawaz 1983, 39). Herds of cows leaving Tripoli each morning and returning to the city every evening attested to the continuing connections between the city and rural areas.[2] Harvesting raw material crops, which were required for both internal industry and foreign trade, contributed to the creation of bonds between the city and the countryside. Peasants coming to the city may have been a bit uncomfortable with its ideas and its novelties, but they would still have found the place familiar and would certainly have used the journey as an opportunity to enter the marketplace. During difficult times visitors may have sought to sell their own labor, and during celebrations they might visit relatives who had migrated earlier. Thus by the middle of the nineteenth century, food and clothing, people, tools, and luxuries had been going back and forth between the two spheres as long as anyone could remember (Toledano 1990, 196–206).

The very structure of the city illustrates the intimate connection between the urban space and its rural hinterland. The commercial district of a city was often geographically contiguous with its principal hinterland. In Damascus, the city was divided between areas servicing the grain trade, a "localist" area with "intimate ties with the grain and meat-producing hinterland" on one hand, and on the other, the central rectangle, which was oriented toward external trade

---

2. Faroqhi 1989, 3–34, describing Abdel Nour's work (Abdel Nour 1982a). Cf. the remarks on Narbonne and Angoulême in chapter 1.

and "high Islamic and imperial culture." Merchants often acted as mediators between the urban and rural economies (Schatkowksi Schilcher 1985, 16).

When approaching the city of Mosul from the Tigris, a peasant would have crossed over a bridge of boats and, immediately inside the gate, would have found himself inside the city's busy commercial center. This hub extended from the currency exchange in the geographical center, in a cone shape, to the river. The cone included all of the city's major institutions: the small shops where goods were manufactured and sold, grouped in large bazaars; the khans for merchants and travelers; the citadel housing the government and troops, and the great mosque (al-Janabi 1981, 17–19, 25; Raymond 1985, 228–71). Thus, all the most important functions of the city opened immediately onto the countryside, expressing the critical connection between those inside and those outside the city walls.

**Change in the Nineteenth Century**

Urban structures and economic institutions had been connected with the surrounding countryside for centuries, but military, economic, and demographic changes had led to increasing interdependence. The circumstances of war and other military requirements fueled some of the growth in agricultural production in the nineteenth century. For instance, Ibrahim Pasha, the son of Muhammad 'Ali, the ruler of Egypt, required large amounts of grain to feed his army of occupation in Syria in the 1830s. At the same time, the presence of such an extensive military force provided the security necessary for the safe harvest of the crops. Rural security also meant that the taxes could be collected. These taxes, often taken in kind, provided more food for the army (Sluglett and Farouk-Sluglett 1984). As the need grew even greater, new lands were brought under cultivation.[3] During the Crimean War, both the Ottomans and their European allies needed extra food for their forces. Cereal prices leapt upward, making investment in agriculture increasingly attractive.

During the nineteenth century, growing Middle Eastern populations continued to require increasing proportions of their own crops, both for food and

3. For the notion of the Syrian "desert line" and the expansion of the area under cultivation in the nineteenth century, see N. Lewis 1987, 15–24, 49–57.

local industries.[4] The countryside fed the city population and provided the wherewithal for its manufacturing at a time when synthetic fertilizers and pesticides could not dramatically alter output, when many areas farmed without the benefit of irrigation, and when mechanization was still in its infancy.[5]

At the same time that local and regional needs were growing, demand for Middle Eastern crops was expanding into ever broader circles. Global interest in the region's rural products reflected recurrent European political crises, population growth, industrialization, and better communications. Algerian grain fed Napoleon's armies, and quarrels over the debts that the French had contracted in purchasing it led to the invasion of 1830. Britain's repeal of the Corn Laws in 1846 opened previously protected markets to Middle Eastern exports. Exports of agricultural goods were not restricted to grain. Thus, when the American Civil War cut off supplies of New World cotton in the early 1860s, Middle Eastern producers and officials responded not only by planting more cotton, but also by beginning work on the ginning factories needed to process the crop and the railways needed to transport it. The cultivation of silkworms led to the production of raw silk, Lebanon's most important export crop, which increased dramatically during the pébrine epidemic in France. Tunisia's growing oil exports provided essential materials for Marseille's flourishing soap industry, while increasing demand fed the wool trade of Mosul. Growing demand for raw materials in the mechanized factories of Europe encouraged massive exports of both cotton and wool.[6]

Heightened interest in agricultural produce at home and abroad led merchants to develop innovative strategies to secure their own supplies. In both

4."During the nineteenth century the population of the ... Middle East [specifically Turkey, Greater Syria, and Iraq] increased by roughly 300 percent, from somewhere between 11 to 12 million to approximately 32 to 33 million." Owen 1981a, 287.

5. In Tunisia, droughts caused declining harvests during many years of the first half of the nineteenth century, to the extent that the authorities were often obliged to import grain (Valensi 1985, 222–23).

6. İslamoğlu-İnan 1987; Pamuk 1987; Kasaba 1988; Owen 1981a, 111; Owen 1981b, 532–33; Valensi 1985, 224; Shields 2000, chapter 5. The literature on the social and economic consequences of the new emphasis on production for the world market is growing. See Doumani 1995; Cuno 1992; İnalcik 1973a; Khater 2001; Tucker 1985; Quataert 1983; Rafeq 1983; Raymond 1974.

the settled agricultural and pastoral sectors, merchants acquired increasing control over the means of production as a way of guaranteeing their commodities.[7] Their direct investment in the rural areas increased over the century, leading to more intricate connections between cities and their hinterlands, and changed the ways in which families acquired wealth and power.

## Agriculture

The consumption of food reflected the most fundamental interaction between the cities and their hinterlands. Although some space was set aside inside city walls for cultivation, large cities remained dependent on rural people to produce the ingredients for their meals. In both prosperous and in difficult times, the dinner of an urban family in the nineteenth century would be based on wheat. For less affluent families, and in times of hardship, city dwellers literally survived on wheat, the most important commodity in most of the nineteenth-century Middle East.

Peasants planted the seeds, cultivated, watered, tended, and worried over the crops. In a good year their labor-intensive harvest might yield eight grains of wheat for each one they had put into the soil. Those eight grains would have to be divided, one to be set aside for the next fall's sowing, some to feed the family until the next harvest, and some to pay the tax collector. Anything left over could be sold for cash or traded for necessities. Floods, drought, or insecurity in the countryside could destroy the crops and with them both the peasants' income and the food for the urban and rural population.

Images of the peasant walking into the city marketplace alongside a donkey cart overflowing with grains, fruits, and vegetables tell only a small part of how the surplus from the countryside came to the urban center. In most places, indeed, regular market days saw an influx of farmers from the rural hinterland into the cities to sell whatever crops they might have over and above what they needed to feed their families and pay their debts.[8] Far more of the

7. It is important to note the development of stratification within the peasantry, with wealthier peasants also engaged in the struggle for the rural surplus. Because this chapter deals with connections between city and countryside, I have not included a discussion of the consequences of class changes in the countryside. See Cuno 1992; D. Khoury 1997a.

8. Cuno (1992, 49–55) described the market system in Egypt.

food found in the cities, however, reflected the methods by which urban people came to control the agricultural surplus during the nineteenth century: taxes, credit, and landownership.

Urban investment in rural products was hardly new in the Middle East during the nineteenth century, as urban merchants had long retained ties to agricultural producers. Nonetheless, a combination of growing local and international demand drew astute urban investors with the prospect of both wealth and power. Indeed, many historians have sketched a transition during the late eighteenth and nineteenth centuries as power was increasingly shifting from those with strictly urban property and investments in long-distance luxury trade to those with strong rural connections who acquired their wealth from the products of the city's rural hinterland.[9]

*Tax Collection*

Taxes were essential to the Ottoman state, and from its inception, taxation on agricultural produce of all kinds had formed the main staple of the empire's revenue. For a time, taxes were based on extensive cadastral surveys, and revenues from specific lands were assigned to individual military leaders and officials to compensate them for their services to the empire. Changes in the military and bureaucratic structures of the empire rendered the old system of paying "traditional" military leaders superfluous. On the other hand, centralized bureaucratic tax collection that would have required moving tax collectors to the site of all the farming villages would have entailed prohibitive expense in the far-flung Ottoman Empire.

By the end of the sixteenth century, direct collection was gradually evolving into a system of tax farming, in which prominent urban notables bid for the right to collect the taxes and then sent a lump sum to the central government. As long as the tax collector provided the amount agreed, the central government had little interest in how much was demanded from the peasants, the

---

9. Schatkowski Schilcher commented that this power changed internal politics in Damascus: "The success of the grain cartel transformed provincial politics from the mid-nineteenth-century onwards, for the profits made in the countryside eclipsed those of the overland urban trade in luxury wares which had been the economic base of the dominant urban faction since the eighteenth century." (1991a, 173, 181). Faroqhi (1989, 13–14) also reviews this issue.

time when the taxes were to be paid, or the form in which they were demanded. During periods of decentralized government, tax collecting provided both a route to, and a reflection of, wealth and power. By the beginning of the nineteenth century, many tax farms had become hereditary, allowing elite families to consolidate the wealth that came from control over tax collection, and, ultimately, the power that came from control over the food supply of the city population. The Ottoman government's intermittent attempts to rationalize and centralize tax collection during the nineteenth century did not succeed in ending the use of various kinds of contract tax collection.[10]

The three major elements over which the central government ceded control—the amount, timing, and type of tax collection—had enormous impact on both the peasantry and the urban population. Tax farmers could, and often did, claim exorbitant amounts in taxes, leaving the peasants too few of the eight grains for their own use. That could lead directly to famine, not only in the countryside but also in the city. The interconnecting web becomes clear here: if the seed grains were no longer available because of extortionate taxation, the next crop could not be planted, the family would not be able to eat, the peasants would flee the land and correspondingly less food would be available for the city during the succeeding year.

Taking taxes at irregular times and switching from taxes in kind to taxes in cash also had a significant impact upon the city; these variations changed the relationships between the city and the countryside. Sometimes tax farmers estimated payment before the crop was harvested, with payment to be made after harvest. Of course, before the grain could finally be brought in and handed over, the farmer might incur losses in harvesting, through hail, or through the voracious locusts that all too frequently devoured the crops. In that case, estimated taxes based on the yields that the tax farmer had projected months earlier would reflect a huge proportion of the final crop. Some tax farmers demanded payment before the harvest, and the peasants had to borrow money in order to pay. In the absence of banks, the cultivators were

10. For a description of the classical system, see İnalcik 1973b. For the reforms, see Shaw 1975. Barkan argued that the standardization of tax rates had inherent problems, caused by the lack of uniformity in previous taxes, local customs, and local production conditions (1940, 354, 357–58).

forced to rely either on a rural elite that was present in some places, or, more commonly, on the urban elite.

When the tax farmers demanded that taxes be paid in cash, this created ripples throughout the rural economy. Changing to taxation in cash sometimes meant a change in the kind of products that peasants grew. If the cultivator needed cash to pay taxes, he or she had to be careful to grow a crop that could be sold on the market. In places with adequate irrigation, a second crop, perhaps cotton or rice, could be grown during the summer for sale on the market. In places where peasants were unable to acquire cash from the sale of a second crop, the introduction of taxation in cash, like increasing taxes, simply led to greater indebtedness among the rural population.[11]

*Money Lending*

When the rural population was forced to borrow money as a result of high taxes, cash taxes, or tax demands in advance, the lenders were usually located in the city. Urban moneylenders provided advances against part of the next year's crop so that peasants could pay taxes. Whatever the demands of the tax collectors, few cultivators had ready money for the ordinary expenses associated with farming. They often purchased on credit from merchants, with the loans payable at the harvest. The lender sold grain for seed or food back to the cultivators, often at prices higher than he had originally paid to the farmers themselves. Sometimes the peasants borrowed additional money for animals or other expenses. Debts often took years to pay off, and in spite of the Islamic prohibition on usury, interest terms were often excessive, and repayment periods could range from twenty to as much as sixty years.[12]

The credit available to peasants tied them directly to urban moneylenders, who competed with the tax collectors for access to the rural surplus (Rafeq

11. Owen (1981a, 37) described larger repercussions in some places. It is worth pointing out that, miserable as the peasant's lot undoubtedly was, the fact that a certain level of agricultural production was able to continue at all meant that there must have been at least some room for maneuver and/or "resistance." See Scott 1985, especially 28–47.

12. Rassam to Canning, 9 August, 6 September 1845, Great Britain, Foreign Office (FO) 195/228 (National Archives, Kew); Meriwether 1987. See also Rafeq's article in this volume (chapter 4) and Jennings 1973.

1984a). Lending money to the rural population was not only a lucrative activity for the merchants, who received substantial interest and could impose harsh payment terms, it also secured their access to rural commodities. In 1858, Christian Rassam (d. 1872), one of the leading merchants of Mosul, who had been British Vice-Consul since 1839, agreed to hand over all the grain he received (15 percent of the harvest) to pay the grain tax. His profit would come from the irrigated summer cash crops: he would receive half of all the cotton, sesame, and rice. From this half, he would pay all taxes on the summer crops, the money for a conscription levy, the costs of seed, and repairs to irrigation works. Nonetheless, that still left him an estimated profit of 20 percent of the irrigated summer crops.[13]

Urban creditors were clearly tied into the economy of the countryside, and the sheer amount of money owed to these agricultural moneylenders sometimes appeared as a threat to the government. When the crops seemed likely to fail, as in 1845, the governor of Mosul specifically forbade the townspeople to demand their debts from cultivators, fearing that the small surplus, if paid to the creditors, would leave him with nothing left to collect as taxes. This competition was dangerous for the merchants, as Rassam pointed out: if the government took the entire surplus, the urban creditors might lose not only their interest, but also access to the crops which constituted their merchandise.

To protect the peasantry from the poverty that could be brought on by the high interest rates on agricultural loans (up to half of the crop if the lender provided irrigation and maintenance as well as tools and seed), a rudimentary agricultural savings bank was established in Mosul in 1884. Richards, the British consul, described the working of the bank and explained its lack of success:

> This bank lends to those in need at the rate of 1 per cent per month, with a lien on the borrower's land for twice the amount, such loans not being made for a period exceeding a year. If the loan be not returned with interest at the end of the year the property given as a guarantee will be sold, and the amount due to the bank recovered from the proceeds of the sale, the surplus,

13. Rassam to Alison, 10 July 1858, FO 195/603 (National Archives, Kew) ; "Correspondence between Mr. Rassam and the Pasha of Moossul 1858."

if there be any, being returned to the borrower. It appears that these conditions have had a considerably deterrent effect upon many peasants who otherwise would have been only too glad to profit by so useful an institution. . . . I am given to understand that the experiment so far is not generally considered a success.[14]

The experiment in commercial credit continued, but peasants still relied primarily on the familiar moneylender. *Salam* contracts, under which speculators bought crops well before the harvest, were common throughout the region because they provided the peasant with the capital needed for agriculture while providing merchants with much coveted agricultural products. Although technically illegal under Islamic law, these contracts seem to have been ubiquitous in the Middle East and significantly increased the connection between urban and rural populations. Valensi noted the existence of *salam* contracts for Tunisian oil in the 1830s. Doumani described the system as applied to oil from Nablus; Cuno, for rice in the Egyptian Delta; and Shields, for wool from Mosul.[15] This indebtedness gave the urban tax collector or moneylender secure access to crops to sell and substantial control over the adjacent countryside, a means of control that, Meriwether argued, was more powerful in the long term than mere tax collection (1987, 69–70).

*Landowning*

By the middle of the nineteenth century, new demands and expanding markets encouraged urban merchants to increase and diversify their involvement and investment in the countryside. There were clearly enormous profits to be made from lending money, from the sale of wheat, from the skyrocketing demand for rural produce in neighboring areas, and from foreign demand for agricultural goods. In order both to ensure their access to the crops that would provide their profits, and to lessen their dependence on rural food producers, urban dwellers increasingly sought to become landowners during the nineteenth

14. British Parliamentary Papers 1884–85, 180, Richards report for 1884. Quataert 1973, 137–8; 1980.

15. Valensi 1985, 226, 236; Doumani 1995, 14, ch. 4; Cuno 1992, 55–56; Shields 2000, ch. 4.

century. At the same time, the Ottoman government wanted to centralize its power throughout the empire, a part of its "self-strengthening" impulse. That required, first, more efficient tax collection, and second, the encouragement of reliable elites willing and able to help control the countryside. The urban merchants wanted more secure access to rural goods, and the government wanted to register land and make sure it got its share of the rural surplus. These two trends, urban investment in the countryside and the government's desire for regular revenue collection, came together in the Ottoman Land Law of 1858.[16]

Historians have debated the impact of the 1858 Land Law, which provided title deeds to land to those who could prove long-term habitation or continuous cultivation. The law seems to have had varying effects in different places. Land tenure changes resulted in large plantation agriculture in a few places in the Ottoman Balkans, Egypt, and scattered areas elsewhere in the Middle East.[17] In the mountainous parts of Syria and Lebanon, numerous peasants did

16. Burke 1991, 29. For connections between the central government's relationship with the new rural moneylending and landowning groups and their political implications, see Burke 1991, 29; Meriwether 1987, 70–73; Cuno 1992, 106–9; İnalcik 1991, 17–53. For usury in Anatolia, see Jennings 1973 and Issawi 1980, 351, 356.

17. "Dead" or uncultivated arable land (*mawat*) was also available for sale. This is thought to be the origin of the large plantations that developed during the nineteenth century to produce cash crops for the world market. These large plantations(*çiftliks*) are a source of great controversy. See Keyder's introduction in Keyder and Tabak (1991) and the articles by Veinstein (1991) and İnalcik (1991). In Mosul, Vice-Consul Rassam claimed that notables, conspiring with local officials, would try to frighten the peasants with a large tax or imminent conscription to force them to flee, and this would enable them to purchase an entire village for a small amount. The foreign representatives in the city were troubled by these sales, because it meant that they would not have free access to the products of the land, nor would they be able to engage in moneylending to the people farming the crops. Başbakanlık Arşivi (Prime Minister's Archives, Istanbul), Irade, Dahiliye 30, 679, reports on the sale in 1860 of fourteen pieces of arable land found deserted, and may refer to the results of this sort of behavior. Rassam to de Redcliffe, 12 February 1855, FO 195/394. In 1919 a British report on Mosul described the practice of imprisoning peasants who refused to sell their land (Great Britain 1919, 21). Marcus (1989, 138) described abandoned villages around Aleppo during the eighteenth century, the result not of conscious efforts to dispossess villagers, but of heavy tax burdens occasioned by war and general rural insecurity.

register their lands and claimed ownership. In southern Iraq, peasants feared that registering their land was simply a trick, making them more visible to the government and therefore more eligible for exploitation (principally higher taxation and conscription). In many cases they simply agreed to have the tax collector or the tribal shaykh register their property for them. Of course, the collector or the shaykh registered the land in his own name. The implications of this new control over land could be substantial in some places. For example, when one merchant owned an entire village, all the surplus produce would be marketed through him, an explanation for some merchants' objections to the new practice. In the tribal lands of southern Iraq, the shaykhs' registration of land dramatically changed the relationships among tribal members. In time, the tribesmen became share-croppers on land officially belonging to the chiefs (Quataert 1991, 38–49; for lower Iraq, see Jwaideh 1984, 333–56, and Farouk-Sluglett and Sluglett 1983a).

Geographical variations alone do not account for some of the more dramatic disagreements over the impact of the land laws on urban-rural relations. The arguments center round whether the law simply legitimized preexisting realities or created new ones, and whether it changed production or relationships between peasants and landholders. Some argue that the Land Law meant continuity, and was simply making legal a de facto reality. In this view, some tax collectors had already developed a relationship with the villages that was very similar to ownership. The tax collector or creditor decided what to plant, made sure people worked the land, lent money to the farmers for seed, helped maintain irrigation, and collected most of the crop either as payment for interest or as taxes. These historians argue that there was little change as a result of the new legislation. The older system of hereditary tax farming (*iltizam* or *malikane*) was, they argue, essentially indistinguishable from landownership anyway, and agricultural products continued to be shared between urban merchants and government officials (Sluglett and Farouk-Sluglett 1984, 416; Owen 1981a, 140).

Others argue that the impact of the new laws in Egypt and the Fertile Crescent was enormous. Pointing out that even hereditary tax farms were often confiscated by the state, some historians have claimed that, by creating true private property, the new laws introduced dramatically different relationships into the countryside. Particularly in places where government officials and urban notables acquired title deeds, the law created a whole class of absentee urban landlords at the same time that it transformed peasants into landless rural laborers. Cuno points out that the very existence of these documents transformed peasants' rights, as officials increasingly refused to recognize transactions that were not substantiated by the new deeds. As the rules changed, peasant claims lost their legitimacy and their families lost their autonomy, becoming merely hired hands on an urban notable's estate.[18]

It seems clear in any case that, whether or not the Land Law changed the status of the parties and the nature of the relationship between city and countryside, the underlying situation continued, changed in degree or method rather than in nature. Whether the urban elites owned the land, or merely collected the taxes and lent the capital, the nineteenth century witnessed a growing tendency for them to be more directly in control of producing the wheat, of grinding the flour, of marketing the grain, and of determining the prices that city people would pay for their bread.

### Controlling the Rural Surplus: Urban Consequences

The city's constant need for grain clearly left urban dwellers dependent upon the countryside. When harvests were bad and bread became expensive, the city people rioted, attacking grain stores and trying to block grain exports. In Sivas and Erzurum, in the years immediately before the revolution of 1908, city dwellers and villagers sacked granaries in protest over food shortages, high prices, and excessive taxes (Schatkowski Schilcher 1991a, 177; Quataert 1991, 45). Through their investment in grain, those who lent money to the peasants demanded their taxes, collected their rents, and marketed their products and thus became an increasingly powerful elite, not only in the countryside, but also in the city. Their success in controlling the marketing of crops also meant that they were able to manipulate the food supply. Indeed, control over wheat meant essentially the power of life and death. Historians have described "created famines" during the second half of the nineteenth century in both Baghdad and Damascus, the result of merchants purposely keeping wheat away from the urban markets, hoarding it in the hope that scarcity would result in higher

18. Cuno 1992, 202–3. Nowshirvani (1981) claimed that this did not happen in Iran, where most landlords remained on the land.

prices. In both places, de facto monopolistic cartels resulted from alliances between urban merchants and "corrupt" government officials (Fattah 1997, 99–150). Aiming to control the market, they limited exports, required that all trade should take place through members of a small cartel, and prevented foreign interests from becoming involved in the grain trade (Schatkowski Schilcher 1991a, 167–90; Fattah 1991, 152, 157).

Abraham Marcus noted the existence of "created famines" in Aleppo in the late eighteenth century. Despite government responsibility for ensuring the urban food supply, local profiteering exacerbated famine conditions. Especially when the authority of the central state was weak, local notables were able to evade price controls and to keep back grain from the market by storing it either in the villages or in urban warehouses. Marcus described the resourcefulness of the elite in profiting from scarcity during the famines of the 1780s and 1790s, when the janissaries and the notables managed to buy up all the grain brought to Aleppo. Wheat, flour, and bread vanished from the shops and markets during the daytime; at night the city came alive as black marketeers sold the new stocks at twice the officially allowed price. "Residents purchased their bread on dark street corners from dealers who charged exorbitant prices for inferior loaves." The situation was so desperate that the governor himself bowed to reality and also bought bread for the troops at black market prices (Marcus 1989, 134). No wonder, then, that the urban population ransacked the granaries and attacked officials in times of famine (see Burke 1989, 1991 and chap. 8 below).

At the same time, the cartels functioned to keep out foreign competition. British representatives complained constantly about price manipulation, oppressive taxes, and favoritism. In late nineteenth-century Baghdad, it seems that famines may have been created partly to freeze out foreign competitors, a form of manipulation that necessarily involved the collusion of the provincial government. Famine prices ruled in the grain market, and starvation seemed imminent. The government railed hypocritically at monopolists and hoarders while working hand in glove with these very profiteers, to the point where it stubbornly refused to distribute grain from its own ample stores even as the population of Baghdad and its environs clamored for food. Many grain merchants were ruined and the market became dominated by government-allied merchants (Fattah 1991, 151–58).

Eleven years later, the grain cartels again drove up prices, and again the provincial government's grain reserves were not made available. Famine threatened, despite a prohibition on grain exports, as the local government ignored orders from the central government in Istanbul to open its own granaries and those belonging to individual merchants. When prices were driven as high as they could go, the merchants and governments finally sold their grain, and Baghdadis were once again able to eat. Hala Fattah points out that these "famines" had important political uses, in mitigating the influence of foreign interests, in reinforcing the importance of ties to the powerful notables and officials of the city, and in facilitating the latter's acquisition of great wealth.[19]

Although control over wheat had been important in endowing the urban notables with wealth and power before the beginning of the nineteenth century, soaring global demand greatly increased the profits to be gained from providing credit and investing in the countryside. Urban food requirements continued to rise as city populations grew. At the same time, industrialization and improvements in transport proceeded apace, creating rapidly expanding demand for certain products from the Middle Eastern countryside. In some areas, this new demand for export crops encouraged a few city notables to invest in the countryside not only as tax collectors and moneylenders but also as entrepreneurial owners of farm land and of the machinery to process the crops. As those areas switched to cash crops for the world market, investing in wheat-growing lands became even more attractive, since the demand for bread in areas producing nongrain export crops had to be met from the remaining grain areas.

## The Pastoral Economy

The gradual process by which merchants increased their control over grain production found an echo in the pastoral economy. Just as there was a fundamental interdependence between the merchants who needed grain and the

19. The British challenged the tax farmer's right to market the crop that he collected as taxes, calling it a hidden monopoly that contravened the provisions of the treaty, which the British and the Ottomans had signed in 1838. The Ottoman government disagreed: "Ottoman bureaucrats insisted that once the multazim discharged his liabilities to the Treasury, he was free to dispose of the produce in any manner he saw fit." Fattah 1991, 160–2.

rural population who provided labor, skills, and access to the soil, so there was a degree of mutual reliance between the city merchants who needed wool and the nomads who grazed the sheep. Tensions mounted between the absentee "owners" and the producers as urban people moved gradually toward more control and ultimately ownership of land and sheep, in an effort to secure supplies.

Nomads living in the hinterland had long cultivated intricate connections with urban centers. These pastoralists were crucial as consumers of the city's goods, as purchasers of the rural products sold in urban markets, as guarantors or destroyers of the rural security needed for trade and cultivation, and as producers of essential raw materials for city looms and urban tables. More important, during the nineteenth century, pastoral products became the principal items of both regional and international trade. Large numbers of sheep were transported on the hoof from northern Iraq to be slaughtered for meat in Syria and Egypt, and their wool became an important commodity. Urban dwellers were unable to raise large numbers of sheep for meat and wool within the city as they had neither the space nor the skills; sheep were raised by nomads living in the hinterland. The story of how the merchants acquired access to those crucial products in northern Iraq provides a good example of economic interaction between the city and the rural areas, another story of mutual dependence.

Although some nomads subsisted solely on the products of the animals they grazed, many Middle Eastern pastoralists ate wheat bread. They acquired the flour in the villages and cities in exchange for animal products: meat, hides, skins, milk. These animal raisers could be found frequenting city markets when their relations with the government were good. When they failed to pay their taxes, when the government involved itself in the details of internal tribal successions or political struggles, or when the nomads encroached on farmland because fodder was scarce, the government tried to punish them by refusing to allow them access to urban markets. The nomads' resistance to urban domination and the merchants' dependence on the nomads became most evident when the government tried to enforce these prohibitions. Having come to depend upon wheat as a dietary staple, the nomads responded by raiding villages, creating insecurity on the roads, and attacking other tribes. The insecurity that they created outside the city affected not only the merchants but the entire population, since it halted all transport and prevented all commerce. When the nomads disrupted the harvest, wheat would not be available in the cities. When they attacked transport, goods could not go in or out. The nomad's control over security, combined with their ability to disrupt production, explains the increasing frequency of government campaigns into the countryside to pacify the tribes. In 1857, the head of the 'Anayza confederation demanded free access to urban markets before ending hostilities with the provincial government. Merchants worried about the Shammar tribes, anticipating plunder as soon as the governor of Baghdad refused them access to the city's markets in 1862.[20]

In an evolution similar to that by which the merchants took control over agricultural production, urban entrepreneurs increasingly came to dominate the region's wool production. As Middle Eastern wool became a "crop" demanded by Europeans, merchants sought new ways to secure adequate supplies. In the past, merchants had simply sent agents to the nomadic tribes at the sheep shearing in order to choose and purchase fleeces. As demand for wool increased, the merchants began to speculate, paying in advance for later delivery of fleeces, thereby securing their future merchandise. Advancing money made the urban merchants dependent on the honesty and goodwill of the tribes while putting the nomads in debt to urban dwellers.

Even this system did not provide enough of a guarantee for many of the merchants of Mosul. It soon became clear that speculative loans would not produce adequate stocks, and merchants began to purchase their own flocks. Still, the urban merchants possessed neither the skills nor the land to graze the sheep, and intensive animal husbandry was still many decades in the future. Hence they hired various tribes in the hinterland to raise the sheep for them, and to "harvest" the fleeces on their behalf. Thus, in spite of their ownership of the animals, they were unable to achieve independence and control over production (N. Lewis 1987, 43–44; Shields 1992, 773–89).

During disputes between the nomads and the government, particularly when the urban markets were closed to them, tribal leaders understood that the merchants' dependence upon them offered a new kind of power. They could make it difficult for merchants to claim their fleeces, or they could raid

20. Rassam to de Redcliffe, 14 December 1857, FO 195/394; Rassam to Bulwer, 26 May 1862, FO 195/717.

the merchants' sheep being grazed by another tribe. The new organization of wool production led city merchants and nomads to become dependent upon each other and tied up in the other's political struggles. The results could be seen in the evolving political power of the nomads and in new political alignments within the city (Shields 1992; Nowshirvani 1981, 572). Merchants found themselves in economic control as long as things went well, but when tensions reached a high pitch, they found that their dependence on both products and security forced them to compromise, if only briefly.

Tensions reached that point in 1860, after two years of wrangling between the government of Mosul and the Shammar tribal confederation outside the city. The governors of Mosul and Baghdad disagreed on who should be recognized as paramount shaykh of this large and important confederation. The paramount shaykh had a crucial role in the countryside, protecting transportation and keeping other groups from plundering villages. In early 1860, the local government deposed Shaykh Farhan, creating protest throughout the countryside not only from Farhan's supporters but also from the local population. It soon became evident that the new paramount shaykh was unable to keep order, as Farhan's supporters began to pillage neighboring villages and raid caravans. But when they plundered some sheep owned by Mosul merchants the uproar became overpowering. The urban merchants condemned the local government and demanded action to recover 30,000 sheep stolen in the raid, sheep owned by the city's notables. In response the governor marched into the desert, accompanied not only by his cavalry, artillery, and irregulars, but also by "a motley group of upwards of 200 people from Moossul chiefly owners of sheep" (Shields 1992, 781).

## Mutually Dependent Power

The intensifying connections between the urban merchants on one hand and nomads and peasants on the other required that the city become involved with its hinterland not only as a source of supply and as a market but also as an integral part of an interdependent economic and political unit. Taxation and landholding (and control over food and seed) combined to create a powerful urban merchant class and also an increasingly powerful rural population, whose power derived directly from their role as irreplaceable producers of the city's most essential commodities. They seldom expressed their discontent in ways that would create transformative change; nonetheless, their ability simply not to produce or to disturb others' production gave them some ability to mediate their own increasingly impoverished living conditions.

Even as urban commercial control over the countryside grew and peasants became increasingly dependent upon urban elites, the rural populations were also able to exert some form of control simply because they were the people with the labor and the skills, and sometimes the property, to control production itself. As we have seen, one of the most common and effective forms of peasant protest was simply not to produce (Scott 1985, 28–47). If demands for taxes, conscription, or labor became too high, the rural population refused to farm, fled, or hid. If peasants refused to pay taxes, the government sent troops to collect the amount due to ensure that adequate food supplies reached the cities. In extreme conditions, especially following such official efforts, peasants abandoned entire villages in massive rebellions against the government and the urban notables.[21] The merchants needed good relations with the peasantry, because control over grain contributed to the acquisition of political influence within the city itself. In times of hoarding, popular anger could jeopardize their positions and threaten their power. Philip Khoury has argued that the Damascus notables who attained power after 1860 achieved their prominence largely because of their control of tax farms. Many of the urban notable families participating in the informal Hawran cartel would eventually form the root soil in which Syrian Arab nationalism grew in the late nineteenth and early twentieth centuries. When the embattled Ottoman government failed to protect or adequately supply the local population during World War I, the Damascus-based Syrian Arab nationalists were able to supply the Hashimite-led Arab Revolt of 1916–18 with logistical support through the Hawran (Fawaz 1983, 90; P. Khoury 1983, 12, 19, 27–28, 31, 44–45).

Even power was at least partly interdependent. The urban elite's control over wheat left them in a position to exploit and endanger both the livelihoods of the peasants and the food of the city dwellers. At the same time, urban merchants desperately needed rural produce in order to be able to make their own fortunes and engage in long-distance trade. Despite the urban elite's monopoly

21. Schatkowski Schilcher 1991b, 50–84; Burke 1991, 24–25. For passive resistance, see also Quataert 1983, 18–25, and Scott 1985.

of wealth and the control that they were able to exercise, the rural populations could retaliate by acting in a variety of ways to endanger the livelihoods of the urban notables.

## Manufacturing

Viewing the rural population simply as agricultural producers would be to ignore their important connection with manufacturing. Peasants not only provided a large market for urban-based production, but during the nineteenth century their labor responded to growing demand from urban entrepreneurs. Peasants manufactured textiles both as a migrant labor force within the cities and as the labor force for a growing putting-out system. Largely because of the need to pay taxes in cash, rural populations agreed to use their skills as laborers to produce goods beyond the immediate needs of their own households.

In the new agricultural conditions of the nineteenth century, many urban laborers were transplanted peasants. They worked in both the cities and the hinterlands, forming yet another human bridge between the two realms. In Manisa, one of the leading textile production centers in the province of İzmir, urban weavers wove in the winters and worked as agricultural laborers during the rest of the year. They maintained their connections with the hinterland, connections that "sustained many weavers in the highly competitive conditions that prevailed during the nineteenth century" (Quataert 1993a, 83).

Many other rural people sold their labor to urban merchants while staying at home. Textiles provide the best known example of this system of putting-out. Merchants often took cotton and wool for spinning or yarn for weaving into the countryside, where people spun and wove at home in the off-season or when farm work was finished for the day. Even the delicate finishing processes were done in the countryside. Girls embroidered cloth in villages throughout the province of İzmir, using silk and gold thread made in Istanbul.[22]

Although some rural people produced for the city, many urban workers depended on the rural hinterland for both markets and materials. Indeed,

22. Quataert (1993a, 82–85) suggests that in areas of greater agricultural productivity, peasants would spend less time with commercial manufacturing. In those areas, weaving would be an urban occupation. In poor areas, peasants wove much of the cotton, and households engaged in both agriculture and manufacturing.

many of Mosul's workers earned the money to pay for their bread by creating the products that the peasants required to produce their wheat. Thus, farriers shod horses and mules, and woodworkers and blacksmiths created farm implements, horseshoes and horseshoe nails, chains, and harnesses for beasts of burden. Some city workers created textiles strictly for rural consumption. Weavers created coarse indigo-dyed fabric made from locally spun yarn that would be purchased only by nomads and peasants (townspeople preferred other textiles despite the low cost and durability of this fabric). Common urban products intended for rural consumption included striped fabrics for men's robes, wool and cotton for cloaks, and felt for hats. By the end of the nineteenth century, Mosul's estimated one thousand hand looms were weaving these specialized fabrics to market in the rural areas surrounding the city.[23]

Urban workers also depended on the rural hinterland for their materials. Tanners and butchers relied on pastoralists and dye-stuff collectors. Urban laborers pressed olives and sesame seeds; cleaned, carded, and spun both cotton and wool; milled flour, baked bread, and processed dairy products. Bakers needed flour, millers needed wheat, spinners and weavers needed cotton. Even after foreign textiles and yarn were imported into the city, Mosul's weavers still received substantial amounts of cotton yarn spun in the villages surrounding the city by both men and women seeking extra income.[24]

### Interdependence: The Arguments

Arguments over the nature of urban-rural relations in the modern Middle East have been raging for decades. While some historians see two distinct realms engaged in continuous conflict, others insist on long-term ties between city people and those living in the cities' hinterlands. Ira Lapidus argued that during the later Middle Ages there had been extensive contact between Middle Eastern cities and their rural hinterlands. Albert Hourani and Kenneth Cuno agreed, claiming that city and countryside had been mutually interdependent,

23. Issawi 1988, 74, quoting FO 195/2243.

24. *Salname-i Vilayet-i Musul*, 1308, 1310, 1312, 1325 and Archives du Ministère des Affaires Étrangères (Paris), Correspondance Commerciale; Mossoul 1:66–67, 2:321–38, 331, 338, 421; Rassam, 4 August 1863, FO 195/771; Great Britain, Naval Intelligence Division, 1917–18, 174.

tied even before 1800 by market and credit networks. According to Roger Owen, it was even a stretch to differentiate the two into separate realms: "Indeed, so intimate was the connection with the rural hinterland that it is certainly wrong to think of the city as belonging to a different economic or political order" (Owen 1981a, 45). On the other hand, Gabriel Baer argued that, by the modern era, integration had ceased. He went further, arguing that the economic disconnection between urban and rural populations was accompanied by a cultural chasm evident even in agricultural style and religious practice. Baer argued that Egypt was home to two exclusive worlds, urban and rural, which were essentially different, economically exclusive and alienated from each other. If we include pastoralists among rural populations, the adherents of this belief in the disconnection and animosity between the city and the hinterland become quite numerous. Recent scholarship cited in this essay suggests, however, that by the modern period, the cities and the countryside constituted reciprocally dependent economic entities whose needs had become intertwined. By the nineteenth century, rural people did not conduct their exchange predominantly with their neighbors using barter, but produced the essentials that permitted cities to flourish, exchanging them either as taxes, as cash, or to repay credit (Baer 1982, 49–100; Hourani 1968; Lapidus 1967; Gran 1987, 27–41; Cuno 1992, 3, 9–14).

The debate over the processes and results of nineteenth-century agrarian change arises from the larger controversy over models of transition. Attempting to define relations between the city and the countryside, historians have been guided by arguments over the stages through which Middle Eastern economies were passing. If Peter Gran's argument that exchange had long taken place in cash and that agricultural laborers produced for the market is accurate, it would allow historians to argue that some forms of capitalist development had indigenous roots in the Middle East. If the Middle East was wallowing hopelessly in a subsistence economy until the beginnings of contact with Europe, modernization theory would seem to apply to the region, encouraging historians to find the roots of development in contact with the outside. A transition from a monetized traditional economy to production for global markets would reinforce the claims of world-systems theory proponents that the integration of the Middle East into the world economy was a result of the emerging global system with Europe at its core. The debate relates to larger historiographical disputes about the nature of capitalism, some arguing that trade led to the development of capitalist structures, and others finding the roots of capitalism in internal struggles between the rising and declining classes within society.[25]

Despite differences over the larger theoretical issues, historians of the nineteenth century appear to agree that agrarian change reflected larger transitions in the relations between the Ottoman government, urban elites, rural populations, and a growing European presence. Interactions between city and countryside changed as the government responded to the merchants' needs for more direct access to the wealth being produced by the peasants. This chapter argues that previously existing ties between the city and the countryside intensified over the last century of Ottoman rule as urban people acquired more direct control over the products of the countryside, and that gaining this control had dramatic consequences for both urban and rural populations.

## Conclusion

During the nineteenth century, with demand for the products of the countryside increasing, important local merchants and officials grew wealthy and powerful as the countryside produced food and raw materials for their tables and their businesses. Margaret Meriwether describes the holdings of the Jabiris, a prominent Aleppo family, in a town 64 kilometers distant from Aleppo. The Jabiri family owned outright "twelve orchards of olive trees, three vineyards, three gardens, several orchards of various kinds of fruit trees, some land . . . a soap factory, two wheels for grinding grain, two olive presses, and ten shops." The family not only owned the land that produced the raw material, in this case olives, but also the press that extruded the oil, a soap factory in which the oil was processed, and shops in which it was sold. Clearly this urban family in the first decades of the nineteenth century obtained wealth from the countryside and invested it not only in land but also in the equipment to process its own product, exhibiting a sophisticated—and lucrative—understanding of vertical integration. As the nineteenth century wore on, such crops became

25. Gran 1987, 27–41; Cuno 1992, 3, 9–14. See Gran's review of Cuno's book (1994, 289–91); Brenner 1976, 30–75; Brenner 1977, 25–92; Hourani 1981, 26–27; Owen 1981a, 45; Hansen 1981, 477.

increasingly important in both foreign and regional trade, and the urban merchants who had invested in them profited handsomely from the new global demand (Meriwether 1987, 68–69). Urban merchants in the Middle East gradually came to acquire control over rural production, evolving from being collectors of crops as taxes on behalf of the government to becoming creditors who collected the surplus on their own account. As they needed to make their supplies even more secure in an age of increasing demand, urban dwellers became the owners of the means of production, in this case land and tools. The same process took place in the pastoral economy, as merchants moved from simply buying wool to contracting for a still-unharvested clip, and finally to purchasing flocks of their own.

Greater direct urban control over the rural surplus had widespread repercussions not only in the countryside, where indebtedness and landlessness increased, but also in the city. Merchants used their control over grain supplies to manipulate prices, in some cases even inducing famine. Their ownership of flocks brought political consequences as it tied the city even more closely to the nomadic pastoralists.

To argue that city and countryside existed in two essentially separate spheres no longer seems tenable in the light of recent scholarship on the Middle East and North Africa. As economic historians turn away from meta-models of development and follow the lead of social historians, more details of the consequences of urban-rural dependence will provide an increasingly comprehensive picture of the limits and possibilities of the shared space encompassed by Middle Eastern cities.

# 3

# Political Relations Between City and State in the Middle East, 1700–1850

## DINA RIZK KHOURY

☙ AS WITH ALL historiographies of multiethnic empires, that of the Ottoman Empire has always been subject to the vagaries of nationalist politics. Until recently, most of those who studied cities in the Arab provinces tended to view Ottoman control as inimical to the development of an urban civil society that remained only partially integrated into the Ottoman "system." Implicit in this analysis was the view that the cities formed part of a local identity, defined either in "nationalist" terms or in terms of a form of "urban patriotism" that worked against any meaningful integration into the Empire. This was especially true of scholars who studied Cairo, Baghdad, and the North African cities where the Ottoman presence often appeared to be tenuous. Such scholars tended to rely on local sources, rarely utilized the Ottoman archives in Istanbul, and were only superficially familiar with the overall history of the Ottoman Empire. The focus of such studies was often the urban notables, *a'yan,* who were seen as the upholders of local interests against "predatory" imperial demands.

Although this kind of scholarship predominated until the 1980s and still has its strong defenders, it is being gradually supplanted by two newer trends. The first of these represents a recognition on the part of both Western and Arab historians that the four centuries of Ottoman rule left a powerful imprint on urban life. Ottoman as well as Arab sources are now utilized, and scholars are increasingly likely to establish links between the Ottoman government and urban society. The work of Abdeljalil Temimi and his center in Tunis is the best example of this trend in the Arab world, and the recent work of a widening circle of Western historians offers a major departure from earlier scholarship.[1]

The second recent trend in scholarship on Ottoman history is an Islamist one that seeks to reexamine the Ottoman Empire as a viable political alternative to its successor national states, with their repressive regimes and dependent economies. In intention and scope, this trend runs parallel to the rehabilitation of the Habsburg Empire now being undertaken by some scholars of Eastern and Central Europe. Those who write from this point of view express differing views of the Ottomans, some echoing the conservatism of religious scholars, others the fiery radicalism of Jamal al-Din al-Afghani.[2] The most interesting among them have come from the liberal Islamist tradition that seeks to revive the autonomy of civil society and that symbiosis of cultural outlook between the state and urban society that supporters of this view believe existed under the Ottomans.[3]

If the general tendency of scholars who study Arab cities was to look at the Ottoman presence as something external to the social life of the city, their counterparts who study the Ottoman Empire from the center, utilizing the Ottoman archives, are more apt to assign to the Ottoman state a greater degree of control over its urban centers. Focusing primarily on western Anatolian and Balkan cities where Ottoman control was strong, historians have tended to generalize from the experiences of these cities. Furthermore, they tend to speak of the Ottoman Empire as an undifferentiated homogeneous unit, without questioning what the Ottoman Empire really meant. Thus, major regional differences between, for example, Ottoman authority in Cairo, Aleppo, Baghdad, or the cities of the Hijaz, are merely acknowledged and glossed over without

1. For the most recent survey in the English language of Arab historiography of the Ottoman Empire, see Barbir 1996a; see also Abou-El-Haj 1982. Abdeljalil Temimi founded the Centre d'études et de recherches ottomanes, morisques, de documentation et d'information (CEROMDI) at Zaghouan, Tunisia, and publishes the journal *Arab Historical Review for Ottoman Studies.*

2. See al-Shinnawi 1980–83. For a radical Islamist perspective, see al-'Azzawi 1994.

3. Wajih Kawtharani has published several interesting books on this theme; see Kawtharani 1988, 1990.

calling for a reconsideration of what such differences actually contributed to the nature of Ottoman state hegemony.[4]

In part this is due to the type of the sources examined. By their very nature, the voluminous archival sources generated by the Ottoman bureaucracy, and now generally available in Istanbul, create the illusion that the Ottoman state was in full control of its population. These documents, which include tax-farm registers, complaints by ordinary citizens, imperial orders, and detailed registers of expenditure, give the impression of an efficient state good at recording its revenues and responding to crises of all sorts. Yet we know very little about the actual workings of the state at the provincial level, largely because, with some notable exceptions, there have been very few monographs based on the use of a combination of local and imperial records that have explored the ways that the power of the state impinged on the lives of ordinary subjects.[5]

The major barrier to a less state-centered interpretation of Ottoman urban society derives from the biases of scholars who spent their formative years in a political milieu in which the modern secular Turkish state played a predominant role in remapping social urban society and identity. However, the past decade has seen a number of attempts to bridge the gap between those who study the Ottomans from the Turkish perspective and those who study them from the Arab perspective. In part this has been inspired by contemporary Islamist challenges to the secular Turkish state and the drive to find commonalities of experiences between Arab and Turkish Muslims. However, among historians who write in Western languages, the driving force has been the development of closer contacts, professional and institutional, between scholars who write on the two areas and the beginnings of a dialogue between the two scholarly communities at a time when "traditional" secular, modernization, and nationalist paradigms are coming under closer and more critical scrutiny.[6]

4. See İnalcik and Quataert 1994. Of all the contributors, only Suraiya Faroqhi attempts to discuss the implications of such differences among urban centers on the definition of empire.

5. Singer 1994; Ze'evi 1996; Peirce 2003; Ergene 2003; and Çanbakal 2006 deal with the sixteenth to the early eighteenth centuries; Grehan 2007 focuses on consumer culture in the eighteenth century.

6. See Akarlı 1993 and Kayalı 1997. For the earlier period, see Singer 1994; Ze'evi 1996; and Masters 1988.

I hope it will be evident from this brief overview of the historiography of the political relations between the Ottoman state and urban society that a promising new scholarship is emerging that builds on the work of earlier historians, sometimes incorporating their perspectives, but also slowly transforming our understanding of the relations between state and city. In what follows, I will try to incorporate the work of these scholars and attempt to make some tentative conclusions on the basis of their work. I will focus in my analysis on the major and well-studied cities of the empire located in the Fertile Crescent: present-day Turkey, North Africa, and Cairo, by far the best documented city in the empire.

I have excluded Istanbul because its position as imperial capital raises a number of issues that do not pertain to other cities within the empire, and dealing with such issues is quite difficult in a short essay.[7] More frustrating for the generalist is the lack of systematic studies on state and urban society relations in Iran during this period. This can partly be explained by the lack of political stability in the country after the defeat of the Safavids by the Afghans in 1722 and the subsequent disruption created by the imperial ambitions of Nadir Shah. By the last quarter of the eighteenth century, political power was fragmented among different regional power elites. The establishment of Qajar rule in 1797 gradually built up the state structures, yet most studies of Iran under the Qajars focus on the second half of the century when the modernizing reforms began to take hold. Significant studies have been undertaken on land tenure and the relation of the ulama to the state, but little has been done on the relationship of the state to various urban institutions prior to 1850 (Lambton 1953, 1987; Algar 1969; Arjomand 1984; and Etthadieh 1983).

7. In addition, although there are several studies of Istanbul during earlier periods, there is remarkably little on the period between 1750 and 1950. One exception is Çelik 1993, although her main focus is the built environment; see also Duben and Behar 1991, on families and fertility; and Rosenthal 1980a, on the Istanbul municipality. Suraiya Faroqhi has written on Ankara and Kayseri in the sixteenth and seventeenth centuries (1984, 1987). One of the few studies in English on the Anatolian towns of the interior in the nineteenth century is Erim's article on Erzurum (1991).

## State and Urban Society, 1700–1850:
## From Centralization to Decentralization?

The Ottoman state was formed as a principality on the edges of the Byzantine Empire in the late medieval period. By the early sixteenth century it had defeated its main Christian rival and conquered many of the Middle Eastern cities that had been under the control of the Seljuk and Mamluk dynasties for centuries. Straddling much of southeastern Europe and the Middle East, the Ottomans became the inheritors of both the Byzantine and the Seljuk and Mamluk methods of urban governance. From the Byzantines they borrowed the belief that provisioning cities and armies was the prime motor of preserving social order and of expanding empire. This provisionalist vision largely explained the attempts of the government to regulate the flow, and set the prices, of primary goods.[8] On the other hand, the legacy of the Seljuks and Mamluks can be inferred from Ottoman attempts to fix prices and control the quality of essential articles produced by the artisan population of the city. This was in the spirit of an Islamic vision of a "moral economy" in which the ruler had the mandate to ensure that exploitation of any kind was held in check.[9] The rule of sharia and state law in the city was maintained through the local Islamic court by judges appointed by the central government and was enforced by the police of the provincial governor. Hence, a "moral" and provisionalist ethic informed the series of laws (*qanunnamler*) that were appended to the censuses undertaken by the Ottomans after the conquest of all Middle Eastern cities from Aleppo to Cairo.

The central question for us in this brief overview of the political relationship between the state and the urban communities is whether such regulations worked between 1700 and 1850. The overwhelming consensus of scholarship is that if such controls over Ottoman economy and population had worked at one time, they were in serious trouble by the second half of the eighteenth century. Some maintain that the government's abilities to

8. For a discussion of this aspect of Ottoman economic philosophy, see Masters 1988, 186–215.

9. See Burke 1989; Grehan 2003; and Sami Zubaida's chapter in this volume (chapter 8).

impose legal and administrative controls were quite effective in the sixteenth century, but appear to have receded largely because of the prolonged fiscal and military crises of the seventeenth and eighteenth centuries. They draw their conclusions from studies of such large urban centers such as Istanbul, Cairo, Aleppo, and Damascus as well as a number of Balkan cities. According to such analysis, the state was able to rule through rotating provincial governors trained in the palace household and by posting provincial military forces, both infantry and cavalry, whose loyalty was more to the central government than to provincial governors based in the large urban centers. The sultan ensured the loyalty of his military by rotating his troops' assignments to urban outposts and by reassigning military prebends to those who best served his empire (İnalcik 1979).

For a variety of reasons, this system had begun to break down as early as the end of the sixteenth century. The process culminated in the eighteenth century in the disintegration of state control and the emergence of local power holders (cf. Thieck 1985), which meant that the state's military and administrative control in the major urban centers passed into the hands of local political elites. Local urban power holders acquired leverage and control over regional economies, sponsoring commercial growth based on control of both the agricultural hinterland and of international trade. At the same time, state controls over the movement of primary products as well as the provisioning of cities and armies eroded in the face of the twin pressures of international demand for such products and the state's inability to compete effectively with local merchants and contractors. Much like some states in the late twentieth century, the Ottoman state began to contract out some of the process of tax collection as well as the provisioning of cities and armies. Thus, by the late seventeenth century, the Ottoman state had developed a conscious policy of contracting out its administrative and military functions as a means of coping with its financial and military troubles. This policy backfired after 1750, when local power holders who had sometimes started their careers as agents and tax farmers for the government challenged its supremacy, often by outright rebellion as in Egypt, the Balkans, and northern Palestine (for example, see McGowan 1994; Joudah 1987).

Local power holders, members of political and bureaucratic provincial households, came to dominate the urban economy, its major administrative positions, and the policing of the city. Those who write urban history from the provincial perspective tend to view the first sixty years of the eighteenth century as a period of economic prosperity, urban renewal, and consolidation and also as a period of the articulation of regional identities and cultures. Those who write from the perspective of the center regard the second part of the century as a period of administrative chaos, military defeats by Europe, and rebellion by local power holders. Both groups view the first decades of the nineteenth century as a transitional period in which ideas of administrative and military reform were discussed and implemented. The reforms were initiated by Sultan Selim III in 1792, carried out successfully by Muhammad 'Ali, the autonomous ruler of Egypt after 1805, and subsequently crowned by a series of measures in the Ottoman Empire, beginning with the abolition of the old and unruly military forces known as the janissaries in 1826 and culminating in the edicts collectively known as the Tanzimat reforms promulgated between 1839 and 1876.[10]

The reforms of the nineteenth century marked a drastic break with past practices of governance. They were based on new Western-inspired models that often ran contrary to the provisionalist and "moral" vision of the premodern state. In concrete terms, this meant that subjects in urban centers were now to regard themselves as citizens, with certain rights and obligations; they were to pay taxes directly to the state rather than to tax farmers who had been local grandees, and those local grandees who had gained a measure of autonomy from the state were now either politically marginalized or incorporated into the provincial administrative structures of the state, such as local administrative councils. Although the state and the local judicial system had tried to maintain some measure of control over prices and the organization of guilds until the eighteenth century, these controls gradually eroded as a result of competition from European goods and were sometimes abolished or viewed as monopolistic in the nineteenth century.

If this narrative of a modernizing state draws too unproblematic a picture of the transition between early modern and modern, it is because until

10. For the provincial perspective, see Cohen 1973; Schatkowski Schilcher 1985; Rafeq 1970, 1975, 1977; Marcus 1989; Fattah 1997. For a central state perspective, see Shaw and Shaw 1976–77; Genç 1976; and McGowan 1994.

recently it presented a fairly neat explanation of the transition from the decentralization and apparent chaos of the eighteenth century to the modern order and rationality of the nineteenth. It also posited a convenient break between the premodern and modern and infused nineteenth-century Middle Eastern states, such as the Egyptian and Ottoman states, with overwhelming power to transform urban and rural societies. This is a narrative that is being questioned by the most recent scholarship on the Middle East, although it still dominates the way most introductory books portray the transition to modernity in the area.[11]

There has been some serious questioning of the extent and effectiveness of Ottoman control of the economy and the administration of urban societies outside major urban centers like Aleppo and Damascus. In fact, what is gradually coming to light is the tenuousness of Ottoman dominion over such cities as Cairo, Baghdad, Mosul, and Izmir in the sixteenth and seventeenth centuries.[12] Even Aleppo and Damascus experienced major rebellions throughout the period of "centralized" control. Thus, it is hard to make blanket statements about the state's control of urban society that gradually disintegrated in the face of the rise of local power holders in the eighteenth century, when such controls seem neither to have been uniform for all cities in the empire, nor to have remained unchallenged for any length of time. Furthermore, most recent scholarship is pointing toward a new understanding of the eighteenth century. Rather than merely focusing on the politics of rebellious provincial grandees and ineffective administrators, scholars are beginning to look in a new way at the workings of the system of tax farming, exemptions, and stipends that pervaded the relations between state and society in the eighteenth century.

Traditionally, the development of tax farming has been considered to be a sign of the diminution of state control over resources in favor of local notables and local power holders. However, rather than seeing this as a harbinger of the

---

11. See B. Lewis 1979; Shaw and Shaw 1976–77; Davison 1963; and Cleveland 2004, all of which provide a good introduction to modern Middle Eastern history. However, the transition between the eighteenth and nineteenth centuries remains problematic.

12. Toledano 1990. For Izmir, see Goffman 1990; for Basra, see D. Khoury 1991 and Abdullah 2001. For Syria in general, see Abdel Nour 1982a; for Aleppo in the seventeenth century, see Masters 1988. For Mosul, see D. Khoury 1997a.

end of the old regime, scholars are now viewing it as a means of incorporating wider sectors of provincial urban society into the Ottoman system by giving them a stake in it.[13] Work on Aleppo, Mosul, and Diyarbakır has shown that the extension of the tax-farming system helped create a local gentry that drew its support from Istanbul, challenged the traditional elite of the city, and provided the backbone of support for the Tanzimat reforms (Thieck 1985; Meriwether 1987; Masters 1991). Furthermore, work on the Mamluk power elite in Cairo, viewed until recently as the quintessential independent regional grandees of the eighteenth century, has demonstrated the intimate political and cultural links between this elite and the government in Istanbul (Hathaway 1997). Scholarship on eighteenth century Cairo, most notably that of Marsot (1984a), stresses the continuity between forms of political control and urban organization that existed in Cairo in the eighteenth and early nineteenth centuries. Khaled Fahmy's study (1997) of Muhammad 'Ali, while focusing on the new perception and implementation of the "new order" in the conscripted army, is careful to place the "founder of modern Egypt" within the factional political culture of the high Ottoman elite of the early years of the nineteenth century. Finally, Juan Cole (1993) has demonstrated the potency of "traditional" ulama and guild networks in mobilizing popular support for the nationalist revolution in Egypt as late as the 1870s.

All such work amounts to a serious challenge to the traditional paradigms that posit a clear narrative of a strong state with effective power over its urban population, giving way to a decentralized and chaotic period, only to end in the Tanzimat and Muhammad 'Ali's reforms, which reimposed state control over urban society. The modernizing Ottoman and Egyptian states of the nineteenth century had to build on alliances that cut across the state/society divide and exhibited remarkable continuities in administrative practice between the late eighteenth and the first half of the nineteenth centuries. The break with past practice only came after the second half of the nineteenth century with the introduction of new administrative regulations, new commercial and penal codes, and the development of a new group of provincial Ottomans that would challenge the older group on whose goodwill and

---

13. Salzmann 1993; see also her doctoral dissertation (1995), which is based on a study of tax-farming practices in Diyarbakır.

support the earlier reforms had been built.[14] The continuity in the structures of power and in class and group alliances between the eighteenth and nineteenth centuries is perhaps as important as the break implied in the borrowing of the Western models of reform and their vocabulary that occurred in the nineteenth century.

Finally, as more studies of smaller urban centers are being carried out, it is becoming imperative to deconstruct such territorially rooted terms as "Egypt" and the "Ottoman Empire." That is to say, it is somewhat misleading to speak generically of political relations between state and urban society in these regions based on analyses of a few cities that were particularly crucial to the empire. Studies of Jerusalem, Bulaq, Nablus, Tunis, Algiers, southern Iraq, and northern and central Arabia have demonstrated the variegated experiences of urban communities and the relationships to centers of power (N. Hanna 1983; Doumani 1995; Fattah 1997; Ze'evi 1996; L. Brown 1974; Valensi 1977). The ramifications of these differences in urban experiences of state power are profound. This new scholarship challenges the conventional view that urban communities in the Middle East lacked autonomy, had no legally defined civil institutions independent of the state, and were hence incapable of balancing the power of the state. What emerges from these studies is the degree to which the balance of local forces and the nature of the political economy of different urban centers largely determined the extent of state control, maintaining a degree of civic autonomy and ensuring the local organization of society.

Given this variety in the political relations between city and state, how is one to articulate an understanding of the nature of power relations between the two? It is useful to turn to a work on the comparative history of these relations in Europe. In his introduction to *Cities and the Rise of States in Europe*, Charles Tilly draws our attention to the close and formative links between the social structures of cities and the nature of the states that rules over these cities. Central to his thesis is the view that cities "shaped the destinies" of states, in as much as they circumscribed the abilities of the latter's ruling elites to

14. The classic work on Syria is P. Khoury 1983. See his reassessment of some of his conclusions in P. Khoury 1990; see also Roded 1984. For Egypt, see Toledano 1985 and 1990; and Cole 1993, 23–52, 84–109.

control resources and mobilize populations to wage war.[15] Two implications of Tilly's work are relevant to our discussion of the relationship between city and state. First, state policies and controls were conditioned by the social matrix of the city itself, that is, the nature of the indigenous power elite, the ability of the state to co-opt them, and the nature and availability of resources in the city. Second, and as a consequence of the first, it is difficult to speak of a homogenous and uniform relationship between the state and the various different urban centers in the Middle East (Tilly and Blockmans 1994, 8).

Perhaps the best approach is to devise a tentative categorization of urban centers based on their position in the regional and international commercial order as well as on their position within the Ottoman imperial system. Four categories emerge, although it should be stressed that these are quite fluid, with a number of cities falling into more than one category. First, let us consider cities that were provincial administrative centers, centers for mobilization and provisioning, as well as centers of trade. These included the largest cities of the empire such as Damascus, Aleppo, Baghdad, Mosul, and Cairo. Second, there were port cities, which served as conduits of international and regional trade and in some instances as frontier provinces of the Empire. Of particular importance here are the cities of Izmir, Acre, Basra, Tunis, and Algiers. The third category consists of interior towns and cities with smaller populations and fewer connections to the provincial and imperial centers of power. Unfortunately these are the least studied cities in our period; the work of Doumani on Nablus (1995), N. Hanna on Bulaq (1983), and Reilly on Hama (2002) are good examples of an emerging trend of studies of these smaller centers. Finally, the fourth category is of urban pilgrimage centers such as Karbala', Mecca, Medina, and Jerusalem that were often governed under different administrative arrangements. Large infusions of capital from endowments financed at times by powers at least nominally hostile to the Ottomans (for example, the Qajars) were the mainstay of these centers' economies. The relationship of their elites to the central government was often determined by the degree of their dependence on appointments to manage such endowments

---

15. Compare the view of Hohenberg and Lees (1995) that the autonomous status of European cities tended to retard the development of nation states: see also Tilly and Blockmans (1994).

at the local level. The local elites of Karbala' and Najaf maintained a level of autonomy commensurate with their ability to support themselves and their civic organizations outside the channels of imperial endowments.[16] For brevity, I will focus on the first two categories.

## Cities as Administrative, Commercial, and Provisioning Centers

Cairo, Damascus, Aleppo, Mosul, and Baghdad were the principal administrative centers in the Arab provinces of the Empire. Ensconced in their local government buildings, citadels, and sharia courts were governors appointed from Istanbul, a number of military regiments known as janissaries, and judges appointed to their offices by the highest Islamic legal authority at the center of the empire. Ideally, these three components of Ottoman rule in the major administrative centers of the Empire were to balance one another, each reporting directly to a different authority in Istanbul, but this system of administrative checks and balances had largely ceased to function by the beginning of the eighteenth century. In an effort to devise a workable system of provincial administration to replace the rather chaotic situation in the provinces in the wake of the conclusion of the Treaty of Carlowitz in 1699, the central government initiated a two-pronged policy. On the one hand, it negotiated an agreement with provincial political and economic elites over two essential issues, mobilization for war and taxation.[17] Increasingly, wealthy local families became the backbone of the provincial administrative apparatus, providing the state with provincial governors and bureaucrats. On the other hand, the state initiated a fiscal policy that gave long-term proprietary rights to local tax farmers drawn from outside the provincial bureaucratic elites. Urban conflicts during the eighteenth and early nineteenth centuries were partly caused by the tension these policies ultimately produced between, on one hand, the locally based Ottomanized elite and, on the other, groups of urban and rural gentry who had benefited from the expansion of various entitlements but were finding

16. Cole 1985; Faroqhi 1994b; on the political implications of financing imperial endowments in Jerusalem, see Peri 1983.
17. Abdel Nour 1982a provides a very good overview of what these changes entailed in the Syrian cities.

themselves obliged to succumb to the predatory demands of a well-entrenched provincial elite.

Three features had emerged in all our cities by the 1750s. First, the governors had acquired more policing, provisioning, and military functions than before. They were mostly self-made men who had begun their careers in the numerous military or paramilitary regiments stationed in the provinces. In their bid to turn themselves into a political elite, they acquired urban or rural tax farms and built an urban constituency by transforming themselves into households. The ‘Azms of Damascus, the Jalilis of Mosul, and the Mamluks of Baghdad were able to obtain and maintain their positions in the first half of the eighteenth century because they were effective in mobilizing and financing mercenaries and local paramilitary forces to maintain internal security and wage war against foreign enemies.[18] Egypt presents an administrative anomaly in this provincial system. Its governors were drawn from the Ottoman elite of the center but maintained very little authority in the province. The real rulers were the Mamluk beys, who governed under special institutional offices such as *shaykh al-balad* (city chief) and *amir al-hajj* (leader of the pilgrimage). Notwithstanding the uniqueness of the Egyptian form of political power, Jane Hathaway has demonstrated that these Mamluk households fit within the general Ottoman nomenclature of provincial elites in this period. The Mamluk beylicate was an Egyptian adaptation of an Ottoman form of provincial political leadership. Like governors in other major administrative centers of the empire, the Mamluks were granted their positions as large tax farmers, and privatized offices that allowed them to subcontract the collection of taxes to various elites within urban society in an effort to win their allegiance. Governors set up elaborate households modeled on the imperial one, purchased slaves to run their private households as provincial bureaucracies, won clients through largesse and intimidation, and attempted, sometimes quite successfully, as in the case of the Mamluks in Egypt and Baghdad, to monopolize the receipts of foreign and domestic trade in an alliance with large merchants and landowners. Only the governor

18. See Schatkowski Schilcher 1985; Barbir 1980; Rafeq 1977; Bodman 1963; D. Khoury 1997a; Nieuwenhuis 1981; Lier 2004; Crecelius 1981; and Hathaway 1997. All the conclusions in this section are based on these sources.

of Aleppo was unable to control the economic life in the city, largely because the office of principal tax collector (*muhassil*) remained outside his influence and was usually monopolized by members of the local elite (Bodman 1963, 36–37; Thieck 1985).

Central to the governors' control of urban resources was the development of a stable tax farming system that allowed the elite and their allies to monopolize agricultural revenues over long periods of time and, as the main collectors of urban artisan and commercial taxes, to maintain control over the urban economy. By the second half of the eighteenth century, when the Ottomans were finding it increasingly difficult to finance their wars with Russia, these local governors maintained a large measure of autonomy. The Mamluk Qazdağli household of Egypt conducted an independent foreign policy, contacting the enemies of the Ottoman state and invading Syria in an attempt to wrest it from Ottoman control. Not all local governors were quite as adventurous, and Ottoman imperial power remained a powerful centripetal force despite the weakening of controls in these administrative centers of the Empire.

Especially after the second half of the eighteenth century, a second trend appears to have been the decline in the independent power of the judge and the market inspector, who were responsible for ensuring that the prices and quality of goods were maintained according to certain standards. Increasingly, the function of maintaining prices and policing the market fell into the lap of local judges who did their policing only when complaints were lodged by artisans. The local police chief (*subashi*), who was drawn from the governor's private household by the second half of the eighteenth century, enforced the rulings of the judge. Despite the fact that market inspectors continued to exist in Middle Eastern cities in our period, their authority and prerogatives had evidently diminished.

Judges, who were appointed by Istanbul, were often drawn from the local pool of religious scholars. When they were not, they often appointed local deputies who were the real arbiters of both religious and state law in the city. They provided an effective balance to the power of the governor and often shielded urbanites from the demands of powerful local men. Until the second half of the eighteenth century, they performed a large array of administrative functions. They called for the mobilization of local auxiliaries when the government needed them; they ensured that the flow of goods into the city remained controlled and that the provisioning of urbanites and soldiers functioned according to government regulations. Together with the local notables and the heads of the quarters they determined the division of the taxes imposed on the population. Clearly, they played a pivotal role in the Ottoman urban administrative structure, and because they often outlasted the governors of the province, they were quite powerful in the city. Grehan (2003) highlighted the centrality of the judge in the Ottoman urban order, arguing that the judge and the courthouse had become the central node of popular discontent in Damascus by the early nineteenth century. Grehan finds this development indicative of the "Ottomanization" of urban popular politics.

By the second half of the century, however, the judges had lost two of their administrative functions to the governors of the city.[19] As the Ottoman government began contracting out the provisioning of troops to wealthy private individuals who were often governors of the province, the judges lost their function as inspectors of the provisioning process. With the privatization of the provisioning process, the governors often bought primary products (that is, mostly foodstuffs) on the open market and were also the owners of the agricultural lands that produced the goods. Hence, the judges lost the power to ensure that the provisioning process did not lay a heavy burden on the local population. They were no longer able to temper the monopolistic practices of the governors and their cohorts among the large merchants and landowners. Furthermore, the judges became obliged to hand over the task of recruiting mercenaries for various military campaigns to the provincial governors, who were now the chief military contractors for the state, responsible for the recruitment and feeding of troops. In this way judges lost another function that had allowed them to check the governor's demands on the local resources of the city and its hinterland.

The third feature, equally crucial to the political life of the urban population, was the function of policing the city. Whereas the janissaries, in cooperation with local quarter chiefs, had been responsible for maintaining the security of the city and enforcing Ottoman law, by the second half of the eighteenth century the police chief answered to the governor rather than to the

---

19. For Aleppo, see Marcus 1989, 173. For the impact of such changes on the political life of the city, see Bodman 1963 and Abdel Nour 1982a, 186–94.

judge.[20] By the end of the century, most urbanites in the larger administrative centers of the empire were increasingly subject to the demands of governors, who suffered few legal checks on their powers to extract taxes, control provisions, and recruit men. As a result of these political shifts, all the major cities under discussion here experienced urban uprisings compounded by attempts at reform on the part of the central government during the first twenty years of the nineteenth century.

### Political Actors in an Urban Setting

The janissaries and the local notables dominated the urban political arena in these major administrative centers. Despite countless monographs on the role of these two groups within urban societies, we retain a very vague understanding of how their role in the local stage was tied to imperial politics. This was due in large part to the factional and fluid nature of their solidarities and the porous nature of their corporate identities. It is essential, however, to try to present a clearer understanding of their changing position within their own societies and within the empire as a whole if we are to understand how these groups negotiated (or survived) the modernizing measures of the state in the second half of the nineteenth century.

Perhaps the most disruptive shift in the political relations between state and urban society in the eighteenth century was the transformation in the nature and role of the military regiments stationed in the major cities.[21] The state had posted janissary regiments in all these cities to ensure security and maintain order. The regiments formed corporate bodies, entitled to their own privileges and provisions, governed by their own rules, and headed by a leader who sat on the local governor's council and was responsible to his superior in Istanbul. A number of developments proved crucial in changing the role of the janissaries in the cities in the eighteenth century. The janissaries became more integrated into the artisan population and urban merchant community that dealt in such primary commodities as grain and meat. In Damascus, for

---

20. This was particularly problematic in Egypt where the janissaries lost such powers to a new element of "mamlukized" households often derived from janissary officer corps; see Marsot 1984a, 5; Hathaway 1997, 32–51.

21. For the political role of the janissaries in Istanbul, see Olson 1974.

example, they came to monopolize the grain trade with southern Syria and the Hawran and established trading links with the coastal cities of southern Syria (Schatkowski Schilcher 1985, 30–35; Rafeq 1975). In Aleppo, they were closely linked with industries that catered to the caravan trade and drew their support from the new settlers who competed with the older more established artisan population. In Cairo, they dominated the craft corporations, collecting their taxes and providing them with protection. In both Mosul and Baghdad they were closely associated with the trade in livestock and meat.

What allowed the janissaries this monopoly over urban life was their capacity to parlay their legal privileges into political capital by transforming themselves into arbiters over urban life. As members of the military estate (*askeriye*), janissaries were tried in their own court, were entitled to daily provision (*uluf*), and were exempt from taxes. The slew of privileges and entitlements, combined with the strength individuals could draw from joining the regiments, provided a powerful incentive for urbanites to buy such privileges for themselves.[22] The Ottoman government had legalized the sale of such privileges in the first half of the eighteenth century, an admission on its part of a practice that had been taking place for some time to allow the janissaries to supplement their income (McGowan 1994, 642–45, 658–72). However, because professional mercenaries became increasingly important in the conduct of war in the eighteenth century, the government became less dependent on the military readiness of the janissaries.[23] As more members of the local population were able to buy into various janissary regiments, their numerical and political strength increased. In Aleppo, for example, it is estimated that by the end of the eighteenth century 15,000 men out of a total population of 90,000 claimed affiliation to the janissaries. They dominated the life of the city until the first decade of the nineteenth century. In Damascus, their support was based in the southern section of the city; they dominated its politics and

---

22. Bodman 1963, 65–66; Raymond 1991; Raymond 1995, 52–59. Raymond elaborates on the links between the janissaries and coffee merchants, stating that a number of coffee merchants found it useful to belong to the janissary corps to strengthen their economic and political positions.

23. Aksan 1998, 1999. I would like to thank Virginia Aksan for allowing me to read these articles prior to their publication and for our many discussions on the janissaries.

effectively challenged the hegemony of the ʿAzm governors. In Egypt, they ran the life of the "little people," protecting them from the exactions of Mamluk governors until they themselves became, to put it in Raymond's term, "mamlukized," integrating a form of princely Mamluk political authority with a following among the regimental officers and the rank and file (Raymond 1995, 28; Hathaway 1997, 32–51).

However, the expansion in the numbers of urbanites who claimed affiliation to the janissaries evidently meant the term "janissary" no longer signified a purely military function. A large number of irregulars often joined the ranks of the janissaries simply by paying their leaders to include their name in the janissary register. In addition, the lack of exclusiveness within the corps meant that pressures on the corporate ethic that held its members together increased. The leadership of the janissary regiments formed political households with followers and retainers and expected allegiance to their households against potential rivals within the janissary corps. By the second half of the eighteenth century the ascendancy of the janissaries in the political life of the cities was seriously threatened. In Cairo, Mosul, Baghdad, and Damascus, the military and bureaucratic elite households who monopolized the office of governor recruited their own mercenary troops who threatened the preeminence of the janissaries in the city. In Mosul, Cairo, and Baghdad, these households were successful either in co-opting or liquidating competitors within the janissary leadership.[24] In Damascus, the janissaries of the Maydan quarter were able to withstand the ascendancy of the ʿAzm household and established independent economic and political links with southern Syria and with the power holders in the coastal cities. In Aleppo, which did not develop homegrown bureaucratic or military households that could challenge the ascendancy of the janissaries, the local challengers were the *ashraf* households who claimed descent from the Prophet. Even in Aleppo, however, the janissaries who had actually run the city at several points in the eighteenth century had lost their control by the beginning of the nineteenth century thanks to the concerted

24. Hathaway 1997, 52–106, presents the most detailed analysis of how this was done by the Qazdağli household in Cairo. For Mosul, see D. Khoury 1997a, 120–41. In Jerusalem and Mosul a sector of the janissaries joined the ranks of the local notables; Ze'evi 1996, 63–85. For Damascus, see Marino 1997.

efforts of the reforming government of Mahmud II and the cooperation of the *ashraf.* In Baghdad, officers in janissary regiments were among the holders of large rural and urban tax farms until the mid–eighteenth century, after which they lost their economic and political ascendancy to Mamluk governors and their households. The violent factional politics of late eighteenth- and early nineteenth-century Baghdad was fueled in part by the downward mobility of this janissary elite (Lier 2004; D. Khoury, 2008).

This brief account of the janissaries leaves us with a very sketchy picture of one of the most powerful groups in urban political life in the eighteenth century. Although we know a great deal about their allegiances in the heat of factional urban politics and rebellions, we do not as yet have a clear picture of how they operated on a daily basis, how they were able to control urban life, the exact nature of their relationship to the central government, or what their various economic roles were. In other words, despite major changes in their composition and their military and policing roles, we still do not have an exact definition of who a janissary was. Studies by Raymond, Rafeq, Schatkowski Schilcher, Bodman, Marcus, Masters, and Hathaway have done much to enlighten us about their political and economic role at certain periods. Yet we still lack a coherent explanation of the changing relationship of these janissaries to the central government at a time when their military role was being supplanted by mercenaries and their policing functions in the city were being threatened by the household troops of local governors. This gap in our understanding is especially critical when we try to explain the transition between the old Mamluk and Ottoman orders and the modernizing measures of Muhammad 'Ali, Selim III, and Mahmud II, all of whom initiated reforms that did away with the system of military privileges. What happened to the janissaries in the wake of these reforms? Why, after Mahmud II's edict abolishing their corps and Muhammad 'Ali's reforms, did they vanish from the political landscape with hardly a whimper after dominating urban life for such a long time?

The second group of political actors in the city was collectively known as the *a'yan* or notables. Even more problematic as a descriptive term than the janissaries, scholars of Syrian and Iraqi cities have expended much effort in devising a more precise definition of who the *a'yan* were in the late nineteenth century, only to end up discussing a miniscule elite (Roded 1984, 63–94;

P. Khoury 1990). Historians of Syrian cities where the role of the *a'yan* has been analyzed for the medieval, early modern and modern periods have done the most systematic studies of this group (Lapidus 1967; Chamberlain 1994; Rafeq 1970; Schatkowski Schilcher 1985; Barbir 1980). Even with the existence of a relatively well-developed body of literature on Syrian cities, the term *a'yan,* used by historians to describe a local civil elite, can obfuscate as well as illuminate the dynamics of state and society relations. Nowhere is this more clearly seen than in the attempts to explain their changing relations to the central government in the transition from the late eighteenth century, during which their independent mediating role between urban populations and the central government was at its most significant, to the second half of the nineteenth century, during which they lost their autonomy as the result of the centralizing efforts of the state.

For historians working on Arab cities, the *a'yan* as a group appear quite amorphous, encompassing men from the scholarly community, men of sacred descent (*ashraf* or *sadah*), merchants, heads of quarters, and sometimes heads of craft corporations. They were a loosely defined civilian elite that helped maintain order and facilitated access to power through informal networks among the various groups in the city. The term has a more specific definition for historians working on the Anatolian and Rumelian areas of the Ottoman Empire. *A'yan* denotes a group of local men, of rural or urban backgrounds, who had become the major power brokers for the Ottoman government by the eighteenth century. The Karaosmanoğlus, Cennetoğlus, and Cihanoğlus of western Anatolia were new men of fortune who made themselves indispensable to the government because of their ability to monopolize violence and trade. Their relationship to the government and their place within the Ottoman provincial hierarchy is much less difficult to analyze than that of the congeries of people in Arab cities designated as *a'yan* at least since the late medieval period. In contrast, the Anatolian and Rumelian *a'yan* were a social group that emerged in the seventeenth century and were successfully subjugated to the centralizing state by the reform measures of the nineteenth (McGowan 1994).

Albert Hourani's paradigm of "the politics of notables" (1968) has dominated the field despite some attempts to modify it. According to Hourani, local notables acted as mediators between the government and the local population, deriving their legitimacy from their ability to maintain a precarious balance between the need of the population to mitigate government demands and the need of the government to maintain a semblance of imperial order in the cities. Theirs was a politics based on forms of patronage and social connections enhanced by wealth but not necessarily tied to it. The nineteenth century reform measures, according to Hourani, undercut the mediating abilities of these local elites by co-opting them into provincial administrative structures.

Although quite effective in presenting a partial explanation for the factional politics of elite households in the late eighteenth and early nineteenth centuries, the "politics of notables" paradigm does little to explain changes in the meaning of the term "notables" or the composition of the group it designated between 1700 and 1850. Nor is it especially useful in explaining the political dynamics that governed the relationship between political power holders in Egypt and the representatives of the Cairene population. More recently, work by some historians has begun to refine, if not overturn, the paradigm.[25] It is becoming clear that by the second half of the eighteenth century the term "notable," while still used in official documents and local histories to denote a group of local representatives, had come to denote a group of people with different economic backgrounds and political roles vis-à-vis the state. The catalysts for such change were the transformation in the taxation system in the empire and the introduction of new tax-farming arrangements.

By the seventeenth century the Ottoman government had devised a system of taxation that allowed local notables to divide the tax burden among the urban and rural populations. This was a principle that had been followed previously but had only applied to the collection of dues from different quarters where locally elected representatives had divided up the taxes among the inhabitants. It had not applied to the collection of market and artisan dues. By the eighteenth century, these urban dues as well as all kinds of rural taxes were apportioned and sometimes collected by the notables or their representatives. In effect, the notables became agents for the state. Long before becoming its

---

25. Marcus 1989 warns against viewing the notables as representative of the local elements against the interests of the government. Schatkowski Schilcher 1985 draws a clear picture of the redefinition of the word "notable" in late eighteenth-century Damascus. For seventeenth-century Palestine, see Ze'evi 1996, 63–67. For the second half of the nineteenth century, see P. Khoury 1983, 1990.

administrators in the second half of the nineteenth century, their mediating role had already been seriously compromised. In their work on Aleppo, Bodman (1963) and Masters (1990) found that the hostility the local population felt toward these notables in the second half of the eighteenth century went a long way to explaining the rise of the *ashraf* and the janissary households as the true upholders of local interests. Thieck (1985), Meriwether (1987), and Masters (1991) have shown that a section of those designated by the local population and the government as *a'yan* had become the main beneficiaries of the new fiscal policy that allowed them to purchase long-term tax farms and to keep portions of rural revenues over generations. By the end of the eighteenth century, they had become a service gentry whose interests were tied to the state.

The fiscal and administrative policies of the state were pivotal in transforming the stratification among the *a'yan* as a group. In Aleppo, for example, the cohesiveness of the *ashraf* as a corporate group, with privileges and exemptions, was strained by the development of a powerful elite able to lionize the tax-farming market and develop elite households. Those less adept at using the system to their advantage, as the *ashraf* households and larger landowners had done, found in their allegiance to the state a means of maintaining a political role in the city to counter the ascendancy of the wealthier local elite. A similar pattern of division and group alliances emerged in Mosul during this period, but with different actors and different political results. In Damascus, class and group alliances were again somewhat different, but it is clear from Schatkowski Schilcher's work (1985) that the notables as a group were no longer easily identifiable as a political bloc, and their mediating role was being usurped by the janissary leadership, or by clients of the 'Azm family.[26]

The implications of such work for our understanding of local groups and their relations to the state are important. First, it is an oversimplification to speak simply of a stratum of independent *a'yan* as representatives of local interests and as mediators with the state in the late eighteenth century. Long

---

26. Schatkowski Schilcher (1985), Thieck (1985), Masters (1990, 1991), Meriwether (1999), D. Khoury (1997a), and Ze'evi (1996) make a distinction between political households and notables in the provinces. They posit that the notables developed a clear corporate, if not class, identity by the nineteenth century. Ze'evi locates the change in the seventeenth century.

before the nineteenth-century administrative reforms, a section of the local population, dubbed as notables by the local literati, who often came from their ranks, had become part of the Ottoman administrative system through their apportionment of taxes and through their control of tax farms over the generations. Second, like the janissaries, the notables themselves had become divided along economic lines that created political boundaries between those who had a great deal (notable households) and those of more modest means (service gentry). It is important to try to analyze the implications of such divisions for the relationship of these local actors to the central government. Third, we need to deconstruct the term "notable" itself; although it continues to be used as a descriptive term, it is also highly charged ideologically. It carried political meanings for those who used it to denote relations of power as well as to mask such relations. Finally, it is important to contextualize the use made of the term in the literature if we are to understand how the place of notables in urban society in the late eighteenth century differed from that in the late medieval period. Both biographical dictionaries and local histories use the term in a generic fashion that is often rather misleading. To understand how individuals were initiated into the stratum of the *a'yan* by contemporaries, it might be useful to undertake a textual analysis of histories and of government documents of the period, keeping in mind that the term does not define a clearly articulated "estate," but a mutable, disparate collection of individuals who were invested politically and economically in inventing and reinventing themselves as notables. By historicizing the moment of their inclusion into this ill-defined category, we will be able to understand their fluid role within urban society. Furthermore, a textual analysis will allow us to understand the enduring ideological pull that the term notable maintained as a means of social identification for upwardly mobile urban groups, despite drastically different historical contexts.[27]

The pattern of relationships between the state, local governors, janissaries, and local notables that held for most of the eighteenth century began to

27. For particularly interesting analysis of the shifting definitions of notability, see Vashitz 1984. Class itself is not merely a category that is identifiable by economic markers and an "integral" consciousness; it is also, to use a much abused term, an "invented" category imbued with contested meanings in the political arena.

unravel by the beginning of the nineteenth. In the cities of both Syria and Iraq the tensions created by the changes in local solidarities were exacerbated by the reforms initiated first by Selim III in 1792, and later by Mahmud II starting in 1812, culminating in the abolition of the janissaries in 1826. Ibrahim Pasha's invasion of Syria in 1831 only added fuel to an already tense situation. In Egypt, the French invasion and Muhammad 'Ali's eventual liquidation of the Mamluks ushered in a period of military reform and fiscal reorganization. Perhaps the clearest break with the eighteenth century was the disappearance of the janissaries as a corporate group, if not as a political factor, from urban life, and the liquidation of the bureaucratic and military households that had dominated these urban centers. Yet the central questions about the internal roots of this dynamic remain unanswered. Was this forcible ending of old political forms a measure enacted by reforming sultans and strong autocrats who drew their inspiration from European models? Or did the apparent violence with which these changes were enforced really conceal continuities in group alliances and relations between the state and urban society?

Although it is important not to underestimate the changes in the relations between the state and urban society in the second half of the nineteenth century, it is essential to keep in mind that the process of modernization was based on the internal historical dynamic of these relations that had been in the making at least since the beginning of the eighteenth century. Thus, despite what appears to be the loss of administrative control by the central government to locally based governors, these governors themselves initiated processes that touched on security, the recruitment of mercenaries, and the erosion of controls over urban markets, which did much to facilitate the reforms of the second half of the nineteenth century. Especially significant in this period was the erosion in the autonomy of the judicial system in issues of recruitment and provisioning, and its subordination to the power of local political households, a process that accelerated in the nineteenth century under the pressures of the centralizing state. At the same time, the expansion of the system of tax farming and entitlements that appears to have eroded the central state's control over resources allowed it to create a wider base of support among ordinary subjects outside the classical system of estates that had existed in the seventeenth century (Abou-El-Haj 1991; Salzmann 1993; Masters 1991; D. Khoury 1997a). If we take these developments as indications of the transition to a new order, it becomes evident that such an order was born and rooted in the internal dynamics of the old even as it initiated new methods and vocabularies of control.

## Port Cities and the state

While the specific ways with which state control and urban local forces interacted were quite different in Cairo and Mosul, there were discernible patterns that allow us to make generalizations about state and urban society relations. It is more difficult to make broad statements about such relations for port cities such as Izmir, Acre and Basra, or Algiers and Tunis, because the historical evolution and the political power relations that developed in them were quite different. It is instructive to discuss each one briefly if only to demonstrate how the local, regional, and imperial interacted and shaped the political life of these port cities.

The eighteenth century was marked by a restructuring of the commercial ties of the Mediterranean with Europe on one hand and the increasing European penetration of Indian Ocean trade on the other, developments that transformed trading patterns in the area (Frangakis-Syrett 1991a; Owen 1981a, 1–82). In the eastern Mediterranean, European demands for grain, cotton, and silk spawned an expansion of regional economies based on trade in these goods. Port cities such as Acre and Izmir emerged to service such trade, acting as conduits between agricultural interiors and European markets. Local grandees, such as the Cennetoğlu and Karaosmanoğlu in western Anatolia, Zahir al-'Umar in Galilee, and Ahmad Jazzar Pasha in Acre, monopolized agricultural revenues and ensured that they had the lion's share of trade with Europe. French merchants, who dominated the trade of the eastern Mediterranean until the Napoleonic invasion, had no choice but to deal with these grandees.

Tunis and Algiers, the frontier port cities of the Ottoman western Mediterranean, present a distinctive version of the interaction between Ottoman forms of government and limitations created by shifts in the balance of economic and political power in the area. In Tunis, the Husaynids, an Ottomanized local dynasty, were able to forge an autonomous state built on the wealth created by privateering and trade with France on one hand and taxes extracted from the countryside on the other. They succeeded in creating the rudiments of a proto-national state under the umbrella of Ottoman rule. In Algiers, the Ottoman elites remained a military overclass (*ocaks* or deys), distinct from the local population and almost completely dependent on privateering and the slave trade. When profits from piracy declined in the late eighteenth century, the rulers of Algiers found themselves unable to withstand pressure from European commercial interests. Unwilling to forge effective links with the local elites, the eighteenth-century deys saw their control eroding as Algiers was gradually transformed into a proto-colonial city, in which European trading communities began to settle and play a dominant political role.[28]

The maritime trade of the Persian Gulf gradually became dominated by Britain, which established factories in Bandar 'Abbas and Bushire on the Persian side and Basra on the Ottoman side. The British found that they had to deal with two political contenders in the area, tribal confederations, who set up market towns and small trading ports in response to the expansion of trade with India and Europe, and local power holders in Basra and Baghdad, who were anxious to monopolize trade, customs, and profits (Fattah 1997, 13–61). Much of the vicissitudes of the political life of the cities under discussion here consisted of maneuvering between European traders, indigenous merchants, local power holders, and the Ottoman state. Yet the ways in which these forces worked in each of our cities is quite distinct.

Izmir was a city of European and minority migrants and merchants and was never a major administrative center in the empire.[29] As such, it retained the aura of a port city with a large degree of autonomy and control by merchants. It developed as a large trading emporium in the seventeenth century, thanks to the settlement of European merchants anxious to circumvent Ottoman prohibitions on the export of primary products from the Empire, and soon came to challenge the monopoly of Istanbul over the grain trade of western Anatolia. By the eighteenth century, European merchants found their principal allies

28. For my analysis of Tunis and Algiers I have relied on Julien 1970, 273–335; Mantran 1970; Raymond 1970; Valensi 1977; and L. Brown 1974. I use the term proto-colonial to denote a town that does not have the administrative structures of colonial rule but in which European mercantile interests are maintained by an active foreign trading resident community. For further discussion of the distinctions between proto-colonial and colonial cities, see Prochaska 1990, 1–28.

29. My information on Izmir is based on Goffman 1990 and particularly on Eldem, Goffman, and Masters 1999. I have also used Veinstein 1976 and Frangakis-Syrett 1991b.

in the grandees-cum-warlords who controlled large agricultural tax farms and maintained security in western Anatolia through the mercenary bands they employed. It was a workable compromise, allowing European merchants and their local agents, usually Ottoman Christians and Jews, to circumvent Ottoman controls over customs and the movement of primary products.

Izmir became a port town that linked a regional network of trade and power to Europe. Because it had developed out of the needs of the merchant community of the area and had no history as a locus of administrative control, the presence of Ottoman officials in it was overshadowed by the power of the landowning grandees based in western Anatolian towns such as Manisa. Goffman, who has done extensive work on the city during our period, finds that the Ottoman government was only able to enforce its writ sporadically, and it adjusted its demands to the reality of the local situation.

The European and minority population shaped the spatial grid of the city and dominated its economic and social life. Jewish merchants controlled the tax farm of the customs house; Christians and Jews built churches and synagogues and practiced their religious observances quite openly; Europeans bought tax farms from the government and built their own quarter with cafés and wine shops. European and minority merchants were exempt from Ottoman law through the capitulations. In a city so dominated by European merchants and their allies, a dual legal system, one for foreign and one for local merchants, seems to have worked more effectively than anywhere else in the empire. Yet, in the eighteenth century, the Ottomans were able to counter such local autonomy through two strategies. The first was the development of an alliance with Ottoman Muslim merchants that allowed the latter to limit the Europeans' direct access to internal markets. The second strategy was to invest the office of local judge with wide powers to adjudicate on issues of trade between European and Ottoman merchants. In the absence of a strong Ottoman administrative presence, the judge became an important arbiter in Ottoman and European matters. The situation in the city began to change in the early nineteenth century when the government curtailed the power of local grandees, and in consequence the Greek minority emerged as the main agents of the trade with Europe (Frangakis-Syrett 1991a). The role of non-Muslim minorities in the political life of the city became more visible as the indigenous Muslim power elites were liquidated. In the second half of the nineteenth century Ottoman control over Izmir became more tenuous once again as the city was transformed into a proto-colonial port town, an enclave of European commercial and political power on the northern littoral of the eastern Mediterranean.

Further south, on the coast of northern Palestine, the city of Acre developed into the stronghold of a tribal leader who built his economic base on tax-farming privileges and the monopolization of the trade with the French (Cohen 1973; Joudah 1987). The governor of Sidon, then the major trading town on the southeastern Mediterranean littoral, administered Acre. Until its conquest by Zahir al-'Umar, it had been a small port where French merchants and Corsican corsairs had established themselves in an attempt to escape the customs dues of the governor of Sidon. Zahir had begun his career as a tax farmer in the hills of northern Palestine, trading in cotton and oil with French merchants. By the middle of the eighteenth century he had conquered Acre, set up a government in alliance with regional merchants who treated the port as a tax haven, and proceeded to monopolize the sale of cotton, forcing French merchants to buy it through him at fixed prices.

The Acre of Zahir al-'Umar was a small commercial state, based on the returns from trade and outside the administrative control of the central government. It drew its strength from the migrant population of greater Syria who found in its prosperity an opportunity for employment and trade. Thomas Philipp found that its mercantile community was drawn from minority immigrants, Melkites, Greek Orthodox, and Jews from Syrian cities. They drew their strength from their ability to work with Europeans, to service Zahir al-'Umar's financial demands and to draw on the support of networks of powerful men in Damascus and Istanbul. The city was run as a family patrimony, and its ruler was the main arbiter of justice and political power in the area (Philipp 2001). Unlike Izmir, which was never ruled directly by the warlords of the western Anatolian interior, Acre in many respects resembled the small commercial city states so common in the Aegean and the Italian Mediterranean: it was only nominally Ottoman, if at all. After several attempts to win recognition from the Ottoman government, Zahir al-'Umar allied himself with the Mamluk rulers of Egypt, who invaded Syria and threatened the Ottoman central government by allying themselves with its enemy, Russia. Unable to maintain his ascendancy in the area because of the instability of his local power base and the hostility of the central government, Zahir was defeated. Ahmad Pasha al-Jazzar, a former Mamluk from Egypt, succeeded in staving off Napoleon's army and set up a quasi-Ottoman form of rule based on his own household of retainers, but he continued to follow the monopolistic trading practices of his predecessor. However, the drop in the price of cotton combined with his inability to create a stable political environment drove the minority merchants away, and Acre gradually lost its place as a commercial town to Beirut and Haifa. In contrast to Izmir, where Greek merchants emerged as the most powerful brokers in the face of receding Ottoman control, the Syrian Christian immigrant minority in Acre found itself increasingly under attack from the community of Muslim religious scholars who had gained preeminence in the city.

The relationship of Tunis and Algiers to the Ottoman government can be analyzed from two perspectives. From the perspective of Istanbul, these cities were frontier outposts, essential to the expansion of Ottoman control over western Mediterranean trade and the struggle of the state against the Spanish, Venetians, and French. The central government's concern was limited to maintaining a strong military contingent and absorbing within its administrative framework the privateering activities of the infamous "Barbary corsairs," the most notable being the Barbarossa brothers of Algiers. From the local perspective, the prerogatives of the central government were circumscribed by the nature of distinct local institutions and pressures created by the increasing commercial might of the French and British in the western Mediterranean.

Ottoman North Africa has been described by one scholar as the "forgotten frontier," in part because twentieth-century historians often overlooked the region's centrality to the Ottoman state in the sixteenth and seventeenth centuries (Hess 1978). Both Algiers and Tunis presented unique local adaptations of Ottoman administrative structures with different results. The military importance of Algiers for the Ottomans lay in its position as the major port town for the privateers who attacked European ships in the western Mediterranean in the sixteenth century. The Ottomans contracted out the business of waging war against the infidels to sea captains based in Algiers and drawn from all over the Mediterranean world. In the circumstances of the "reconquista" of the Iberian peninsula by the Most Catholic Kings in the fifteenth and early sixteenth centuries, the line between privateering and fighting a Holy War was a fine one. The Ottomans appointed the privateers as governors, supported them with a fresh influx of troops from Anatolia, and had no choice but to allow the military regiments (*ocaks*) to rule the city quite independently of the central government. As in other cities of the empire, the military leadership of these groups formed political households and reinforced their strength by fresh recruits from Anatolia (Mantran 1970, 254–56). The descendants of marriages between the Turkish soldiery and local women were excluded from the elite, a situation unique in an empire in which the ranks of the military had become replete with local elements by the eighteenth century. Raymond believes that this policy explains in part the weakness of the Algerian political elite and their inability to build up institutions that provided the basis of a modern state (Raymond 1970, 266).

The prosperity of Algiers in the seventeenth century was fueled by piracy and the slave trade. Its internal affairs were run by coalition of powerful merchants (*ta'ifat al-ru'sa'*) drawn from the corsair leaders within the population and the Ottoman military establishment (Julien 1970, 302–24). Tal Shuval's work on Ottoman Algiers has qualified our understanding of the eighteenth century as one of unmitigated political and economic decline. According to Shuval, the period brought stable government and a measure of prosperity that only dissipated during the last decades of the century (Shuval 1998, 2000). The constant attacks by European powers on the "Barbary corsairs" succeeded in limiting that trade. The concessions granted to European merchants and the growth of rival port towns such as Bône ('Annaba) relegated Algiers to a peripheral position. Furthermore, as Ottoman power in the western Mediterranean waned, Algiers lost its centrality to the state as a frontier outpost. The internecine struggles between its power elites, combined with their predatory policies toward the rural population of Algeria, contributed to the inability of Algiers to cope with European pressure. Historians portray the late eighteenth and early nineteenth centuries as an inevitable prelude to the fateful incident between a French merchant and the dey that led to the colonization of the city in 1830 (Raymond 1970, 278–85).

Tunis presents us with a conundrum. The city had been the administrative capital of the pre-Ottoman Hafsid state and, unlike Algiers, which retained its character as an unruly frontier and corsair port, the Ottomans found that Tunis had a relatively strong administrative tradition on which they would build their provincial government. Yet the commercial role of Tunis was the most critical element in the definition of its relationship with the central government. Its elites were able to maintain a great deal of autonomy because they did not rely on the central state to dole out resources, and its local merchant class were strong partners with the Ottomanized local rulers, a situation that had no parallel in any of the major administrative centers of the empire. These reasons may justify its inclusion in the category of port cities.

During the seventeenth century, the city built its prosperity on the corsair trade and on the influx of some 80,000 Moriscos expelled from Spain in 1609 (Julien 1970, 307). The administration of Tunis was taken over by the leadership of the janissaries (deys), and the governor appointed by Istanbul became a mere figurehead. Deys ruled the province with the cooperation of the admiral of the fleet (*kapudan bashi*), and the city had a large European merchant community with well-established commercial houses. Unlike Algiers, the activities of its corsairs seem to have been more strictly regulated and less central to the economic well-being of the government. By 1714, however, the military elites, who were often drawn from Anatolia, lost ground to an Ottomanized local bureaucratic household, the Husaynids, who established themselves as a hereditary ruling dynasty in Tunis. As in other administrative centers in the empire, the autonomous beys of Tunisia were able to subordinate the military regiments by relying on irregulars drawn from the sons of Anatolian janissaries and local women (*kuluoğlular*) and by striking an alliance with local notables in Tunis (L. Brown 1974, 57). The Tunisian court adapted an Ottoman form of political and administrative control to Tunis by building an elaborate household with an internal bureaucracy steeped in the rituals and hierarchy of elite provincial households elsewhere in the empire (L. Brown 1974, 104–6). Rural areas that paid tribute to the state were known as *bilad al-makhzan,* and the governors undertook two annual expeditions to collect rural taxes. They co-opted rural leaders by appointing them as cavalry (*sipahis*) and used them quite effectively to counter the power of the janissaries. In the city of Tunis itself, the Husaynid beys built an alliance with merchant princes and tax farmers who formed a local political elite with remarkable longevity.

To bolster their control of the urban population the governors followed a two-pronged approach. On one hand, they removed the task of policing the city from the military regiments and delegated it to the civil authority of the heads of quarters who adjudicated disputes through customary law (*'urf*) (L. Brown

1974, 122–23). On the other hand, the beys worked at building an institutional framework with a clear hierarchy of bureaucrats, at the top of which was a military and bureaucratic elite attached to the household, supported by a judicial and clerical local establishment, and a slew of other formalized consultative bodies such as the city council (*diwan*) and the council of merchants (L. Brown 1974, 98–99). By the beginning of the nineteenth century, the Husaynids had succeeded in creating relatively stable government institutions based on the support of a well-defined political class. The Ottoman sultan remained as a figurehead and an example to emulate, although his authority over his western Mediterranean provincial capital was purely nominal.

There seems to be unanimity among historians of Tunis that the modern history of the nation state goes back to the founding of the Husaynid dynasty in the eighteenth century. Thus, Brown's book on Ahmad Bey, the first modernizer of Tunis, takes care to place him in the context of the political culture of the eighteenth century. Unlike other areas of the empire, the narrative of the modern period does not start with the Westernizing reforms of the nineteenth century but with the founding of the proto-national state under the Husaynids. The question that needs to be asked is why Tunis presents such an anomaly. Are its distance from the center of power and its pre-Ottoman historical experience sufficient to explain its exceptionalism, or should one look more closely at the way the Ottomanized elite were able to create alliances and connections to civil society despite the diversity of that society?

Basra presents us with another variation of a port city. It was the main gateway for Indian goods into the empire. Because India was one of the main trading partners of the Ottomans, control of the city and its trade was very important for the state (Özbaran 1972; D. Khoury 1991; Fattah 1997; Nieuwenhuis 1981; Abdullah 2001). Until the Ottoman conquest in 1539, it was a tribal commercial town, dominated politically by the Muntafiq federation, with a strong independent merchant community and a trade diaspora that hailed from India, Arabia, and East Africa. The Ottomans established it as an administrative center, from which they attempted to control the Indian and Persian Gulf trade, and also set up a mint to control the flow of bullion in and out of the empire to and from the India trade. To counter the Portuguese presence in the Indian Ocean, they made Basra a center of a fleet and the *kapudan bashi*, the admiral of the Ottoman fleet, remained a powerful presence in the city until the second half of the eighteenth century. Unlike Izmir and Acre, Basra was not a commercial port developed by European merchants or renegade warlords: it was at the heart of the Ottomans' vision of themselves as a maritime and commercial power in Asia. However, by the late eighteenth century, several factors had combined to transform Basra to a political appendage of Baghdad and to curtail the prosperity and independence of its merchant community.

By the eighteenth century the Mamluk governors of Baghdad had become indispensable to the Ottomans as military contractors who protected the eastern frontiers of the empire and controlled the tribal populations that threatened the security of trade through Iraq. Like their counterparts in Mosul, Damascus, and Egypt, they proved effective in transforming their households into small bureaucracies, and in recruiting and financing mercenaries. As part of the return for their loyalty, they were gradually allowed to turn Basra into a political and commercial satellite of Baghdad. Basra's administrative status was downgraded from a province in the sixteenth century to a dependency of the province of Baghdad in the late eighteenth. The highest Ottoman office holder was the lieutenant governor (*mutesellim*), who was appointed by the Mamluk governors of Baghdad, assisted by a judge, a small contingent of janissaries, and a council of local notables. Two other administrative posts attest to the position of Basra as a major trading center: the *kapudan bashi*, who was appointed by Istanbul at the beginning of the eighteenth century and controlled a fleet of some fifty to sixty ships, and the *shahbandar*, who was the head of the merchants and the main controller of the customs house. In most respects, Basra had the administrative trappings of a typical Ottoman city.[30]

However, the division of power within the city differed somewhat from that in Baghdad or other cities in the Fertile Crescent. Basra had always had a strong merchant community with commercial and family ties to the tribal leadership in its hinterland. The great merchants sat on the local council, intermarried with the local elite, and were often central to the resolution of conflicts between tribes and city government over control of land and sea trade

---

30. Abdullah 2001, 29–36, 99–120. Most of the material on eighteenth-century Basra is based on Abdullah's work; for late nineteenth- and early twentieth-century Basra, see Visser 2005. For the impact of Baghdad's policies on the regional trade network, see Fattah 1997.

routes. While other cities in the empire were gradually being dominated by local landowning elites whose wealth was based on increasing demand for agricultural goods, Basra's merchant community drew its economic strength from long distance trade, establishing commercial houses along the Persian Gulf littoral and in the Indian coastal cities (Abdullah 2001, 83–98). Perhaps because the sources of their wealth did not depend on an agricultural tax-farming system deeply embedded in the local system of power, they were able to exercise a measure of control and retained a fair degree of social and geographical mobility. They seem to have had more power to mediate conflict, resist the demands of power brokers, and control the commercial life of the city than their counterparts in the administrative centers of the empire. Their ascendancy in the city may go some way to explain the relative marginality of military and paramilitary groups in its political life.

However, Basra's merchant community found itself subject to the same pressures as in other cities in the empire. The Mamluk governors of Baghdad began appointing local judges and administrators and engaged in an active policy of diverting the caravan trade from Basra to Baghdad. Furthermore, they made several attempts to turn Baghdad into the main stop of the riverain trade, thus diverting important customs dues from Basra. By the second half of the eighteenth century the governors of Baghdad appointed the *kapudan bashi,* and in consequence his fleet declined to twelve ships (Abdullah 2001, 30). This policy of subjugating the administrative apparatus of the city and diverting its trade receipts had deleterious effects on the merchants. Wars with Persia and a series of natural disasters compounded the problem and led merchants either to relocate their operations to newly emergent port towns on the Persian Gulf or to migrate to India.

More significant for future developments in a number of port towns in the empire was the growing power of the British trade representative in Basra. Challenging the power of the Mamluk governors and the local lieutenant governor, he interfered in matters of local government and challenged the supremacy of the larger merchants in Basra. As in Aleppo, he found allies among the Christian (mainly Armenian) trading community who became partners in the British trade in the area. Unlike in Izmir, however, the growing power of foreign merchants in Basra did not mean that the city became a colonial port town. It remained an important administrative center in Iraq, and at some point in the nineteenth century, the writ of its governors was extended to the port towns of the Persian Gulf littoral, such as Kuwait and al-Hasa.

I have sketched this brief history of five port towns to demonstrate the variety in patterns of relationship between state and urban society in the Ottoman Empire. Notwithstanding the difficulty of making generalizations, these cities shared some common features. Europeans and their trade became essential components of the power structures in these cities, although there was great variety in the manner in which the local and the international interacted. Furthermore, the state had much less control in these cities than it did in the major administrative centers of the empire. By the mid–nineteenth century the five port cities had taken different trajectories. Izmir was transformed into a proto-colonial port town, Acre declined as an independent port, Algiers was colonized, Tunis became the center of an autonomous modernizing state, and Basra was to be incorporated into the administrative structures of the reforming state. However, beyond providing the narrative of the different paths these cities took, one needs to ask why these port cities presented such different scenarios. Relying for a clarification on the obvious external determinants such as distance from Istanbul or integration into the world market does not provide us with a satisfactory explanation. For instance, why did Algiers and Tunis take such radically divergent routes despite similar positions vis-à-vis Europe and Istanbul? The same question could be asked for Izmir and Acre. For a more satisfactory explanation one needs to look more systematically at the nature of power structures within these port towns and place them in the imperial and regional context.

## Conclusion

There is evidently much to be done in the historiography of cities in this crucial transitional period in Middle East history. This brief incursion into the political relations between city and state in the years that spanned the long eighteenth century has brought into focus the need for a more analytical approach to three interconnected issues.

First, there is a need to question such monoliths as the Ottoman Empire. Although historians of the Ottoman state have tended to take a normative stance toward relations between state and urban society, focusing on the workings of central state institutions within a limited geographical area and generalizing to other areas, historians of the Arab provinces have often gone to the other extreme, giving preference to the study of urban history without making sufficient efforts to link such history to the wider imperial context. Although recent scholarship is moving away from this polarization, we still lack a general typology of the determinants of the differentiated experiences of state and urban society relations. Focusing on regional or urban history, as some scholars have recently done, presents us with a viable alternative to state-centered analyses and will certainly help in the deconstruction of the Ottoman monolith. However, such studies need to be undertaken with two important caveats: they must avoid the nationalist/national state paradigms, and they must move away from the essentialist manner of viewing urban centers as extensions of classical "Islamic" cities with different sets of actors (janissaries, guilds, notables).

Second, there is a need for a closer examination of the intricate ways in which state and urban society interacted over space and time. Tilly's statement about the determining role that alliances between urban social groups and the state played in shaping the nature of the state is something of a truism. Beyond stating the obvious, however, we need to explore how the patterns of interaction between state and society shaped the power of the state at the local level and limited the options of its elites at the center. If we keep in mind that the relationship between the state and the societies it governed was at all times limited by the strength of the alliances it could contract, it becomes easier to move on from the orientalist and neo-orientalist debates about the autonomous nature of the Middle Eastern state and the legacy of dependent urban elites in the "undemocratic" nature of Middle Eastern societies (Sadowski 1997). Although the term "negotiations" has become the mantra of anthropologists and political scientists who use it to describe state and urban society relations in areas marked by the absence of autonomous judicial and municipal bodies, it is nevertheless a useful term to employ in describing such relations in the Middle Eastern context. The years between 1750 and 1850 were marked by intense negotiations between a wide sector of urban society and the state over issues of administrative control, entitlements, and exemptions. However, the results of such negotiations different widely in the various cities of the empire and were dependent on the political economy of particular cities, the nature of their power elites, the degree of resistance on the part of their populations, and the centrality of the city to the maintenance of the empire.

Finally, we need a more satisfactory explanation of the relations between cities and the state in the transition to the reform period. The modernizing reforms of the second half of the nineteenth century put an official end to the "premodern" system of relations, bringing rationality and principles of management to government. Yet most studies of urban societies in the second half of the nineteenth century demonstrate how a new and more diverse urban elite continued to view the state as an arena of negotiation for office despite the emergence of a rationalized bureaucracy. In addition, the transformations in the prerogatives of the provincial judicial establishment, the marginalization of the janissaries as an effective military force, and the creation of a larger pool of claimants to the state's resources furnished the bases for the reforms of the nineteenth century. The Tanzimat reforms of the nineteenth century added a new dimension to changes already at work in the late eighteenth century by investing the state with wide powers to pass new laws and create new institutions. However, it is important to keep in mind that these laws remained normative well into the second half of the century, their implementation remaining dependent on the success of the alliances struck with provincial urban populations.

Recent studies of Middle Eastern societies have demonstrated that the modern Middle Eastern state remains a hybrid, combining a system of entitlements and exemptions with rationalized bureaucracy. Suad Joseph has located such hybridity in the persistent importance of family and communal networks, used as protection against autocratic state structures, and political scientist Diane Singerman has found that urban populations have discovered in entitlements and exemptions, in other words, what is often defined in the old parlance as venality, "avenues of participation" in the national state (Joseph 1997, 64–71; Singerman 1995). Such studies of late twentieth-century Middle Eastern urban societies provide us with new paradigms that allow us to look at our data more creatively, and they point to the continuities with the past. They make it possible for us to root the modernization project of the nineteenth-century state not simply in European models of development but in the localization of such models by urban populations.

# 4

## The Economic Organization of Cities in Ottoman Syria

### ABDUL-KARIM RAFEQ

❧ IN A VARIETY OF WAYS, the contemporary economic organization of Middle Eastern cities still bears the imprint of centuries of interaction between Islamic, customary, Ottoman, and European legal and economic institutions. In Syria, this interaction was characterized by alternating conflict and accommodation over time, and the result was a high degree of sophistication and adaptability in business practices. Very often Islamic law conflicted with Ottoman law in these matters, but pragmatic solutions were devised, in line with custom and tradition, to accommodate local practice. In Anatolia and the Balkans, for example, business practices were adapted to conform to pre-Islamic Turkic or pre-Ottoman Byzantine practices. This is evident in the application of interest in matters of credit and loans in the sharia courts in Anatolia and the Balkans. Islamic law does not permit the taking of interest, but interest had been a feature of Byzantine and pre-Islamic Turkic financial dealings. Sultanic orders approving interest were thus communicated to the courts and implemented by the strength of Ottoman law. Judges in the Syrian Islamic courts were initially reluctant to apply interest to credit transactions, but they were eventually prevailed upon to do so by Ottoman decree.[1]

European influences also played a role in shaping the economic organization of Middle Eastern cities, particularly after the mid–nineteenth century.

---

1. See the quotation from Masters 1988 in chapter 1, note 50.

104

Prior to the Industrial and French Revolutions, mercantilist Europe coexisted alongside the traditional economy and society of the Middle East and protected its interests in the Ottoman Empire largely through commercial treaties known as the capitulations. In time, the capitulations became extraterritorial rights granted to European merchants and their local protégés. In the nineteenth century, industrial, capitalist Europe destabilized the traditional economy and society of the Middle East and brought new institutions and new social classes into existence, with different business practices and political platforms influenced by Europe. Thus the guilds, introduced under the Ottomans, underwent deep changes under the impact of industrial Europe. Many of the traditional institutions were abolished and new institutions emerged, such as the commercial courts established in Damascus and Aleppo in the early 1850s.

### The Guilds in the Syrian Cities

The backbone of the traditional economy and society of Syrian cities under the Ottomans was formed by the guilds, referred to in the court records as *ta'ifas*, groups. These were autonomous groups of craftsmen engaged in production, marketing, and services. The major sources of information about the guilds are the Ottoman court records, which are available for some Syrian cities from the 1530s.

The controversy over the existence of guilds in Arab-Islamic cities before the Ottoman period has not been entirely resolved (Cahen 1970). Despite the fact that there were crafts and craftsmen at the time, there were no craft organizations with corporate bodies, apparently because the Islamic sharia and its associated institutions were considered the only authoritative sources for organizing every aspect of life. When disputes arose among the crafts, the *qadi* (judge) and the *mufti* (jurist) looked into the matter. The market-inspector (*muhtasib*) then played a major role in checking weights, prices, quality of work, and the ethics of the profession at large.

The creation of guilds in the Syrian cities under Ottoman rule was an extension of similar institutions in Anatolia and the Balkans, which were no doubt influenced by earlier Byzantine and European guilds. Their flourishing in Syria under the Ottomans is reflected in the growing commercial activity of the cities locally, regionally, and internationally, a fact well attested by the creation of a large number of caravanserais (*khans*) in the Syrian cities, which profited tremendously from trade in and beyond the vast Ottoman Empire (Raymond 1979–80, 1984, 1985). The shift in commercial importance in the nineteenth century from the internal caravan cities to seaports such as Beirut, which could accommodate steamships carrying European goods, although damaging to local manufactures, did not affect the overall commercial activity of the cities. While handling a diminishing quantity of local products, those cities became engaged in marketing European products as well.

The guilds were autonomous or voluntary bodies of craftsmen and merchants, organized both for protection and for the maintenance of standards of excellence in work. In the course of time, they developed sophisticated organizations of their own. Members of the same craft established themselves as a guild, chose their own head (shaykh), laid down the rules of their profession, fixed the price of their commodities, merged with, or separated from, other guilds, or dissolved themselves as guilds according to their own interests. Their appearance before the judge in the Islamic court was largely intended to legalize their decisions and seek endorsement of their actions. The Ottoman government did not control the guilds and only occasionally interfered in the appointment of some of their heads or senior administrators. The role of the traditional *muhtasib,* who had been dominant in the Islamic cities prior to the establishment of the guilds, was considerably diminished after the consolidation of the guilds, which usurped much of his functions. However, certain guilds of importance to the government, such as the guild of butchers (*qassabin*), which supplied the people and the army with meat, and the guild of builders (*mi'mariyya*), which supervised the safety of public and private buildings, were under government control. The butchers' guild had its head (*shaykh al-qassabin*) who was elected by the members of the guild, and beside him there was the *qassab bashi* who apparently represented government interests. The builders seem to have been more controlled than the butchers; their head was directly appointed by the government and given the title of *bashi,* hence *mi'mar bashi.*

The number of guilds varied from one city to another and from one period to another. At the peak of guild activity in the Syrian cities in the seventeenth and eighteenth centuries, there were between 160 and 180 guilds in Damascus and Aleppo and slightly fewer in Hama. In the late nineteenth century, the *Qamus al-sina'at al-Shamiyya* (directory of Damascene crafts), co-authored by Qasimi and 'Azm, lists 435 occupations, including many modern ones, such as lawyer (*muhami*) and engineer (*muhandis*) (al-Qasimi 1960). But there is no proof that each one of these 435 crafts or occupations was organized into a guild.

Some guilds died away because their products could not keep up with the changing fashions, such as makers of old-fashioned headgear.[2] Other guilds lost their importance and their sales diminished because the social classes for whom they had catered had become poorer, as in the case of the furriers (*al-farrayin*). New guilds also emerged occasionally to satisfy new demands and changing lifestyles. For example, after much controversy among the ulama over its merits, coffee drinking was finally legalized in the latter part of the sixteenth century. According to the Damascene biographer Najm al-Din al-Ghazzi, the Yemeni scholar Abu Bakr al-Shadhili al-'Aydarusi, who was the first to legalize coffee-drinking, pointed out its advantages in relieving the mind, keeping a person awake, and enabling him to perform his night prayers. Sufis were among the first to drink coffee (al-Ghazzi 1979, 1:113–14, 2:126). Consequently, guilds for coffee sellers (*ba'i'yin al-bunn*), coffee roasters (*muhammissiyin al-bunn*), and coffeehouse owners (*qahwiyya or qahwatiyya*) emerged.[3] Coffee from Yemen, most of which was imported on the return journey of the Damascus pilgrim caravan, generated much activity in the Syrian cities and came to constitute a major component of the trade accompanying the pilgrimage. Similarly, when tobacco smoking was legalized by the jurists in the first quarter of the eighteenth century in Damascus, Cairo, and Istanbul, among other places, a number of guilds engaged in various aspects of the tobacco business emerged. The Damascene Shaykh 'Abd al-Ghani al-Nabulsi, a Hanafi jurist and prolific author, authorized tobacco smoking in a treatise entitled *al-Sulh bayna al-ikhwan fi hukm ibahat al-dukhkhan* (Peace among friends concerning the legalization of smoking (al-Nabulsi 1924). Nabulsi considers that smoking is like food: if it hurts you, avoid it, if it does not, why not indulge?

2. Directorate of Historical Archives, Damascus, Law Court Registers (henceforth LCR), Damascus, 45:58, 28 Sha'ban 1132 (5 July 1720).

3. LCR, Aleppo 15:493, 4 Ramadan 1039 (17 Apr. 1730) 15:639, 14 Rabi' I 1042 (29 Sept. 1632); 25:298, 25 Muharram 1079 (5 July 1668); Damascus, 101:2, 2 Jumada II 1151 (17 Sept. 1738); see also Rafeq 2001.

The chief administrator of the guild was the shaykh, who was elected by a majority of the senior members from among the master craftsmen in their ranks. After his election he would be officially endorsed by the *qadi*. Piety, correctness, and an upright character were more important than professional expertise for the choice of shaykh. If the shaykh worked against the interests of the craft members or breached their code of ethics, he would be deposed by majority vote and the judge would respect the decision. In the larger guilds like the butchers, whose activities were spread throughout the city, district shaykhs in the various quarters were answerable to the chief shaykh of the whole guild. This was also the case for the Jewish butchers who had a shaykh of their own.[4] Since promotion from one professional rank to another in the guild was an occasion for celebrations mixed with Sufi practices, whose nature and scope has yet to be studied, a *shaykh al-mashayikh* (head of the shaykhs), who apparently had Sufi, rather than professional, precedence, seems to have officiated at these ceremonies (Qudsi 1885, 15–30).

The guild shaykh was aided by a number of officers whose numbers, titles, and positions changed over time. The important officers included the *naqib*, who deputized for the shaykh, and the *yikit bashi* (rendered in Turkish *yigit bashi*) who acted as assistant to the shaykh. Like the *naqib*, the *yikit bashi* was chosen by the shaykh and occasionally deputized for him. Another officer was the *mu'arrif* (the identifier) who helped the shaykh in collecting the taxes imposed on the guild as a whole, by identifying each guild member and imposing on him the relevant tax in accordance with his work and income (Rafeq 1991).

Like its medieval European counterpart, each guild had three professional ranks: the apprentice (*al-ajir* or *al-mubtadi'*) at the beginning level, the journeyman (*al-sani'*), and the master (*al-ustadh* in Persian, shortened into *usta*, or *al-mu'allim* in Arabic). There was no time limit for remaining in each rank. Excellence, good character, and, more importantly, gradation within the ranks were the main criteria for promotion. Outsiders were not allowed to practice the craft. Journeymen, however, tended to stay in their rank for long periods because the masters sometimes delayed their promotion on purpose to avoid competition, and also because there might be no openings at the masters'

4. LCR, Aleppo, 15:709, 25 Muharram 1044 (21 July 1634); 15:805, 26 Dhu'l-Hijja 1045 (1 June 1636).

level. The master, who was entitled to have an independent workshop, had to acquire *gedik* (equipment) and *khilu* (the right to use vacant premises), which amounted to licenses. These were costly, owned in part or as a whole by individuals who were not necessarily craftsmen, and were not always available. The price of the *gedik* and the *khilu* varied according to the type of the craft and the geographical location of the workshop (Rafeq 1991, 503).

The guilds were involved in three major activities: production, services, and marketing, and there was a clear division of labor within each category. There were dyers of red and dyers of blue, dyers of silk and dyers of cotton, and dyers of all colors. In one example, it was agreed before the judge in Aleppo in 1588 in the presence of the shaykh of the dyers (*shaykh al-sabbaghin*) that the dyers who specialized in dark blue were not to be interfered with by the dyers of other colors.[5] Specialization in dark blue dyeing seems to have continued over the centuries; thus in 1761 a dye shop in Damascus was mentioned as specializing in dying dark blue.[6] There were also separate guilds for dyers according to the material and the color they dyed. In Aleppo in 1626–27, a shaykh was nominated head of the guild that specialized in the red dyeing of linen from Malatya (*ta'ifat al-sabbaghin li'l-sabgh al-ahmar li'l-kham al-Malti bi-Halab*).[7] There was also specialization in the guilds offering services. There was a guild of porters who carried the goods of European merchants (*ta'ifat al-'attalin al-ladhin yahmilun ahmal ta'ifat al-Afranj bi-Halab*) and another guild of these who carried the goods of local merchants (*ta'ifat al-hammalin*). There was also a guild of auctioneers (*dallalin*) specializing in gallnuts (*dallalin al-'afs*), a guild of auctioneers brokering Malatya linen, and a guild of auctioneers at large. Specialization in marketing is equally evident in the creation of separate merchant guilds and the existence of specialized markets. Craft guilds were usually separate from the merchant guilds that marketed commodities produced by the former.

Work was done in independent workshops, which were encouraged by the legal authorities. Partnerships were discouraged. In one case a judge stated

---

5. LCR, Aleppo, 6:307, awakhir Rabi' Awwal 996 (late Feb. 1588).

6. LCR, Damascus, 169:140, 26 Rajab 1174 (3 Mar. 1761).

7. LCR, Aleppo, 15:112, 24 Muharram 1036 (15 Oct. 1626); 15:212, 21 Dhu'l-Qa'da 1036 (3 Aug. 1627); 15:238, 25 Muharram 1037 (6 Oct. 1627).

that each craft master should work in an independent workshop and should not resort to partnership because it is harmful to the Muslims (*yashtaghil kullu wahid minhum fi dukkan mustaqill wa-la yashtarikun fi'l-'amal li-anna fihi dararan li'l-Muslimin*).[8] Partnership was apparently discouraged for fear of the monopolization of commodities, price rises, and the consequent accumulation of wealth by a few persons, which would endanger equal opportunities for individual workers. The guilds succeeded in ensuring a balanced income for their members with a minimum of competition and eventually brought about a degree of social stability. This situation continued until the mid–nineteenth century, when the traditional economic system broke down under the impact of goods from industrial Europe, and competition with European goods made it imperative for local industrialists to engage in partnerships.

To offset the limitations imposed by traditional work regulations and to meet the demands of an expanding market, the guilds resorted to advanced economic practices that illustrate their dominant economic role at the time. Mergers occurred among related guilds: for example, the separate guilds of makers of swords, knives, daggers, bows, and shields merged in Aleppo in 1629 under the headship of a single shaykh. Similarly, the guilds of cooks (*tabbakhin*), of meat-roasters (*shawwayyin*), and of makers of meat pies (*sanbuskiyya*) merged under one shaykh.[9] Such mergers were necessitated by the challenge of the market. They were usually initiated by the most influential of the merging guilds in order to maintain better control over the distribution of raw materials, to stabilize and maintain prices, and eventually to eliminate competition among members and provide equal opportunities for them.

As the role of the guilds became consolidated in the urban economy of Syria in the seventeenth and eighteenth centuries, the constraints laid upon them by increasingly outdated traditions and practices became onerous and limited their ability to expand their activity. Thus the makers of leather shoes (*ta'ifat al-qawwafin*) in Damascus protested to the judge in the early eighteenth century against the dyers of cow hide (*ta'ifat al-baqqarin*) for refusing

8. LCR, Aleppo, 22:248, 14 Ramadan 1049 (8 Jan. 1640); for the egalitarian aspect of the guilds, see Rafeq 2002b.

9. LCR, Aleppo, 15:380, 22 Jumada I 1038 (17 Jan. 1629); 15:761, 17 Rabi' II 1045 (30 Sept. 1635).

to increase their daily quota of hide to meet the increasing demand for their products. The dyers of cow hide responded by saying that they had to satisfy the needs of other guilds that used hide. The matter was referred to the official Hanafi jurist (mufti) who ruled that the makers of leather shoes should not force the dyers of cow hide to increase their quota. In his decision to maintain the status quo, the jurist was evidently oblivious of the dynamics of a free market economy.

To counter these legal impediments, and in order to diversify their investments, some of the larger individual guilds would attach minor guilds to themselves through a system of *yamak* relationships. The Turkish term *yamak* (Arabic *yamaq*), which literally means companion, or assistant, occurs in the Syrian court records either on its own, or in its Arabic equivalent *taba'*, or jointly with the latter term. Through this relationship, which fell short of a merger, the major guild would control the products of the minor guild and occasionally make the latter process and market its by-products. It also involved the sharing of taxes between the two guilds. Each guild in the *yamak* relationship would normally retain its shaykh, although the attached guild sometimes did not have one. The guild of slaughterers (*masalkhiyya*) was *yamak* to the guild of butchers (*qassabin*). The latter's role was crucial in marketing the products of the slaughterers. The guild of tanners (*dabbaghin*) competed with the butchers in controlling the slaughterers because the latter provided them with hide. The guild of ice makers (*buzjiyya*) was *yamak* (also mentioned as *taba'* in the same document) to the guild of ice-cream makers (*aqsamawiyya*) and shared with the latter the same shaykh.[10] Likewise, two guilds making different types of caps (*al-'iriqjiyya* or *'irqyaniyya* and *al-tawaqiyya*) were *yamak* to the guild of tailors (*al-khayyatin*). They reworked the by-products of the tailors into caps and also shared the payment of taxes with them.[11]

Disputes over claims of *yamak* relationship between the guilds were referred to the judge. On one occasion, the shaykh of the guild of owners of coffeehouses (*al-qahwiyya*) was obliged to make monetary contributions to

10. LCR, Aleppo, 15:805, 26 Dhu'l-Hijja 1045 (1 June 1636).

11. LCR, Aleppo, 4:135, 6 Rabi' II 1052 (4 July 1642); Damascus, 45:58, case dated 28 Sha'ban 1132 (5 July 1720).

the army. He asked the guild of coffee sellers (*ba'i'yin bunn al-qahwa*) to participate in the contributions because they were *yamak* to the owners of coffeehouses. The coffee sellers declined to pay, denying that they had ever paid contributions in the past or had ever been *yamak* to the owners of coffeehouses. The judge called on a group of trustworthy witnesses who affirmed that the sellers of coffee were not *yamak* to the owners of coffeehouses and that at no time in the past had they made any contribution to them. The judge therefore prevented the owners of coffeehouses from molesting the sellers of coffee. The multiplication and the diversity of the guilds in Ottoman Syria and the control which the major guilds exercised over the affiliated guilds attest to the development of capitalistic patterns of a sort.

As autonomous bodies, the guilds had important economic, fiscal, and social roles. They distributed raw materials among their members, supervised the quality of production, fixed the prices of their products and regularized their marketing, and assigned the amount of taxes each member had to pay. Of no less importance was the social role that the guilds played in integrating the religious communities within their ranks.

The shaykh of the guild controlled the distribution of raw materials among the members of his guild to ensure equal opportunities for all. The dyers in red of Malatya linen in Aleppo, for example, deposed their shaykh in 1626 because he wanted to have more than his usual share of linen for dyeing. They installed a new shaykh and agreed with him that the linen should be distributed equally among them and that no member should seek more than his share.[12] The shaykh of the guild of carpenters (*al-najjarin*) was responsible for distributing imported timber among the members of his guild, to each in accordance with his capacity and his ability to work. The shaykh was also to set the price of timber.[13] Members of the guild of *khurdajiyya* (sellers of miscellaneous wares) in Aleppo agreed among themselves that imported wares, like combs and cutlery, should be distributed equally among them by the shaykh of their guild. Any member who violated this agreement would be liable for punishment.[14] Likewise, the members of the guild of sellers of pottery (*ta'ifat*

---

12. LCR, Aleppo, 15:112, 24 Muharram 1036 (15 Oct. 1626).
13. LCR, Aleppo, 11:76, 22 Muharram 1027 (19 Jan. 1618).
14. LCR, Aleppo, 15:804, awa'il Muharram 1046 (early June 1636).

*ba'i'yin al-fakhur* or *al-fukhkhar*) agreed that their shaykh would distribute the locally made pottery and the imported pottery among them.[15]

The shaykh of the market was also responsible for the good behavior and correctness of the merchants under his jurisdiction. Mischievous merchants were ousted from the market by the consensus of fellow merchants and the approval of the judge.[16] The shaykh himself could also be held accountable for his own behavior. If a shaykh requested money illegally from the members of a related guild, the latter could dispute his claim in court. The shaykh of the druggists (*al'altarin*) in Damascus, for instance, requested that the auctioneers of perfumes and drugs (*al-badayi' al-'itriyya*) in the market of Bzuriyya should pay one-third of their earnings to him. The latter refused to pay and testified before the judge that there was no precedent for their paying any money to the shaykh of the druggists. The judge concurred with their deposition.[17]

The quality of production was also maintained by guild regulations, which explains why nonmembers were not allowed to practice a guild's profession and why no products could be sold outside the specialized market where a specific commodity was sold, thus enabling the head of the market (*shaykh al-suq*) to monitor the provenance, quality, and price of the product. By exercising a monopoly over a particular craft, the guild provided the consumer with protection against poor workmanship and fraud. The guilds involved in textile production, for example, laid down the type of material to be used in each manufacture, assigned the proportion of cotton to silk in both the warp and the weft, specified the number of threads to be incorporated in each type of cloth, and set forth the measurements of cloth produced in pieces. The guild even went to the extent of specifying the weight and measurements of a silk piece before and after dyeing. Members of the Aleppine *ta'ifat al-haririyya*, also known as *ta'ifat al-'anatiyya*, who made silk robes, referred to in Aleppo as *'anatiyya*, agreed among themselves in 1608 that the robes they produced should be of two types: the first was to be made of ten thousand threads and was to measure ten *dhira*'s in length and one *dhira'* in breadth, and the second

15. LCR, Aleppo, 15:446, 8 Rabi' II 1039 (25 Nov. 1629).

16. LCR, Aleppo, 25:124, 19 Sha'ban 1058 (8 Sept. 1648); Damascus, 51:119, 8 Rajab 1135 (14 Apr. 1723).

17. LCR, Damascus, 107:16, khitam Rabi' II 1154 (14 July 1741).

was to consist of thirteen to fourteen thousand threads and have the same measurements as the first. Any deviation from these specifications would expose the maker to punishment by the shaykh of the guild. The craftsmen also agreed that the *muhtasib* (market inspector) should not have any say in their affairs. The reelers of thread (*ta'ifat al-mulaffifin*) appeared in court alongside the *haririyya* and pledged to provide silk spools containing no less than ten thousand threads.[18]

By producing silk cloth made of thirteen to fourteen thousand threads, Aleppo led the Ottoman Empire in producing fine silk cloth in the early seventeenth century (İnalcik 1979). By keeping the *muhtasib* out of their affairs, the guild of the *haririyya* was upholding a pattern while also indicating the loss of authority of this traditional official over the internal organization of the guilds. The ban on the *muhtasib* meddling in the affairs of the guild of the *haririyya/'anatiyya* was reasserted again in 1628 when the guild agreed to produce three brands of silk cloth: a superior type made up of twelve thousand threads that should not fall below ten thousand threads, a medium type consisting of eight thousand threads, and an inferior type of five thousand threads.[19]

A commodity that had wide demand could be retailed in more than one market. A case in point were the woolen cloaks (*'abat*, colloquial plural *'ubi*) which were sold in Suq al-'Atiq and in Suq Khayr Bek in Aleppo. Members of the guild of cloak sellers (*ta'ifat ba'i'yi al-'ubi*) agreed before their shaykh and the judge to sell their cloaks in either market.[20]

The guilds also fixed the prices of their products, taking into consideration the devaluation of the currency and the need to prevent inflation. Any breach of the fixed prices was severely punished, morally and materially, by the shaykh of the guild, who had the support of the judge in these matters. The creation of specialized markets made it easy for the shaykh of the market to control the price of merchandise as well as its quality. It also enabled the buyer to purchase the commodities he needed with ease and satisfaction.

Bulk goods sold in gross were available in a specialized caravanserai (*khan*) located either in the market (*suq*) retailing the same commodity or close by.

18. LCR, Aleppo, 10:870, awakhir Dhu'l-Hijja 1016 (mid-Apr. 1608).
19. LCR, Aleppo, 15:288, 4 Jumada II 1037 (10 Feb. 1628).
20. LCR, Aleppo, 10:605, awakhir Rajab 1017 (early Nov. 1608).

The person in charge of the *khan* was known as the shaykh or *mutakallim* (literally spokesman) and it was his responsibility to lease space in the facility.[21] Guilds of specialized auctioneers were responsible for selling bulk goods to retailers.[22] The auctioneers of gallnuts, for example, were located in Khan al-Sabun (soap) in Aleppo. In 1615, at the request of the head of the merchants in Aleppo (*shahbandar madinat Halab*), of several merchants, and of the shaykh of the guild of brokers (*samasira*), the judge ordered the auctioneers of gallnuts to leave Khan al-Sabun because of their mischief, which had damaged the interests of the merchants.[23]

The nature of the office of the *shahbandar* and of that of *bazar bashi* (chief merchant) is not known with certainty from the sources. In cases involving disputes among merchant guilds or among groups of merchants, both officials appear to have used their moral, and, one would assume, expert, authority to bring disputes to a satisfactory conclusion. From the context of several cases, there seems to have been one *shahbandar* in each city, although there was more than one *bazar bashi*.[24] The shaykh of the suq, on the other hand, had direct authority over the merchants of his suq. He was chosen by them and authorized by the judge. In one case, the merchants of Suq al-Dahsha in Aleppo, who were Muslims and Christians selling textiles, agreed to the conditions set by their shaykh after he threatened to resign. His conditions were to establish three categories of taxes among them (high, medium, and low), that he should be the sole distributor of textiles to them, that he should have a share of textiles equal to theirs when distribution occurred, and that each merchant should work independently of the other merchants and confer with the shaykh on matters of mutual interest. When the merchants accepted these conditions in front of the judge, the shaykh withdrew his resignation and agreed to resume his functions.

To sell their goods beyond the city, the merchants usually sold on credit to retail merchants in smaller towns. The latter exhibited their goods in their

21. LCR, Aleppo, 15:661, 8 Sha'ban 1042 (18 Feb. 1633).

22. See, for example, LCR, Aleppo, 15:204, 9 Shawwal 1036 (23 June 1627).

23. LCR, Aleppo, 15:735, 23 Jumada II 1024 (20 July 1615).

24. See, for example, LCR, Aleppo, 15:758, 7 Dhu'l-Hijja 1044 (24 May 1635); Damascus, 17:10, 11 Rabi' I 1101 (23 Dec. 1689); 17:82, 3 Rabi' II 1101 (14 Jan. 1690).

shops and also traveled to nearby villages where markets were held on specific days. There were also fortnightly fairs and seasonal fairs that attracted nomads selling their products and buying what city products they needed. Europeans frequented these seasonal fairs mainly to buy horses, which were exported to Europe in large quantities in the nineteenth century to satisfy the need of the newly established courts in central Europe, mostly the kings and princes of the House of Hohenzollern.

The taxes imposed on the guilds were farmed out by the government to the highest bidder. With the help of the identifier (*mu'arrif*), the shaykh of the guild assigned the amount of taxes each member had to pay in accordance with his work and his financial situation. Working members had to pay for nonworking members because taxes were collectively imposed on the guild. When extra taxes were imposed on the guilds to defray the expenses of war or other necessities, the amount of money each guild was to contribute was agreed upon by all the shaykhs of the contributing guilds.[25] Also, when the governor of the province or other top officials bought commodities on credit from the merchants, the shaykhs of the merchants usually acted as guarantors for the officials. Occasionally, the *bazarbashi* also acted as guarantor.[26]

A major aspect of the functioning of the guilds was their integration of members of the various religious communities within their ranks through a work ethic that emphasized expertise over religious affiliation. Because the majority of the population was Muslim, the majority of the guild members were normally Muslim. But in matters of expertise in which one community had come to monopolize a certain craft, the guild as a whole was limited to members of that community. Jews, for instance, monopolized the guild of smelters of silver and gold (*ta'ifat murawbissi al-fidda wa-al-dhahab*) in Aleppo in 1590. The judge of Aleppo confirmed a Jew, Shamwil al-Yahudi (Samuel the Jew), as shaykh of this guild.[27] The guild of sculptors (*nahhatin*) in Damascus whose membership in 1689 amounted to twenty-seven, was predominantly Christian, and the guild of builders (*mi'mariyyin*) was almost entirely monopolized

25. LCR, Aleppo, 15:820, 26 Shawwal 1046 (23 Mar. 1637).

26. See, for example, LCR, Damascus, 17:10, 11 Rabi' I 1101 (23 Dec. 1689); 17:82, several cases dated 22 Rabi' II 1101 (2 Feb. 1690); 17:86, 24 Rabi' II 1101 (4 Feb. 1690).

27. LCR, Aleppo, 7:4, 29 Rajab 998 (3 June 1590).

by Christians. The majority of the members of the guild of silk-spinners in Aleppo in 1626 were Christians, and a Christian was endorsed by the Muslim judge as shaykh of this guild with the concurrence of the Muslim members.[28] Christians seem also to have monopolized the guild producing woolen caps (*al-'iraqi al-jukh*) in Aleppo in 1632.[29]

In the mixed guilds with members from two or three religious communities, the members worked smoothly with each other. The guild of butchers (*qassabin*) was and still is limited to Muslims and Jews, both of whom insisted on the lawful slaughter of animals according to their religious practices. The guild of druggists (*'attarin*) was also composed of Muslims and Jews, both of whom were experts in making and selling perfumes and in preparing herbal medicines. In Aleppo, for instance, the delegations of druggists appearing in the Muslim court as representatives of their guild included almost equal numbers of Muslims and Jews. In February 1660, a delegation of druggists appearing before the court in Aleppo to discuss matters of interest to their guild included nine Muslims and eight Jews. A majority of Jews and a sprinkling of Muslims and Christians made up the guild of money changers (*sarrafin*) in Aleppo in 1618.[30]

Christians figured alongside Muslims in the guilds of bleachers (*qassarin*), saddlers (*barad'iyya* and *samarjiyya*), weavers (*hiyyak*), and dyers in red (*sabbaghi al-ahmar*) among other guilds. Muslims, Jews, and Christians figured in a number of guilds such as dyers (*sabbaghin*), blacksmiths (*haddadin*), tailors (*khayyatin*), bakers (*khabbazin*), surgeons (*jarrahin*), and a host of other professions as indicated by the professional surnames carried by members of all three communities (Rafeq 1993b, 2004).

Only a few guilds were restricted to members of particular ethnic groups. The makers of light shoes (*khaffafin*) in Aleppo in 1588, for example, had two guilds, one for the Rumi (Turkish) members (*ta'ifat al-khaffafin al-Arwam*) and one for the Arabs of Aleppo (*ta'ifat al-khaffafin min abna' al-'Arab bi-Halab*).[31] This example clearly indicates the closure of the local guilds to ethnic aliens.

---

28. LCR, Aleppo, 15:83, 9 Dhu'l-Qa'da 1035 (2 Aug. 1626).

29. LCR, Aleppo, 15:619, 26 Dhu'l-Qa'da 1041 (14 June 1632).

30. LCR, Aleppp, 11:76, 22 Muharram 1027 (19 Jan. 1618).

31. LCR, Aleppo, 6:165, early Safar 996 (early Jan. 1588).

Egyptians figured in the guild of water carriers (*saqqayyin*) and constituted half the eight members of this guild in Aleppo around the middle of the eighteenth century.[32] Algerians figured as messengers (*su'at*) and watchmen (*hurras*). In the eighteenth century, they were employed in large numbers as mercenary troops.

Religion played an important role in business practices and ceremonies. Much respect was accorded to the members of the religious minorities in the guilds. The Jewish butchers in Aleppo, for example, were allowed to sell meat at a price slightly higher than that allowed to the Muslim butchers so as to provide for the poor within the Jewish community.[33] The fact that non-Muslim members in the mixed guilds were included in the delegations representing the guilds before the court is a clear indication of their importance as active members in the profession. In the ceremonies marking the promotion of a guild member from one professional rank to a higher one, the appropriate religious rituals were performed. For a Muslim, the *Fatiha* (opening *sura* of the Qur'an) was uttered; for a Christian, the Lord's Prayer; and for a Jew, the Ten Commandments.[34] The Islamic courts also recognized the oath of a Christian on the gospel and the oath made by a Jew on the Torah.[35]

The orderly relations that existed in the mixed guilds between members belonging to different religious communities reflect the degree of tolerance and of professional respect that non-Muslims enjoyed in a Muslim-dominated society. Mixing in the workplace was also reflected in mixing in the residential quarters where families from the various religious communities lived next to each other and generally maintained good neighborly relations.[36] No wonder, therefore, that no sectarian conflicts of the type that flared up in the Syrian cities around the middle of the nineteenth century had taken place in the three preceding centuries.

32. LCR, Aleppo, 4:(no pagination), ghurrat Rabi' II 1052 (29 June 1642); 5:196, 22 Shawwal 1058 (9 Nov. 1648).

33. LCR, Aleppo, 6:265, end Safar 996 (29 Jan. 1588).

34. Qudsi 1885, 15–30.

35. LCR, Aleppo, 2:48, 7 Dhu'l-Hijja 1001 (4 Sept. 1593).

36. See, for example, Rafeq 1988b; on the generally peaceful coexistence between the religious communities in Ottoman Syria, see Rafeq 2003a, 2004, 2005. For a detailed statistical survey, see the summaries of the quarter populations of Aleppo in 1900 assembled (from Kamil al-Ghazzi 1926) in the tables in Gaube and Wirth 1984, 427–34.

Among the Muslim craftsmen, religious precedence and descent from the Prophet (*sharif*) were valued. One alim (scholar), who belonged to the guild of sawyers (*nashsharin*), was exempted from the payment of irregular taxes because he was a leader in prayer (*imam*) and a preacher in the Friday prayer.[37] The influential guild of tanners (*dabbaghin*) in Aleppo was reported in 1593 to have had two shaykhs: one for the tanners who were *ashraf* (descendants of the Prophet) and another for those who were not. The two shaykhs agreed that hide delivered to them for processing should be divided into four parts: one part for the *ashraf* tanners, of whom there were fewer, and three parts for the rest. It was also agreed that bachelor tanners should have half the share of married tanners.[38] Thus, social and economic considerations as well as the religious status of members were also taken into account by the guild. It is not known how long the division of the tanners into *ashraf* and non-*ashraf* lasted, but this division is significant in the history of Aleppo, where the *ashraf* played an important political and military role in the life of the city.

Women are not mentioned in the court records as guild members despite the well-known fact that they provided cheap labor in the privacy of their homes. They were engaged mainly in cotton spinning, mat making, embroidery, and sewing, and sometimes acted as auctioneers of secondhand clothing. In one case, a woman was assigned by the judge in Aleppo in 1627 a half share of the fat from which wax was made to be given to her daily by the shaykh of the guild of wax makers (*shamma'in*) in the slaughterhouse alongside the male members, each one of whom was to receive a whole share.[39] It is not known whether the woman was a full member of this guild and was given half a share because of her gender or whether she was deputizing for her handicapped husband. On a lighter note, the court in Damascus reported a case in 1710 in which a female who stole money from another woman declared in the court that she was a member of the guild of thieves (*ta'ifat al-sarraqin*).[40] Peasant

37. LCR, Damascus, 21:275–76, 1 Jumada II 1101 (5 Mar. 1593).

38. LCR, Aleppo, 2:152, 17 Dhu'l-Hijja 1001 (14 Sept. 1593).

39. LCR, Aleppo, 15:237, 5 Safar 1037 (16 Oct. 1627); cf. 25 Muharram 1037 (6 Oct. 1627).

40. LCR, Damascus, 33:91, 24 Ramadan 1119 (19 Dec. 1707); for women's labor and their absence from the guilds in Hama, see Reilly 2002, 83–84.

women played a major role in agricultural work and very often outdid their lazy husbands, but there is no mention of their constituting guilds on their own or with the men.

Information on child labor in the cities is difficult to ascertain. Most of those employed in the guilds at the beginning level as apprentices (*ajir* or *mubtadi'*) seem to have been youths who had reached the age of adolescence. In one case from Damascus in 1722, a master cloth printer (*tabba'*) made a legal contract before the *Shafi'i* judge employing his adult nephew for two *'aqd*s, each of three years' duration. The nephew's daily pay was six *misriyya*s (one piaster equalled 40 *misriyya*s), four of which were to be retained by the employer for the daily food, drink, and other needs of the employee and two *misriyya*s were to be paid to him.[41] The contract does not mention whether the employer would offer lodging to the apprentice.

The guilds performed many of the regulating duties now undertaken by a modern urban municipality. In addition to their economic functions, they also cared, among other things, about public health and cleanliness. The tanners, for example, were directed to establish their tanneries outside the populated areas to ensure that the bad odors emanating from animal skins and the flies and insects gathering around them would not cause discomfort to the inhabitants. No tanner was allowed to practice his profession in his own residence, not only because this breached the general rules of the guild that work had to be done in specially assigned places, but also because it constituted a health hazard. In Damascus between the sixteenth and nineteenth centuries the tannery remained outside the quarter of Bab al-Salam and the walls of the city, where water to clean the skins, space to dry them, and a degree of isolation from residential areas were all available.[42] In Aleppo in 1635, in the presence of the shaykh of the tanners, the butchers were urged by the judge not to sell animal skins outside the tannery. The tanners were likewise requested not to buy any skins outside the tannery, otherwise both parties would risk punishment. The tannery of Aleppo was reported at the time to be outside Aleppo (*zahir* Halab), that is, outside the city walls, more specifically in the *qaysariyya* of Muhammad Pasha, the Vizir, outside Bab Antakya (Gate

41. LCR, Damascus, 50:28, 25 Dhu'l-Hijja 1134 (6 Oct. 1722).

42. LCR, Damascus, 28:220, 11 Muharram 1114 (7 June 1702).

of Antioch).[43] The relocation of the tanneries away from the walls of the city is also indicative of the expansion of the city (Raymond 1977b).

Guilds involved in public services were urged to adhere to the instructions issued to them. Members of the guild of earth removers (*tarrabin*) entrusted with removing the accumulated earth within the city were instructed by their shaykh not to deposit the soil in cemeteries, on roads, or on the hills in the vicinity of the city but to take it to specially designated pits or caves.[44] In matters where members of a guild breached the moral code of their craft, they were held accountable for their actions. When members of the Aleppo guild of goldsmiths objected in the court to the misdeeds of fellow members who were cheating the customers and tarnishing the good image of their craft, the judge granted their request by ordering the expulsion of the mischievous members from the goldsmiths' market.[45] In another example, members of the guild of silk spinners were held accountable for any decrease in the weight of spun silk after its being dyed blue. The silk spinners were offered two piasters in wages for every one hundred dirhams of silk spun. After the spun silk was dyed blue, the one hundred dirhams of silk were supposed to weigh sixty-seven dirhams. If they weighed less, then the silk at the time of spinning had probably been treated with oil, which would cause its weight to decline below the officially prescribed weight after dyeing. The spinner then had to make up the difference in weight and would be administered the punishment he deserved.[46] Such self-imposed rules observed by the guild members had a powerful moral and social authority that transcended any laws the government might impose. Even today, when labor courts fail to reach a satisfactory solution between the parties in a labor dispute, an experienced master craftsman, who is respected by all for his integrity, can often achieve better results. Piety and correctness were more important than professional skill in the election of the shaykh and the senior officers because these officers were charged to watch over the morals of the guild members. The degree of discipline, morality, religious tolerance,

43. LCR, Aleppo, 15:767, 15 Safar 1045 (31 July 1635). cf. 12:67, 5 Rabi' II 1032 (6 Feb. 1623); 13:294, 4 Safar 1034 (16 Nov. 1624); 22:88, 22 Sha'ban 1050 (7 Dec. 1640).

44. LCR, Aleppo, 23:184, 19 Jumada II 1052 (14 Sept. 1642).

45. LCR, Aleppo, 25:124, 19 Sha'ban 1058 (8 Sept. 1648).

46. LCR, Aleppo, 22:89, 25 Sha'ban 1050 (10 Dec. 1640).

and the high standards of work that characterized the guilds reflected, and in turn promoted, these same qualities in traditional society as a whole.

At times of insecurity, such as during the eighteenth century when the authority of the central administration declined and power groups in the Syrian cities fought each other, the guild members defended their interests. In Damascus, for instance, members of the guilds paraded in the streets in 1760 carrying arms, tools, and magnificent shields. However, the increasing corruption of the state administration and the deteriorating economic conditions of the majority of the people, particularly the peasantry, tended to compromise the positive effects of the guilds.[47]

### Business Practice in Ottoman Syria

Business practice in Ottoman Syria was a reflection of a combination of the discipline and ethics of the guilds, the corruption of the administration, and the poverty of the people. Financial dealings between individuals are well documented in the court records. In the early period of Ottoman rule in Syria, according to the court records of Hama from the mid-1530s, four categories of credit were common among the local population. In order of frequency, these were selling on credit, that is, delayed payment for commodities sold (*bay' bi'l-dayn*), loan (*qard*), debt (*dayn*), and prepayment for future delivery (*salam*). Out of 1,090 legible cases in the first register of the Hama court, which covers a period of 279 days spread over two years, A.H. 942-43/A.D. 1535–36), 429 cases (39 percent of the total) deal with credit transactions. These transactions were recorded in the sharia court to make them legal. The court accordingly issued *hujja*s (documents) to the contracting parties setting out the terms of the transaction. Table 1 classifies these transactions according to their category, number, and value.

Selling on credit topped the list with a total of 63.4 percent of all transactions and 71.11 percent of the total money invested in these transactions. This

47. Studies of guilds in various cities and provinces make it possible to compare practices in the Empire as a whole: see, for example, Raymond 1973 on Cairo; Shkodra 1973, 1975, on Albania; Baer 1982 on Egypt; Akarlı 1985–86 on Istanbul; Yi 2004 on Istanbul; and Faroqhi and Deguilhem 2005 on the Muslim Mediterranean. For a survey of the social history of labor in the Empire in the nineteenth century, see Quataert 1996; for late nineteenth-century Egypt, see Chalcraft 2004.

TABLE 1

**Credit Transactions in Hama, 1535–36**

| Credit category | Number of transactions | Percentage | Total value in Aleppo dinars | Percentage |
|---|---|---|---|---|
| Selling on credit (*bay bi-al-dayn*) | 272 | 63.40 | 1,155,550 | 71.11 |
| Loan (*qard*) | 96 | 22.38 | 246,287 | 15.15 |
| Debt (*dayn*) | 43 | 10.02 | 121,219 | 7.46 |
| Prepayment for future delivery (*salam*) | 18 | 4.20 | 102,070 | 6.28 |
| TOTAL | 429 | 100.00 | 1,625,126 | 100.00 |

category of credit, which involved delayed payment for commodities sold, was widespread and constituted the core of the subsistence economy at the time. A limited number of creditors, mostly of urban origin, extended credit to buyers by selling them the commodities they needed, very often at inflated prices. The social groups involved in this type of credit, whether creditors or debtors, and the value of the commodities sold on credit are examined in Table 2.

The group with the highest number of creditors (59.56 percent) was composed of the untitled, that is, ordinary people with no social, religious, or ethnic title that might enable us to identify their, status, sect, or ethnicity. Despite their large number, however, the value of the commodities they sold on credit constituted 26.94 percent of the total, that is, less than half the percentage of their number, which indicates the large number of ordinary people involved in the credit market. This is further confirmed by their large percentage (46.91 percent) among the debtors, and also by the large amount of debt (41.2 percent) they owed to others.

The three other groups that topped the list of creditors after the untitled with regard to the large amount of credit they advanced despite their small numbers were the *hajjis*/merchants (that is, those who could afford to go on the costly pilgrimage and were mostly merchants), the military, and the ulama. Although the military were fewer in number (3.68 percent), compared to the ulama (8.45 percent) and the *hajjis* (20.59 percent), the amount of the credit they offered (16.57 percent) was proportionally greater than the amount offered by the ulama (15.57 percent) and the *hajjis* (31.23 percent) in

TABLE 2

Creditors, Debtors, and Value of Credit in Hama, 1535–36

| | Creditors | | | | Debtors | | | |
|---|---|---|---|---|---|---|---|---|
| Social group | No. | % | Credit in Halabi dirhams | % | No. | % | Credit in Halabi dirhams | % |
| Officials | 1 | 0.37 | 12,500 | 1.08 | | | | |
| Treasury | 2 | 0.74 | 50,000 | 4.32 | | | | |
| Military | 10 | 3.68 | 191,473 | 16.57 | 1 | 0.31 | 1,000 | 0.08 |
| Ulama | 23 | 8.45 | 180,027 | 15.57 | 3 | 0.93 | 48,000 | 4.15 |
| Hajjis/ merchants | 56 | 20.59 | 360,875 | 31.23 | 37 | 11.42 | 179,582 | 15.54 |
| Untitled | 162 | 59.56 | 311,310 | 26.94 | 152 | 46.91 | 476,055 | 41.2 |
| Peasants | 7 | 2.57 | 12,880 | 1.14 | 103 | 31.79 | 389,773 | 33.73 |
| Women | 7 | 2.57 | 27,190 | 2.35 | 4 | 1.23 | 2,155 | 0.19 |
| Christians | 4 | 1.47 | 9,295 | 0.8 | 23 | 7.1 | 41,485 | 3.59 |
| Jews | | | | | 1 | 0.31 | 17,500 | 1.52 |
| TOTAL | 272 | 100.00 | 1,155,550 | 100.00 | 324 | 100.00 | 1,155,550 | 100.00 |

percentage terms. The high investment by the military in the credit market was indeed the beginning of a trend that they maintained throughout Ottoman rule in Syria, indicating the major role they were to play in the economic life of the country. Women, Christians, and Jews played relatively minor roles as creditors and debtors; this continued to be the case until the nineteenth century when the two latter groups began to accumulate wealth as middlemen and agents for European merchants and also as entrepreneurs in their own right.

Among the debtors, the peasants ranked after the untitled both in number (31.79 percent) and in the amount of credit offered to them (33.73 percent). This also set a pattern for the future, because of the deteriorating economic condition of the peasantry and their exploitation by the military as creditors and holders of agricultural land grants and also as tax farmers. Most of the commodities the peasants bought on credit consisted of the grain, cotton, and animals that they produced and worked with but were obliged to sell to pay off their debts. By quantifying the types of commodities sold on credit and their value according to the various social groups that dealt in them, important conclusions can be drawn, as Table 3 indicates.

The military headed the list of providers of grain (44.4 percent), which indicates their heavy involvement with the peasants as holders of land grants or as tax farmers. The peasants ranked after women and Christians as creditors of grain (1.77 percent). The untitled ranked first (50.45 percent)among the groups offering cotton on credit. The ulama, the *hajjis*/merchants, and the untitled together accounted for about 96 percent of the textiles given out in credit. The *hajjis*/merchants and the untitled together accounted for about 64 percent of the animals sold on credit, which indicates the involvement of both groups in agricultural dealings with the peasants.

By examining the receiving groups, that is, the debtors, the peasants again figure as the most indebted social group. The types of commodities they bought on credit are very indicative, as illustrated in Table 4. Credit extended to the peasants to buy grain was 72.46 percent of the total, to buy cotton 45.23 percent, and to buy animals 29.22 percent. The peasants' meager purchases of textiles and woolen cloth (7.57 percent and 5.12 percent respectively) can presumably be explained by their modest means. The absence of spices and perfumes from their credit likewise attests to the harshness of their way of life. The military barely figure as debtors.

Two basic facts emerge from sales on credit in the *liwa'* of Hama in 1535–36: the major role of the military in extending credit, mostly to peasants, and the profound indebtedness of the peasants, mainly to urban creditors. In time, the military grew richer by investing heavily in the countryside and by using illegal means of making money while the condition of the peasantry deteriorated.

As holders of land grants (*timariots* or *sipahis*) and tax farmers (*multazims*), the military found the peasantry an easy prey. The *timariots* lived mostly in the towns, rather than on their fiefs, but they abused the peasants who lived and worked on their fiefs. They burdened them with excessive taxation, beat them, and even put them in chains in their private prisons,[48] especially during

---

48. LCR, Hama, 24:471, awa'il 992 (beginning 1585); 25:554, awakhir Muharram 994 (mid-Jan. 1586).

TABLE 3

Creditors: Commodities, and Credit in Hama, 1535–36

| Social groups | No. | Grain | Cotton | Textiles | Woolen cloth | Spices and perfumes | Animals | Miscellaneous |
|---|---|---|---|---|---|---|---|---|
| Officials | 1 | | 12,500 | | | | | |
| | | | (18.78) | | | | | |
| Treasury | 2 | | 2,500 | | | | 25,000 | |
| | | | (6.37) | | | | (25.52) | |
| Military | 10 | 174,150 | 1,535 | | | | 5,288 | 10,500 |
| | | (44.40) | (2.31) | | | | (5.40) | (7.03) |
| Ulama | 3 | 42,290 | 12,150 | 90,140 | 1,210 | | 1,200 | 33,037 |
| | | (10.78) | (18.26) | (32.18) | (1.31) | | (1.22) | (22.11) |
| *Hajjis*/ merchants | 56 | 59,875 | 4,900 | 92,840 | 69,700 | 65,600 | 28,840 | 39,120 |
| | | (15.26) | (7.36) | (33.15) | (75.70) | (84.95) | (29.44) | (26.19) |
| Untitled | 162 | 79,904 | 33,573 | 85,355 | 19,020 | 11,620 | 33,840 | 47,998 |
| | | (20.37) | (50.45) | (30.48) | (20.66) | (15.05) | (34.54) | (32.13) |
| Peasants | 7 | 6,930 | 1,650 | 500 | | | 3,800 | |
| | | (1.77) | (2.48) | (0.18) | | | (3.88) | |
| Women | 7 | 2,500 | | 8,300 | | | | 14,240 |
| | | (0.64) | | (2.96) | | | | (9.53) |
| Christians | 4 | 1,600 | 245 | 2,950 | | | | 4,500 |
| | | (0.41) | (0.36) | (1.05) | | | | (3.01) |
| Jews | — | — | — | — | — | — | — | — |
| TOTAL | 272 | 392,249 | 66,553 | 280,085 | 92,080 | 77,220 | 97,968 | 149,395 |
| Percentage of total value | | | | | | | | |
| (1,155,550) | | (33.94) | (5.76) | (24.24) | (7.97) | (6.68) | (8.48) | (12.93) |

*Note:* Values are in Halabi dirhams with percentage of total values in parentheses.

TABLE 4

**Debtors: Commodities and Credit in Hama, 1535–36**

| Social Groups | No. | Grain | Cotton | Textiles | Woolen cloth | Spices and perfumes | Animals | Miscellaneous |
|---|---|---|---|---|---|---|---|---|
| Military | 1 | | 100 | | | | | |
| | | | (0.03) | | | | | |
| Ulama | 3 | | 12,500 | | | | 25,000 | 10,500 |
| | | | (18.78) | | | | (25.52) | (7.03) |
| *hajjis/* merchants | 37 | 21,770 | 11,100 | 58,087 | 7,350 | 44,000 | 4,645 | 32,630 |
| | | (5.55) | (16.68) | (20.74) | (7.98) | (56.98) | (4.74) | (21.84) |
| Untitled | 152 | 54,964 | 12,607 | 193,818 | 61,120 | 33,220 | 39,693 | 80,633 |
| | | (14.01) | (18.94) | (69.20) | (66.38) | (43.02) | (40.52) | (53.97) |
| Peasants | 103 | 284,240 | 30,101 | 21,200 | 4,710 | | 28,630 | 20,892 |
| | | (72.46) | (45.23) | (7.57) | (5.12) | | (29.22) | (13.99) |
| Women | 4 | 1,475 | | 680 | | | | |
| | | (0.38) | | (0.24) | | | | |
| Christians | 23 | 29,800 | 245 | 5,300 | 1,400 | | | 4,740 |
| | | (7.60) | (0.37) | (1.89) | (1.52) | | | (3.17) |
| Jews | 1 | | | | 17,500 | | | |
| | | | | | (19.00) | | | |
| TOTAL | 324 | 392,249 | 66,553 | 280,085 | 92,080 | 77,220 | 97,968 | 149,395 |

*Note:* Values in Halabi dirhams with percentage of total values in parentheses.

the seventeenth and the eighteenth centuries, when the *timariot*s were at the peak of their power. The peasants reacted to their plight in two ways, either by taking to banditry on the highways or by seeking safety in flight. Many villagers fled their villages, both to the detriment of their lords (who were deprived of their labor) and to the displeasure of their remaining fellow peasants, who had to pay their share of the collective taxes. The *timariot*s used force and also appealed to the judges to bring back fugitive peasants in accordance with the laws promulgated by the state. The judges did not always concur with the requests of the *timariots*, especially when the peasants could prove that they had been settled in their new villages for not less than fifteen years, had family, and paid taxes there (al-Faradi n.d.) According to Halil İnalcik, Ottoman law "forbade the *reaya* to leave their settlement and go elsewhere" because "the Sipahi whose *reaya* fled lost his income. . . . The Sipahi had fifteen years in which to compel a fugitive peasant to return to his land but to do this he needed a kadi's decree" (1973b, 111–12). Such abuses of authority on the part of the *timariots* were common in the Ottoman Empire at the time.

The Syrian ulama came to the defense of the fugitive peasants by condemning the Sultan's orders and the feudal laws that allowed the maltreatment of the peasants. They approved of the peasants' flight because of the injustice they suffered and quoted the example of the Prophet Muhammad who fled Mecca to Medina to avoid persecution by the Meccans. The ulama went to the extent of encouraging the peasants to rise against their oppressors and even to kill them. Ottoman law, the ulama maintained, could be implemented only when it conformed to the sharia (al-Nabulsi 1987–88, 18–20, 28–37).

Throughout Ottoman rule in Syria, the military, more than any other group, both *timariots* and local janissaries (*yerliyya*), maintained their hold over most of the agricultural land as holders of land grants, tax farmers, and as lessees of *waqf* agricultural land. A sample from the court records of Damascus from the period between 20 September 1583 and 8 September 1584 indicates that the military rented property during this period for 158,240 silver *qit'as* (probably *aqche*, the first Ottoman silver coin), which constituted 61 percent of the total rent paid to all social groups during the same period. The military do not figure at all as lessors of property, only as buyers. They bought property to the amount of 9,760 *qit'as*, 13.53 percent of the total. Agricultural property accounted for 57.78 percent of what they bought, 36.89 percent commercial and 5.33 percent residential. The military sold agricultural property valued at 32,000 *qit'as*, or 44.37 percent of all property sold in that year. This clearly shows the heavy involvement of the military in dealings in land, especially agricultural land (Rafeq 1987b, 158–59).

Outside the urban centers, agricultural land was mostly either *miri* (state) land or *waqf* (charitable or family foundations) land. Neither type of land could be sold and owned as freehold (*milk*). Plantations and buildings on these lands, however, could be owned according to Islamic law. Thus, buying agricultural property generally meant buying plantations. In another sample from the court records of Damascus, about 115 years later, in 1700–1, the military again headed the list as lessees of agricultural land. They also ranked second, after the *ashraf*, as buyers of property. They bought 28.08 percent of the land on sale in the countryside of Damascus while the *ashraf* bought 52.94 percent. The military sold less land (26.92 percent) than they had bought. In a second sample from Damascus in 1724–25, the military bought about half the land (50.08 percent) on sale; the remaining percentage was bought by six other social groups. The military sold only 27.99 percent of the land they had bought. The military leased 50.10 percent of all charitable (*khayri*) and family (*ahli*) *waqf* agricultural land that was put out for rent in the 1700–1 sample. They leased about the same per centage (49.53 percent) of *waqf* land in the sample of 1724–25 (Rafeq 1992a, 297–99, 318–20).

*Waqf* agricultural land leased by the military in the sample of 1700–1 consisted of 57.13 percent of charitable *waqf* land and 23.08 percent of family *waqf* land. In the 1724–25 sample, they leased 50 percent and 20 percent respectively. Most of the leases of *waqf* land contracted by the military in both samples broke the three-year limit stipulated by the official Hanafi school of law. To ensure the legitimacy of the longer leases, the military referred them mostly to the Shafi'i judge who, in accordance with his school of law, legalized the leases which were then endorsed by the official Hanafi judge, a procedure which brought the lessees much profit. This is because in the lease contract of *waqf* land, a clause referred to as the right of *muzara'a* or *munasaba*, that is, the right of plantation, allowed the lessee to plant on *waqf* land during the lease period. One-third to three-quarters of these plantations would be the property of the lessee, the remaining portion belonging to the *waqf*. This portion would then be entrusted to the lessee by virtue of another clause in the contract known as *musaqat* (from the Arabic root meaning to irrigate), for which he would be offered an almost standard compensation amounting to 999 out of 1,000 shares of the revenue of the plantations belonging to the *waqf*. The remaining one share went to the *waqf* (Rafeq 1992b, 2006).

Such legal tricks and the substitution of the more accommodating Shafi'i law for the more rigid Hanafi law in the leasing of *waqf* land played especially into the hands of the influential military lessees who took advantage of them to

consolidate their economic standing at the expense of the *waqf* and its beneficiaries. This explains why a number of mosques, schools, hospices, and water
fountains within and outside the cities were neglected or destroyed in the
course of time, because the *waqf* revenues that should have accrued to them
were usurped by influential persons including the military and the urban notables. The twentieth-century Damascene alim 'Abd al-Qadir Badran criticized
the greed of these persons and lamented the disappearance of many charitable
establishments because they had lost their *waqf* revenue (Badran 1960). This
situation was not limited to the main cities. Thus, many streets in Gaza in the
late 1850s still carried the names of mosques that had once existed but were no
longer there or left only traces of their remains (Rafeq 1980).

Fortunes were also made in the cities by offering credit at usurious rates.
In the first Hama court register from 1535 to 1536, loans outnumbered debts.
There were 96 loans (*qard*) against 43 debts (*dayn*). The fact that there were
more than twice as many loans as debts is of great significance in the early
years of Ottoman rule in Syria. This occurred before Ottoman laws and regulations were fully implemented and before administrative corruption transformed financial practices for the worse. Traditionally loans were interest-free,
had no time limit, needed no security, were offered in kind or in cash, and were
intended to help the needy. Hence they were known as *qard hasan*, meaning a
fair, meritorious loan. The 96 loans were offered by the same number of creditors to 124 persons, indicating that a larger number of persons benefited from
them. The ulama ranked first among the lenders (43.79 percent) followed by
untitled people (43.33 percent). The least involved in loans were the military
(1.04 percent), who had the same percentage as the peasants and the Christians. The majority of the persons who sought loans were peasants (59.67 percent). The total value of the 96 loans amounted to 246,287 Aleppo dirhams, or
an average of 2,565 dirhams per loan.

In comparison to loans, debts had a time limit, required security, were
offered in kind or in cash, and were referred to as *shar'i*, meaning they were
legal and in conformity with the rules of the sharia. They also required two
types of guarantors: a financial guarantor (*kafil bi'l-mal*) and a personal guarantor (*kafil bi'l-nafs*), who was responsible for keeping the debtor available. No
interest was explicitly mentioned in the debt transaction. The Islamic court
allowed the investment of money for profit, under the rubric of *murabaha*, in

only two cases: when money belonged to minor orphans or to *waqfs*. *Murabaha* was intended to benefit both beneficiaries.

In the same court register from Hama, 43 creditors gave out debts to 64 debtors. The total amount of debt was 121,219 dirhams, an average of 2,819 dirhams per creditor, which was slightly higher than the average loan. The military ranked third as creditors (16.57 percent) after the *hajjis*/merchants (31.23 percent), and the untitled (26.57 percent). The peasants as creditors totaled a low 2.57 percent, but they ranked high among the debtors (33.73 percent) and were only surpassed by the untitled (41.20 percent).

According to Ronald Jennings, loans and debts in the records of the Islamic courts in Anatolia explicitly carried interest (1973). Apparently, compelling economic causes must have necessitated the application of interest to these transactions in Anatolia. Interest seems to have been deeply embedded in the culture of Anatolia from Byzantine times, and it was also part of the financial practices of the Turks in central Asia before they converted to Islam. Interest was applied in the Ottoman Empire by the orders of the sultan and the concurrence of the Shaykh al-Islam (Grand jurist of Istanbul and of the empire) who periodically issued orders fixing its rate. In a case dated 24 December 1585 from the sharia court in Aleppo, there is mention of a debt contracted by a villager from an Aleppppine creditor at the rate of 11½ for every 10, according to the orders of the Sultan (*bi-mujib al-amr al-Sharif al-Sultani*). The judge apparently tried to avoid the use of the term *fa'ida* (interest) in the transaction, but the rate given equals 15 percent. He also laid its responsibility squarely with the sultan, thus absolving his court and the Islamic sharia from any blame.[49]

The debasement of the currency, first reported in the Syrian chronicles in 1585, and its subsequent continuation caused many financial strains, including a high rate of inflation that affected the poorer classes. When corruption came to permeate all sectors of the administration, especially in the eighteenth century, the amount and volume of debts increased and interest became a common practice even though it was not mentioned by name in the court records. In comparison, loans decreased in number and amount, indicating a less humane financial relationship between individuals and an unrestrained avidity on the

---

49. LCR, Aleppo, 6:107, 2 Muharram 994 (24 Dec. 1585). For other cases, see 3:850 and 10:814.

part of creditors to accumulate wealth by any means. The disparity in wealth among social classes thus widened, and class antagonisms began to develop, which had grave consequences in the nineteenth century.

Despite the sultan's orders legalizing interest and the growing need of the impoverished rural and urban poor to contract debts, the overt application of interest was opposed in the Syrian courts because it was contrary to the sharia. Creditors and debtors therefore had recourse to legal tricks to camouflage interest. Fictitious sales, mainly of soap, appeared in the debt contract as a cover-up for interest. In one case a group of villagers collectively borrowed 800 piasters from a creditor in Damascus in 1738 for a period of ten months. One hundred and fifty piasters of this amount were allocated for the purchase of soap from the lender; the balance of the debt was then paid in cash to the villagers.[50] Judging from the many examples from about that period, the value of soap amounted to about one-sixth of the debt, which gives a rate of interest ranging between 15 and 20 percent. This is about the same rate of interest approved by the sultan in the last quarter of the sixteenth century. In another case of soap interest in 1780 in a debt contracted collectively by villagers to a Damascene creditor, the value of soap amounted to 358 piasters for a debt of 2,200 piasters that was due to be paid in six months. Here the interest was about 16.5 percent. A French report from Damascus in 1852 confirms the use of soap as a cover-up for interest: "Vous seriez étonné, Monsieur le Ministre, si vous voyiez l'usure en action dans ce pays. (Le savon joue un grand rôle dans ces sortes de transaction)."[51] According to this report, interest often amounted to 25 percent.

The transfer of money from urban creditors to rural debtors at high interest benefited an increasing number of creditors composed mostly of military, tax-farmers, and *hajjis*/merchants. In the eighteenth century, many ulama among the urban notables, such as the Muradi family, which produced many official Hanafi jurists, acquired tax farms for life (*malikane*) of villages in the vicinity

---

50. LCR, Damascus, 100:17–18, 12 Ramadan 1150 (3 Jan. 1738); see also Rafeq 1981b, 674–75; see also Rafeq 2002b, 108–18.

51. Ministère des Affaires Etrangères (MAE), Correspondance Commerciale (CC), Damas 3, 12 Janvier 1852. For a more complete version of the text, see Rafeq 1983, 431 n.100, and 1994a, 21.

of Damascus, and this brought the notables added wealth. In time the gap between the rich and the poor widened, with serious social consequences.

When the first devaluation of the currency occurred in Syria in 1585, the contemporary Damascene chronicler al-Ansari reported a rise in food prices in the city. Merchants and notables hoarded foodstuffs with the complicity of Ottoman officials. Thefts were rampant and many suicides were reported, largely due to the deteriorating economic situation (al-Ansari 1991; Rafeq 1974/1993, 143). To express their disapproval of the situation, which deteriorated further over time, the urban poor in Damascus supported any movement against the establishment. The poor included many displaced villagers who had fled from the injustice of the *timariots* in the countryside and sought refuge in the urban suburbs. Early in the seventeenth century the poor of Damascus accepted the reportedly un-Islamic religious teachings of Yahya ibn 'Isa al-Karaki who was opposed by the city's ulama who declared him a *zindiq* (freethinker, unbeliever). A large following gathered around him. In 1610, fearing his growing popularity, the ulama prevailed on the governor of the city to have him executed,[52] but this had no effect on the troubled economic and social situation. Hoarding, monopolization of products, rising prices, thefts, and murders became the order of the day. This was also the case in the eighteenth century when Ottoman authority declined. The contemporary Damascene chronicler al-Budayri reports a schism in Damascene society in the eighteenth century between the poor and the rich to the extent that the poor threw stones at the rich notables standing in procession waiting to receive the new governor, and denounced the notables as hypocrites who aided the rulers in oppressing them (al-Budayri 1959, 12–15, 41, 50–51, 76–77).

Because of widespread and endemic exploitation and injustice on the part of the notables and the government officials, the people eventually lost their sense of justice. Budayri states that on one occasion the Damascenes became restless because the judge did not accept bribes and faithfully administered the law (al-Budayri 1959). Similarly, Mikha'il al-Dimashqi, a later Damascene chronicler, commented on the tyrannical rule of the governor 'Abd al-Ra'uf Pasha (1827–31), saying that because of his excessive sense of justice the people

52. For Yahya al-Karaki, see al-Muhibbi 1869, 4, 478–80; Najm al-Din al-Ghazzi 1981–82, 2, 698–706.

were emboldened to stand against him because they had become accustomed to injustice (al-Dimashqi 1912, 49).

## The Impact of Industrial Europe

Radical changes were to occur in Syria's traditional economy and society in the nineteenth century in the wake of the French and the Industrial Revolutions in Europe and the growing dominance of capitalism. Under Muhammad 'Ali's rule in Syria (1831–40), the country became open to European influence, including the establishment of consulates in Damascus, where there had been none before, the opening of Protestant and Catholic missionary schools, and, more importantly, the influx of European industrial goods, notably textiles, mostly through the port of Beirut. Goods carried by steamer to Beirut found their way into the interior of Syria and beyond, profiting from the building of the carriage road between Beirut and Damascus in 1863 and later from the extension of railways linking the coastal towns with the interior (Fawaz 1983; Rafeq 1984b).

The opening of the Suez Canal in 1869 dealt a heavy blow to Syria's caravan cities and to the economy of the country in general. Pilgrims who used to join the pilgrimage at Damascus in their thousands from Anatolia and the Balkans, and even from Persia, now took the sea route to the Hijaz, which was cheaper and safer. Two major shipping companies, the *Messageries Impériales* and the *Compagnie Russe,* now transported the pilgrims by sea to the Hijaz through the Suez Canal. With the Damascene pilgrimage down to a mere few hundred pilgrims from the fifteen to twenty thousand that used to assemble there with their trade, the city lost much of its revenue. The contemporary Damascene Qasatli commented on the consequences of this shift of route by saying that Damascus had lost the stream of gold that poured into it with the pilgrims (Qasatli 1879, 124–25; Rafeq 2002a). Many Damascene guilds offering services to the pilgrims, such as the makers of the wooden boxes (*maha'iriyya*) that seated the pilgrims on the camels' backs, travel agents (*muqawwimin*), guides and caravan conductors, and makers of dried bread cubes (*buqsmat*) purchased by the pilgrims, saw their business diminish to a trickle. No less affected were the Bedouin tribes in the nearby Hawran villages who had rented thousands of camels each year to transport the pilgrims and the troops accompanying them to the Hijaz (Rafeq 1987a). To add to the losses sustained by the tribes, the Ottoman government adopted a firm policy of disciplining the tribes and strengthening its own hold over the provinces.

Under the impact of industrial Europe, Syria was drained of its raw materials, notably cotton and wool, which were exported to Europe at cheap prices and then partly reexported to Syria as yarn at high prices, but the greatest effect was on the guilds that produced local textiles. Many consumers also believed that European textiles were cheaper and better than local textiles. They appealed to local taste, suited the climate, and satisfied the spread of fashions imported from Europe. Traditional looms were put on sale more frequently than at any time before because they were no longer a commercially going concern. Their prices gradually fell as did the prices of the *gedik* (equipment) and the *khilu* (the right to use the premises) of the workshops manufacturing them and the shops retailing them. Many textile producers went bankrupt and journeymen were increasingly laid off or had their wages reduced. Friction and even clashes developed within the guilds between journeymen and masters. The nineteenth-century Damascene Ilyas Qudsi characterized these clashes as revolts within the guilds between impoverished journeymen and hard-pressed masters (Qudsi 1885, 15).

Out of this chaos, a new class of nouveaux riches began to take shape, composed of middlemen and agents marketing European products. Christians, Jews, and Muslims marketed these products. According to Bowring's *Report on the Commercial Statistics of Syria* on the state of affairs in Syria under Muhammad 'Ali's rule in the 1830s, which was presented to Lord Palmerston in 1839, 107 shops in Damascus sold British textiles with a total capital of 1,600,000 to 2,100,000 piasters. Sixty-six Muslim commercial establishments traded with Europe with capital estimated at between 20 and 25 million piasters, or between £200,000 and £250,000. Bowring went on to say that twenty-nine Christian merchants at Damascus were engaged in foreign trade with a capital estimated at between 4.5 and 5.5 million piastres. Twenty-four Jewish houses in Damascus were likewise engaged in foreign trade with a capital of between 16 and 18 million piasters (Bowring 1840, 94). It is thus evident that the Muslims were in the forefront of the merchants dealing with Europe. However, given the smaller number of both Christians and Jews among the population, the proportion of their number working as merchants was actually much higher than that of the Muslims.[53]

The commercial courts introduced into Syria under Egyptian rule were formally institutionalized after the Ottoman "restoration." A commercial court was established in Aleppo in 1850 and in Damascus in 1855. The composition of the commercial court summarizes the degree of participation of the communities in commerce at the time. In Damascus, for example, the court was composed of fourteen members, half of whom were appointed by the foreign consuls, either their own nationals or their local protégés, while the other half was appointed by the Ottoman government. Of the latter, there were four Muslims, two Christians, and one Jew.[54] This ratio reflects the extent of the commercial relations of each community with Europe in terms of capital and number of houses.

A clash of interest was soon to develop between the impoverished population and the new class of entrepreneurs, of whom only the Christians were targeted in both Aleppo and Damascus. Other factors, both local and foreign, were at play and transformed socioeconomic riots into sectarian warfare. Ever since Muhammad 'Ali had opened Syria to Western influences and advocated a policy of religious tolerance, the Christians had become more visible and assertive, both socially and economically. This not only brought them more wealth but also the hatred of the underprivileged masses. The exemption by the Ottomans of non-Muslims from conscription into the army (which they imposed forcibly upon the Muslims) increased the latter's hatred of the newly emancipated and privileged Christians. The riots in Aleppo in 1850, which were instigated by individuals from the poorer quarters and were exploited interested individuals and powers, were directed against the rich Christians residing in the Judayda quarter, the majority of whom were Catholics who had benefited from dealing with the Europeans (Masters 1990; Masters 200( 156–65). Ten years later, under the impact of the same factors but with a spill over from the communal feuding in Mount Lebanon, Damascus witnessed similar socioeconomic riots that were exploited religiously as in Aleppo (Harel

53. For a study of merchants and traders in Aleppo in the early twentieth century based on a contemporary directory, see Sluglett 2002.

54. MAE, CC, Damas 3, 28 mai 1850; see also Rafeq 1983, 426.

1998; Masters 1990; Rafeq 1988a; Rogan 2004). Even Jidda in the Hijaz was the scene of clashes over commerce in 1858 between local Hijazi merchants and European merchants and their protégés that turned sectarian (Ochsenwald 1984, 141–51).

In Syria, as in Lebanon, religious fanaticism was used as a catalyst to whip up the emotions of the masses against the Christians. The complicity of Ottoman officials in these events is attested by the subsequent condemnation to death of many of them, including the governor of Damascus, by the tribunal headed by the Ottoman Foreign Minister Fu'ad Pasha. The European powers whose interests were threatened were soon involved, as was shown by the dispatch of French troops to Lebanon. Napoleon III was anxious at the time to placate Catholic public opinion in his country and in Rome, divert attention from his internal troubles and foreign failures, and assert France's interests in the Levant vis-à-vis British interests.

What began in Lebanon as a peasant movement among the Maronites of Kisrawan seeking emancipation from the control and exploitation of Maronite feudal nobles (which could not be exploited religiously, since both parties were Maronites) turned into sectarian war in the Shuf and beyond. Here the peasants were both Druze and Maronite and rose in rebellion against oppressive Druze feudal chieftains. The mixture of communities in the Shuf lent itself to exploitation, and soon a movement for peasant emancipation turned into a sectarian war (Makdisi 2000).

In Syria, as in Lebanon, the riots were not primarily motivated by religion. For example, the poor Christians in the Maydan quarter of Damascus were not molested during the riots because they shared common rural origins, neighborliness, coexistence, and also poverty with their Muslim neighbors (Rafeq 1988b). In fact the riots were directed by interested parties against the quarter of Bab Tuma where the rich Christians lived. Furthermore, the Jews were not molested, neither in Aleppo nor in Damascus, despite the immense wealth of a few individuals among them. Traditionally, the rich Jews kept a low profile and did not show their wealth in public, but of course the majority of Jews were poor. It is significant that Syria had not experienced anything similar in the three centuries that preceded the riots. Indeed, the various religious communities had coexisted for centuries and were already integrated under Ottoman rule in the guild system through their work ethic.

Before the nineteenth century, mercantilist Europe had coexisted with the traditional economy and society, but this relationship was to change drastically. The disparity of wealth that had come into being in the Syrian cities under the impact of capitalist Europe lay at the root of the riots. Thus Mustafa Bey Hawasili, the head of the irregular troops, the *zabtiyya,* who wrought havoc in the Christian quarter of Bab Tuma, was heavily indebted to Christian creditors. The likelihood of his participation in their massacre makes his execution by the Ottoman disciplinary court more meaningful (Rafeq 1988a).

The people of Aleppo and Damascus soon put these events behind them. As they had cooperated in the past in the mixed guilds on the basis of merit and expertise, they now again cooperated on an even wider economic basis by introducing partnerships (*shirka* or *sharaka*) in business, cutting across religious barriers.[55] They imported European machines, such as the Jacquard loom, which produced figured weave patterns. Much wealth was accumulated by the emerging class of neo-bourgeois entrepreneurs in the Syrian cities. This was reflected in the building of spacious, sumptuous, even palatial family mansions. According to the contemporary historian Qasatli, a great deal of money was spent on building these mansions in Damascus. Rich members of the various communities participated in their construction, for example, the Muslims 'Abdallah Pasha al-'Azm, Sa'id Efendi Quwwatli and his brother Murad Efendi, and Hasan Agha al-Barudi, the Christians Habib Efendi Sabbagh and Antun Efendi Shami, and the Jews Yusuf Efendi 'Anbar (who expended the most money on his still surviving palatial residence), Sham'aya Efendi, Khawaja Islambuli, and Khawaja Lazbuna (al-Qasatli 1879, 96–97).

Some members of this neo-bourgeoisie, composed of a cross-section of Muslims, Christians, and Jews, would promote the new ideology of Arab national consciousness. Secular in essence, invoking the common Arab cultural contributions of the various religious communities in the past, and anxious to distance itself from fanaticism, Arabism gave all the communities a sense of purpose and of common action for the betterment of the Arab people.

55. For Muslim/Jewish partnerships in late Ottoman Haifa, see Yazbak 1994.

While these developments were occurring in the urban centers, the peasantry were still suffering from the depredations of feudal lords, tax farmers,
and Bedouin tribes. Forced labor (*sukhra*), additional taxes to finance the
army (*i'ane*) (Rafeq 1999), protection money (*khuwwa*), and indebtedness
devastated the countryside. With the enactment of the 1858 Land Law, the
Ottoman government made a bid to regularize the practices of land tenure that
had dominated the countryside for centuries. It was not immediately implemented, and when it was, it only affected the areas under the control of the
government and mostly played into the hands of the influential notables. The
right of usufruct of land, which these notables had enjoyed, soon changed into
a de facto right of ownership, thus turning them into large landowners. Many
of them were absentee landowners to whom the land was a mere commodity to
be exploited together with its peasantry. Many peasants at the time were reluctant to become owners of land for fear of further molestation by the state. The
landowners allied themselves with the Ottomans, and later on with the French
mandatory authorities, to safeguard their interests (Hanna 2004).

When Ottoman rule came to an end in Syria in 1918, a nascent bourgeoisie was still in the making and an entrenched landowning class was in
the process of consolidating its privileges. Faysal's government in Damascus
(1918–20) tried to build up a balanced infrastructure. It introduced many
economic, educational, and cultural projects and also encouraged the private
sector to do the same. But it confronted major difficulties and in the process
alienated a large sector of the population because of deteriorating economic
conditions. The change in the currency and its subsequent devaluation and
the loss of markets in Anatolia and the rest of the Ottoman Empire, which
particularly affected Aleppo, weakened Syria's economy, despite the Arab
government's effort to abolish the heavy taxes that had been imposed by the
Ottomans (Rafeq 1993a, 2003a).

The demise of Faysal's government in 1920 put a hold on the projects it
had attempted to introduce. Under French rule, the large landowners maxi-
mized their gain by engaging in industrial projects, thus becoming a bourgeois
landowning class. Their politics, however, although self-serving, was still dominant when Syria achieved its independence. Later, ideological parties came
to the fore with socioeconomic programs that reached out to the masses of

the population. Of all these parties (Communist, Muslim Brotherhood, Syrian Nationalist, Ba'thist), the Ba'th party was destined to be at the forefront. Upon assuming power, it applied a command (state-controlled) economy and implemented major programs of nationalization. Later, however, mixed projects between the public and the private sectors began to take shape. Privatization was welcomed as long as it was subject to state supervision and aimed at promoting national welfare.

# 5

## Political Relations Between City and State in the Colonial Period

### LEILA FAWAZ AND ROBERT ILBERT

↯ FROM THE VERY BEGINNINGS of Islam, the great cities have played pivotal political roles. By the nineteenth century, cities had developed into new instruments of control as government attempts to modernize required a greater degree of centralization on the part of the state. At the same time, the city was also the place where powers competing with the state were likely to emerge, especially through the new commerce with the West, which was largely administered by the European consular authorities. Processes of urbanization and state control expanded through the twentieth century, first under the French and British mandates and then even more intensively after the midcentury. In Syria and Iraq, men from mostly rural backgrounds took over the state in the last quarter of the twentieth century and gained control of key positions in the cities, which, more than ever, became instruments of the highly centralized state (Batatu 1978, 1999). Large-scale migration from the countryside to the towns also brought rural life into the city. Modernization continues on the material level, and urban ideologies—including nationalism and Islamism—remain the slogans of choice. Leadership in much of the Arab world is now in the hands of people of rural origin, and they will need to continue to control the cities if they are to remain able to impose their will.

We would like to thank Charles Davidson, Ph.D. candidate, and Craig Cohen, alumnus, the Fletcher School of Law and Diplomacy, for their bibliographical research.

141

The nature of the role played by the Ottomans in the urban history of their Arab provinces between the sixteenth century, when they dominated most of the Arab lands, and the fall of the empire in 1918, is portrayed variously by different authors, and here historiography has been both cruel and kind. André Raymond notes that, on the whole, the long period of Ottoman rule over the Arab provinces has been presented negatively or sometimes not even commented upon at all (Raymond 1985, ch. 1). Earlier French and Arab historians tended to contrast the Ottoman centuries in the Arab lands with the glorious achievements of the Umayyads and 'Abbasids, presenting the Ottoman centuries as periods of urban decline, deterioration, and social segregation (Raymond 1994b).[1]

This negative view derives from two quite different historiographical traditions, the first that of French colonialists concerned to present French rule in the eastern Mediterranean and North Africa as a major improvement on Ottoman rule, and the second, that of Arab historians who experienced, or wrote about, the struggle for Arab independence from Ottoman, French, or British rule, often with scant regard for the historical record. Arab nationalists, substantially influenced by the writings of Sati' al-Husri, have tended to portray the Ottomans as colonialists less interested in their Arab territories than in their European and Anatolian provinces, and whose "real" commitment to Islam was quite superficial. The reality, as less ideologically driven historians have shown, was rather different: there is little evidence to suggest that Arabs in the late Ottoman Empire regarded themselves as a "colonized people."[2] Over the past two or three decades, the Ottoman legacy in the Arab world has been looked upon more objectively by Western and Turkish historians, as well as by some Arab historians, often scholars of Arab origin trained in the United States who know both Arabic and Ottoman Turkish and have worked in the Ottoman archives. The new approaches arrived at by this group

---

1. See also Barbir 1996b; Hourani 1991.

2. See Bruce Masters's appraisal of the prevailing views of the Arab population of the Ottoman Empire at the end of the nineteenth century: "The empire, for most Muslims and even some Christians, was simply seen as the only remaining political force capable of forestalling European colonial ambitions" (2001, 176).

generally reflect a more accurate appreciation of the role played by the Ottoman government in the Arab lands.[3]

All Middle Eastern cities underwent tremendous upheavals in the nineteenth and twentieth centuries. Political, social, and economic change in the
nineteenth century forced Ottoman leaders and Muslim thinkers to accept the
social transformations dictated by the Tanzimat reforms, and mass printing
and publishing had significant effects upon the cities. The expansion of trade
with Europe (made possible largely by the development of steamships) largely
transformed the economy of the Middle East (Pamuk 1987; Kasaba 1988).
Before the nineteenth century, trade within the Ottoman Empire was more
important than trade between the empire and Europe (Walz 1978). In the
nineteenth century, the position changed dramatically as the economy became
more Western-oriented. Roger Owen and others have written extensively about
the expanding world economy and its impact on the Middle East, and Smilianskaya has given a vivid description of the effect of the flood of European goods
on such traditional artisan and commercial centers as Damascus and Aleppo.
While local industry and crafts suffered, those involved in organizing the cultivation and export of raw materials, especially cotton from Egypt and silk
and cotton from Greater Syria, often made spectacular fortunes. An economic
revolution was taking place, and the accompanying prosperity even reached
smaller market towns such as Zahleh and Dayr al-Qamar in Mount Lebanon,
which now became centers of local inter-regional trade.[4]

The principal urban beneficiaries of the new trade were the ports on the
eastern Mediterranean, which became the centers of the trade with Europe,

3. Halil İnalcik best represents the historians who did superb work on Ottoman institutions but essentially ignored the Arab provinces. Notable for their exceptional interest in Arab
history and for their knowledge and use of Arabic sources among historians who are Turkish
or of Turkish origin are Engin Akarlı (1993), Hasan Kayalı (1997), and Ekmeleddin Ihsanoğlu
(2001). Among historians who are Arab, or of Arab origin, working on Ottoman historiography are Abdeljelil Temimi (1994), Abdul-Rahim Abu-Husayn (1985), 'Adnan Bakhit (1992),
Karl Barbir (1980), and Dina Khoury (1997a).

4. For a brilliant overview of the subject in global perspective, see Bayly 2004, chs. 3–6.
See also Raymond 1985, 43–46; Issawi 1988; Owen 1981a; Smilianskaya 1972; Fawaz 1983;
Labaki 1984.

especially Alexandria, Izmir, and Beirut.[5] Their prosperity produced entrepreneurs who acted as middlemen for the new trade with Europe. The most
successful among them interacted both with the Ottoman representatives and
with the European consuls, who made many of them consular protégés, thus
exempting them from most local taxes and regulations. In some cities, particularly Alexandria, foreigners benefited particularly from the new economic
opportunities, but in others, particularly Beirut, local entrepreneurs gained
the upper hand. To a very great extent, the Christian minorities and the Jews
dominated trade with Europe, although some Muslim merchants survived the
reorientation of the market and continued to prosper under the new conditions.[6] Those who were unable to adjust suffered the most.

The growth of the new trading centers attracted people to the cities from
the adjacent rural regions in search of work. Not enough has been written about
the population drawn to the city from smaller urban centers and from the
countryside; sources are scarce for the poor and illiterate, especially in times
of peace. It is easier to find information on the merchant elites who bought
and sold lands and registered them in the *mahakim shar'iyya,* the law-courts,
and filed complaints and petitions, and thus left behind a record of their contacts with both Ottomans and Europeans. Some even kept chronicles or wrote
memoirs that are invaluable for historians. Some very good research has been
done on the working classes, but there are few studies on the way in which village and rural life was affected by the growth of the major centers of European
trade in the Middle East.[7] The desire of many country folk to come to the cities
is clear from the growth of the larger cities in the late nineteenth and twentieth

5. Issawi 1969; Kasaba, Keyder and Tabak 1986. For Alexandria, see Ilbert 1996; for Beirut, see Fawaz 1983, and Hanssen 2005. See also Keyder, Özveren and Quataert 1993.

6. See the lists of commercial establishments in various eastern Mediterranean cities in
*Dalil Suriyya wa Misr al-tujjari* 1908 and the discussions in Labaki 1994 and Sluglett 2002.

7. For working class movements, see Botman 1988; Beinin 1988; Lockman 1994; E.
Goldberg 1996. For premodern and modern Cairo, see Abu-Lughod 1971; Raymond 1993.
For nineteenth- and early twentieth-century Alexandria, see Ilbert 1996; Reimer 1997. For
mandatory Damascus, see P. Khoury 1987; Thompson 2000; Provence 2005. For Aleppo,
see Gaube and Wirth 1984; David 1998; Watenpaugh 2006. For Beirut, see Chevallier 1971;
Labaki 1984; Davie 1996; Hanssen 2005. For Haifa, see Seikaly 1995. See also the wide-rang-
ing coverage of late Ottoman provincial cities in Hanssen, Philipp, and Weber 2002.

centuries. Population figures are notoriously inexact for premodern times, but some breakthroughs have been made in research on the cities of North Africa, the central Arab lands, and Anatolia.[8]

The arrival of peasants and, more recently, nomadic peoples, in cities, generated a number of problems whose effects on Cairo have been described by Janet Abu-Lughod (1971) and on Beirut by the anthropologist Fuad I. Khuri (1975). Does the migration of rural groups to an urban milieu result in their urbanization? Or does it do the opposite, transform urban ways of life into rural ones, especially in the poorer quarters where the migrants are concentrated? Or does the city end up with a mixture of rural and urban ways as people move from one milieu to the other? Certainly, where immigration approaches or surpasses natural increase as a source of growth, this evidently produces a mix of urban and nonurban ways and values (Raymond 1973; Abu-Lughod 1971; Khuri 1975).[9]

In some cases, bringing the values of the countryside into the city meant a loss of flexibility and social harmony. Whereas religious communities in the centers of trade on the eastern Mediterranean had always had both commercial, and to some extent social, dealings with each other, communities in the countryside were more isolated. In his classic study of the Mediterranean, Braudel drew attention to the role of geography in social formations and in the differentiation of social and political traditions. For example, when communications were difficult in Mount Lebanon in premodern times, the religious communities of the mountain were more self-reliant than those on the coast. One result was that when a civil war engulfed large parts of Mount Lebanon in the mid–nineteenth century, the rural population that fled came to Beirut, the politically safest and economically most secure port. However, they brought with them their fears and prejudices about the other communities with whom they had clashed with in their home villages (Makdisi 2000). As a result, while their migration to some extent eased the sectarian tensions in the areas they came from, it brought those tensions with them into the city, and, some fifty years later, Beirut began to experience its own sectarian incidents. Thus, one result of rural to urban migration in the nineteenth century

8. See Bernard Hourcade's chapter in this volume (chapter 6).

9. See also Debbas 2001, and Bryan Roberts's classic study *Cities of Peasants* (1978).

was that, while defusing economic or social pressures in their areas of origin, it often simply shifted them to new areas of settlement (Braudel 1975; Khuri 1975; Fawaz 1994).

Urban groups continued to dominate local politics throughout the nineteenth and early twentieth centuries. The city played a major role in center-provincial relations during the Ottoman centuries, and studies of the urban notables have contributed to the understanding of the nature and workings of these relations. In the nineteenth century, as in earlier Ottoman centuries, the Ottoman government used these local notables, or a'yan, as mediators of their will and as barometers of the provincial mood. In 1968 Albert Hourani coined the phrase "the politics of notables" to describe their place in the scheme of Ottoman politics as indispensable mediators who were both instruments of government and checks on its power. Other scholars have shown that there were variations in the behavior of notables in different centers and regions and that internal rivalries among the local elites did much to weaken, or factionalize, the privileged classes.[10]

Although such findings alert us to some of the nuances that need to be taken into account, there is little sense in pretending that the notables were not pivotal in urban life. Even in American politics certain families have gained a degree of "notability," and the public is eager to have its uncrowned royalty to talk and read about. If that notion is projected back to the Middle East, where history weighs more heavily and the first questions posed to any newcomer will inevitably focus on which family he belongs to, where he comes from, whom he knows, and who knows him, one can see, in many ways, how little things have changed. Economic change, social mobility, rapid communications, and other aspects of modern life may have permitted new social classes to emerge, and may have brought about a degree of diversification among the elites, but the same questions are being asked of the new ones.

The new elites also operate in ways that ensure the continuation of family networks at the beginning of the twenty-first century. Where one comes from may matter as much as who one is. The notables may belong to old elites or be nouveaux riches; they may be urban, rural, or tribal in origin or practice, but

10. For insights into the role of the notables, see, for example, Rafeq 1977; Schatkowski Schilcher 1985; P. Khoury 1983; Seikaly 1995; Marcus 1989; Masters 1988; D. Khoury 1997a.

the role of personal connections and personal politics remains. As in many other places, connections help people get jobs and get things done. In fact, the role of the elites has been amplified, not diminished, by the growth of modern bureaucracies. In modern times, new names and new families have been brought into the political game and have joined the economic and social elites, but the principle that a group of go-betweens facilitate social mobility and protect the unconnected continues to be relevant. Modern highways and airports have not made family background and family standing redundant. The medieval biographical dictionaries detailing religious, political, and/or social clout and connections have disappeared, but they have been replaced by Western-type directories like *Who's Who*. Connections are still needed to get things done,[11] an important difference being that social mobility is greater now, partly because of expanding economies and the large-scale movement of populations. Despite this, there is a great deal of continuity in urban and other social networks.

For a while, European colonial rule prolonged the political importance of local elites, since the Europeans often relied on them, or on factions among them, to maintain order in various ways and, in doing so, prepared them to take over the "independent" governments. The nature and intensity of the colonial presence varied in different parts of the Middle East, depending on how important (economically, politically, strategically) the European powers believed continued control of a particular area to be. The rise of nationalism and other events also influenced outcomes. World War II, for example, exhausted the Europeans and helped speed the departure of France from Syria and Lebanon and of Britain from Jordan and Palestine, and eventually from Egypt, Iraq, and Sudan. In the states of the Levant, French and British colonial rule, in the form of mandates granted by the League of Nations at the end of World War I (in theory to prepare the countries under their rule for independence), lasted only for the two decades between the world wars, with different timetables for the departure of the powers from the individual countries after World War II.[12]

11. Personal connections are especially vital in totalitarian states where individuals are not equally protected by the law —if, indeed, they are protected at all.

12. Iraq had become formally independent of Britain as early as 1932.

Although the colonial powers deeply affected the histories of the states that they created and ruled, they did not greatly affect the physical layout of the main cities, in comparison with the situation in North Africa, where the French and the Italians built spacious "European" cities some distance away from the local population. Hence, there is not much lasting physical evidence of Western occupation in the cities of Syria, Lebanon, Jordan, Palestine, or Iraq.[13] In Egypt and the Sudan, where the British came earlier and left later (1880s–1950s), more of a mark was left on urban development.[14]

The mandate period in Syria was marked by strikes and uprisings against the French, but it was also a time of rapid population growth, inflation, agrarian commercialization, and urban development (P. Khoury 1987; Thompson 2000). In 1926, Damascus began a period of growth as the areas between al-Salihiyya and the Old City were rapidly built up. Several modern garden districts (such as al-Jisr, 'Arnus, and al-Shuhada') with large villas were built for French functionaries and other Europeans as well as for wealthy Syrians. In 1929, the urban planner René Danger drew up a master plan for the future development of the city, with Michel Écochard in charge of its implementation. The focus of political activity moved from the Old City to the headquarters of the French High Commission, though the Old City continued to be the locus of social and political organization, each of its quarters having its own hierarchy of shaykhs, ulama, and other a'yan. It was in the city's quarters that nationalism flourished, although physical and social barriers gradually eroded toward the end of the mandate.[15]

On the other hand, the impact of the mandatory powers on particular institutions and political structures was profound. In Lebanon, separated from the rest of Syria in part to give the Maronites an enclave and in part to implement

13. A possible exception here is the work of the architect and "urbaniste"/town planner Michel Écochard (1905–1985) in Damascus and Beirut (and later in Morocco). See Abdulac 1982 and de Mazières 1985.

14. See Debbas 1986; Abu-Lughod 1971. For Cairo, see Raymond 1993, ch. 15 and 16; Volait 2005; for colonial North Africa, see von Henneberg 1996; Çelik 1997; and more generally Wright 1991.

15. For more information on the layout of the city at various periods, see Elisséeff 1965, 1970; Barbir 1980; Raymond 1979, 1979–80; Dettmann 1969; Abdulac 1982; Bianquis 1980; P. Khoury 1984.

a more general policy of dividing the religious communities so as to rule them better, Christian notables could now aspire to rule. During the Ottoman centuries, minorities had to be content with acquiring riches and influence; they could not hope for tangible political power. Under the mandate, however, like the other notables in Lebanon, the minorities played politics with a vengeance (Traboulsi 2007, 88–127). Their national political struggles were concentrated in the capitals where the colonial powers were centered and prepared them for the intense political rivalries of the postindependence period.

In Egypt, the colonial power, Britain, left more of a mark on urban development. In Cairo, substantial growth began in the 1830s, but it was only during the reign of Khedive Isma'il (1863–79) that the city was fundamentally transformed. Influenced by Haussmann's reorganization of Paris, Isma'il ordered the construction of a European-style city to the west of the medieval center, and French city planning principles dominated the design of these districts ('Azbakiyya, 'Abdin, Isma'iliyya). By the end of the nineteenth century, all were well developed, and after the British took control in 1882 they functioned as a colonial enclave. André Raymond remarks that at this point Cairo became two cities, "an indigenous city and a 'European' city." These "two cities" differed from each other in almost every respect, from street layout to the social class of the inhabitants. The streets of the old city were dilapidated, and those who remained there were mostly poor and often unemployed. The western city, in contrast, was the center of tourism, politics, and banking; its population was predominantly European and elite.[16] In 1906, the Belgian Baron Empain founded the new suburb of Heliopolis; by 1947, it had some 50,000 inhabitants (Ilbert 1981; Raymond 1993; Volait 2005).

Alexandria was also transformed. Here, too, Khedive Isma'il was instrumental in building new districts, roads, the first sewage system in Egypt, and the railway station; the harbor acquired new lighthouses and other facilities. Europeans continued to be drawn to the city and to dominate its economy during the cotton boom under British rule. They organized themselves into communities based on national and ethnic backgrounds, each community having its own church or synagogue, clergy, schools, hospitals, cemeteries, journals, and financial institutions. In 1934, a twenty-kilometer corniche was built along

16. Abu-Lughod 1971; Raymond 1993; Zaki 1964; Reimer 1997.

the Mediterranean coast, and the city became a major tourist resort with the construction of numerous hotels, swimming pools, and restaurants.[17]

However, the adoption of technology and other outward signs of modernity did little to disrupt traditional ties of family, clan, region, and religion, partly, as has been noted, because of the arbitrariness inherent in the new political structures. Sometimes, as in Iraq, Jordan, Lebanon, and Syria, the sheer numbers of migrants brought the values of the countryside to the cities.[18] As a result, skyscrapers and modern dress have gone hand in hand with traditional commitments to the extended family and to long-established social traditions. Intermarriage between religions (and between sects) continues to be relatively rare[19] and civil marriage has never been instituted.[20]

Not all migration has been voluntary. Refugees have become a familiar part of the landscape of most Middle Eastern states, where inter-Arab, inter-Muslim, and especially since 1948, Arab-Israeli, tensions have caused populations to move, usually against their will. Refugees have brought with them their memories and their oral histories, and these have shaped their perceptions of the groups that forced their migration. Sometimes, refugees have moved across continents and oceans, and physical distance has tempered their commitment to their original cause or at least transformed the forms of its expression. Often, however, and certainly in the case of the Palestinians in the neighboring lands, the proximity of the land to which they cannot return has fueled their nationalism and brought it into the areas where they have settled.

17. See "Alexandrie entre deux mondes," special issue of *Revue de l'Occident musulman et de la Méditerranée* 46 (1988); Ilbert 1981; Saad El-Din 1993; Reimer 1997.

18. This was particularly true of Iraq. In the census of 1977, 64 percent of the population of Iraq lived in cities and only 36 percent in the countryside, representing an almost direct reversal of the proportions in the 1947 census. See Farouk-Sluglett and Sluglett 2001, 246–49; al-Ansari 1979.

19. Except perhaps in Iraq, where, at least according to anecdotal evidence, there were numerous cross-sectarian marriages between middle-class Sunnis and middle-class Shi'is in the 1940s, 1950s, and 1960s. See Al-Ali 2007, 107.

20. Civil marriage was proposed by the French administration in Syria in the 1930s in a manner almost calculated to offend religious sensibilities; see Thompson 1999, 152–53.

Partly as a result, the cities have become centers of ideological formulations, intellectual exchanges, and power.

Advances in communications have also meant that it has become more difficult to remain aloof from the politics of neighboring states. This is partly because pan-Arabism, at least in theory, does not recognize the national borders drawn up after World War I. Those who espouse the cause consider that they have the right to be involved in the affairs of their neighbors. Cities that have received large numbers of political refugees have absorbed some of the attitudes which successive waves of refugees have brought with them.[21] Modern technology has served national sentiment and contributed to the persistence or deepening of cultural or national differences affected by wars or forced migration.

One of the ways in which the city has served political agendas has been the role it plays as the home of the media. Newspapers, journals, and books are published in cities; television broadcasts the views of the states that control it in and from the cities, and television broadcasts reach into homes all over the Middle East. There is no need to dwell on the power of the media for a Western readership; here, as elsewhere, it is put to the service of those who control it. When the telegraph was used to relay messages during the Crimean War (1856–58), this was considered a major event. A century and a half later, the role of the media in the Gulf War and in the invasion of Iraq in 2003 and its long aftermath has brought home the extent of the media revolution and the intertwining of so many parts of the contemporary world. The city is at the heart of traditional and novel forms of cultural expression and, as a result, plays a key role in giving governments (particularly dictatorial ones) and others a powerful means of expression.

In the twentieth century, no entity has benefited more from the opportunities provided by the media than the national state. At the end of the eighteenth century, Napoleon well understood the power of propaganda, as may be deduced from his statement to the astonished Egyptians when he arrived in Egypt in 1798: "O shaykhs, judges and imams, officers and notables of the

21. Among them, perhaps quintessentially, Amman; see Hannoyer and Chami 1996. More recently, Amman has also received substantial numbers of Iraqi refugees.

land, tell your people that the French are also sincere Muslims."[22] Every group brought to power by elections or by force has used every means at its disposal to propagate its message. In 1923 Mustafa Kemal, the founder of modern Turkey, led a national rebellion from Ankara, not from Istanbul, the former Ottoman capital, that freed his homeland from foreign occupation and created a republic. Ever since, leaders in the Middle East have used the resources of their capital city to propagate their messages. No leader in the Arab world has been as popular as Colonel Nasser, brought to power by the Free Officers' coup d'état in 1952, who broadcast his speeches from Cairo supporting pan-Arabism and denouncing imperialism and Zionism over Cairo radio, *Sawt al-'Arab*, and on television to tens of millions all over the Arab world and beyond.

Eventually, as technology has spread and become cheaper, even dictatorial governments have gradually become unable to exert total control over the media. In the nineteenth century, the revolution in publishing allowed the circulation of antigovernment tracts, and the Ottoman government had trouble controlling them and keeping them out of the empire. In the second half of the twentieth century, opposition groups used tapes and films as well as the printed word, and more recently the Internet, to undermine the viewpoints that they opposed. The most famous case is perhaps that of the revolution in Iran, where the Shah had brought television to the villages only to have it used against him as it broadcast Ayatollah Khumayni's messages from France to his followers in Iran.

Although the spread of technology has diminished the role of the city in politics, as messages can be relayed to wherever the audience is, it has also increased dependence on the state for the provision of social services. In his seminal research on Iraq and Syria, Hanna Batatu has shown that after the coups d'état and revolutions of the late 1940s and early 1950s, the primary employer in Syria, Iraq, and Egypt has been the state, with Damascus, Baghdad, and Cairo as the main poles of attraction for the population.[23] He argues

22. The full text (together with the contemporary chronicler al-Jabarti's commentary) is available in Moreh 1993, 24–33.

23. It is also often the case that the capital city, and perhaps one or two others, are very much larger than those in the second or third tier. Thus Damascus and Aleppo both have about 4 million inhabitants, while the next largest city in Syria is Homs, with 1.6 million. See chapter 6, Table 7.

convincingly that, taken together, the cumulative impact of the social trans-formations of these regimes has been revolutionary, even though each coup d'état or proclaimed revolution on its own may not have been revolutionary. It also accounts for the qualitative changes in the social transformations of the second half of the twentieth century (Batatu 1978, 1984, 1999).

When political power was seized by the populist dictatorships of the 1950s and 1960s, the leadership of the urban notables, which had continued through the first decades of independence, was replaced by the rule of new leaders drawn mostly from the lower classes or from the army, since earlier reforms had opened the ranks of the officer corps to those without private means. By the end of World War II, the young officers were well placed to seize power, particularly after the national humiliations of the interwar period and later of the first Arab-Israeli war of 1948. The urban elites who had dominated politics had failed to free their countries from colonial rule, and in many cases the for-mer colonial powers still retained important privileges. Then came the shock of the 1948 war and the devastating defeat that culminated in the creation of Israel. The traditional *a'yan* thus lost much of their legitimacy, and a new era of (at least initially) popular dictatorships began.

The mix of urban and rural political and social culture brought a new ele-ment into politics after the 1950s, the domination of the countryside over the city. However, the passage of time has shown that the city and its elites might well have the last word. The new leaders still need the city to legitimize their rule and to control and influence their citizens. To some extent, they have "ruralized" the city, but that process is as old as migration and the interde-pendence of city and countryside. They have seized power in many parts of the Middle East, but in doing so have resorted to networks and personal poli-tics, just as the *a'yan* once did. The urban notables may be out of politics in some parts of the Middle East, but their ways of doing business continue; to that extent, the continuity between the past, the present, and the future seems likely to endure.

# 6

## The Demography of Cities
## and the Expansion of Urban Space

### BERNARD HOURCADE

🐾 IN THE CENTURY and a half between Napoleon's expedition to Egypt in 1798 and the end of World War II, the urban population of the Middle East, that is, the area between Morocco and Afghanistan, increased almost tenfold, from 2.8 million to 26 million inhabitants. This very considerable rate of quantitative growth was not peculiar to the Middle East; the whole world, including Europe in the full flush of the Industrial Revolution, experienced similar demographic upheavals during this period, which led to the emergence of a new society dominated by cities.

However, demographic change and the evolution of urban space in the Middle East does exhibit a number of distinct features, influenced by three special factors: the dominant role of the two great megalopolises, Istanbul and Cairo; the diversity of the heterogeneous cultural contexts and regional politics; and the existence of several kinds of cities, differentiated both by their antiquity and the variations in their dominant activity. Hence Isfahan, Casablanca, and Riyadh cannot easily be compared with one another, since each city has an entirely different demographic and urban history.

Istanbul was the fourth largest city in the world in 1800 and Cairo the eighth; both cities ranked ahead of Paris or Peking, but the urban population of the Middle East was less than 10 percent of the total population of the area. In contrast, the level of urbanization in the Middle East had reached 23.8 percent by 1950, relatively close to the world average, and had actually overtaken it by 1970, reaching 39 percent in comparison with the world average of 36 percent.[1] Until the 1930s, most Middle Eastern cities had experienced steady growth in proportion to that of the total population in the states in which they were located, except for those that were directly affected by government activity as capitals (Tehran, Ankara, Damascus, Algiers, Rabat) or those directly linked with the economic activities of the more industrialized states, such as Casablanca, or oil towns such as Ahwaz, Abadan, and Kuwait. Thus, the urban history of the Middle East takes its place within a spectrum comparable to that of other regions of the world, occupying an intermediate position between the industrialized states (Europe, 52.7 percent urban in 1950; North America, 55.8 percent) and the great rural continents (China, 11.1 percent; West Africa, 9.7 percent) although less urbanized than Central Asia or Latin America, (respectively, 30.1 percent and 32.2 percent in 1950).

The point of departure of this particular urban history is the "oriental city," whose model corresponds globally to the traditional city at the beginning of the nineteenth century, with its architecture, spatial organization, and "oriental" social organization.[2] These analytical categories provide an extremely useful frame of reference, giving an overview of the different kinds of demographic and urban transformations taking place in cities in the nineteenth and twentieth centuries. The Ottoman Empire also forms a frame of reference for the urban history of the states involved in its dissolution, whereas other states such as Iran or Morocco remained on the periphery. Finally, the cities were affected to a greater or lesser extent by the consequences of the Industrial Revolution, which were causing major disruptions in Western Europe, together with the opening of the Suez Canal, direct colonization, the discovery of oil, and new cultural influences on the elites. The great cities became the bridgeheads for European industrial society and were transformed accordingly.

By the end of the 1930s, cities had become more heterogeneous. The model of the "oriental city" had been complemented by that of the "dual city,"

1. In 1950, 28.4 percent of the population of the Maghrib, 24.7 percent of the population of the rest of the Arab world, and 19.1 percent of the population of Afghanistan, Iran, and Turkey lived in cities.

2. On this controversial topic, to which we will return later, see Abu-Lughod 1987, E. Goldberg 1991, and Raymond 1994b.

created by the juxtaposition of a new city, inhabited by Europeans or new local elites, with the ancient city, peopled almost entirely by Muslims. This model of the dual city is an approach that has some utility for the analysis of urban space, but it has the disadvantage of being subject to numerous exceptions and deficiencies and cannot be reduced to a simple binary opposition between tradition and modernity.

### The Demographic Emergence of "Dual Cities": Sources and Methodology

Studies of the political, and to some extent the social, history of cities abound, but precise demographic data are rare and approximate as well as often being inconsistent between one source and another. The first "modern" censuses, generally in the Ottoman Empire, date from the second half of the nineteenth century (Karpat 1978, 1985; McCarthy 1981), and reliable statistics for all the cities of the region do not generally antedate the 1930s.[3] Hence this study is based on a selection of fifty cities, comprising, it goes without saying, the most populous but also the most important cities in each of the subregions, so that towns in the less urbanized areas can be integrated into the analysis.

The notion of the "great city," which has been used to construct the sample of fifty cities, is of course relative, since the number of inhabitants must be related to that of the total population of the country at any given date. Thus, if the population of the Middle East multiplied four times between 1800 and 1950 (from about 27 million to about 111 million) a town of 100,000 in 1950 is equivalent to one of 25,000 in 1800. In addition, in certain areas, such as the Maghrib or Iran, towns with small populations (when measured against Cairo or Istanbul) have been kept in the sample, because they play an important political or commercial role, such as Marrakesh, Tangier, Shiraz, and Yazd. In the same way, "mushroom cities," often created in the course of the first half

---

3. Although earlier Ottoman censuses had been fairly reliable; for Anatolia between 1450 and 1600, see Cook 1972. Most of these figures come from monographs on various cities and states in the region. See the references in more general works: Mantran 1989; Ganiage 1994; Avery et al. 1991; Raymond 1984, 1985; de Planhol 1993. For more specific studies of particular areas or cities in the nineteenth and early twentieth centuries, see Gerber 1979 (Syria and Palestine); McCarthy 1983 (Syria and Iraq); Panzac 1987 (Egypt); McCarthy 1989 (Palestine); Schmelz 1994 (Jerusalem); and Riis 1999 (Aleppo).

of the twentieth century, either as capitals (Riyadh, Kuwait, Tel Aviv), as commercial capitals (Casablanca), or for a specific economic purpose (Port Said for the Suez Canal, Ahwaz for oil) have developed into heavily populated centers and constitute a new and original urban type that needs to be integrated into the sample.

In concentrating only on cities with significant populations and regional functions in the nineteenth century and those that became of prime importance at the beginning of the twentieth, the little towns and urban centers of between 3,000 and 10,000 inhabitants have been neglected in spite of the fact that they occupied a position of prime importance in the organization of space and in urban culture, and that they were also closely linked to the rural milieu. In Iran this was true of numerous little towns on the edge of the central desert, with a bazaar, a great mosque often constructed under the Seljuks, towns which might be famous for a special type of carpet. Kashan, Ardestan, Na'in, Nishapur, and Qum played a vital local role as regional centers, but during the period that interests us these towns did not experience the major changes that affected the largest cities. This is also true of the small towns of Anatolia or Morocco that nevertheless have long histories and considerable reputations.

Because many of the figures in the sources are unreliable and often do not relate to the same years, the statistics have been simplified and the populations have been estimated at a number of key moments, the beginning, middle, and end of the nineteenth century, and 1930, 1950, and 1970, in order to arrive at manageable generalizations (Table 5).

## The Influence of the Great Urban Centers

In the eighteenth century the eight largest cities in the Arab world accounted for 5.6 percent of the total population, compared to 4.4 percent of the population of France for the eight largest French cities (Raymond 1985, 66), a fact that tends to confirm the overwhelming and long-standing importance of the urban phenomenon in the Middle East and its decline relative to Europe, which has experienced major urban and industrial revolutions over the past two centuries.

Over the past one and a half centuries the list of the largest cities has undergone a series of changes, and their demographic evolution, though conforming

TABLE 5

**Demographic Growth of Middle Eastern Cities, 1800–1970**

|  | 1800 | 1850 | 1900 | 1930 | 1950 | 1970 |
|---|---|---|---|---|---|---|
| Total urban population | | | | | | |
| in 100,000s | 2,865 | 3,696 | 7,799 | 12,556 | 26,494 | 72,203 |
| (Growth percent per year) | | 0.5 | 1.5 | 1.6 | 3.8 | 5.1 |
| Sample of 50 cities | 1,993 | 2,535 | 4,871 | 7,300 | 14,624 | 37,729 |
| (Growth percent per year) | | 0.5 | 1.3 | 1.4 | 3.5 | 4.9 |
| Other cities | 887 | 1,181 | 2,938 | 5,294 | 11,911 | 34,252 |
| (Growth percent per year) | | 0.6 | 1.8 | 2 | 4.1 | 5.4 |
| Percentage of the sample of | | | | | | |
| total urban population | 69 | 68 | 62 | 58 | 55 | 53 |

*Note:* Population and annual rate of growth.

to a global matrix, has been strongly affected by the history of each city and of each regional subsystem. Only three cities (Cairo, Istanbul, and Damascus) have featured consistently in the list of the ten largest cities in the region between 1800 and 1970. Many of the traditional great cities, with opulent histories, have undergone relative decline in the face of the cities that came into being as a result of political changes in the new states, such as Algiers, Casablanca, Tel Aviv, and even Baghdad, which was still among the largest cities at the very beginning of the nineteenth century but went into decline during the last decades of the Ottoman Empire, only to be reborn as the capital of Iraq (Table 6).

The population geography of the region has been profoundly affected by the sheer weight of the population of the largest cities, particularly Istanbul and Cairo, which accounted for 31 percent of the population of the fifty cities in the sample in 1800 and 22 percent of the total urban population. Moreover, these two international metropolises have kept their dominant position. In 1900, Istanbul was the fifteenth largest urban agglomeration in the world and Cairo the thirty-second. In 1990, Cairo took sixteenth place and Istanbul twenty-sixth, just behind Tehran (Moriconi-Ebrard 1993a, 1993b, 328ff). Although Cairo and Istanbul have remained dominant, it is also the case that the great cities of the Middle East underwent a relative decline over this period, at least

TABLE 6

**The Ten Largest Cities in the Middle East, 1800–1970**

| 1800 | 1850 | 1900 | 1930 | 1950 | 1970 |
|---|---|---|---|---|---|
| Istanbul | Istanbul | Istanbul | Cairo | Cairo | Cairo |
| Cairo | Cairo | Cairo | Istanbul | Tehran | Tehran |
| Aleppo | Tabriz | Alexandria | Alexandria | Istanbul | Istanbul |
| Damascus | Izmir | Izmir | Tehran | Alexandria | Alexandria |
| Baghdad | Alexandria | Tabriz | Algiers | Casablanca | Baghdad |
| Tabriz | Aleppo | Tehran | Tabriz | Tel Aviv | Casablanca |
| Izmir | Tehran | Tunis | Baghdad | Damascus | Algiers |
| Fez | Damascus | Damascus | Tunis | Tunis | Ankara |
| Tunis | Tunis | Algiers | Damascus | Algiers | Tel Aviv |
| Mosul | Fez | Beirut | Oran | Baghdad | Damascus |

in comparison with other cities of the world. In 1950, the four cities with more than a million inhabitants (Cairo, Tehran, Istanbul, and Alexandria) accounted for 22 percent of the urban population of the Middle East, compared to 31 percent for the world as a whole. The relative fall in the combined population of the fifty major cities in the sample, from 69 percent to 53 percent of the total urban population between 1800 and 1970, or that of the ten largest towns in the region, confirms this general tendency and also points to the more rapid growth of small and medium-sized cities, especially after 1900. However, this generalization still gives overwhelming importance to the very largest cities. In certain cases their hegemony is underscored, especially since the 1950s, as in Syria, where the combined population of Damascus and Aleppo has increased from 23 percent of the population in 1870 to 48 percent in 1981 (Table 7).

The ranking and the rhythm of evolution of the five largest cities of the Middle East at the beginning of the twentieth century (Istanbul, Cairo, Alexandria, Izmir, and Tehran[4]) (see Table 8) serves not only to confirm their

4. In fact Tabriz had a higher population than Tehran but was rapidly overtaken by the capital in the first years of the century.

TABLE 7

The Dominant Position of the Major Cities

| Rank | 1800 | 1850 | 1900 | 1930 | 1950 | 1970 |
|---|---|---|---|---|---|---|
| Two largest cities | 22 | 19 | 19 | 15 | 14 | 13 |
| 1 to 5 | 32 | 28 | 30 | 25 | 24 | 23 |
| 6 to 10 | 11 | 11 | 10 | 9 | 10 | 9 |
| Top ten largest cities | 43 | 33 | 32 | 29 | 29 | 27 |

*Note:* Cumulated population of cities by size at various dates in percentage of the total population of the sample of fifty cities.

relative status as regression cities but also the permanence of their lead position in spite of the vagaries of history. The great cities of Anatolia kept their rank order in spite of the stagnation in their population in the wake of the exodus of the Greeks after World War I, but other cities would emerge.

Table 9 confirms that the very large cities have undergone a markedly less dynamic demographic growth during our study period than many of the second rank cities that came to encompass very large populations within a few decades, whether as new capitals, oil cities, or cities of colonization. The enormous size of Cairo and Istanbul during the last century, followed by Tehran or Baghdad, should not conceal the size and diversity of urban realities in the Middle East, punctuated by the stagnation of some old "oriental" cities and the creation or rebirth of a number of others, following the example of Alexandria.

TABLE 8

The Global Demographic Growth of Cairo, Istanbul, Tehran, Alexandria, and Izmir, 1800–1970

| | 1800 | 1850 | 1900 | 1930 | 1950 | 1970 |
|---|---|---|---|---|---|---|
| Cumulative population (1,000s) | 738 | 996 | 2,315 | 2,992 | 6,056 | 15,417 |
| Percentage of total urban population | 26 | 27 | 30 | 24 | 23 | 21 |
| Rate of growth (% per annum) | | 0.6 | 1.7 | 0.9 | 3.6 | 4.8 |

TABLE 9

Differential Demographic Growth According to City Size

| Rank | 1800–1900 | 1900–1950 | 1800–1950 |
|------|-----------|-----------|-----------|
| 1 to 5 | 1 | 0.7 | 0.9 |
| 6 to 10 | 0.9 | 2.7 | 1.5 |
| 11 to 20 | 1 | 2.8 | 1.6 |
| 21 to 50 | 0.9 | 2.4 | 1.4 |
| TOTAL SAMPLE | 0.9 | 2.2 | 1.3 |

*Note:* Annual demographic growth in percentage, size of cities sorted in the earlier year.

## Urban Stagnation at the Beginning of the Nineteenth Century

Between the end of the eighteenth century and the late 1940s, the demographic evolution of cities went through three stages: a period of very slow growth, less than 1 percent per year, for most of the nineteenth century, followed by a moderate increase, of the order of 1.5 percent, between 1870 and 1930, and finally a spurt of very rapid growth that continued to accelerate through the 1970s.

For much of the nineteenth century the urban population increased only slowly, at much the same rate as the population as a whole, which remained overwhelmingly rural. In spite of the antiquity of the urban history of the region, and the pride of place of both Istanbul and Cairo, the urban system in the nineteenth century was thoroughly integrated into the rural world. In Iran, Hans Bobek (1974) and Eckart Ehlers (1992) have described the system of "rent capitalism" (*Rent Kapitalismus*) that enabled small towns and rural markets to live off "rents" from agriculture and carpet weaving without reinvesting in these activities. This kind of relationship, which can be found in most cities well integrated into their hinterlands, such as Aleppo, Marrakesh, or Fez, did not generally encourage migration to the cities, since the economic system was stable, dominated by the rural economy, property rents, and a largely rural population.

The rhythms of growth of the urban population were determined primarily by the general evolution of the population as a whole, which was itself still substantially rural. Throughout the nineteenth century the demography of the

Middle East exhibited high fertility rates and high mortality rates, resulting in very slow growth. Large-scale epidemics of plague and cholera, together with periodic famines, were part of the social history of the region until the end of the century: to cite a few examples, there was a cholera epidemic in Cairo in 1831, a plague in the city in 1835 resulting in 500,000 deaths, a plague in Aleppo in 1837 from which the city took three years to recover (Raymond 1993, 298; Gaube and Wirth 1984, 248, 252), famines in the Maghrib in 1866 and 1868, and cholera in Tehran in 1870–71. With improvements in sanitary conditions and medical treatment and with better communications, mortality rates declined rapidly, ushering in a period of "demographic transition" during the 1930s. The 1950s marked the beginning of a new phase often described as the "demographic explosion," which was accompanied by an accelerated tendency on the part of rural people to migrate toward the cities (Table 10).

During the years of stagnation in the nineteenth century, the urban geography of the Middle East was marked by the uncontested domination of Istanbul and Cairo. One townsman out of five lived in these two great metropolises, which had 360,000 and 263,000 inhabitants respectively. Aleppo, the third largest city, had 120,000 inhabitants and Damascus, 90,000. This rank order changed little throughout the century as each of these cities continued to function as a regional capital and developed accordingly, sometimes affected by the irruption of European influence, but primarily by the domination of their rural hinterlands. In the first half of the century, economic regression struck the whole region and affected prestigious cities such as Mosul, and particularly Damascus, whose populations decreased, as well as cities directly dependent on declining activities, such as Algiers, which was affected by the end of piracy in the Mediterranean and the departure of the Turkish garrisons, and not yet benefiting—unlike Oran—from the effects of French colonization (after 1830).

In contrast, other cities, such as Tabriz, were developing. The Turkish-speaking capital of Persian Azerbaijan was in close contact with Istanbul and with the Tsarist empire, which was already a presence in the Caucasus. Numerous Tabrizi merchants had branch houses in Istanbul, which also served as a refuge for the Persian political opposition. This Persian community in Istanbul was influential in making Tabriz the port of entry for modernization into Iran and thus the real international and intellectual capital of the country, whereas

TABLE 10

**Demographic Growth Between 1800 and 1970 of the Ten Largest Cities in 1900**

| City | 1800 | 1850 | 1900 | 1930 | 1950 | 1970 |
|---|---|---|---|---|---|---|
| Istanbul | 360 | 391 | 950 | 691 | 1035 | 2835 |
|  |  | 0.8 | 1.8 | -1.1 | 2 | 5.2 |
| Cairo | 363 | 305 | 570 | 1139 | 2426 | 5950 |
|  |  | 0.3 | 1.3 | 2.3 | 3.9 | 4.6 |
| Alexandria | 10 | 105 | 370 | 608 | 1025 | 2130 |
|  |  | 4.8 | 2.6 | 1.7 | 2.6 | 3.7 |
| Izmir | 60 | 110 | 225 | 154 | 270 | 758 |
|  |  | 1 | 1.4 | -1.3 | 2.8 | 5.3 |
| Tabriz | 80 | 110 | 200 | 250 | 289 | 450 |
|  |  | 0.6 | 1.2 | 0.7 | 0.7 | 2.2 |
| Tehran | 45 | 85 | 200 | 400 | 1300 | 3744 |
|  |  | 1.3 | 1.7 | 2.3 | 6.1 | 5.4 |
| Tunis | 60 | 80 | 177 | 234 | 489 | 761 |
|  |  | 0.6 | 1.6 | 0.9 | 3.8 | 2.2 |
| Damascus | 90 | 80 | 154 | 216 | 563 | 970 |
|  |  | -0.2 | 1.3 | 1.1 | 4.9 | 2.8 |
| Algiers | 40 | 30 | 140 | 336 | 480 | 1393 |
|  |  | -0.6 | 3.1 | 3 | 1.8 | 5.5 |
| Beirut | 6 | 40 | 120 | 150 | 350 | 939 |
|  |  | 3.9 | 2.2 | 0.7 | 4.3 | 5.1 |

*Note:* Totals in thousands and annual rate of growth.

Tehran, the official capital since 1786, remained an unimpressive city where the rulers resided only in winter and which had no public buildings other than the Ark, or "Kremlin," surrounding the Gulistan palace (Adle and Hourcade 1992; Zarcone 1993).

In Anatolia, the rapid development of Izmir was due to its coastal location, which facilitated its function as an interface with European countries, partly because of its large Armenian, Greek, and Jewish population, but also because of the presence of a large number of Europeans, who were able to buy houses and land in the city under the terms of the Land Law of 1867. In the course of the nineteenth century, which was marked by a series of crises within the Ottoman Empire and by the stagnation of Qajar Iran, as well as by the reforms of Muhammad 'Ali in Egypt, Alexandria developed into a new metropolis of international standing. The insignificant "outer harbor" of Cairo became a city of 105,000 inhabitants in 1848, of whom 5,000 were foreigners, and 232,000 inhabitants in 1882, of whom 49,000 were foreigners. Similarly Beirut, a small town of 6,000 inhabitants in 1800, had grown to 140,000 by the beginning of the twentieth century, benefiting from its position on the coast and its relative distance from both Cairo and Istanbul.

## The Effects of Colonization and Modernization

After this long period of stagnation, the second phase of the demographic evo-lution of Middle Eastern cities was marked by an acceleration of the rate of growth (about 1.5 percent per annum) and by the effects of modernization policies between 1870 and 1930. The first large-scale efforts at urbanization took place under the aegis either of colonization (Algiers, Casablanca) or of the modernizing royal house of Egypt, where the upheaval and turmoil ini-tiated by Muhammad 'Ali (1805–48) came to some completion under Khe-dive Isma'il (1863–79), during whose reign the Suez Canal was inaugurated in 1869. The population of Cairo rose from 315,000 in 1863 to 374,000 in 1882, reaching 1.3 million in 1937. Cairo accounted for 60 percent of the urban pop-ulation of Egypt in 1907 (21 percent of the total); in 1927, half the population of Cairo had not been born in the city.

The Universal Exhibition of 1867 and the transformation of Paris car-ried out by Baron Haussmann that had so impressed Khedive Isma'il had also impressed Nasreddin Shah, who began to tear down the old Safavid city walls of Tehran after his return from Europe and sketched out the rudiments of an urban policy. The Persian capital nevertheless remained a somewhat inferior city; electricity was not introduced until 1906, and the first motor vehicles (apart from those belonging to the Shah) did not arrive until 1912. However, the Constitutional Revolution of 1906 and the discovery of oil in 1907 facili-tated the strengthening of central authority and the development of the capital, while other cities, such as Isfahan, Shiraz, and Yazd remained on the periphery of the political and economic storms that were engulfing the countries of the Mediterranean basin at the time. During these years Damascus and Aleppo also remained on the margins and only underwent modest development, while Baghdad, also under foreign domination, began to recover from a long period of decline and counted some 250,000 inhabitants in 1930.

In Turkey, the cities of the interior, with the exception of Eskişehir, were also bypassed by industrialization and modernization. In 1900, a town as bustling and prestigious as Bursa could count only seventy-five silk-weaving establishments. In contrast, Istanbul and Izmir attained their apogee. At the end of the nineteenth century Istanbul began to experience some early warnings of the decline that would set in during the 1920s. The population of both cities grew very quickly (2.6 percent per annum for Izmir, 1.8 percent for Istanbul). In 1886, Istanbul had 873,000 inhabitants and remained substantially cosmopolitan, since the Muslim population only formed 44 percent of the whole; 17.7 percent were Greeks, 17.1 percent Armenians, 5.1 percent Jews and 15.3 percent foreigners, many of whom were non-Ottoman Muslims (Mantran 1996, 299). In the first years of the twentieth century, Istanbul's population was more than a million, but this rapid increase was due mostly to an influx of *muhajirs*, refugees from the Balkans, the Caucasus, Crete, or the Crimea.

Under the direct influence of colonization or the various imperial conquests, a second type of city developed during the years between 1870 and 1930, particularly in the Maghrib. Unlike the cities of Egypt and Anatolia, which had historic connections with European countries, the cities of North Africa had remained largely cut off from foreign influence. The only nonindigenous inhabitants in Algeria were the soldiers of the Turkish garrisons; there were only 130 foreigners living in Morocco in 1830. Urban development was sudden and rapid, directly linked to the influx of colons whose presence was supported by military operations, rather than the result of internal migration. This was especially true of Tunis and the coastal cities of Algeria. Algiers itself had barely 30,000 inhabitants at the time of the French conquest, but had 136,000 in the census of 1901 (336,000 in 1930), while Oran had a population of 89,000 (172,000 in 1930). Morocco underwent a similar experience half a century later, because Lyautey's urban policy was not fully executed until after World War I. In spite of the long history of urbanization in Sharifian Morocco,

Casablanca, which barely existed at the end of the nineteenth century, grew to 163,000 inhabitants in 1931 (and almost 700,000 in the 1950s), whereas Marrakesh, which remained the largest city in Morocco for several years (195,000), developed slowly because of its location in the interior, although more rapidly than Fez. The old imperial capital, which had a population of some 90,000 at the beginning of the century, fell victim to its opposition to colonization and only had 112,000 inhabitants in the census of 1931.

The discovery of oil and the creation of ports or industrial cities linked directly to foreign enterprises brought a number of cities of a novel kind into being, often built up from nothing. This was the case of Port Said, which housed the builders of the Suez Canal, of Abadan, which did not exist when the first cargo of Iranian oil was loaded on to a merchant ship in 1912, and of Ahwaz, which became the headquarters of the Anglo-Persian Oil Company.

World War I and the fall of the Ottoman Empire marked the end of this period of urban history, characterized partly by the establishment of new urban structures, but also by the dominant influence of the heritage of the past and of traditional society. Urban renewal had remained largely confined to the great cities, particularly the coastal cities in direct contact with the European world, but it also owed much to the initiatives of individuals or local elites whose role was innovative although often limited to an empirical adaptation of the old cities to new techniques and ways of life. At the end of World War II, the nation-states of the Middle East were still heavily influenced by the rural world that dominated the population, economy, culture, and society. The modernization of the cities by the elites and the creation of "European" quarters did not encourage the migration of peasants toward the cities, but a new dynamic had begun to emerge.

## The Beginnings of the Urban Revolution

The period after World Wars I and II was marked particularly by extremely rapid urban growth stemming from four principal causes: the acceleration of world demographic growth due to the decline in mortality rates, rural to urban migration, processes of state formation, and most significantly, the more thoroughgoing entry of the Middle East into the international economy, both industrial and urban. This new dynamic was at its height between 1945 and the 1980s. In this context, the decline of Istanbul and the cities of the Anatolian littoral seemed to symbolize a fundamental break with the old urban system.

Some 300,000 Greeks, Armenians, Jews, and foreigners left Istanbul within a few years, with the result that in 1923 the former Ottoman metropolis had no more than 720,000 inhabitants, almost all Turks. The town lost the cosmopolitan, multiconfessional, and international character that had been a vital part of its identity over the centuries, and it also lost its political function to Ankara, the new capital, which had only 74,000 inhabitants in 1930. It would take several decades for the great metropolitan city on the Bosphorus to construct a new identity and once more discover a new rhythm of rapid development. Izmir, and to a lesser extent Alexandria, underwent a similar trajectory. During these years of decline, and in spite of the continuing prestige of the former Constantinople, Cairo became the new leading city of the region, with a population of 1.2 million in 1930 and 2.5 million in 1950, more than twice that of Istanbul.

In the first half of this century the capitals of the new states developed extremely rapidly. Many of them had previously been small towns without much of a past but now benefited from the activist policies and the capital investments of the new governments. Most of these cities had been built on virgin sites, or at least on sites largely devoid of major symbolic significance. In 1930 all these soulless new cities had populations of fewer than 30,000 inhabitants, except Ankara, which had a previous existence as a small industrial town, with 74,000. After World War II a new stage in the demographic evolution of these cities began, in which they experienced extremely rapid growth, but they remained fairly modest capital cities: Ankara had 290,000 inhabitants; Amman, barely 100,000; Riyadh, 83,000; Rabat, 189,000; Kuwait, 115,000; and Beirut, 350,000.

During the interwar period the older capitals, often casualties of industrialization but benefiting from a prestigious architectural, social, and cultural heritage, discovered a new dynamic, sometimes at the expense of the other great cities of the past, which had not had the chance of becoming national capitals. This was true of Baghdad with regard to Mosul and of Tunis, Algiers, and especially Damascus, which inexorably overtook Aleppo to reach a population of 563,000 in 1950. Tel Aviv was a special case because the capital of the new state of Israel, which had only 30,000 inhabitants in 1930, mushroomed to

567,000 in 1950 because of the massive influx of immigrants, while Jerusalem remained a medium-sized city of only 123,000. A new stage of demographic evolution began in the beginning of the 1950s, when all cities, great and small, were exposed to modernity and took part in the "urban revolution" as part of the new processes of state formation.

### Regional Variations in Demographic Growth

In spite of important differences in the demographic evolution of each of these cities, as a function of their antiquity, size, or economic purpose, there is little variation between the evolution of the various regions, which tends to confirm the general homogeneity of the "cultural zone" extending between Morocco and Iran (Table 11). This homogeneity was particularly evident in the nineteenth century, when growth rates were low everywhere. At that time the "Islamic city" was the common model for most cities, none of which had yet been profoundly affected by modernization and close relations with Europe. In the second part of the century, the cities of Anatolia and Egypt grew more rapidly (1.6 percent per annum) than those of the Fertile Crescent (Damascus, Aleppo, Baghdad, Jerusalem, Beirut, 1.1 percent per annum) or of the Arabian peninsula (San'a', Medina, Mecca), which remained large towns, of the Maghrib (1.3 percent), still not greatly affected by colonization and Iran (1 percent), still on the periphery of the industrial world.

TABLE 11

**Comparative Regional Evolution of Middle Eastern Cities, 1800–1970 (annual growth rate)**

|  | 1850 | 1900 | 1930 | 1950 | 1970 |
|---|---|---|---|---|---|
| Middle East | 0.05 | 1.3 | 1.3 | 3.5 | 4.9 |
| Anatolia | 0.4 | 1.6 | -0.8 | 2.9 | 5.7 |
| Egypt | 0.8 | 1.7 | 2.1 | 3.5 | 4.4 |
| Fertile Crescent | -0.1 | 1.1 | 1.8 | 4.9 | (3.8) 4.8 |
| Arabian Peninsula | 0.9 | 1.3 | 1.5 | 3 | 9 |
| Maghrib | 0.5 | 1.3 | 2.3 | 3.2 | 4.1 |
| Iran | 0.8 | 1 | 1.2 | 3.4 | 4.6 |

At the beginning of the twentieth century, these minor variations became more marked, a consequence of two trends with contrary effects. These were, on one hand, the end of the Ottoman Empire, which brought about a decline in the urban population of Anatolia, and on the other, the heyday of French colonization in the Maghrib, which resulted in an average annual increase of 2.3 percent in the population of North African cities between 1900 and 1930. In the same period the cities of Egypt and the Fertile Crescent benefited from the crisis in Anatolia, but Iran and the Arabian peninsula were still not greatly affected by urbanization, their cities developing at the same pace as that of the largely rural population as a whole.

Between the 1920s and the late 1940s Middle Eastern cities again grew as a unified whole, much as they had done in the first half of the nineteenth century, but in a very different context. First, the urban population throughout the area grew faster (although still less than 3 percent per annum) than the population of the country in general, and second, the modernization of the political systems and the international integration of the local economies imposed a common development model, dominated by the cities. Here the only exception was the Fertile Crescent, with an average rate of growth of 4.9 percent per annum between 1930 and 1950, but this was almost entirely due to the atypical case of Tel Aviv (15.8 percent), without which the annual rate would have been 3.8 percent.

The beginning of the second half of the twentieth century saw the eventual acceleration of the urban growth of Iran and especially of the Arabian Peninsula (9 percent between 1959 and 1970), whose cities had shown some signs of development before World War II but now reached unparalleled growth rates with the more thoroughgoing exploitation of the region's oil. Even the cities of Egypt and Anatolia rediscovered a dynamism that to some extent recalled their glorious days at the beginning of the nineteenth century. But later this urban development became more homogeneous, taking in the rural world and being characterized by the development of a large number of small and medium-sized cities but also by the emergence of great metropolises with several million inhabitants throughout the Middle East and North Africa— including Tehran, Baghdad, Ankara, Riyadh, Casablanca, and Algiers.

Thus, between 1800 and 1950 three kinds of demographic growth can be found in the various regions:

• Iran and the Arabian Peninsula, which share some common characteristics in spite of their very different cultural and demographic contexts, since
their cities only developed relatively late as a consequence of the oil economy.

• The Maghrib and the Fertile Crescent, which were on the margins of
Europe and the Istanbul/Cairo tandem. Their marginalized cities stagnated
until the beginning of the twentieth century when they experienced a spectacular renewal as a result either of colonization or of the creation of the various new states.

• Egypt and Turkey, whose urban population had been growing since the
end of the nineteenth century because of the hegemonic role of their two great
metropolises that had long had continuous relations with industrial Europe.
The decline of Istanbul during the first half of the twentieth century lasted
only three decades, and the former capital soon began to compete again on the
same level as Cairo.

## The Transformations of Urban Space: The Oriental City and the Role of Pious Endowments in Urbanization

At the beginning of the nineteenth century almost all of the cities of the
Middle East, with the exception of Istanbul, corresponded in their entirety
to the often described model of the "oriental city." The principal cities were
all surrounded by ancient walls (Cairo, Aleppo, Damascus, Marrakesh, and
Jerusalem)—even if they were sometimes almost in ruins, as in the case of
the walls surrounding Tehran, Isfahan, and Baghdad. In some cases even
the new quarters or the gardens were surrounded by walls, as in Fez Jadid or
San'a'. Closing the gates every evening, as took place in Jerusalem until 1880,
was carried out partly for security reasons but also to underline the authority
of the political powers and to stress the identity of the city in contrast to the
rural world beyond it.

In these "traditional" cities, the royal palace, or the governor's palace, and
the great mosque were often the only significant buildings, together with the
suq or bazaar whose entrance was often built in the grand style. Urban space was
usually divided according to various activities whether economic—the organization of artisans by specialty—political, or religious. Even the residential
quarters sometimes had areas given over to religious minorities, whether Jewish (*mellahs*) or Christian. These minorities were often quite widely dispersed

within the city, as in Istanbul, Aleppo, and Damascus, at least before clustering in one or two quarters became more or less the rule in the nineteenth century,[5] again sometimes spontaneously, but often by decree, as in Rabat, with the creation of a Jewish mellah on *habus* land. These Christian or Jewish quarters were often under the protection of the prince and thus situated near the palace walls, as in Cairo, Fez, Marrakesh, and Shiraz. No spatial extension was possible for these quarters within the medinas, and their population densities became excessive in the course of the nineteenth century, making living conditions very difficult. For their part, the Muslims were able to establish themselves in gardens *intra muros* and later outside the walls when the population began to increase significantly.[6]

The plan and organization of the network of streets in the medina was not very different from that of contemporary European cities: narrow winding streets, indifferent sanitation, and the obstacles created by the presence of numerous pack animals.[7] Only a few roads leading to the Palace were widened for reasons of security or prestige. The suqs and bazaars surrounded the great mosques in cities such as Damascus, Mashhad, Aleppo, and Cairo, and great urban undertakings resulting in wide avenues or great piazzas like those of Isfahan or Istanbul were quite exceptional.

Although urban life was not administered by a sole central authority, as was the case in Europe, it was by no means anarchic. The traditional cities were administered locally by a combination of different local powers and of the solidarity that existed in the quarters, the guilds of artisans and merchants (*hirfa*),

5. de Planhol 1997, 284. See also chapter 7 in this volume by Gudrun Krämer.

6. However, the population of the "new suburbs" of Aleppo (al-Jamaliya, al-Niyal, al-Hamidiya, al-Sulaymaniya, al-Saliba al-Saghir, and al-'Aziziya, which were constructed between 1868 and 1895) was 8 percent Muslim, 8 percent "other," 11 percent Jewish, and 73 percent Christian in 1900. See Gaube and Wirth 1984, 434.

7. One of the key tasks of the municipalities founded (often by European residents) in the wake of the Ottoman Law of Municipalities in 1877 (Lewis 1979, 399) was the organization of sewage systems and the means of providing clean drinking water; for Alexandria, see Reimer 1997, 118; for Jerusalem, Kark 1980; for Istanbul, Rosenthal 1980a. The Galata Municipality and the Commissione di Ornato (in Alexandria; see Reimer 1993) were both founded before 1877, but, for a number of reasons, their scope and effectiveness was limited. For a useful study of several late Ottoman municipalities, see Lafi 2005.

ethnic groups, and religious authorities.[8] Each guild had police, judicial, and fiscal powers; each quarter (*hara*) of the traditional cities had a strong individual identity and was "run" by a respected shaykh who acted as mediator with the authorities. These various communities (*ta'ifa*) long remained capable of managing most of the medinas, even the largest ones. Thus, in Cairo there were 100 quarters and 250 guilds, with 350 shaykhs both elected and recognized by the state authorities (Raymond 1994b). They were used particularly by Bonaparte to calm down the disturbances that broke out all over the city. The *shaykh al-balad* in Algiers and the night-watchman of the suq in San'a' had sole charge of these places; in San'a' this official was called the "shaykh of the night" (Mermier 1996).

Waqf or *habus* also played a particular role in the organization and administration of cities. At the heart of urban space, *waqf* properties, with their inviolable character, guaranteed the occupants of buildings with this status a form of security and permanence that partly served to protect them from the dramas of history. Thus fountains, public baths, schools, libraries, shops, mosques, caravanserais, and even dwelling houses that had been made *waqf* were assured of being maintained and kept in order, in so far, at least, as the foundation remained in existence and the *mutawalli* performed his duties honestly. It also enabled the rent from rural *waqf* lands to be diverted to various urban functions. Hence *awqaf* were a significant component of the "rent capitalism" that was a feature of the economy of the whole of the region (Ehlers 1992).

The institution of *waqf* was also used by poor or minority populations to protect themselves from hardship. In Tunis, where the growing influx of Europeans after 1815 gave rise to a wave of speculation in urban property, the poorer homeowners founded *habus* to protect themselves from the speculators. In 1840, 14 percent of property transactions were of *habus* properties, compared with only 4.2 percent in 1800 (Hénia 1995). Similarly, the Christians made use of this Muslim institution to protect their churches, schools, and houses, especially in Aleppo, where there was in any case a considerable overlap between Muslim and Christian *waqf* (David 1997).

However, the capacity of *waqf* to "immobilize" urban real estate often functioned as an obstacle to the development of cities and to urbanization in

---

8. Raymond 1980. See also chapter 4 in this volume by Abdul-Karim Rafeq.

general, and as such affected most of the larger cities of the region after the mid–nineteenth century. It is certain that the institution of *waqf* was vital in keeping up the traditional inner cities (medinas) and had the effect of making urban developers prefer to construct new quarters outside the old walls or to build new cities, where the juridical, political, and cultural problems associated with *waqf* were less acute. This was especially true of areas exposed to European colonization, such as Morocco.

In spite of its efficaciousness within the confines of the traditional oriental city, the traditional methods of managing urban space had difficulty in adapting to rapid urban growth. For example, by obstructing certain property transactions, the *waqf* status of many buildings often hindered the renovation of the medinas (David and Hreitani 1984). In Iran the town of Mashhad was an exception, because most of the surface area of the city—some 58 percent of its 7,000 hectares in 1974—belonged to the Astan-i Quds Razavi, the *waqf* that administered the shrine of the Imam Reza. The administrators of this *waqf*, probably the largest of its kind in the world, were able to develop an active and modernizing urban policy, which has been continued to this day (Hourcade 1989).

### Early Modernization

The second part of the nineteenth century was conspicuous for the beginning of several large-scale urbanization projects. The renovations carried out by enlightened monarchs, keen to modernize their capitals on European lines, gradually transformed the great cities. The first stage often took the form of the destruction of the ancient walls that enclosed the old cities, where the growth in population density was making living conditions increasingly uncomfortable.

In Tehran, the old Safavid walls, some nine kilometers in length, were destroyed on the orders of Nasreddin Shah in 1870–71 and replaced with a new perimeter wall with a circumference of 19.2 kilometers, along the lines of the one around Paris, with twelve richly decorated monumental gates. Within the city however, urban renewal was limited to the construction of a number of broad avenues to the north of the palace, although this did endow Tehran with the first elements of urbanization indispensable for a modern capital city.

In Cairo, the projects planned under Napoleon were quite limited and only actually carried out under Muhammad 'Ali. These included the removal of the *mastaba*, or stone seats, in front of the shops, the law on the width of streets, enacted in 1845, the opening of the "new street" (al-sikka al-jadida, later the Boulevard Muhammad 'Ali), the construction of the Great Mosque, and so forth. However, the khedive preferred to develop Alexandria, the new city, and the Egyptian capital was transformed under Isma'il. Within a few years, under the direction of 'Ali Mubarak, a Western-style city was laid out to the west of the old town, toward the Nile. The surface area of the city, which had barely increased in half a century, doubled between 1863 and 1882, when it covered 1,260 hectares.

In Istanbul, which had expanded extensively beyond the perimeters of its ancient walls, there was a comparable burst of development during the Tanzimat period (1839–78), which was remarkable both for its modern features and its original architecture. In 1836, Mustafa Reşid Pasha had set out the general principles of urban planning that would be developed in more detail in the first urban ordinance issued by Helmut von Moltke in 1848. This was only very partially applied to the outer quarters of the city, and not at all to the city center, whose reconstruction was less the result of planning than of a number of fires that destroyed several quarters and enabled them to be rebuilt according to modern styles and norms. In 1856, 650 houses were burnt down in Aksaray and 3,000 in Beyoğlu in 1870; there were more fires in 1910 and 1917. This endowed the "Frankish quarter" with the modern architecture that gave it international prestige. Since 1856 several streets had been lit with gas lamps; there was a tramway in Pera in 1869, and the Galatasaray lycée opened its doors in 1868.

However, in spite of these various attempts to modernize the urban space of Middle Eastern cities, most of them still retained their traditional characteristics at the end of the nineteenth century. Midhat Pasha, governor of Baghdad between 1869 and 1872, had the city walls razed to the ground, but the city continued to stagnate. In contrast, Jerusalem began to be modernized after the occupation of Palestine and Syria by Ibrahim Pasha in 1831, although the city walls remained intact. In fact modernization was generally fairly limited in all these cities, with no overall plan; most of them were like Fez, San'a', and Marrakesh, where the city walls remained intact and there was little in the way of urban development.

Population growth brought about intense crowding within the walls, and sometimes occasioned the construction of wretched popular quarters just outside the city walls, together with bourgeois or aristocratic quarters and secondary residences at some distance from the city centers. In Tehran, the extension of the city northward began most notably after 1860, when the little canal diverting the river Karaj was completed, making it possible to plant orchards and pleasure gardens near the dusty city. The same happened in Fez with the development of large houses in the new city (Fez Jadid), and in the western part of San'a' where the gardens were surrounded by walls.

## Dual Cities and New Cities

The great urban transformations took place after 1870, with the acceleration of colonization in Algeria, the construction of the Suez Canal, the conquest of Morocco, the British presence in Egypt and the Middle East in general in the early twentieth century, and the various grants of independence and autonomy after 1930. In the context of accelerated urban growth, these changes brought about the division of some cities into two parts, with the construction of a "European city" alongside the "native city" or medina. This model was particularly prevalent in the Maghrib; good examples are Algiers, Meknès, Marrakesh, and Rabat.

As well as the "extensions" that have just been mentioned, the construction of entirely new cities such as Casablanca, Ahwaz, and Ankara, on much the same lines as Alexandria, was carried out in the context of a full-fledged urban program, under the aegis of determined and ambitious politicians, often with the assistance of European engineers and architects. In 1937, Mustafa Kemal commissioned the French architect Henri Prost to redesign the historic center of Istanbul, although his plans were not to be implemented for a further twenty years.

In Cairo, between 1882 and "independence" in 1936, a second, colonial city was constructed between the old city (the citadel, Old Cairo, Khan al-Khalili) and the Nile. Lord Cromer, the British Agent and Consul-General between 1883 and 1907, played a leading role in putting the finishing touches to the projects begun under Isma'il. However, this modern city, so very different from the old city, was not entirely cut off from it. It was highly cosmopolitan (150,000 foreigners in 1927, compared to 69,000 in 1870), and frequented especially by the new Egyptian bourgeoisie. Things changed in the early twentieth century, with the construction by Baron Empain of the new city of

Heliopolis, to the north of Cairo, which began in 1906. The building of this garden city with hotels, clubs, and luxury houses proceeded very slowly over the first few years (there were fewer than 30,000 inhabitants in 1930), but it marked an important cultural and geographic departure.

Similarly, the modern residential quarters at Zamalek, on the left bank of the Nile toward Giza, were more clearly cut off from the city and virtually reserved for the British. The Egyptian capital thus became fragmented into a number of different cultural and urban entities, but this segmentation was a long way from the much more absolute segregation so distinctive of the colonial cities of the Maghrib. In fact, there was no medina in Cairo, as was also true of Istanbul and Alexandria; the old cities were not homogeneous, and perhaps more importantly, there was a significant local modern bourgeoisie. These cities were the first to integrate modernization, and as such developed an urban landscape less sharply contrasted or potentially conflicting than in countries where Europeanization was more recent or closely linked to a direct colonial presence.

Although they retained their old walls, Aleppo and even Damascus were not really "partitioned" because the modern quarters constructed during the mandate remained closely linked to the old city. In Aleppo, the first constructions outside the walls appeared around 1870; during the French mandate the urban architect René Danger proposed an overall plan whose main purpose was to respect the old city, while constructing two broad avenues to separate the administrative quarters from the area at the foot of the citadel, a project only completed after World War II. The very slow development of the city, even the construction of the railway station, did not result in the creation of a separate modern town. In Hama and Beirut, however, urban development was essentially bipolar, while in Jerusalem, whose population was declining at the beginning of the twentieth century, the new Jewish quarters built after 1860 outside the western walls of the city remained relatively little developed before 1933.

The cities of Iran altered very little before the 1930s; Western influence remained limited, and the British presence was largely confined to the oil-rich province of Khuzistan. It was not until the reign of Reza Shah Pahlavi, between 1933 and 1940, that Tehran began to be thoroughly redesigned, with the construction of wide avenues cut through the city walls, piercing to the heart of the traditional city. The erection of modern buildings for ministries and public services, and the first hotels, finally turned the city into a modern capital. The construction of wide straight boulevards in the style of Haussmann was planned for other cities, but was not implemented. Hence, the cities of Iran had no double-track development, and there was no antagonism between old and new parts of the city. The social segregation that now exists in Tehran between the old quarters around the bazaar and the Ark and the summer quarters of Shemiran toward the north only developed gradually after World War II.

In the Maghrib, on the other hand, French colonization created a very distinct urban form, of two adjacent cities, one containing the "European" city, built according to a plan, with broad streets to facilitate the circulation of motor vehicles and low housing density, and the other of an unmodernized medina, where very little had changed, still surrounded by its old city walls. Taken to its extreme, the logic of these garden cities, often influenced by the social and modernist ideas of the Saint-Simonians, resulted in the construction of completely new cities far away from any "native" city—as in Casablanca or Kenitra (Port Lyautey)—or some little distance away, as in Meknès, Marrakesh, and Rabat.

This was particularly true of Morocco, under the policy directed by Marshal Lyautey, who became resident-general in 1912. Initiated before World War I, this colonial urban policy aimed to maintain the architecture, urban structure, and "indigenous" culture and society in general, without much overt interference, while facilitating the rapid development of European-style cities that would reflect and respond to economic imperatives and encourage the immigration of colons (Wright 1991). This was why the cities of the interior, Marrakesh and especially Fez, were underdeveloped in comparison with the coastal cities where the colons lived in large numbers. It was the same in Algeria, where the coastal cities, linked by the railways, and the cities in the zones where colonial agriculture was practiced, were often inhabited by a majority of non-Muslims (see Table 12).

Between 1900 and 1930 the urban population of the Maghrib doubled, largely because of the development of the Europeanized cities, but also because these cities required workers and local laborers employed in construction and other new activities. This poor population could not live in the European city and took up residence in the medinas, where population densities quickly rose

## TABLE 12

### The Population of Cities in the Maghrib in 1930

| | 1930 | | 1901 | |
|---|---|---|---|---|
| | *Population (1,000s)* | *Muslims (%)* | *Population (1,000s)* | *Muslims (%)* |
| Algiers | 337 | 33.5 | 135 | 22.2 |
| Oran | 172 | 21.2 | 89 | 14.8 |
| Constantine | 105 | 51.2 | 49 | 48.6 |
| Bône | 69 | 44.6 | 39 | 48.6 |
| Phillippeville | 48 | 50.2 | 21 | 33.4 |
| Tlemcen | 46 | 73.6 | 35 | 69.5 |
| Sidi bel-Abbes | 46 | 33.5 | 26 | 24.7 |
| Blida | 39 | 70.1 | 29 | 66.1 |
| Tunis | 234 | 43.9 | | |
| Sfax | 40 | 71.9 | | |
| Sousse | 25 | 52.5 | | |
| Bizerta | 23 | 60.2 | | |
| Kairouan | 21 | 95.2 | | |
| Marrakesh | 195 | 84.5 | | |
| Casablanca | 163 | 52.5 | | |
| Fez | 112 | 80.7 | | |
| Tangier | 60 | 58.3 | | |
| Meknès | 57 | 64.5 | | |
| Rabat | 55 | 51.1 | | |
| Salé | 26 | 81.2 | | |

*Note:* Based on Ganiage 1994, 460. The indigenous non-Muslim population consisted largely of Jews, who outnumbered the Europeans in Marrakesh (22,000 as against 8,500) and formed 7 percent of the non-Muslim population of Algiers, 11 percent of Oran, and 15 percent of Tunis.

to unacceptable levels (500 inhabitants per hectare), and living conditions were made even worse because of the lack of modern facilities. The traditional methods of managing urban space were no longer able to function, and some of the notables began to leave the old city quarters, often abandoning their traditional residences. The 1930s were also marked by the beginnings of a crisis in the medinas, which became more obvious in the 1960s with the creation of bidonvilles, packed with those who could no longer live in the overpopulated and chaotic old city centers.

In the new industrial cities, which had no medinas, this dual urbanism was not so obvious. Half of the population of the industrial and port city of Casablanca was Moroccan in 1930. In other cases, such as the phosphate mining town of Khouribga, the local population was actually forbidden to take up residence in the city. In addition, miners were recruited by force from the rural areas and were settled in worker cities. The new petroleum cities that were constructed in the first half of the twentieth century were also subject to town planning; Abadan was the first city of this kind, built from nothing by the Anglo-Persian Oil Company next to the refinery and the port. A virtual British city was built by the company, with the red bricks for the concert hall actually imported from Britain for the purpose. The city and the architecture of the villas and public buildings were designed on the basis of the professional, social, and ethnic status of the various employees: accommodation for the families of those of high rank; accommodation for bachelors, British technicians; and accommodation for non-British technicians and workers, most of whom were Indians until the signing of the petroleum agreement in 1933. Social, cultural, and sporting facilities, the most modern in Iran, were also segregated, for the British and for the "others." The development of Ahwaz in the interior was more complex, since the city was not only the capital of the Iranian oil industry but the administrative center of the province of Khuzistan. It had large numbers of British residents but also a significant Iranian population, particularly of migrants from the Iranian plateau (Arak, Isfahan, Kashan). The homogeneity of the population, all concentrated around a single industrial activity, explains why the city as a whole, and the center in particular, was constructed in a colonial style, and always retained that character. Although the oil cities were probably the first in Iran to be electrified, the traditional cities of the area, such as Dizful and Shushtar, developed much more slowly and have kept much of their elaborate traditional architecture down to the present time.

From the 1930s onward, the creation of capitals for the new states in the region produced cities whose structures often resembled that of the industrial cities just described. Riyadh, located on a site that had been occupied intermittently by the Sa'ud family since the 1820s, became the starting point of the conquest of Najd in 1902 and later Ibn Sa'ud's de facto capital. The growth of the city took place at the behest of the ruling family and thus in a highly centralized fashion. It was still a small city of fewer than 100,000 inhabitants when it was officially declared the capital in 1953, but grew at an impressive rate with the construction of suburbs and clusters of new buildings as well as a city center with administrative and public service facilities. The plan of Riyadh was thus that of a modern, almost European city, since influential local bourgeoisies continued to live in the cities of Mecca, Medina, and Jidda, which had virtually no modern quarters before the 1950s. The "dual city" phenomenon did exist in the Arabian Peninsula, but on a scale comparable to that of most of the rest of the region, with the coexistence of long-established cities with new cities that owed their construction to oil or to the emergence of the new states after World War I. In the same way, Amman, Kuwait, Tel Aviv, and certainly Ankara were built and designed on modern functional lines, whereas the villages or little towns that had originally occupied the sites either disappeared completely or occupied an insignificant place in the spatial development of the new capitals, whose urban character had only the most distant connection with that of the "Islamic city."

The demographic development of the cities of the Middle East since the early nineteenth century is unique on the level both of demography and urbanization. On a global level, the growth of the population was roughly comparable with that of other regions outside Europe. The specificity of the great antiquity of an urban network of "oriental cities" and the preponderant role played by Istanbul and Cairo did not produce a particular kind of urban growth, since the development of cities at this time was largely a function of European influence or domination, followed by independence and the formation of new states. The mass of the rural population generally remained on the margins of the cities, and the massive waves of rural to urban migration did not appear until rather later in the "urban revolution." In contrast, the existence of the historic cities, the European presence in a colonial, imperial, or economic context, together with the actions of local political leaders or a modernizing bourgeoisie produced a unique form of urbanization, associating tradition and modernity, so typical of the Middle East, but differing from one region to another.

In a remarkable work of synthesis on the history of the urban morphology of the Middle East, Eckart Ehlers shows how the "Islamic city," so characteristic of the region, became transformed after 1900 in different ways according to geographical region (Ehlers 1992). He distinguishes five different types for the Islamic world as a whole:

• In North Africa, what was left of the medina became separate from the new European city in the 1900s, and this situation continued almost unchanged until the 1950s, apart from the extension of the modern city toward the Muslim city and the appearance of the first bidonvilles.

• In the Turco-Iranian world the old cities were modernized in the 1930s (breaching of the city walls, the construction of wide avenues) and hardly changed until recent times with the planned development of a new city around the ancient center.

• In the Arabian Peninsula, apart from San'a' and the towns of the Hijaz, there were no "Islamic cities," with the result that the planned modern city appeared "immediately" in the 1950s.

• In Central Asia the ancient cities were left in place but linked to the new Russian cities, which engulfed them completely during the 1950s.

• In Muslim India, as in the Maghrib, the historic city and the British-built city were separated, before the whole entity was restructured and reconstituted as a more homogeneous whole.

Hence, between 1800 and 1950 the identity and development of Middle Eastern cities was reconstituted and reformulated as a function of a series of complex interrelations between long-established Islamic cities and modern cities. The demographic weight and the spatial extent of the two types of living space were at roughly the same level at the beginning of the twentieth century, which tended to encourage political and cultural antagonism, but which also produced oversimplistic analyses stressing conflict rather than the dynamic function of intermediate areas and social strata, the transitional entities that would come to dominate urban society.

# 7

## *Moving Out of Place*

### Minorities in Middle Eastern Urban Societies, 1800–1914

#### GUDRUN KRÄMER

 MINORITIES HAVE PLAYED a prominent role in the history of Middle Eastern societies, urban as well as rural, and the minority question continues to be highly relevant in contemporary politics. If minorities have mostly been studied in the context of modern nation-building processes, they are of equal interest with regard to the profound changes in urban society that were caused by, or related to, the transformations of socioeconomic, political, and cultural thought, practice, and organization that in spite of much criticism continue to be described as "modernization."

These transformations, which in some cases date back to the eighteenth century and in others only began to make themselves felt toward the end of the nineteenth, slowly accumulating in certain areas, and causing rapid if

I would like to thank Thomas Berchtold (formerly of the Freie Universität Berlin) who as my research assistant and the critical reader of earlier drafts of this paper made it possible for me to reach further beyond my own field, and to enjoy doing so. Since work on the manuscript was completed several years ago, new studies have been published that I have not been able to systematically consult and integrate in my paper. This applies in particular to *Revue des mondes musulmans et de la Méditerranée* 2006, 107–8, 109–110, *Identités confessionelles et espace urbain en terres d'islam.*

not traumatic ruptures in others, affected the lives of the entire population, whether majority or minority, Muslim or non-Muslim. Yet it was the role of the non-Muslims, whose part in the newly evolving spheres of commerce and culture was becoming quite conspicuous and whose share in the population of the major Middle Eastern cities was rising sharply at the same time, that caught the eye of observers, local as well as foreign. The assumption that non-Muslims acted as "agents of change" and "channels of modernization",[1] roles ascribed to ethnic minorities in all kinds of societies, and in addition, that they derived extra benefits from integration into a world market dominated by the Europeans not only because they were minorities but also because they were non-Muslim, merits special attention.

Three sets of questions will be central to what follows: first, the question of boundaries, social as well as physical, so deeply relevant to the structuring of urban space and social interaction in Middle Eastern as in any other society. To what extent were these boundaries modified or possibly entirely redrawn in the course of modernization, and who were the "agents of change" here? More specifically: was the very concept of minorities an "invented" one, similar to other "imagined communities," such as tribes and nations, that were emerging at the same time to be quickly transformed into highly effective social actors? Second, to what extent did the effects of modernization on local urban societies constitute a break with established patterns of interaction between Muslims and non-Muslims? Third, how general was the phenomenon, and to what extent was it characteristic of Middle Eastern urban society in the nineteenth and early twentieth centuries as a whole?

The subject is in many ways a difficult one. Not only are we looking at diverse physical settings ranging from old inland cities of commerce, learning, pilgrimage, or production to port cities, some of them old but newly expanding, others entirely new, situated in different political contexts and developing according to specific parameters, but we are also looking at a wide range of individuals, groups, and communities distinguished by origin, creed, language, and status who lived as minorities among a majority population that, outside Iran, was in most cases either Arab or Turkish Sunni Muslim: Albanians, Berbers, Kurds,

---

1. Although Davison 1982 refers to the non-Muslim minorities as "agents of change," he does not share the entire set of assumptions outlined above.

and Nubians; Christians, Jews, and Zoroastrians; Druzes, Alawis, and Alevis who might or might not be included in the Muslim community depending on convenience and political circumstance; Ahmadis, Babis, and Baha'is who were widely regarded as heretics by the local majority, no matter whether Sunni or Shi'i. Following established patterns of perception and representation concerning the very concept of "minorities" in the period under review, this paper will focus on non-Muslim communities, more particularly Christians and Jews.

Two biases marking the present study ought to be mentioned at the outset: one is the emphasis on large cities at the expense of many of the smaller ones that has characterized Middle Eastern urban historiography in general until recently, although this seems to be rapidly changing (Blake 1980).[2] The other is the striking imbalance in the treatment of the various non-Muslim communities.[3] Thus the documentation on Jews and Jewish life in Middle Eastern cities, ranging from broad overviews to individual case studies, and covering anything from community organization to costume, culture, and cuisine,[4] is considerably richer than on any other ethnic or religious minority, including the much more numerous Christians. Research on Middle Eastern Christianity still tends to privilege politics, church matters, and missionary activities over broader concerns inspired by, say, historical anthropology.[5] Overall syntheses of Middle Eastern urban development in the eighteenth and nineteenth

2. Several interesting studies of smaller towns are presented in *Villes au Levant* (*Revue du monde musulman et de la Méditerranée* 55–56 [1990]); Panzac 1991; Dumont and Georgeon 1992; Hanssen, Philipp, and Weber 2002. See also the annotated bibliography by Bonine et al. 1994. For relevant case studies, see Grangaud 2002 and Lafi 2002; Abu'l-Sha'r 1995; Reilly 2002; Hanssen 2005.

3. For overviews, see Courbage and Fargues 1997, Masters 2001, Braude and Lewis 1992, and Hourani 1947.

4. For overviews, see Deshen and Zenner 1982, 1996; H. Goldberg 1996; A. Cohen 1973. Bernard Lewis (1984) pays less attention to the modern age. Subregional studies include Stillman 1991, Abitbol 1980, Levy 1994, Weiker 1992, Rodrigue 1992, Shaw 1991, and Sarshar 2002. For case studies focusing on Jewish urban society, see, e.g., Karmi 1994, Deshen 1989, 1994, and Gottreich 2007.

5. Heyberger 1994, 2003; Atiya 1968. For case studies, most of which do not focus on urban society, see Hajjar 1962; Sanjian 1965; Haddad 1970; al-Bishri 1980; Joseph 1961, 1983; Philipp 1985. For Iran, see Sanasarian 2000; Stümpel-Hatami 1996; Schwartz 1985; Hartmann 1980; Gabriel 1971.

centuries are rare.[6] The focus will therefore be on those cities and communities that are better covered than others, and apart from the Ottoman capital, Istanbul, they mostly happen to be in the Mediterranean and the Ottoman Arab East. Hence major cities like Nablus, Jidda, Tabriz, or Shiraz will figure much less prominently in the narrative, not necessarily for lack of material and critical study (of which there are several excellent ones), but because non-Muslims played only a minor role in their urban economy and society. High diversity combined with considerable gaps in knowledge make it all the more hazardous to generalize, and the following will therefore often resemble a patchwork rather than a tightly woven analysis of the role of non-Muslim minorities in modern Middle Eastern urban societies.

## Starting Points

### *The Legal Tradition and Social Practice*

The old and somewhat stale debate over whether non-Muslims were generally oppressed under Muslim rule, "second-class citizens" suffering from unrelenting Muslim fanaticism and oriental despotism, or whether tolerance was the distinguishing mark of Islam and non-Muslims its most favored beneficiaries, need not detain us long. In fact, neither the "black myth" nor the "white" one, referring as they do to different times and places, to "dark ages" and to "golden" ones, do justice to the complexities of the historical experience, which rather unsurprisingly was characterized by various shades of gray.[7] More to the point are a number of other issues: the relevance of religion to social cohesion, stratification, and interaction in Middle Eastern urban society, the impact of legal norms on social practice, and the link between socioreligious distinctiveness and sociopolitical tension.

---

6. Apart from Raymond 1985, Eldem, Goffman, and Masters 1999, and Wirth 2000, several articles discussing the notion of the "Islamic," "Arab," or "oriental" city are particularly helpful: Raymond 1994b, Panerai 1989, and Abu-Lughod 1987.

7. For the "black myth," see notably Bat Ye'or 1985 or Gilbert 1976; for the "white myth," referring in particular to the "golden ages" of peaceful coexistence in Umayyad Spain, Fatimid Cairo, or the heyday of Ottoman power in the sixteenth century, see, e.g., Qasim 1987; for more judicious judgement, see M. Cohen 1994; Masters 2001; and several works on Ottoman Jewry, especially Levy, Shaw, and Weiker (above, note 4).

In contradistinction to earlier, more rigid, notions of ethnicity, anthropologists, sociologists, and historians have come to the realization that ethnic identities are not meta-historical "givens" but the outcome of specific contexts, often consciously created or "constructed." Ethnic boundaries are consequently seen as contingent and changeable, if not fluid.[8] That still leaves the question of who has the power of definition and what the parameters of changeability are. All the evidence indicates that until the beginning of the twentieth century (and beyond), religious affiliation served as one of the most important markers of group identity in Middle Eastern as well as in many other societies. It was not the only marker, and it was not necessarily always decisive, but it did matter in the context of urban life and space.

As in any other culture and society, legal norms and social practices reflected power relations, and in this equation local non-Muslims most often formed the weaker party. Although many outward signs of distinctiveness were adopted by other groups and strata of society, including first and foremost the elite, some were imposed on, or denied to, its weakest elements only, non-Muslims as well as subject Muslim groups,[9] not to mention women of all communities (D. Khoury 1997b). Finally, distinctiveness is not identical to tension. Indeed, it has been argued that the very fact that religious distinctions were so clearly marked, and so much taken for granted, made it possible for people to mingle freely in the public sphere (Marcus 1989, 39–48), provided they kept their place.

The status and treatment of non-Muslims in Muslim societies has varied greatly over time and space. Islamic legal concepts and popular attitudes were partly based on Qur'anic references that are often ambiguous and inconsistent, reflecting changing relations between the early and still highly vulnerable community of Muslims and their non-Muslim environment, allowing later commentators to select those passages that suited their own argument (Friedmann 2003; McAuliffe 1991; Humphreys 1991, 255–73; A. Khoury

8. Barth 1969; Anderson 1991. For a lucid discussion of the issue and its relevance to Middle Eastern urban history, see Reilly 1996, or, from an anthropological approach, Valensi 1986.

9. The latter point has been made by a number of authors, including Khuri 1990, 86–93, and M. Cohen 1994, ch. 6. In this context, see also Stillman 2003.

1994). During the early Muslim conquests (*futuh*), actual practice responded to local conditions and accordingly varied considerably from one place to another. One primary concern seems to have been to draw a clear and visible boundary between Muslims and non-Muslims, which could be done through dress codes, headgear, or hair styles, marking the person (Muslim as well as non-Muslim) rather than space. Islamic jurisprudence (*fiqh*), which was elaborated well after the Muslims had established themselves as masters on former Christian, Zoroastrian, and pagan territory, attempted to impose stricter limits on current practices.[10] Following essentially theological criteria, Muslim jurists distinguished between two categories of infidels (*kuffar,* sing. *kafir*): first, the pagans or polytheists (*mushrikun*), who worshiped more than one godhead and had not received a book of revelation, with whom there was to be no social intercourse, ranging from shared food to intermarriage, and who were to be fought until they either converted or were killed or enslaved; second, the "people of the book" (*ahl al-kitab*), more precisely the Christians, the Jews, the Sabaeans, and the Zoroastrians, whose faith was founded on a book of revelation and with whom social intercourse was licit. In practice, and largely irrespective of these distinctions, the vast majority of non-Muslims living in the lands of Islam (*dar al-islam*) were granted protected status that in certain respects assimilated them to the status of "people of the book" so that not just the Zoroastrians, whose religious status continued to be debated, but also (in time) Buddhists and Hindus no longer stood in danger of being expelled, killed, enslaved, or converted to Islam, though (licit) social intercourse with Muslims continued to be severely restricted.

In accordance with the Qur'anic injunction, "(There shall be) no compulsion in religion" (Sura 2:256), the status of these non-Muslims was secured by a contract of protection (*dhimma*), which guaranteed their life, body, property, and, with certain restrictions, also guaranteed their cult. The "Pact of 'Umar" (whose attribution to the second caliph 'Umar b. al-Khattab is contested) laid down a number of restrictions on the conduct and movement of

---

10. For the Sunni legal tradition, see Fattal 1958 and Zaydan 1988. The most liberal of the Sunni schools was the Hanafi one, which dominated in the Ottoman Empire and which granted non-Muslims equal rights with regard to property and parts of criminal law (notably *diya*, blood money), but not in the fields of testimony or inheritance.

non-Muslims, especially regarding dress and hair styles, the use of arms and horses, worship, the height of houses as well as the construction, extension, and repair of churches, synagogues, and temples (the latter especially relevant to urban development), which served not only to identify the *dhimmi*s physically like any other group of society, but to mark them as social inferiors (M. Cohen 1999, ch. 4; Noth 1987). Protection was granted against the payment of tribute, dues, and taxes of various kinds. Only gradually did two main categories evolve without, however, ever being consistently defined: a land tax (*kharaj*), which soon came to be imposed on all owners of lands that at a certain moment had been registered under that category, regardless of their religious affiliation, and a poll or capitation tax (*jizya*, based on Qur'an 9:29) to be paid in cash, kind or services that was to be levied on all able-bodied free adult *dhimmi* males of sufficient means.[11]

The various schools of Islamic law (*madhhab*, pl. *madhahib*) varied considerably in their definition of *dhimmi* rights and obligations. (Imami) Shi'i jurists differed from their Sunni counterparts in that they generally declared non-Muslims (if not all non-Shi'is) to be ritually unclean (*najis*), rendering social contact more difficult than in Sunni lands, a position that became particularly relevant in Iran after the Safavid conquest in 1501–02. It is important to remember that this concern with purity and impurity was shared by other major non-Muslim groups in Iranian society, first and foremost the Jews and Zoroastrians, who were just as intent on defending their own communal boundaries as were the Shi'i jurists.[12] Theory, therefore, was by no means uniform.

11. One the whole, monks and clerics were not taxed. However, the poor were not always exempted, so that the tax burden could cause great hardship to them or their community, respectively. For the technicalities of taxation in the Ottoman Empire, especially the *jizya* (Turkish *cizye*) until its abolition in 1855–56, see Shaw 1975; Weiker 1992, 53–57; and Karmi 1984, 87–97. Kuroki 1998 offers fascinating insights into taxation practices, as does Klein-Franke 1997.

12. (Sunni) Muslim conceptions of purity have received recent scholarly attention; see Gauvain 2005 and Maghen 1999. For Zorostrian notions, see Choksy 1989 and Boyce 1991. In modern Iran, reference was generally made to the work of Baha' al-Din al-'Amili (1547–1621), a leading Shi'i scholar under Shah 'Abbas I (r. 1587–1629). The relevant writings of Muhammad Taqi al-Majlisi (1594–1659, also known as Majlisi-yi Awwal) and his son Muhammad Baqir (1627/8–1698/9, al-'Allama al-Majlisi), must have made a significant impact: for the

What is more, practice frequently did not conform to normative prescriptions and popular attentions—it could be more lenient at times, but it could also be harsher. Given the localized nature of power and politics, government rulings were not necessarily applied in the provinces, and one ruler did not necessarily follow his predecessor's policies. The actual situation of the *dhimmis* was more closely conditioned by a number of economic and political factors: the utility of non-Muslims to a given society or more particularly to its rulers, whether of the community as a whole or of some of its members (for example, artisans, merchants, bankers, or physicians); the economic and political circumstances prevailing within the individual Muslim territory or locality, and its relationship with the major non-Muslim powers of the day. To some extent, these correlations remained valid until the modern age. At the same time, basic legal notions retained their normative force, affecting popular attitudes until well into the twentieth century, and if at any given time non-Muslims overstepped the limits, this could be condemned as a breach of the established code by Muslim scholars and their followers. Condemnation was usually coached in moral terms, accusing non-Muslims of "ostentation," "arrogance," and "overbearing manners." These charges were to be heard over the centuries, and figure prominently in accounts of eighteenth- and nineteenth-century intercommunal conflict.

By the Middle Ages, non-Muslims had become minorities in virtually all areas of the Middle East.[13] Economic and ecological changes, migration, political pressure, or conversion to Islam, which tended to be more widespread among certain Christian denominations and the Zoroastrians than among the Jews, all contributed to a considerable reduction in their numbers. As

---

latter, see Moreen 1992. However, neither Moreen 1981, Gregorian 1974, nor McCabe 1999 refer to a specific legal code as relevant to their period of investigation. For eighteenth- and nineteenth-century Shiʻi scholarship, see Tsadik 2003. The precise impact of these norms on urban life, notably the organization of space, remains to be examined. One known effect was the interdiction against non-Muslims living close to mosques or even getting close to them.

13. See Courbage and Fargues 1997, chs. 4–6, who register considerable demographic growth among Christians and Jews under Ottoman rule. For conversion to Islam, see especially Valensi 1997; also Humphreys 1991, 273–83; Gervers and Bikhazi 1990. García-Arenal 2002 also covers the nineteenth and twentieth centuries.

communities formed and reformed, certain features remained essentially the same: in return for submission to Muslim rule, non-Muslims enjoyed considerable autonomy in the spheres of personal status and family law (marriage, divorce, adoption, legacies, and wills), worship and education, constituting largely self-contained units with their own religious, legal, social, educational, and charitable institutions. Communal autonomy amounting to relative freedom from government intervention appeared most clearly in the Ottoman millet system (derived from the Turkish term for ethnic-religious groups or communities, *millet*, Arabic *milla*) as it had evolved by the nineteenth century.[14] By 1914, the Ottoman authorities had recognized more than ten different millets (all of them non-Muslim: neither the Shi'is and Druzes nor the 'Alawis and Alevis were legally recognized as distinct communities, though they actually functioned as such) that were headed by their religious and lay leadership. The most numerous and heterogeneous were the Rum (often referred to as "Greek") Orthodox, followed by the Armenian millet (which at times represented not just the members of the Armenian Apostolic Church but also other Middle Eastern Christian communities, mostly Monophysites) and the Rabbanite (as opposed to the Karaite) Jewish millet, which was considerably more homogeneous in religious terms (though not necessarily in broader cultural terms) than its Christian counterparts.

Several points need to be emphasized when speaking about communal autonomy. First, communal ties were not necessarily exclusive and communal boundaries were not watertight: like their Muslim contemporaries, non-Muslims could be members of various cross-cutting units and associations, notably urban neighborhoods, corporations, or guilds, also offering services, orientation, and a certain measure of social cohesion.[15] In spite of strict interdictions on the part of their religious authorities, non-Muslims seem to have resorted

14. Masters 2001, chs. 1 and 2, especially 61–67. For origins and definitions, see also Braude in Braude and Cohen 1982, 1:69–88, and Davison 1982, 320. For a list of the millets, see Sousa 1933, 89n2; for the competences of the communal leadership of the Rum Orthodox, Armenian, and Rabbanite millets as defined by imperial decree in the 1830s and modified by new Organic Laws in 1862, 1863, and 1865, respectively, see Davison 1963, ch. 4. In Safavid and Qajar Iran, Christian, Jewish, and Zoroastrian communities equally enjoyed a large measure of communal autonomy, although this was not institutionalized; Hartmann 1980, 35–37; Afary 2002.

15. See chapter 4 in this volume by Abdul-Karim Rafeq.

to Muslim courts and mediators rather more freely even on matters of marriage, divorce, and inheritance than is generally assumed.[16] Therefore the individual was not completely submerged in the group, and communal leadership was not the only channel of communication with the authorities. Although taxes were in most cases levied on the community as a whole, to be collected either by its head, a government agent or a tax-farmer, requests for tax exemption were made and granted on an individual basis, bringing the individual taxpayer into direct contact with the authorities. Second, the millet system in its institutionalized form served purposes of taxation and administration and was more relevant to dealings at government level than to the cohesion and actual functioning of local congregations. The millet of the Rum Orthodox, for instance, included millions of people of different origins and languages spread over extensive territories, ranging from ethnic Greeks, Albanians, Bulgars, Rumanians, Russians, and Serbs to Arabs, for whom the Ecumenical Patriarch of Constantinople served formally as their spiritual head and representative, but who looked primarily to their local leadership to maintain their local institutions on a day-by-day basis. Hence the continued relevance of the local context to an understanding of Middle Eastern urban society, particularly with regard to Jewish communities and congregations, among whom hierarchies were less pronounced than among the Christian churches.

*Occupation: The "Ethno-Religious Division of Labor"*

The boundaries defined by Muslim jurists on the basis of religious affiliation could easily translate into prescriptions for segregation, pertaining not only to dress and norms of social interaction, but also to occupation and space. Although in most parts of the Middle East there was no forced segregation, professional specialization and the residential concentration of ethnic groups and communities were very common. The former has been described as an

---

16. For the complexities of the situation, see Hacker 1994; for case studies from Ottoman Arab cities, see Marcus 1989; Al-Qattan 1992, 1999; Masters 2001, 31–37; and A. Cohen 1984, ch. 6; for courts, taxation, and tax exemption, see also Karmi 1984, 14f, 30, 89f. Much the same phenomena could be observed with regard to the Jewish *mellah* communities in Sharifian Morocco, whose social boundaries as Deshen (1996) has specifically emphasized, were permeable. See also Gottreich 2007.

"ethnic division of labor," in which non-Muslims specialized in certain economic roles and functions, some of which were regarded as undesirable, lowly, or ritually unclean by Muslims.[17] The paradigm has since been thoroughly revised, for there was, as a rule, no rigid division of roles and functions, and though specialization existed, its patterns varied greatly from one location and one period to the other. The one major area of exclusion concerned the military: according to the so-called Pact of 'Umar, *dhimmis* were not allowed to carry arms (although practice frequently diverted from that rule, particularly in rural areas that were difficult to control), and thus were generally not able to join the military elite. Outside the military sphere, however, it was by no means rare to find Muslims and non-Muslims working together in trades and crafts, including guilds (*ta'ifa, sinf, hirfa*) when and where they existed.[18] In some instances, Christian or Jewish guilds were affiliated to the local organization representing all members of a particular craft or trade, but in others they seem to have functioned independently. Crafts and the trade with gold, silver, precious stones, or textiles, such as gold and silver smithing, tailoring, and silk weaving, money changing, money lending, usury, or pawnbroking, which Muslim scholars disapproved of for religious reasons, were often in the hands of Christians and Jews, as was the production and sale of alcohol. In Egypt,

17. Interestingly, the relevant literature mostly dates from the 1950s and 1960s: Sussnitzki 1966, Gibb and Bowen 1969, Brunschvig 1962, and Coon 1958, 162. But see also Khuri 1990, 91–93.

18. In several places, lists of crafts and professions have been preserved, whose problematic nature is discussed in Philipp 1984a and 1984b, who looks specifically at two examples from Isfahan and Damascus: Mirza Husayn Khan Tahvildar, *Jughrafiya-yi Iran*, ed. Manuchehr Setudeh (Tehran 1342/1963) and al-Qasimi's *Qamus al-sina'at al-Shamiyya* (1960). For the Ottoman Empire, see Quataert 1993a, 1996; or İnalcik and Quataert 1994, 586–604, 695–709, 890–98. Berchtold's (2001) comprehensive study has not yet been published. For case studies including data on non-Muslims, see Raymond 1973–74; Ghazaleh 1999; Rafeq 1991; Masters 1988, 53, 82–88; Reilly 1996, 2002; A. Cohen 2001; Goffman 1990, 85–90; Gerber 1976; Serjeant and Lewcock 1983, 167–69, 394f; K. Brown 1976, 140–54. For Iran, where conditions varied greatly over time and from one location to the other, see Floor 1975, 2003; Keyvani (1982, 176–84, 195–217, 296–311) states that although non-Muslims played a considerable role in urban crafts and trade in the seventeenth century, they did not formally participate in guilds. For a detailed description of Iranian crafts and craftsmen, including their techniques, locations, and origins, see Wulff 1966.

Copts dominated public administration and the collection of taxes (to a large extent as a function of their literacy and experience); also in Egypt, garbage collection (unclean work associated with the feeding of pigs) was handled by lower class Copts, in San'a' by lower class Jews.

Like minorities in many other parts of the world, the Christians and Jews were well represented in international trade and commerce. In the absence of institutionalized safeguards, long-distance trade was based essentially on personal trust, which was more easily established and maintained on the basis of kinship and family ties. Thus like the Hadhrami merchants and traders in Southeast Asia, Indians in Africa, or Jews in Europe, Middle Eastern Armenians, Greeks, and Jews engaged in trading networks, often in cooperation with Muslim partners or under royal patronage. The link between prosperity and patronage merits attention: the Armenian merchants of New Julfa, a suburb of Isfahan, flourished as long as the Safavid Shahs actively used and protected them in the sixteenth and early seventeenth centuries and lost their wealth and status when the latter were no longer willing or able to do so. The royal merchants of Mogador (al-Sawira/Essaouira), who were established, financed, and closely supervised by the Moroccan Sultans, saw their fortunes decline when the central government (*makhzan*) lost the will and capacity to support them toward the end of the nineteenth century, and trading patterns shifted to their detriment.[19]

In the Ottoman Empire and the Maghreb, individual Christians and Jews, often in fierce competition with one another, held some of the most lucrative tax farms or served as money lenders (*sarraf*), brokers, or bankers (*simsar, dallal*) to the local governors. That placed them among the richest segments of society, but it also rendered them vulnerable: wealthy but powerless, they played a role similar to the European court Jews. Favors could be withdrawn, fortunes confiscated, and lives taken. The *dhimmi*s knew it, perhaps better than other subjects, and they took care to act accordingly: they kept their place, maintained low profile, avoided ostentation, and cultivated good relations

19. On the Julfa merchants, see McCabe 1999, 122–98, 257f; for Mogador, see Schroeter 1988, chs. 2 and 5, 34–50; for the Algerian Bacri and Busnach families, see Kortepeter 1994; for eighteenth-century Aleppo and Damascus, see Masters 1992; Philipp 1984a; and Bouchain 1996.

with the political elite, which they were unable to join, short of conversion. To the rulers, *dhimmis* could prove most useful as long as they remained what they were supposed to be: "productive, loyal, and silent."[20]

*Urban Space: Quarters, Neighborhoods, and Ghettoes*

If the concept of an ethnic-religious division of labor has recently come under attack, the same is true for the notion of spatial segregation. Three issues have been central to the debate: the social and functional unity of the city, the homogeneity of urban quarters and neighborhoods, and the distinctiveness of non-Muslim neighborhoods. In the light of new research and evidence, the traditional notion of the Middle Eastern city as rigidly divided into quarters sealed by solid gates and inhabited, over long periods of time, by homogeneous groups of people bound together by common origin, religion, or occupation (Gibb and Bowen 1969, 1:276f) has had to be considerably modified, to be replaced by concepts emphasizing, once again, the permeability of boundaries and their changeability over time.

There is no doubt that, as in the rest of the preindustrial world, Middle Eastern cities were characterized by a certain degree of spatial and residential segregation based on ethnicity, religion, or occupation rather than the "horizontal" element of class—although craft and occupation do, of course, as a rule correlate with class and status, and ethnicity and religion could be related to class and status, too.[21] However, empirical study reveals a great variety of spatial patterns even within individual countries or regions and constant demographic flux and reflux over time. In some cities, the various quarters (*mahalla, hayy, hara, huma*) do not seem to have been clearly marked at all.[22]

20. Weiker 1992, 3. Boyce 1991, 162, speaks of "protective obscurity."

21. For a superb case study of nineteenth-century Cairo, see Alleaume and Fargues 1998. For Damascus in 1700, Establet and Pascual 1994 show greater social heterogeneity within individual living areas. For eighteenth-century Hama, see Reilly 2002, app. 1 and 2. For Aleppo in 1900, see Gaube and Wirth 1984, 427–34.

22. Towns in Yemen and Algeria provide interesting examples: According to Serjeant and Lewcock 1983, 144–47, quarters in nineteenth-century San'a' were not clearly defined and not known to the "man in the street." Kopp and Wirth 1990, who provide interesting data on urban development under Ottoman rule (1872–1917), do not deal with the issue systematically. In twentieth-century Sa'da, the second largest town of northern Yemen, quarters seem

In many others, quarters were known and neighborhoods relatively homogeneous ethnically, but neither was sealed with gates, let alone walls. In others, all quarters or neighborhoods were enclosed by gates, and when this was the case over extended periods of time, it was usually indicative of general insecurity or intercommunal tension. All over the Middle East, Jewish quarters or neighborhoods were most likely to be set apart from surrounding living areas or enclosed by gates or even walls, not necessarily for security reasons but for practical ones, first and foremost to reduce the distance to the closest synagogue, bath, or kosher butcher to a minimum (Schroeter 1994).[23]

The traditional view that ethnic quarters form a characteristic, and essentially static, feature of Islamic urban organization was critically examined by Greenshields (1980). He suggested taking what he called "ethnic clusters" rather than ethnic quarters, which were all too often vaguely defined, as the basic reference, defining them as "spatial clusters of members of particular ethnic groups within a city greater than those expected from a random distribution of all people within the city" (121), without making any prior assumptions concerning social ties within the various clusters or their distinctiveness, segregation, or isolation, whether social or physical. Greenshields argued that ethnic clusters must originate and grow through population redistribution, either

---

to have been well defined albeit (no longer) sealed with gates; Niewöhner-Eberhard 1985. In eighteenth-century Constantine, "quarters" were not a relevant unit; Grangaud 2002, 90–104; the same was true of nineteenth-century Sétif; Bahloul 1996.

23. In nineteenth-century Aleppo, only the Jewish quarter seems to have been sealed off by a gate; Gaube and Wirth 1984; in late eighteenth-century Damascus, all Jews lived in the *mahallat al-yahud*, yet it was not exclusively Jewish; Al-Qattan 1992. For the Maghreb, see Deshen 1989; Gottreich 2007; Schroeter 1988; K. Brown 1976, 34–39; Le Tourneau 1949, 217f; and Udovitch and Valensi 1984. For Yemen, see Serjeant and Lewcock 1983, 391–431, and Lingenau 1994. In Iran, the situation varied from place to place and even where clustering was very dense, it was as a rule voluntary, not enforced; see Sarshar 2002, 104f. In nineteenth-century Kerman, Jews and Zoroastrians as the major non-Muslim minorities in town lived in segregated quarters inside and outside of the city walls, respectively, with heavily protected houses testifying to their deep sense of insecurity; English 1966. In nineteenth-century Shiraz, Jews were allegedly forbidden to live outside their quarter *(mahalle)*, to share food and drink with Muslims and to move outside their quarter in the rainy seasons for fear of pollution; Loeb 1996. Loeb described Iranian Jews as "outcastes"; but see also Afary 2002.

collective or individual, which may follow different motives and patterns. This could involve the immigration of homogeneous groups (military units, members of the ruling class, transferred populations, or refugees); collective regroupings within cities (for example, the establishment of ethnic quarters in the towns of North Africa, Yemen, and Iran); or individual movements based on kinship ties, the presence of holy sites, changed socioeconomic status, or mutual distrust. Clustering could be government-planned, forced (caused by natural disasters, epidemics, famine, war, political instability, or persecution), or voluntary (caused by demographic pressure or the individual motives mentioned above).

For obvious reasons, collective transfer and relocation are generally better documented than individual migration. They include most notably forced transfer and resettlement as it was practiced for centuries in the Persian as well as the Ottoman Empires (*sürgün*), although it should be emphasized that deportations took place for economic as well as political or security-related reasons and were not restricted to non-Muslims (Hacker 1992; McCabe 1999, ch. 2; Perry 1975). It was still reflected in the mass deportation of Armenians in 1914–15 (a substantial number of Armenian refugees found refuge in Aleppo and Beirut after 1920) or what has been euphemistically called the population exchange between Christian Greeks and Muslim Turks after World War I. Government-planned regrouping of ethnic groups that had previously lived intermingled with the rest of the population or voluntarily chosen to live together is exemplified in the creation of the closed Jewish quarter (*mellah*) of Fez in the early fourteenth century, followed by the foundation of similar quarters in other Moroccan towns such as Meknès and Marrakesh, the Yemeni capital San'a' or the Iranian city of Kerman, which had strongly protected Jewish and Zoroastrian quarters in the nineteenth century. Nothing similar seems to have existed in the Ottoman Arab East. The chief reasons for the creation of closed quarters, which were often established near the citadel or royal palace, appear not only to have been to reduce intercommunal tension (whose rise, of course, needs to be explained in each case) and to better protect the *dhimmi*s, but also to prevent their spreading over town (for socioeconomic as well as religious reasons, including notions of ritual purity and pollution).

Regroupings within the city could also be based on security considerations, but organized by members of the community or communities concerned rather than the authorities. Ottoman Damascus provides a good example (Sack 1989, 21, 61–67; Sauvaget 1934, 459–53; Sauvaget 1941, 1:150f). In medieval times, shops and workshops owned by Muslims were situated inside the Christian and Jewish neighborhoods and many mosques were built inside the (predominantly) Christian quarters. In the seventeenth and eighteenth centuries, intense intercommunal tensions brought about a greater search for security and ethnic homogeneity. Although intermingling continued in some areas and urban property was still co-owned by Muslims and non-Muslims, in others self-protection was carried so far as to cut off all connections between individual streets and quarters. Yet, insecurity and the search for protection just exemplified and stressed so strongly by Sauvaget in his studies of Aleppo and Damascus were not the only factors involved in ethnic regrouping and clustering. Like the Jewish quarter of San'a', the Jewish *mellahs* in Sharifian Morocco, Algeria, and Tunisia were not always close to the citadel or royal palace and hence to the government. Frequently, economic rather than political or security-related considerations, notably the availability of vacant land, dictated the selection of a new location.

The key notions concerning urban space, then, are "neighborhoods," which as a rule formed around particular streets or even parts of streets, rather than well-defined and physically closed off "quarters," and the voluntary clustering rather than the forced segregation, let alone the ghettoization, of specific ethnic or religious groups. Like others, non-Muslims tended to concentrate in specific areas or neighborhoods.[24] This was particularly true of the Jews, among whom this tendency appears to have been more marked than among either

24. Abu-Lughod (1987, 166) speaks about a process of "long-term voluntary sifting and sorting"; Schatkowski Schilcher (1985, 21–26) emphasizes that in Damascus, ethnic groups were spatially only rarely isolated from the dominant group. See also Degeorge 1994, 52f, and Al-Qattan 1992. Similar results emerge from Hama (Reilly 1996, 221, and 2002). For Aleppo we have a number of highly sophisticated analyses, mainly distinguished by the emphasis they put on persistent ethnic segregation (Raymond 1992, 153–56) or the changing patterns of mixing and segregation (David 1990, 1997); see also Gaube and Wirth 1984, 64–66, 113–19, 191–200, 427–34. For in-depth studies of Jerusalem, documenting the changing patterns of intermingling and segregation from the Middle Ages to the present, see Arnon 1992 and Ben-Arieh 1984. For Beirut, see Khalaf and Khoury 1993, ch. 2; for Istanbul, see Mantran 1962, 48–66; Çelik 1993, chs. 1 and 2; and Karmi 1984, 131ff.

Christians or Muslims. The crucial question always remains that of exactly how migration and clustering were initiated, and to what extent the decision was related to religion, and more specifically to notions of ritual purity and pollution. In this regard, two spheres were especially sensitive: mosques and baths. It seems that in Iran, non-Muslims, being regarded as ritually unclean (*najis*), were not allowed to live close to mosques or even to be in the vicinity of mosques. The same applied to certain sites and cities in Morocco, although non-Muslims were not generally considered impure in Sunni legal thought (Maghen 1999, 364).[25] Significantly, many shrines or saints' tombs were often visited by Muslims, Jews, and Christians alike, who all believed in the special power (*baraka*) attached to them. As for baths, which at least in Sunni lands, non-Muslims were entitled to use alongside Muslims, physical contact was either avoided or carefully structured, for instance, by obliging non-Muslim men to wear colored string, amulets, or even bells so as to signal their presence; non-Muslim women used separate days or times of day for their visits (M. Cohen 1994, 131ff; A. Cohen 1984, 76–86; Marcus 1989, 42; Masters 2001, 6). Apart from mosques and "sacred space" more generally, physical boundaries were not always clearly defined, and there was ethnic intermingling in most Middle Eastern cities. Most of all, physical boundaries were not static. Relocation and regrouping was often the result of demographic growth (presupposing sociopolitical conditions that allowed for expansion), and social and economic motives rather than insecurity and politics narrowly defined.

It remained the case that while non-Muslims generally shared the same material culture, social values, and important religious practices with their Muslim neighbors, they generally saw themselves as parts of different "imagined communities," and were seen as such by others.[26] It would be especially interesting to explore exactly what these "imagined communities" consisted

25. See above, note 12.

26. On the spaces, opportunities, and limits of urban conviviality, see Georgeon and Dumont 1997 and Masters 2001, ch. 1. Izmir/Smyrna provides an interesting case study; see Georgelin 2005. Although the city lies beyond the boundaries of the Middle East as commonly understood, studies of Ottoman Salonica offer fascinating insights into urban conviviality; see notably Anastassiadou 1997 and Mazower 2004.

of, and how far they reached: the neighborhood, the city, the Armenian Apostolic Church, Christianity, the Sephardi congregation in Salonica, Sephardi Jewry, world Jewry. In any case, non-Muslims were generally not included in the urban political elites, and they had no responsibility for urban life or public order outside their own community or neighborhood.

## The Nineteenth Century: Reform, Differentiation, and Complication

Traditional notions of how non-Muslims ought to live and behave in a Muslim society were still largely in force when the combined effects of socioeconomic, legal, and cultural change began to transform their role and status, particularly in the Ottoman Empire and the territories more or less controlled by it from the mid–nineteenth century onward; although Qajar Iran also witnessed socioeconomic, cultural, and legal change, there have been few studies of its impact on local non-Muslim urban communities. The growth of European trade and influence, internal migration, political, legal, educational, and cultural change, which led to increased social differentiation, profoundly altered the profile and internal structure of local non-Muslim communities as well as their status and role within urban society. Change was not uniform: it affected the various minorities in a highly uneven manner, depending, inter alia, on criteria of origin (indigenous or immigrant), geographical distribution (local or transnational), and denomination or sect, which in their turn were partly correlated with language, cultural orientation, ties to specific European powers, and nationality or legal status more generally. A community was hardly ever transformed as a whole. As a rule, individual Christians and Jews, or individual Christian and Jewish families, managed to benefit from increased educational and economic opportunities, gaining access to the legal protection and privileges now offered by the European powers. Their successes and failures were then projected back on the communities they belonged to and were thought to represent.

*Legal Change: The Tanzimat, the Capitulations, and European Protection*

In the Ottoman Empire, the legal innovations of the Tanzimat period (1839–76) revised or at least modified certain provisions of Islamic law, culminating in the formal abolition of the poll tax (*jizya*) and the proclamation of legal equality between Muslims and non-Muslims.[27] This element of the broader reform movement reflected European pressure to move beyond traditional notions of tolerance and protection and to grant non-Muslims full rights of citizenship, itself a novel concept in Ottoman political thought (and, it should be added, a fairly recent one in Europe as well). For the Ottoman Empire to cede to this pressure was one way to prove itself "civilized" and worthy of inclusion in the European concert of powers (which indeed it was at the Congress of Paris in 1856)—a fact that could not but compromise the reforms in the eyes of many Muslims who resented any change in their relationship with local non-Muslims, let alone change brought about by European demands and expectations.[28]

The so-called Noble Rescript of the Rose Chamber (*hatt-ı şerif* of Gülhane) of 1839 professed to confirm Islamic law by guaranteeing all Ottoman subjects, Muslims as well as non-Muslims, "perfect security of life, honor and property" (according to the sharia). The Imperial Rescript (*hatt-ı hümayun*) of 1856 went considerably further, proclaiming legal equality of all Ottoman subjects (who continued to be labeled as such rather than as citizens; in the nationality law of 1869, the term *tebaa* was used for the former military and administrative elite, *askeri,* as well as for the tax-paying population, more specifically the non-Muslims, *reaya*). The *jizya* was replaced by a military exemption tax (*bedel-i askeri*). Though it was abolished by the Young Turks in 1909, non-Muslims were not drafted into the Ottoman army until shortly before the

---

27. See Mardin's article on the Tanzimat (1995, 183–86). The term is best translated as "regulations." In the same period, the Iranian government improved the legal protection of local non-Muslims without offering them legal emancipation; see Floor 1983. It seems that Zoroastrians benefited from contacts with their coreligionists in India: restrictions on religious buildings were lifted in the second half of the nineteenth century, and the *jizya* levied on them was abolished in 1882; Boyce 1991, 209–12, 218ff. Though the constitution of 1906–7 declared all Iranian citizens to be equal, Jews appear to have remained subject to some discriminatory legislation until 1926, when it was finally abolished under Reza Shah. See Loeb 1996, 249; Afary 2002, 162–74; and Tsadik 2003, 405–8.

28. It should be emphasized that at least until 1856, the Ottoman reforms were not so much inspired by European precedent and pressure as by domestic concerns; see Mardin 1995 and Abu-Manneh 1994.

outbreak of Word War I.[29] Particularly important in an urban context, legal emancipation also implied that many of the restrictions on the construction, repair, and extension of churches, synagogues, schools, baths, hospitals, or cemeteries that had been part of the Pact of 'Umar were lifted. Significantly enough, government approval was still required for new construction in areas inhabited exclusively by the respective (non-Muslim) community and any kind of repair or construction activity in mixed areas. Practice did not always follow the law.[30]

The Tanzimat reforms did not abolish religious personal status law, nor did they eliminate all outward signs of difference such as dress, hairstyle, and so forth, which continued to be observed in certain parts of the Empire (Davison 1982; Quataert 1997; Stillman 2003). At the same time that legal equality was declared and non-Muslims in growing numbers came to be included in municipal, provincial, and national assemblies that were either newly created or endowed with wider authority, the millet system was preserved. Hence, several powerful markers of religious distinctiveness remained in force until the dissolution of the Ottoman Empire.[31] Legal emancipation did not necessarily pave the way for the political and cultural integration of non-Muslims, either individually or collectively, whether into the Empire where the new concept of "Ottomanism" was propagated from the 1860s, or into the new entities, nations-in-being, that succeeded it after World War I (Khalidi et al. 1991; Kayalı 1997).

European influence went considerably further than merely pressing for equal rights for all Ottoman subjects. In the nineteenth century, two

29. Zürcher (1999) provides an important introduction into an underresearched field; see also Kunt 1982. For case studies illustrating negotiations on the ground, see Karmi 1984, 99–104, and H. Goldberg 1990, 47–51.

30. Paragraphs 6 and 7 of the *Hatt-ı hümayun*, quoted from the French translation in Young 1905–6, 2:5. For the effects on Istanbul and several other Ottoman cities, see Karmi 1984, 21–24.

31. Kunt 1982; Levy 1994, chs. 16–18; Ma'oz 1968; and Lafi 2005 provide overviews. For Istanbul, see Karmi 1984, ch. 6; for Haifa, Yazbak 1998. Jerusalem, Tripoli (Lebanon), and Beirut provide markedly different settings; see Gerber 1985; Sulayman 2001; and Hanssen 2005. For the impact of the reforms on a peripheral Ottoman province, see H. Goldberg 1990 and Simon 1994.

instruments were used that had existed before, but which now acquired a force they had hitherto lacked: the capitulations and European protection of local subjects. Continuing earlier Islamic as well as non-Islamic practices, the capitulations (*ahdname*-s, *imtiyazat*) were originally (reciprocal) treaties of commerce and protection between Muslim rulers and Christian princes or republics, guaranteeing the lives and property of their subjects, most of them diplomatic envoys, merchants, pilgrims, or travelers, while in the territory of the contracting parties (van den Boogert 2005).[32] On Muslim territory, the treaties exempted the foreign subjects from Islamic criminal jurisdiction and local taxation, notably the *jizya* imposed on the local *dhimmis*, placing them under a separate jurisdiction which, as early as the thirteenth century, was exerted by local foreign consuls. (It must be emphasized, though, that as soon as litigation involved more than one "nation," and more particularly subjects of the sultan, they entered into the jurisdiction of the Ottoman qadis and law courts. Privilege and autonomy were thus not identical with exterritorial status.) By the mid–nineteenth century, the system of capitulations, based partly on written treaties and partly on custom, had moved far beyond its original parameters. Initially voluntary and reciprocal, the capitulations had assumed the binding character of international treaties. At the same time, their scope had greatly expanded, involving privileges of autonomous jurisdiction as well as important trading facilities, fiscal exemptions, and special rights of control over customs duties exerted by the capitulatory powers which by that time included most European states as well as the United States of America and Brazil. The capitulations were unilaterally abrogated by the Ottoman government in 1914, but it was only in 1923 that the Treaty of Lausanne finally decreed their abolition; in Iran, they were abolished in 1928, and in Egypt under the Treaty of Montreux in 1936.

Intimately linked to this development, foreign protection that had originally been granted only to consular agents and employees (notably the so-called *dragomans*, from the Arabic *turjuman*, interpreter), assumed unprecedented dimensions when hundreds, if not thousands, of local subjects acquired

---

32. For the evolution, functions, and abuses of the system, see also Sousa 1933, Darling 1995, and Ahmad 2000. For their Moroccan equivalents, whose effects never reached Ottoman proportions, see Schroeter 1988, 165–78, 201, and Bowie 1976.

certificates of foreign protection (*berat*-s, hence the Ottoman Turkish term, *beratlı*, protégé) in the course of the eighteenth and nineteenth centuries, which, until new and rather more restrictive regulations were agreed upon in 1863, were hereditary. On the whole, Muslims hesitated to seek protection from a foreign power, whereas non-Muslims were quick to see the advantages of being exempted from the *jizya* when and where it was still imposed, as well as being offered quite substantial legal, fiscal, and economic privileges (van den Boogert 2005).[33] It was not only individuals that came to enjoy foreign protection, but entire non-Muslim communities. Strictly speaking, protection only applied to their clergy, monks, and religious institutions, including churches, monasteries, pious foundations, and holy sites, but European protection and patronage, vaguely defined and resting mostly on custom, gradually extended much further to include the body of the faithful as well. And we are speaking of large numbers: thus in 1774, the Ottoman-Russian Treaty of Küçük Kaynarca, followed by more extensive concessions in 1830, placed the Orthodox Church, with its several million ethnic Greek, Albanian, Bulgarian, Serbian, and Arab members, under Russian protection. In the nineteenth century, Russia protected the Rum Orthodox and Armenian communities throughout the Ottoman Empire, with independent Greece increasingly seeking to exert its influence over ethnic Greeks. France claimed the exclusive right (although contested and increasingly challenged by the Austrians, the Vatican, Spain, Sardinia, and later Italy) to protect the Roman Catholics and the Uniate churches including Armenian, Syrian, and Coptic Catholics and the Maronites, and here again, considerable numbers were involved. Lacking long-time religious or historical bonds with local minorities, Britain protected what was left: the Protestants, the Druzes, and the Jews in Palestine. Only French and Russian rights were, with important reservations, recognized by the Porte, whereas Austrian or British claims rested merely on custom, although they were no less effective.

Several points have to be made when discussing the impact of foreign protection on Middle Eastern non-Muslims. First, while certain communities

33. For individual countries and communities, see Homsy 1956, Hopwood 1969, Schlicht 1981, Frazee 1983, Farah 1986, and Friedman 1986. For Aleppo, see Masters 1992, 2001, ch. 3, and (with caution) Shalit 1996; for Damascus, Schatkowski Schilcher 1985; for Beirut, Fawaz 1983, 85ff.

such as the Rum Orthodox and the Catholics came to enjoy foreign protection, others, like the Egyptian (Orthodox) Copts or Karaite Jews did not. Even when a community was collectively placed under foreign protection, this did not imply that the lives and fortunes of all its members were transformed, for as a rule, it was only the educated and well-to-do middle and upper strata that were able to obtain foreign status and to benefit from the privileges attached to it.[34] Regardless, however, of whether local non-Muslims were in fact affiliated to a foreign power, they were increasingly perceived as "local foreign minorities."[35] Second, in most cases, foreign protection or even nationality did not involve foreign origin. Many of the individuals enjoying foreign status of some kind (and this itself was often ill-defined) had not actually immigrated from France, Britain, Russia, or Italy, or even from areas controlled or occupied by them, but were members of the local population. Third, no political loyalties needed to be involved in the relationship between the protégés and their protecting power. The choice of a particular European nation was usually based on convenience and could be changed if that seemed advantageous; members of the same family (for example, the Poche family in Aleppo) could have different protecting powers, remain local subjects, or become stateless. Choice also depended on opportunity: though many local consuls (who were themselves often of local origin and were sometimes consuls for several different powers) were quite ready to sell certificates and increase the number of their protégés, thereby augmenting their income as well as their standing and influence, some of their governments were not.

As a matter of fact, European racism and snobbery could be directed against local non-Muslims just as much as against Muslims: Greeks, Armenians, Syrian Christians, and Jews were frequently grouped together as "Levantines," and the connotations of the term—greed, pushiness, dishonesty, and shallowness—were not positive. Not all European powers were intent on acquiring protégés among local minorities that until recently had enjoyed low status and in many cases continued to do so, particularly when this threatened to create

34. The case of Egyptian Jewry illustrates this point rather well; see Krämer 1989, 29–36, and with different figures, Shamir 1987, 33–67.

35. For an excellent illustration of the ambiguities of legal status and identity, see Ilbert 1996, vol. 1, chs. 3 and 7.

difficulties with the Muslim authorities.[36] The Décret Crémieux of 1870 that extended French citizenship to some 30,000 Algerian Jews was thus an exceptional effort to co-opt an entire non-Muslim community, although it did not in fact extend to the Jewish congregations in the south of the country, notably in the M'zab (Ansky 1950; Kateb 2001, 190–93).

The capitulations left their imprint on urban society. Istanbul, Izmir, Cairo, or Alexandria all provide examples of their negative effect.[37] Foreigners found it relatively easy to evade paying taxes and rents, and to avoid arrest or confiscation, suspects merely had to claim foreign protected status, for without the consent of the consul in charge police could not arrest them or take them to court. The vexing complexity of codes, courts, and procedures was only reduced when the capitulations and the Mixed Courts dealing with cases involving foreign protégés and local/Ottoman subjects were abolished in the course of the twentieth century (Cannon 1988; N. Brown 1993).

*Demographic Growth and Change*

Legal emancipation and growing ties to Europe coincided with considerable demographic growth among local non-Muslims that reached its climax in the early 1880s. Better hygiene in the face of the epidemics that continued to plague Middle Eastern cities until well into the nineteenth century played a role in this process,[38] as did high birth rates among local Christians and Jews.[39] As their numbers augmented, their share in the urban population increased.

36. Lord Cromer's disparaging comments on local Copts and Armenians bear out the point rather forcefully: Cromer 1908. For a neutral definition of the term "Levantine," the intermediary par excellence, see Eldem 1991, n. 3.

37. For Istanbul, see Rosenthal 1980a, chs. 6, 7, and 11, and Scheben 1991, 174–77, 198, 234. For Egypt, see, for example, the memoirs of Sir Thomas Russell Pasha (1949), former commander of the Egyptian police; Krämer 1989, 19, 29–31; Ilbert 1996, vol. 1; and Reimer 1997, 127ff.

38. Panzac 1985, 64ff, supplemented by case studies; see, notably, Dumont 1992; Kuhnke 1990, ch. 4.

39. See the basic data in Courbage and Fargues 1997, 58, 64f, 105f, 124f; Karpat 1985, and McCarthy 1983, 1989; also Levy 1994, chs. 10, 11. Algeria under French colonial rule provides a special case; see the excellent study by Kateb 2001. For Iran, Gilbar (1976) includes data on foreign residents, whose number rose from 150 in 1850 to some 1,200 in 1904 (154), but he does not mention local non-Muslims.

Population pressure in its turn led to increased density within existing neighborhoods or quarters as well as dispersal over the city as a whole. In addition to demographic growth there was considerable migration from rural areas and from abroad, demonstrating the attractiveness of certain cities and territories within the Ottoman Empire, Egypt, and the Maghreb, which was, of course, not restricted to non-Muslims. Reflecting the shift of trading patterns, economic growth, and activity from inland to port cities, population growth was particularly marked in Beirut, where the number of Christian residents rose from about 50 to 66 percent of the urban population between 1860 and 1920.[40] In Alexandria, cosmopolitan port city par excellence, non-Muslims made a significant contribution to the general atmosphere, even though they were never more than one-third of the population, and foreigners (Muslims as well as non-Muslims) accounted for about one-fifth. In late nineteenth-century Istanbul, non-Muslims made up some 40 percent of the population, and even in inland Aleppo, they accounted for 28 percent. Baghdad witnessed a spectacular growth of its Jewish population, from about 3.3 percent in 1794 to nearly 35 percent in 1893. Immigration could not but change the composition and internal organization of the existing non-Muslim communities, and local community leaders, anticipating the financial burdens and potential social problems linked to this massive influx, did not always welcome the newcomers.[41] While it is true that most migrants were young and poor, they were also achievement oriented and generally hard working. Many brought special skills, experience, new ideas, and in some cases capital, giving a new impetus to the local economy and community. Some could also rely on international networks of family and kinship ties, which were particularly useful in the fields of commerce and finance.

40. On what follows, see Courbage and Fargues 1997, 76, 99. For Beirut, see Fawaz 1983, 28–43, 60; for Alexandria, Ilbert 1996, 1:91–98, 361–76; for Istanbul, Çelik 1993, 38; Karmi 1984, ch. 1, is not entirely consistent; for Aleppo, Gaube and Wirth 1984, 196; for Baghdad, Deshen 1994, 684. For migration among Middle Eastern Jewish communities in general, see Stillman 1991, 38–41.

41. In Cairo and Alexandria, they made several attempts to have the authorities impose some limits on the immigration of Jews without the necessary means of subsistence; Krämer 1989, 11f. For similar problems in Ottoman cities, see Karmi 1984, 24f, and Nahum 1997, 93f. Deshen (1994, 685f) refers to unrest within the Jewish community of Baghdad.

Egypt provides a striking example of the multiplication, growth, and diversification of local non-Muslim communities (Krämer 1989, 8–10, 59ff).[42] From the 1860s to the 1920s, Egypt was a country of immigration. If some of the immigrants came to escape from political instability or persecution at home (Syrian Christians, Eastern European Jews), most were attracted by the hope of a better life, social advancement, or rapid enrichment. Laissez-faire economics and the capitulations created highly favorable conditions for enterprising individuals, which were further guaranteed by the political, economic and, if necessary, military pressure of the European powers headed by Britain. After the British occupation in 1882, immigration began to soar, reaching its peak in the decade 1897–1907. Foreign colonies were formed and existing communities transformed, including Greeks, Italians, Syrians, Armenians, and Jews from all parts of the Middle East, the Mediterranean, and Europe. Large-scale immigration continued well into the 1920s, bringing the number of foreigners living in Egypt up from about 15,000 in the 1850s to 100,000 in the 1880s and over 200,000 in the years after World War I (and again it should be remembered that foreign nationals could very well be of indigenous origin and that most non-Muslims did not have foreign status). Immigration from abroad was accompanied by migration within the country. In the 1880s, the center of commerce, industry, and administration shifted definitively to Cairo and Alexandria. The non-Muslim provincial middle and upper-middle classes joined the general trend of migration to the big cities, which offered better communal and educational services, better protection against attacks both on individuals and on entire communities (such as, for instance, ritual murder accusations leveled by Christians against local Jews) and much more entertainment. With the exception of the Copts and many Greeks, it was only the poorer, less educated, or less enterprising who stayed behind, and many Christians and Jews who lived in provincial towns actually commuted on a daily or weekly basis to Alexandria, Cairo, or the larger cities in the Delta.

42. See further Collins 1984 and Shalabi 1993, Philipp 1985, and Kitroeff 1989. The Copts, being entirely indigenous, have to be analyzed separately; see notably al-Bishri 1980 and Motzki 1979.

*Socioeconomic and Educational Change*

The overall impact of European economic penetration and competition on local crafts, manufacturing, trade, and industry remains controversial. Divergence of opinion is due not only to regional variations depending on the location of specific towns and areas (coast or inland, trade routes old and new, security, accessibility, etc.), but to differences in interpreting their effects on the local economies and their various sectors, notably textiles.[43] There is, however, no controversy concerning the prominent role played by non-Muslims in the newly expanding, and often highly profitable, trade with Europe, which in the case of the Ottoman Empire assumed new dimensions after the Anglo-Ottoman commercial treaty of 1838 (Treaty of Balta Liman), followed by the Franco-Ottoman Treaty of 1839, both of which had profound effects on the local economy. With certain local variations, a pattern evolved which in many instances had begun to form well before:[44] trade and commerce with neighboring Muslim territories, often classified as "internal," was largely in the hands of Muslims; trade with Europe was dominated, but by no means monopolized, by local Christians, Jews, and foreign residents (as a rule Europeans or Americans),[45] while both Muslims and local non-Muslims had a share

43. For a general overview, see Owen 1993. Once again, the discussion has largely focused on the Ottoman Empire; see Pamuk 1987; İslamoğlu-İnan 1987; Kasaba 1988; and Quataert 1983, 1993a. For Morocco, see Schroeter 1988, ch. 1. For Iran, see Floor 2003, and for an interesting case study illustrating the capacity of "traditional" industries to adapt to changing demands, Helfgott 1994. See also note 44 below.

44. For Ottoman trade and commerce 1600–1914, see Faroqhi in İnalcik and Quataert 1994. For non-Muslims, see especially Issawi 1982; Bağiş 1983; Eldem 1991; Masters 1992; Fawaz 1983, chs. 6 and 7; Philipp 1985; and Bittar 1992. In Morocco, local Jews had played a prominent role in trade well before the Anglo-Moroccan commercial treaty of 1856 that ushered in the era of free trade; Schroeter 1988, chs. 3, 5, and 6. To the extent, however, that non-Muslims became associated with European influence and protection, they tended to be replaced by Muslims: Cigar 1981. For Jewish peddlers, see Deshen 1989 or Simon 1993. In contrast, local non-Muslims in nineteenth-century Iran do not seem to have played a prominent role in money lending, banking, or international trade even with Europe; see Migeod 1990, 179–94; Floor 1979, 1976; and Nashat 1981.

45. Rafeq 1988a, 429–30, specifically emphasizes the fact that in nineteenth-century Damascus, Muslims were very much part of the local financial elite, holding an important

in trade between the cities and their hinterlands, which often took the form of petty trade or peddling. Put differently, Muslims continued to control trade and commerce in inland cities such as Damascus, Aleppo, Homs, or Nablus, which was primarily local or internal, whereas local non-Muslims and resident foreigners played a conspicuous role in the commercial activity of port cities (Istanbul, Salonica, Izmir, Alexandretta [İskenderun], Beirut, Tunis, or Alexandria), which was largely long distance and international. In the same way, small-scale finance generally remained in the hands of local Muslims, whereas local non-Muslims and foreigners figured prominently in large-scale and high-profit banking and finance.

Two factors may help to explain the extraordinary role of non-Muslims, both local and foreign, in European trade and commerce as well as in the economy more generally, one cultural, the other social and occupational (and again, both are to a certain extent connected). When and where they existed, religious sympathies and cultural affinities tended to facilitate contacts between local non-Muslims (Christians for obvious reasons more so than Jews) and European merchants, diplomats, and missionaries. As a rule, European consuls and commercial agents preferred non-Muslims, more specifically Christians, to Muslims as their partners, agents, and employees.[46] Muslims, in their turn, were generally more reluctant to enter into close business relationships with Europeans (although not with local non-Muslims) or to be employed by their consulates or embassies. The decisive matter was not so much that Maronites, Armenians, or the "Greek" Orthodox felt attracted to France, Britain, or Russia or that the French, British, or Russians acted out of sympathy with their fellow Christians in the East—they rarely did. Mutual dislike and negative stereotypes were in fact quite pronounced. But local non-Muslims

---

share of the trade with Europe. The same applies not only to Homs, Hama (Reilly 1996 and 2002), and Aleppo (Sluglett 2002), but also to Fez, whose Muslim merchants in the late nineteenth century controlled much of Moroccan international trade (Cigar 1981), and to the cities of Qajar Iran.

46. Philipp (1994) indicates that, to the extent that it existed between Catholic Frenchmen and Oriental Christians, religious sympathy did not necessarily influence commercial and diplomatic relations. As Al-Qattan puts it so well, the business of money tends to be "blind to the color of religious affiliation" (1992, 207).

had a great deal to gain from association with an outside power that offered them important legal and fiscal privileges, providing them with "escape routes from *dhimmi* status" (Marcus 1989, 45). To the Europeans, local non-Muslims could be eminently useful: they knew the local markets, they spoke the languages required, and they had the necessary contacts at both ends of the exchange (Halliday 1992).

Languages and managerial skills were of utmost importance in this context, and they grew with the expansion and modernization of education that was so characteristic of nineteenth-century reform in the Ottoman Empire, Egypt, North Africa, and, albeit to a lesser extent, in Iran. As far as non-Muslims were concerned, expanded education was closely related to European, and later also American, missionary and educational efforts, which were marked by intense competition among the various churches, governments, and nations.[47] Catholic (mostly French and Italian) missions dated back to the Middle Ages and took renewed force during the Reformation; the Maronite college in Rome had been founded in 1584. Muslims, who were not only restrained by cultural sentiments and political loyalties, but also by the severe sanctions placed on conversion from Islam, offered little hope of success to the missionaries.[48] Hence, their efforts were mostly directed at local Christians and Jews, leading to the formation of new Catholic and Protestant churches, greatly to the dismay of the older communities from whom they had split; some of these churches were later recognized as separate millets by the Sublime Porte (Masters 2001).

From the early eighteenth century, missionary influence gradually expanded, spreading from local Catholics and Uniate churches in Lebanon and Syria to other Christian denominations as well as to the Jews. American Protestants opened their first missionary school in Lebanon in 1834 and in Egypt in 1854. Institutions of higher learning followed suit: Robert College

47. In addition to Somel 2001, Fortna 2002, and Courbage and Fargues 1997, see the case studies by Deguilhem 1998, Tibawi 1966, Labaki 1988, and Georgelin 2005. For religious and educational renewal among Egyptian Copts, see Reiss 1998. For Iran, see Stümpel-Hatami 1996, 67–80; and Sanasarian 2000, ch. 1. Waterfield 1973 offers a church perspective.

48. See Peters and de Vries 1976–77; for practical applications, see Gervers and Bikhazi 1990 and García-Arenal 2002. In the Ottoman Empire, capital punishment for apostasy was abolished as part of the Tanzimat reforms, but there still remained disabilities in civil law, concerning notably legacies, testaments, and inheritance from which apostates were excluded.

was founded in 1863, the Syrian Protestant College (later the American University of Beirut) in 1866, and the Catholic Université Saint-Joseph in 1875. Education on modern lines was by no means restricted to foreign missionary schools (which frequently held the additional attraction of giving free tuition), but was offered by foreign secular institutions, communal notables and, last but not least, the Ottoman state.

Although for some time Jews lagged behind, educational change became increasingly noticeable among them as well.[49] In the first half of the century, most local Jews had had little formal education. From the 1860s on, Jewish education in the Maghreb, Egypt, the Levant, and Iraq was gradually transformed from traditional methods of religious instruction (local equivalents of the Ashkenazi *heder, talmud torah, yeshiva*) into a modern system adapted to European, notably French, standards, which was specifically designed for oriental Jews. An important role was played by the Alliance Israélite Universelle, founded in 1860, which propagated a secular outlook inspired by French culture and therefore met with some resistance on the part of Jewish religious circles and the general public.[50] After World War I, only the poor or the observant still sent their children to inexpensive community schools. The middle and upper classes (and this holds true not only for Jews and Christians, but also for many Muslims) preferred to send their children, including a growing number of girls, to foreign private schools, many of them actually run by Catholic or Protestant missionaries. Nevertheless, it is important to bear in mind that the large majority of local non-Muslims remained illiterate.

The combined weight of religion, education, and language played an important part in the rise of the non-Muslims in the changing regional economy of the nineteenth and early twentieth centuries. Great importance came to be attached to appropriate skills, experience, and networks: local Christians and Jews had been traditionally involved (often in sharp competition with one another) in those trades and occupations that were most needed in

---

49. For modernized Jewish education and its sociocultural effects, see H. Cohen 1973, ch. 4; Stillman 1991; Levy 1994; and H. Goldberg 1996. For Iran, see Nikbakht 2002.

50. On the Alliance Israélite Universelle, see Chouraqui 1965, Marmorstein 1969, Laskier 1983, and Rodrigue 1990; also Karmi 1984, ch. 5.

the expansion of finance, commerce, and industry: money changing, money lending, usury, pawnbroking, and so on, which blended into modern forms of banking, administrative and clerical work both in the expanding state bureaucracies and in private business as well as some of the liberal professions (Findley 1982; Krikorian 1977).

All over the Middle East, Armenians, Greeks, and Jews had acted as money changers, money lenders, brokers, and bankers on a local and regional level, not necessarily involving transactions with European partners. The case of the Syrian Jewish Farhi family serves to illustrate the ups and downs of their status and fortune as well as the transition from premodern to modern forms of credit and finance (Philipp 1984a; Bouchain 1996).[51] In the Ottoman capital, Armenians and Jews emerged as powerful financiers (known as "Galata bankers" after the residential quarter where they lived) increasingly trying to shape urban structures and politics as well. There were families such as Sassoon and Kadoorie (Kedourie) in Baghdad (and Shanghai and Hong Kong), Farhi in Damascus or Busnach and Bacri in Algiers who had acquired wealth and status as traders, money lenders and bankers in the eighteenth century and who were able to secure their position in the course of the nineteenth. Others such as Sursuq (Sursock) and Bustros in Beirut and Alexandria, or Cattaoui, Mosseri, and de Menasce in Cairo gradually moved from fairly humble beginnings in trade or money changing to more profitable and prestigious positions in commerce and banking, ultimately leading to positions of great wealth, status, and influence within their respective communities, if not local society as a whole. There were also the "rags-to-riches" stories described by Reid (1970). Toward the end of the nineteenth century, family businesses became increasingly diversified. Investment in land and real estate, infrastructure, construction, and, although to a lesser extent, industry were added to banking and trading. The web of business contacts tying together individuals and families from various ethnic and

51. A study of the Armenian Dadian family illustrates the social and cultural aspects of nineteenth-century reform and change; Ter Minassian 1995. For the Galata bankers, see Rosenthal 1980a and Seni 1994; for the Sassoon family, Deshen 1994; for Bacri and Busnach, Kortepeter 1994; for Sursuq and Bustros, Fawaz 1983, 89–95; for Cattaoui, Mosseri, and de Menasce, Krämer 1989, ch. 2; and Ilbert 1996, vol. 1, ch. 5; for the Jewish merchant families of Morocco, Schroeter 1988, 34–50.

religious backgrounds was reinforced by intermarriage, creating strong links within the individual ethnic and religious groups and, to a certain extent, even among them (Collins 1984, 44–57, 128–31; Tignor 1980).

*Internal Differentiation*

Even before the nineteenth century, Christian and Jewish communities in the Middle East had been stratified, hierarchical, and decidedly status-conscious: culturally, however, they had been relatively homogeneous, if one leaves aside the fine distinctions of rite and language characteristic of Ottoman Jewry and the Rum Orthodox Church. Socioeconomic and cultural change, reinforced by large-scale migration to the urban centers, deepened existing cleavages and created new status groups. Social differentiation was reflected in a growing diversity of lifestyles, education, language, culture, nationality, and, as a result, identity. Socioeconomic change and demographic growth also modified power relations within the various communities, as a new commercial and professional middle class began to challenge the dominance of the clergy and the local notables.[52]

After 1856, communal councils (*meclis-i milli, majlis milli*) were established in most cities of the Ottoman Empire and began to work, with greater energy, for social and educational reform, better housing, the rehabilitation of decaying living areas, and better care of the poor in general. The urban poor are frequently ignored in the literature, as attention remains focused on the cosmopolitan notables and the polyglot middle class whose economic interest and cultural outlook connected them to and identified them with the modern sectors of the economy and to Europe. But alongside them there remained this lower class, more or less assimilated to local custom, speaking a local dialect that did not necessarily identify them as non-Muslims, sharing the same material culture, eating the same food, celebrating the same festivals, and adhering, by and large, to the same social and cultural values as their Muslim neighbors and compatriots. Not surprisingly, we know little about the quality and intensity of daily contacts and relations between Muslims and non-Muslims outside the spheres of economics and religion. What we do know is that poverty,

52. See the contributions by Barsoumian on the Armenians (1982) and Clogg on the Rum/Greek Orthodox (1982); for Egyptian Copts, see Atiya 1968, 104ff; for Egyptian Jews, see Krämer 1989; for Istanbul Jews, Levy 1994 and Karmi 1984.

illiteracy, and bad health often made the poor dependent on the charity of the community or their wealthy coreligionists, reinforcing vertical loyalties, and tying them to their richer coreligionists rather than to their Muslim (or Christian, Jewish, and Zoroastrian) neighbors.

Although it is difficult to obtain precise figures on the social composition of Middle Eastern non-Muslim minorities, particularly the Christians, there are some features characterizing Jewish communities from San'a' to Istanbul and Izmir, and from Baghdad to Damascus and Cairo.[53] Detailed data from Egypt after 1918 yield similar results (Krämer 1989, 14f, 52ff): In Cairo and Alexandria, the lower class may have constituted up to 25 percent of some 75,000 Jews living there. As a rule, they had little formal education and were mostly engaged in small-scale trade and various crafts; a significant part was without regular income or openly unemployed, and quite a few lived off begging. The lower and upper middle classes together amounted to some 65 percent of Egyptian Jewry, comprising an estimated 15 percent employees, 15 percent craftsmen, at least 30 percent merchants and commercial agents, and about 5 percent professionals. At the top there stood a small but very wealthy upper class of bankers, import-export merchants, landowners, entrepreneurs, and managers, comprising between 5 and 10 percent of the community, among whom a limited, and almost closed, circle of Sephardi families acted as a kind of Jewish aristocracy. It was this affluent, educated, and cosmopolitan middle and upper class, which exerted considerable influence on the local economy, that shaped the image of Egyptian Jewry as a whole. Wealth, which in most cases was accumulated and invested locally, constituted the single most important factor of upward social mobility. Technical, managerial, and language skills in some cases offered alternative routes of advancement, and both were to a certain extent correlated with regional or ethnic origin and cultural orientation.

*Urban Residence*

The domain where growing social differentiation was most visibly expressed was residence. From the mid–nineteenth century, migration within cities

---

53. For Istanbul and Ottoman Turkey in general, see Weiker 1992, Karmi 1984, and Dumont 1982; for Baghdad, Deshen 1994 and Dumont 1992; for Damascus, Frankel 1997, especially ch. 3; for San'a', Serjeant and Lewcock 1983, 394ff.

was as a rule voluntary, following individual choice and preference, rather than being caused by political pressure or general insecurity. Of course, it was not that security ceased to matter or that dispersal was irreversible. Twentieth-century Beirut provides striking proof that even at an advanced stage of modernization, and indeed very much as a result of it, ethnic groups could choose to relocate in segregated areas, or be forced to do so. What Khalaf and Khoury (1993, ch. 2) called the "territorialization of identity" and what could equally be described as a "confessionalization of space" in fact continued well established patterns of expansion and contraction, or flux and reflux. Demographic growth and socioeconomic advancement, with the greater affluence that resulted from it, led first and foremost to structural change and greater population density within existing quarters and neighborhoods, which, as has been repeatedly stressed, need not date back very long. (To make matters more complicated, place names tend to linger, and the fact that a quarter was called "Armenian" or "Greek" or "Jewish" did not necessarily imply that Armenians, Greeks, or Jews were still in a majority there.)

In the Jewish and Christian quarters of Damascus, a number of large houses were built in the second half of the nineteenth century, especially in the Christian quarter of Bab Tuma (Sack 1989, 37, 41ff, 72–80). Some of this construction documented intensified missionary and religious activity that surged after the Ottoman reform edict of 1839. Almost all churches and related buildings, such as monasteries, seminaries, and schools, seem to date from the late nineteenth and early twentieth centuries, when the previous restrictions had been abolished and when, under the special protection of the Ottoman governor, Christians were able to acquire extensive urban property. In Baghdad, the Jewish quarter expanded vastly in the course of the nineteenth century, chiefly as a result of large-scale migration of Jews from rural Kurdish areas as well as from Iran and Syria (Deshen 1994; Golany 1994). High density and expansion were accompanied by migration toward districts that were either more modern, having only been established in the nineteenth century (this usually involved the wealthier strata), or adjacent to the previous living area or quarter (mostly caused by demographic pressure and involving the middle and lower strata as well). For obvious reasons, the two cannot always be readily distinguished.

Migration within the city removed large sections of the middle and upper classes physically and culturally from their poorer coreligionists, who continued to live in predominantly Christian or Jewish neighborhoods, grouped around their respective churches, monasteries, or synagogues. While clustering along ethnic and religious lines often persisted in the new residential areas, even if only in individual buildings, the composition of neighborhoods tended to reflect social stratification rather than ethnic or religious origin. Most writers have emphasized the break-up of ethnic quarters as part of a "movement towards a new social organisation based on socio-economic class status" (Greenshields 1980, 130),[54] weakening the link between kinship and residence particularly among the elites.

New towns or quarters created by the European colonial powers in the late nineteenth and early twentieth centuries for their own nationals and parts of the local "foreign" minorities provide a special case. Examples include the "dual cities" of Morocco (for example, Fez, Marrakesh, or Rabat) that were specifically created not only in order to preserve the historical "Arab" or "Muslim" cities intact, but also to separate the colonizers from the colonized. Janet Abu-Lughod (1980) went so far as to describe the guiding principle as "urban apartheid".[55] In other places such as Cairo, Alexandria, Tunis, or Tehran, the boundary between the historic city (*madina, kasba*) and the modern quarters heavily influenced by European tastes and inhabited predominantly by Europeans and local foreign minorities was less obvious. In a number of cases, the modern city cut deeply into the historical core (Algiers, Baghdad, or Istanbul), whereas in Beirut or Kuwait the old city was completely destroyed. Modern European concepts of urban planning and architectural style were not restricted to the new towns and urban quarters largely built by and for Europeans or those parts of the local population most closely tied to them. They were also reflected in the ultimate goals of the Tanzimat reformers, soon to be followed by the rulers of Iran, who aimed at replacing what

54. Baer 1969, 216–18, and Zubaida 1989, 69, support this view. Yazbak's study of nineteenth-century Haifa (1998) shows (especially chs. 4 and 6) that the trend was by no means universal and that at least in this Palestinian coastal town, "sectarian" clustering remained strong.

55. The following is based on Blake and Lawless 1980, 178ff, and *Revue du monde musulman et de la Méditerranée* 73–74 (1994). For Fez, see Escher and Wirth 1992, 41–56, 80f; for Tunis, Santelli 1995. For Cairo, where this process can be observed in great detail, see Raymond 1993 and Scharabi 1989, 50ff.

they saw as urban chaos and anarchy by order, hygiene, and beauty, eventually leading to dramatic changes in urban planning, architecture, and building techniques.[56]

Sociocultural differentiation, migration, and the weakening of ethnic clustering can be illustrated particularly well by looking at Cairo, and once again, the process is best documented with regard to local Jews.[57] Until the mid–nineteenth century, most Jews had lived in the "Jewish quarter" of Cairo, the *harat al-yahud*, situated in the Bab al- Sha'riyya quarter that was part of the historical core of the city. The more prosperous families lived in large courtyard houses (*hawsh*), which combined living and work areas, the poorer families in crowded rented apartments. Only a few families remained in Old Cairo (*misr al-qadima*), where the Jewish cemetery was located. The Jewish quarter was no ghetto, for residential concentration was entirely voluntary, but it offered its inhabitants protection and allowed them to lead a traditional Jewish life. In the late 1860s, individual members of the old Sephardi families began to leave the *hara* to settle in areas to the west and north of the old city, where Muhammad 'Ali and his successors had encouraged the elite to build and settle.[58]

In the years preceding World War I, some of these residential areas such as 'Abbasiyya or Isma'iliyya lost their exclusive character and became

56. The best example is the Ottoman capital itself; see Rosenthal 1980a, Çelik 1993, and Barillari and Godoli 1996; also Panzac 1991, 1:97–120, and Dumont and Georgeon 1992. For the Ottoman Arab provinces, see Hanssen, Philipp, and Weber 2002. Inspired by the examples of Paris and Istanbul, Nasir al-Din Shah ordered extensive construction and development on "modern" lines in Tehran in 1867. See Adle and Hourcade 1992.

57. For what follows, see Krämer 1989, 62–67. For ethnic quarters in the medieval period, see Goitein 1971, 2:289–99; Behrens-Abouseif 1986, Denoix 1992, 81–91; and Sayyid 1998, 178–90. For the *harat* in Ottoman Cairo, see N. Hanna 1991, 160–66. Under the French, most *hara* gates were destroyed in order to be able to better control the quarters and their inhabitants, and the city was divided into new administrative units (*aqsam*, sing. *qism*). However, neighborhoods dominated by certain ethnic or religious groups continued to exist, and some of the gates were restored in later periods. For the Muhammad 'Ali period, see Alleaume and Fargues 1998 and Ibrahim 1992.

58. See Scharabi 1989, 51f, 56; for a map of the residential distribution of ethnic minorities in 1877, see 75; for a ranking of quarters according to the social status, income, nationality, and religion of their inhabitants, see Collins 1984, 128 and appendices, using data from 1882 and 1894.

middle-class neighborhoods; the upper class then moved into newly developed quarters along the Nile, notably Zamalik, Garden City, Roda (al-Rawda), Giza, Ma'adi or Heliopolis, where they constructed spacious villas in Ottoman revival style (Raafat 1994; Ilbert 1981, ch. 5). From the late nineteenth century, the wealthy families were followed by the middle class. Upward social mobility among the lower and lower-middle classes was generally reflected in a move from the *hara* to lower-middle class areas that were inhabited by large numbers of non-Muslims such as Sakakini (including Daher), Bulaq, Bab al-Luq, and 'Abidin. Those who rose even further in status moved on to more prestigious areas such as 'Abbasiyya, Azbakiyya, Isma'iliyya, and Heliopolis, where other minorities and foreigners lived. Needless to say their move was part of a wider phenomenon, involving Muslims as well as non-Muslims. In his study of the Egyptian elite under Cromer (1893–1907), where he also analyzed urban property, Collins (1984, 87, 115) registered a massive flow of wealth and power from Muslims to foreigners, foreign protégés, and minorities, which he considered to be one of the most profound changes in Egyptian urban society during this period.

## Conflict and Cooperation

Within the Ottoman Empire and Egypt, the abolition of the *jizya* and the declaration of legal equality between Muslims and non-Muslims signaled an end to traditional notions of superiority, submission, and protection (*dhimma*), which for centuries had ruled their relations. Non-Muslims were free to leave their traditional enclaves where they had previously existed and to enter spheres from which they had formerly been excluded. Physical boundaries were largely removed, and social space opened up. Improved legal status and economic success filled non-Muslims with a new sense of confidence and security, expressed in all kinds of ways. Most non-Muslims abandoned the distinctive garb they had previously worn, or been obliged to wear, and dressed according to modern Ottoman or European fashion; they no longer stepped down from the pavement when a Muslim came along; the rich built sumptuous houses for themselves like other members of their class, flaunting their wealth rather than hiding it. In short: non-Muslims moved out of place, and many Muslims resented it, particularly since this move was so obviously related to European influence and intervention.

Of course, the social boundaries rooted in traditional legal and religious notions that were, by and large, recognized by all Middle Easterners, did not fade away easily. As a rule, people remained perfectly aware of where "the other" was to be "placed" and which religious or ethnic group he or she belonged to, and ethnic affiliation continued to matter to urban life. The Tanzimat preserved the millets as frameworks of reference, identity and, from time to time, also of collective action, offering solidarity and services and thereby creating and demanding loyalties. Even among the cosmopolitan elites, who were less dependent on communal institutions than their poorer coreligionists, the "vertical" element of religious and ethnic identification was never fully supplanted by the "horizontal" element of class. Case studies from various places, no matter how cosmopolitan, point to the underlying sense of ambivalence and the subtle (and sometimes not so subtle) interplay of cooperation and conflict that characterized intercommunal relations throughout the period—and beyond. On one hand, physical and social spaces where Muslims and non-Muslims could meet, mix, and associate were greatly expanded beyond the realm of economics where they had always interacted and often cooperated. For the middle and upper classes, European-style clubs, coffee houses, and restaurants offered new forms and venues of sociability; theaters, opera houses, music halls, and cabarets provided new kinds of entertainment; literary, musical, and cultural circles brought together men (and even some women) from different walks of life; the press created a new media of expression and information. Like Muslims, non-Muslims took an active interest in the revival of the Arabic language and literature which became known as the Arab renaissance or awakening (*nahda*).[59]

On the other hand, closer contact also exposed deep-seated anxieties and animosities among all parties concerned. This was not merely a matter of "false

59. For the debate on the contribution of Arab Christians to the *nahda*, which earlier research had rated very highly, and which now seems to have been somewhat exaggerated, see, e.g., Khalidi et al. 1991. For various facets of urban conviviality, see notably Georgeon and Dumont 1997. Case studies serve as a reminder that the mega-trend of socioeconomic change and legal emancipation affected different localities, groups and individuals in a highly uneven manner and that social status was extremely important in providing opportunities for interaction, and in the formation of self-views and perceptions; see, e.g., Sulayman 2001.

consciousness," to use a vulgarized Marxist concept, masking the real issues: class struggle or competition over status and socioeconomic resources more generally, though competition over resources did, of course, play a role in this context. Anxiety and animosity mostly remained latent or confined to an inter-personal level, but they could also flare up in collective violence. It is significant that several of the worst incidents occurred in mid-nineteenth-century Aleppo (1850) and Damascus (1860), which at that time were becoming integrated into the new economic circuit dominated by Europe. Since local foreign-protected non-Muslims were highly conspicuous in supplying credit at rates of interest that were often ruinous to both urban dwellers and farmers, they were widely held responsible for rural indebtedness. But what the protesters resented just as much was an unprecedented Christian presence in the public sphere: they resented the renovated churches, the ringing of bells, and all kinds of manifestations of newly acquired wealth and status: non-Muslims, particularly Christians, were visibly overstepping the limits set by custom and religion.[60] The most dramatic incident with the widest impact was the Damascus massacre of July 1860 that, among an estimated population of 10,000–12,000 Christians, left several thousand dead (realistic figures are in the range of 2,000–5,000), causing massive destruction in the Christian quarter of Bab Tuma.[61] The violence fed on present grievances and age-old religious stereotypes; it expressed the worn-out charges of "osten-tation" and "arrogance," and it followed established patterns. Tension and dis-satisfaction with the existing state of affairs had previously been deflected onto local non-Muslims, and in a recurring pattern, fear of foreign invasion, anger over rising prices, or resentment of government injustice had been vented on Christians or Jews living among the Muslim population. But it must be empha-sized that this was not a religious war against local non-Muslims (the Jews and

60. In spite of intensive study, the nature and assessment of these events still remain dis-puted; see notably Reilly 1996, 219–21; Masters 1990 and 2001, ch. 5; Harel 1998; Yazbak 1998, ch. 6, and note 61 below.

61. The narrative is based on Fawaz 1994, chs. 4 and 6; Schatkowski Schilcher 1985, 87–100; and 'A. Hanna 1985, 235–75. Ghazzal 1993, 54f, 162f, stresses the strong hostility felt by local Muslims toward local Christians in the 1840s. In this context, Burke (1989, 48) has spoken of acts of "ritual violence"; for a specific incident, see Olson 1977, 198–210. In his study of rural Lebanon, Makdisi (2000), questions the existence of sectarianism before the impact of colonialism and the advent of the modern state.

poorer Christians living in the Maidan quarter were left unmolested and quite a few of their Druze and Muslim neighbors, including prominent notables, offered the victims protection). The same is true of the Alexandria riots of June 1882, which served as the pretext for British military intervention (Ilbert 1992, 1:211–32; Reimer 1997, 171–82; Schölch 1972; Cole 1993).

Mistrust, competition, and religious prejudice not only marked relations between Muslims and non-Muslims but also among the various Christian denominations, and between Christians and Jews. Indeed, it is much more useful to think of intercommunal relations (at least outside the Maghreb and the Arabian Peninsula, where the number of local Christians was insignificant) not in terms of a binary Muslim/non-Muslim relationship but of multiple relationships among (various groups of) Muslims, Christians, Jews, or Zoroastrians allowing for considerable variation over time and place.[62] Intra-Christian friction in itself was by no means new. It was exacerbated by the activities of Catholic and Protestant missionaries that led to the establishment and sociopolitical rise of new churches, weakening the older, mostly orthodox Christian communities of the Middle East. Christian-Jewish animosity, deeply rooted in religious prejudice, was intensified by Christian resentment of the emancipation of the Jews who previously had been considered socially inferior to them, and it was aggravated by economic competition. It is interesting to note that while the dislike was indeed mutual, in virtually all instances of overt tension the Christians appear as the active party, with local Jews trying to maintain their low profile or at the most to stage defensive action. The series of ritual murder or "blood libel" accusations launched by local Christians (often actively supported by European consuls, teachers, and missionaries) against local Jews, of which the so-called Damascus Affair of 1840 was only the most notorious, illustrate this point.[63] Intercommunal tensions and apprehensions

62. The point is very well illustrated with regard to the Christian communities in eighteenth- and nineteenth-century Aleppo; see Masters 2001, chs. 4–6. Students of Ottoman Jewry have emphasized the loyalty of Ottoman Jews to the state, especially in the face of Christian abuse and aggression; see Levy 1994, 108–12, 121–23; and Karmi 1984, 48–56. For Ottoman loyalty and tensions between local Greeks and Jews in Izmir, see Nahum 1997, chs. 4 and 5.

63. For ritual murder accusations in the Ottoman Empire, see Karmi 1984, 16–18, on Istanbul; Frankel 1997 on Damascus; and Dumont 1992 on Baghdad. For Egypt, see Landau

made people resort to or reactivate well-established strategies of communal mobilization for self-defense.

The social rise of local non-Muslims, or rather of their recomposed middle and upper classes, was possible because the precolonial "ethnic division of labor" had never been rigid, because legal emancipation freed them of previous disabilities, and because the European powers granted them protection. Their role as intermediaries in the economic as well as the cultural and linguistic spheres, and their function as channels, buffers, or filters of change, made it easier for non-Muslims to attain status and wealth (Davison 1982). But this process was accompanied by a process of marginalization that assimilated all non-Muslims, no matter whether indigenous or immigrant, to foreign interests. Seen in historical perspective, the link between confessional and political affiliation, real or presumed, was by no means new, nor was it confined to relations between Muslims and non-Muslims: the treatment of Shi'i Muslims in the Ottoman Empire and of Sunnis in the Safavid domains had followed the same logic. Egyptian Copts certainly did not all benefit from European rule, and among the "local foreign minorities" there were many individuals who were neither of foreign origin nor had access to foreign protection. Nor could the non-Muslim commercial and financial elites in their entirety be classified as a "comprador bourgeoisie," as much of their wealth was not only accumulated locally, but also invested in the local or the regional economy (Kasaba 1988, 114f).

Still, as in other societies at other times, perceptions often mattered more than facts: local non-Muslims were widely seen as protégés of the European powers and the main beneficiaries of an economic restructuring that cost the Ottoman (Egyptian, Moroccan, Iranian) state its control over national resources and many craftsmen and traders their jobs and income. Their socioeconomic role exposed the minorities as dependents—no longer of the Muslim rulers or notables but of the colonial powers and the colonial system as a whole. One form of vulnerability was thus exchanged for another. After World War I, non-Muslims lost much of their previous utility. Mediation in economic

---

1973 and Krämer 1989, 60, 62, 113, 225, and 228f. For a sophisticated analysis of another incident in Alexandria, see Ilbert 1987, 1992.

and cultural terms was either discredited because of its close link to the colonial system or contested by a rising Muslim middle class aspiring to the same place and functions that had been assumed by non-Muslims in the course of the nineteenth century. The dangers of marginalization became fully apparent after the fall of the Ottoman Empire and the gradual formation of separate states on its former territory, and they were profoundly impressed on the fabric of urban history.[64]

64. Tempting as it is, the larger issues of modernity and the rise of an indigenous (transcommunal and nonsectarian) middle class in the early twentieth century cannot be addressed here; for valuable recent additions to the debate, see Hanssen 2005 and Watenpaugh 2006.

# 8

# Urban Social Movements,
# 1750–1950

## SAMI ZUBAIDA

➤ IN BROAD OUTLINE, a pattern of urban politics can be discerned in the major cities of the Ottoman Empire in the eighteenth century, with continuities into the nineteenth in most of them. Popular movements, protests, riots, and rebellions are best considered in the context of the urban politics of that period. Toward the end of the nineteenth and the beginning of the twentieth centuries, a gradual transformation in the forms and frameworks of urban (and now "national") politics took place, which also transformed the forms of popular organization and mobilization. We witness the emergence of *modern* politics, a concept that will be elaborated further below. This chapter is organized around this emergence of modernity, first examining the old patterns of urban politics and popular movements and then defining political modernity in terms of the newly emerging patterns.

### "Traditional" Urban Politics

Who are the main actors on the urban political scene? What are their sources of power and what are the stakes and issues of contention? The rulers of the Ottoman city were the military classes, *askaris*. At the top of the hierarchy was the pasha, the centrally appointed governor, with his personal retinue of soldiers and functionaries. Usually appointed for one year (though a number of individuals held office for both shorter and longer periods), his primary concern was to try to extract as much revenue as possible (partly to recoup the investment he had made to acquire the office and to make a profit and partly to remit revenues to the central treasury in Istanbul) and to maintain order and allegiance to his lord, the sultan. The janissary regiments were another regular military power in most Ottoman cities, known in Egypt as *ocak*s, with their commanders, usually called *agha*s. These forces played different roles in different cities at various times. They became particularly important at times of crises and instability, when they assumed greater control and almost arbitrary powers, as we shall see in the case of Aleppo in the 1780s and 1790s. In Istanbul and many other cities, the janissaries had particularly intimate connections with the urban population, especially the craft guilds.[1] A janissary regiment would often attach itself to a particular guild as partner and protector, and some of the men would actually enroll as practitioners of the craft, which did not leave much time or inclination for soldiering. In some cities, such as Aleppo and Cairo, the *ocak*s were divided between those who were long established and almost native to the city and those who were stationed there on a tour of duty. The former, naturally, tended to form long-term attachments to the guilds, though, at times, many other soldiers attempted to impose their "partnership" on tradesmen (al-Jabarti n.d., 1:633–34).

Mamluks were another category in the military power elites of Ottoman cities, most notably in Egypt during our period, but also in Iraq and Syria. In eighteenth-century Cairo the Mamluk amirs (with the title of beg or bey) were the virtual rulers, deploying large numbers of well trained and disciplined men, and benefiting from wide networks of influence and alliances with local notables and urban strata. There were rivalries, however, between Mamluk households, each around an amir and his slaves and freedmen, controlling vast sources of revenue from rural tax farms, taxes on urban trade, and sundry exactions. They also traded and often established monopolies in various commodities.[2]

The nonmilitary components of the urban elites consisted of the local urban notables, in varying patterns of affiliation to the politico-military

1. For the organization of Ottoman provincial government in the "classical age," see Kunt 1983.

2. On Mamluk organization and politics in Egypt, see Hathaway 1997, especially ch. 3. For Syria, see Grehan 2003; for Iraq, see Lier 2004.

rulers. The elite ulama (that is, not the general run of ulama), the *mashayikh*, heads of Sufi *turuq* (orders), the *ashraf* (descendants of the Prophet) all derived their status from their religious rank, fortified with personal wealth, endowments, tax farms, and networks of kinship and patronage. Positions of leadership were often kept and passed on within notable families, for example, the office of *naqib al-ashraf,* or of *mufti* (Marcus 1989, 56–63; Thieck 1985, 117–68). Similarly, the shaykhs of Sufi *turuq* were often either the real or eponymous descendants of the founder saint, making their offices also hereditary. Hence notability, wealth, endowments, and power tended to be concentrated in particular families. Merchant and ulama families overlapped, and the control exercised by the ulama over sectors of the urban economy forged links with merchants and landlords. Thus both religious and merchant elites participated in Hourani's "politics of notables." Formally, these notables were subservient to the imperial politicomilitary elites, but in practice, the latter, being for the most part alien to the city, and in the case of the pashas only enjoying short terms of office, became dependent on the local notables for effective rule. In many Iraqi and Syrian cities, some notable families were instrumental in the provisioning of the city with food from the surrounding rural hinterland.[3] As such they controlled vital levers of power, and the military elite had to work through them.

In Cairo, Mamluk households acted as the focus for political affiliations and factions, described by Hourani as "élites created by men possessing political or military power, composed of freedmen trained in the service of the current heads of the household, and held together by solidarity which would last a lifetime" (Hourani 1968). The various rival households formed a core surrounded by religious leaders, commanders of regiments, popular guilds, and the inhabitants of particular urban quarters. The Mamluk households were enmeshed within the urban fabric through their economic as well as politicomilitary power. They controlled tax farms, which were major sources of revenue, some of it in the form of agricultural goods in which they traded, often using their military powers to create monopolies in certain goods, to corner markets, and sometimes to coerce merchants to buy.[4]

---

3. See Hourani 1968, 41–68. On Iraqi cities, see Fattah 1997 and D. Khoury 1997a.

4. Hathaway 1997 deals extensively with the household of 'Ali Bey and his contemporaries.

Below these power elites there were various segments of the urban population, *ra'aya*, subject to political rule and fiscal exactions. Many were organized into corporate bodies, each a tax-paying unit. The craft guilds were so
organized, under a craft master, and the guilds determined conditions of work,
remuneration, supplies of raw materials, standards of work, and prices. These
elements were also subject to regulation by the judicial authorities (the *qadi* and
the *muhtasib*). Urban quarters, which were often separated from each other by
high, gated walls, had chiefs, *shaykh al-hara*, and occasionally organized gangs
of young men, *futuwwa*, constituted another corporate tax-paying unit. Organized quarters and neighborhoods were also units of collective responsibility
before the *qadi* for legal or moral infractions in their locality (Marcus 1989,
326–28). Christian and Jewish communities were also constituted as corporate tax-paying units, and as such were often the subject of the most severe
exactions, as we shall see.[5]

Having identified the main social components of the city, let us turn to
the dynamics that stimulated urban politics. These were primarily "material" considerations, to do with taxes and food. Pashas might pay considerable sums for their office (in the early nineteenth century, estimated at about
200,000 piasters, which they tried to recoup at a profit, often an enormous
one: thus 'Ali Pasha, expelled as governor of Aleppo in 1775 after only four
months in office, departed with 700,000 piasters, and some of his contemporaries did even better (Marcus 1989, 95–96). At the same time, lesser functionaries, officers, and soldiers were also trying to enrich themselves. In the
eighteenth century, the imperial treasury in Istanbul levied various regular
taxes, which were occasionally supplemented by extraordinary levies decreed
by the sultan. Governors and other officials imposed additional taxes and
exactions, sometimes for particular projects such as military campaigns to
subdue tribes. They also imposed fines and penalties on various groups for
real or fabricated infractions.

Religious minorities were often subjected to demands for money, usually
in the form of *'awn* or *avania*. Particularly outrageous impositions would be
made on Christians and Jews, such as restrictive dress codes, or, as in Cairo

5. Abdul-Karim Rafeq has emphasized the multiconfessional nature of many of the craft
guilds. See chapter 4 in this volume, and Rafeq 1991.

in the late eighteenth century, the obligation for all those named after bibli-
cal figures (prophets to Muslims) such as Abraham or Joseph, to change their
names (al-Jabarti n.d., 1:639). The order would be rescinded on the payment of
a negotiated (hard bargaining) sum to the governor and appropriate officials.
Lower officials and soldiers engaged in various extortions from vulnerable
individuals or from guilds and quarters. These exactions fell on all sectors of
the urban population, including the a'yan, notables, but the latter were better
placed to bargain and exert pressure. The mass of poorer urban dwellers suffered disproportionately, and under particularly rapacious pashas, such as 'Ali
Pasha in Aleppo, people could hardly earn enough to discharge all their ordinary and extraordinary tax burdens.

Food provisioning of the cities was another source of enrichment for the
official class. During times of scarcity of basic foods, governors, officials, and
janissaries manipulated prices by hoarding and controlling supplies to make
maximum profits while the urban population went hungry. Local merchants,
and even local ulama, were often complicit in these operations.[6]

These conflicts over revenues and provisions formed the basic framework
of urban politics: intraelite conflict over shares of the spoils, and conflicts
between elite and population over the volume of fiscal exactions and the price
of basic foods. Under normal circumstances intraelite conflict was managed
through bargaining, threats, and the balance of power between the parties.
The urban populations had few avenues of effective action, and under conditions of excessive fiscal oppression were for the most part quiescent: "But
only infrequently did the resentment break out in open political protest, and
then mostly in the form of small outbursts of despair rather than massive and
organized action" (Marcus 1989, 100). Marcus cites examples of these actions
in eighteenth-century Aleppo. Women occupied the minaret of the Great
Mosque in 1751, interrupting prayers and abusing the governor for inaction
on the famine. In 1778, crowds dragged the qadi to the governor's palace with
demands that the governor be executed for not alleviating food shortages. In
1787, women gathered in the courthouse and cursed the notables while the
qadi took refuge in the citadel. We shall presently consider further examples
from Cairo.

6. For the provisioning of Iraqi cities, see Fattah 1997.

There is a common view in the literature on Muslim cities that the notables, and particularly the ulama, acted as the leaders of public opinion, representing the grievances of the populace to the rulers, and under extreme conditions leading demonstrations and even riots in support of them.[7] This view has been convincingly challenged by Marcus and Baer for eighteenth-century Aleppo and Cairo. Marcus wrote that the local leaders "represented certain groups and clienteles, not the public in general. In exercising their influence they also exploited various segments of the population. They practiced the politics of hierarchy and subordination, not of consensus" (Marcus 1989, 101). This theme will be further elaborated in the discussion of Cairo politics.

There were occasions, however, when notables, ulama, and even janissaries did put themselves at the head of popular forces, although only when they were the main protagonists in the struggle, pursuing their own interests, and mobilizing popular discontent against the authorities as part of that process. Marcus (1989) and Thieck (1985) illustrate this very well in the context of the widespread disturbances in Aleppo in the last quarter of the eighteenth century. As mentioned earlier, a particularly extortionate governor, 'Ali Pasha, was expelled from the city in 1775. His exactions were directed against all sectors of the population, including the rich and powerful. His downfall, however, came only when he ordered the janissaries to march under his command on a campaign into the countryside to subdue the tribes. Their officers challenged his right to command them, and 'Ali Pasha backed down. They subsequently took advantage of his weakness to demand his departure, which they eventually forced with the support of a jubilant population: "As the expelled pasha rode to the outskirts thousands of triumphant residents, including many women, stood in the streets, jeering and spitting in contempt" (Marcus 1989, 88). Their joy did not last, however. The janissaries, at times in league with the *ashraf* (also armed), and at times in open conflict with them, made it impossible for any governor to rule effectively till the early nineteenth century. If

7. For instance, Ernest Gellner's model of "Muslim society" portrays urban communities led by the ulama with the rule of the sharia, separate from the rulers and skeptical about their legitimacy; see Gellner 1983, 54–56, 79–81. See also Zubaida 1995. This view is commonly held by Islamist and nationalist historians and sociologists; see, for instance, Sayf al-Din 'Abd al-Fattah Isma'il 1992.

anything, the rule of the janissaries was worse than that of the pashas, since they imposed on the population, rich and poor, ever more innovative exactions, fines, extortions, and manipulations of the food supply and prices. In the fights between the janissaries, their *ashraf* rivals and successive pashas, the urban population suffered increasing misery and insecurity, though sectors of the townsfolk were occasionally mobilized on one side or the other. Their force, however, was marginal to determining outcomes: it was the size of the armed groups that mattered.

Hence, in the case of eighteenth-century Aleppo, popular movements were limited to rare, sporadic, and short-lived riots. Some of the common people occasionally participated in fights between elite factions and governors. They never initiated these fights and were ultimately almost always the losers when the triumphant faction turned on them for further exactions. Let us now examine a number of interesting parallels and differences in the case of Cairo in the same epoch.

## Cairo

The picture of Cairo in the late eighteenth century emerging from studies such as those of Raymond (1968) and Baer (1977) reveals a high level of active popular dissent. The last quarter of the century saw disturbances and crises resulting from struggles between the main Mamluk factions, led by Murad and Ibrahim, and successive Ottoman pashas. The military formations of Mamluks, *ocaks* (janissaries), the pasha's forces, and sundry other groupings took different and sometimes shifting sides. In the process the urban population suffered arbitrary exactions and harassment and pillage by the soldiery. This period culminated in the invasion and occupation of Egypt by Napoleon in 1798, which lasted until 1800. Various acts of resistance and two revolts characterized this period, in which the urban population participated prominently. The factional strife between Mamluks, pashas, and different military formations continued after the departure of the French and culminated in 1805 in the investiture of Muhammad 'Ali as governor in preference to the incumbent pasha, which was ultimately ratified by the sultan. Sectors of the popular urban classes also participated in the struggles leading to this event. What do these episodes tell us about urban social movements at that time?

André Raymond (1968, 1973–74) gives a vivid picture of the popular quarters of Cairo in the eighteenth century, identifying the quarters inhabited by the popular classes in terms of their economic activity. They were often centered around trades related to food: abattoirs, butchers' markets, fruit and vegetable trades, tanneries, oil presses, and charcoal works. The neighborhoods of many of these trades were disdained by the bourgeoisie, whose living quarters were separate from them. The chronicler al-Jabarti expressed the bourgeoisie's prejudices and fears regarding these neighborhoods in the terms used to designate their inhabitants: *ahl al-hiraf al-safila, al-amma, al-nas al-dun,* and in their threatening aspects: *al-usab* (gangs), *al-shuttar* (louts), *al-ghawgha'* (the populace), *al-awbash* (criminals), *al-harafish* (the rabble). These quarters included al-Husayniyya, al-Rumayla, al-Hattaba, and al-Utuf, all outlying suburbs of the city, and as such were perceived as marginal or external, in al-Jabarti's terms *al-ahya' al-barraniyya* (Raymond 1968, 111). Like all city quarters, these were corporate entities, some with their own gates separating them from the outside and their own chief, the *shaykh al-hara,* with policing and leadership functions. The locational identity of these quarters was reinforced by their association with particular trades and corporations and particular Sufi *turuq.* Thus al-Husayniyya was dominated by the butchers' guild, which was associated with the Bayumiyya order. The greengrocers' corporation and the Rifa'iyya order were similarly associated with Rumayla. Gangs of young men defended the quarter against external threats, sometimes enforced the shaykh's orders within, and engaged in real or ceremonial fights with youths from other quarters.[8] It was these gangs that were feared in the disturbances and disorders which overtook the city in the late eighteenth and early nineteenth centuries.

In addition to these popular quarters, another element contributed to the popular manifestations of Cairene politics. This was the university/mosque of al-Azhar, and in particular its students. While the higher ulama, some of whom were professors at Azhar, generally avoided involvement in popular manifestations, the teachers at *kuttabs,* the imams and *khatibs* of small mosques, the

---

8. Najib Mahfuz's novel *Malhamat al-Harafish* (1977) presents a vivid picture of life and politics in the old urban quarters.

clerks of sharia courts, and sectors of the student body were often prominent participants in protests and revolts. This is the class described by al-Jabarti as *al-muta'ammimin*, the turbaned.

Raymond (1968, 119) distinguishes two periods of intense popular activity: 1675–1735, followed by a period of calm till about 1780 when agitation returned, continuing till 1805 when Muhammad 'Ali established firm control and ushered in a long period of effective repression. Raymond relates this periodization to economic fluctuations and fiscal oppression. The first period was one of food shortages, with prices fluctuating upward, accompanied by a progressive debasement of the currency. Typically, the crowds would gather at the foot of the citadel calling for measures to ameliorate shortages. Some would get out of control and attack and pillage grain stores and the surrounding shops. The authorities reacted sometimes with severe repression and sometimes with edicts regulating supplies and prices. al-Rumayla, near the citadel and grain stores, was often the center of these activities. In 1722, crowds rioting because of food shortages stoned the beys on their way to the *diwan*. A protracted series of protests and riots occurred in 1715 as a reaction to the pasha's attempt to introduce a new debased *para* and forbid the use of earlier coinage. This resulted in the closure of all the markets (often part of the disturbances, if not as a protest by the traders, then out of fear of popular anger). Despite retreats by the authorities, the situation did not return to normal for a month.

Raymond argues that popular activity in this early period resulted primarily from economic conjunctures, and it ceased during the subsequent decades of relative stability in food supply and prices. The second period of activity, later in the century, started with similar economic grievances but took on an increasingly political form, culminating in the revolts against the French occupation in 1798–1800, and in popular participation in the struggles leading to the installation of Muhammad 'Ali in 1805.

The context of this politicization was the system of despoilment/exaction/pillage set in motion by the Mamluk beys Ibrahim and Murad in the 1780s and the Ottoman attempt to remove these beys with popular support. The beys' exactions and open thefts affected many members of the bourgeoisie, including wealthy ulama, and a number of *awqaf* provisioning various categories of Azhar students (notably the blind). It followed that certain members of the bourgeoisie and ulama, their interests directly harmed by the pillage, put themselves at the head of popular movements against the beys. In 1786, the violent attack by one of Murad's Mamluks on a butcher, Ahmad Salim, who was also a shaykh of the Bayumiyya, occasioned a revolt in al-Husayniyya. The beys were obliged to negotiate with Shaykh al-Dardir, a prominent alim and patron of this order. The Cairenes were ultimately disappointed by the failure of the Ottoman attempt to subdue the beys, who resumed their pillage, and protest activity intensified. In 1787 merchants and craft guilds rebelled against a Mamluk attempt to raise a forced loan. Many similar incidents followed, in which the solidarities of guild/*tariqa*/quarter were instrumental. al-Azhar students rioted in 1777 and 1785 against attempts by Mamluk beys to deprive them of their *waqf* allocations (Baer 1977).

Hence the revolts of the latter decades of the eighteenth century were clearly linked to economic factors. However, the revolts became political to the extent that the grievances resulted from the oppressive exactions on the urban population carried out by Mamluk amirs. Inter-elite conflicts, between Mamluks, Ottoman pashas, and prominent bourgeois notables involved the popular classes in their struggles. In the revolts against the French, a further dimension, the religious, was superimposed on these two.

The revolts against the French, especially the one in 1800, saw a considerable degree of organization on the part of the popular classes. One feature was the building of barricades, with large numbers of insurgents sheltering behind them. The 1800 revolt was led by Ottoman units, which organized and directed popular militias. Each quarter contributed its own militia, and a gun factory was established in which local artisans were employed. Rich merchants contributed supplies (Baer 1977, 226–27). The struggle had the aspect of a Muslim or "native" war against the Christian invader (an aspect that will be elaborated below). Popular participation, reflecting, as it did, the solidarity of quarter, guild, and *tariqa*, was ultimately organized and directed by professional soldiers, but the events of 1805 can, perhaps, be seen to have thrown up a more autonomous popular leadership.

The context of the 1805 events was the struggle for power between the Ottoman pasha Ahmad Khurshid and Muhammad 'Ali, the leader of the Albanian Ottoman troops originally sent to fight the French, in which Mamluks, janissaries, and various military units participated. The inhabitants of Cairo had their own grievances against fiscal excesses as well as arbitrary oppression and pillage by soldiers. The pasha's edicts restraining the soldiers (issued after the mediation of al-Azhar ulama over the demands of popular demonstrations) were ignored. Subsequent popular agitations were increasingly well organized, involving, at one stage, a siege of the Citadel that prevented provisions from reaching it. Popular leaders emerged at the head of these agitations, such as Hajjaj al-Khudari, head of the greengrocers' guild in al-Rumayla, and Ibn Sham'a, the shaykh of the butchers (Raymond 1968, 116; Baer 1977, 241–42). Ultimately, the Porte acquiesced in Muhammad 'Ali's military superiority and sent a messenger nominating him as pasha. The messenger was welcomed by an enormous demonstration consisting mainly of popular masses and janissaries and headed by the two leaders. The same quarters and suburbs feature as the sources of popular movements: al-Husayniyya, al-Rumayla, al-Utuf, and so on. However, the triumph of Muhammad 'Ali and his consolidation of power saw a rapid return to calm and normality; the popular movements subsided, and their leaders were forgotten (Raymond 1968, 116).

### The Question of Political Modernity

The forms of politics described so far can be distinguished as "premodern." The question then arises as to the nature of political modernity. Michael Walzer characterized it in the following terms:

> A politics of conflict and competition for power, of faction, intrigue and open war is probably universal in human history. Not so a politics of party organisation and methodical activity, opposition and reform, radical ideology and revolution. . . . The detached appraisal of a going system, the programmatic expression of discontent and aspiration, the organisation of zealous men for sustained political activity: it is surely fair to say that these three together are aspects of the modern, that is, the post-medieval political world. (Walzer 1966, 1)

In *The Revolution of the Saints,* Walzer goes on to argue that the Calvinists of the English Civil War were the first to develop this form of politics. He goes on to specify the general conditions that make this form of politics possible: the separation of politics from the household, the appearance of free men (without masters), the rational and pragmatic consideration of political methods (as in Machiavelli), and, crucially, the rise of large-scale and inclusive political units, as in the modern state, beginning with the absolutist destruction of feudal seg-mentarity in Europe (Walzer 1966, 1).

In these terms, the forms of politics described so far are decidedly pre-modern. Interelite politics is clearly one of "conflict and competition for power, of faction, intrigue and open war." Solidarities are based on personal loyalties and patronage (as in Mamluk households), kinship, and, in the case of the popular classes, neighborhood, guilds, and *turuq*. Crucial to all these is a strong "materialism," an orientation toward economic interests. The ulti-mate stakes in practically all political struggles were revenues, and for the city population, food prices, fiscal oppression, and other arbitrary exactions. Popu-lar movements were generally spontaneous and short-lived, revolving around immediate grievances. As such, they were far from "sustained political activ-ity." The issues had nothing to do with reform or revolution of "the system"; such a concept would have been quite alien. Popular aspirations were always for the appearance of a just prince who would bring stability and security. It can be argued, then, that premodern politics was materialist and nonideologi-cal. Yet how can such an argument be sustained for a milieu that was evidently imbued with religious precepts?

Having traced the pattern of urban movements in several Arab cities in the nineteenth century, Burke concludes that riots did not consist of acts of aim-less violence, but were indeed directed against particular targets that were the locus of their grievances: "The burden of the foregoing," he states, "is that there was indeed a popular ideology of social protest in the Middle Eastern societies which centered upon the application of the sharia by a vigilant Muslim ruler" (Burke 1989, 47–48; cf. Grehan 2003). He goes on to enumerate the various economic provisions of the sharia whose application was demanded by the protesters, including restrictions on taxation and debasements of the coinage and the prohibition of usury.

There is no doubt that the demand for justice and for a just prince was at the center of popular protest. Notions of justice are inevitably religious and customary (the two not being always distinct in the popular, or even the learned, mind). Indeed, even in interelite conflicts one party would denounce the other as traitors or deviants from religious prescriptions (al-Jabarti n.d., 1:621–22). The language of righteousness and justice was intimately tied to religion, although this is not to say that there was a precise notion in the *sharia* of what actually constituted legal and illegal taxes and coinages. From the earliest times, Muslim rulers had levied taxes and other dues dictated by administrative fiat rather than canonical sanction, and the ulama and *fuqaha'* for the most part abstained from raising legal objections. The exceptions were situations of conflict, disorder, and crisis in which the weight of fiscal oppression, food prices, and plain pillage were regular features, and in which protests whether by ulama, rival princes, or the populace always laid their claim to justice in religious, that is, *shar'i,* terms. Religion and legality provided a *vocabulary* of demands and contests rather than a determinate notion of alternative political or legal orders. Burke and others have described these forms of contestation and opposition as "moral economy." The argument here is that it is best to regard this economy as a language of contestation rather than as a precise description of an existing or desired system.

Within this ideological sphere of contest, the existing system of rule is taken as given: the object is to make the prince just or to exchange him for a more just ruler. The only form of radical transformation envisaged is that of the end of time. Although messianic notions thrived in both Sunni and Shi'i Islam, they did not engender significant urban movements in the period under discussion, though they did in the rural and tribal hinterlands, as exemplified most notably by the Sudanese *Mahdiyya.*

Another religious element in urban social movements was the role of the ulama and the mosque. The mosque was the point of assembly and the locus of the expression of grievances for most demonstrations and protests, and the minarets the loci of public calls to action. The crowds almost always took their grievances first to prominent ulama and attempted to enlist them as leaders and spokesmen to convey their grievances to the princes. Naturally, this led many observers to suppose that the ulama were the leaders of the urban populace and their representatives before the authorities. As we have already intimated, this view has been strongly challenged by some writers on the subject, most notably for Egypt by Gabriel Baer.

Baer distinguishes between the high ulama, the teachers at al-Azhar, the holders of high office, and supervisors of large foundations and the lower ulama, clerks, *maktab* teachers, muezzins and imams at small mosques, and above all the students of al-Azhar (Baer 1977, 228–42). The lower ulama played a prominent part in popular movements and frequently led them. They were, however, regarded by the rulers and the bourgeoisie as part of the lower orders and not as intermediaries and representatives who had access to the ears of authority. These, and in particular the students, notably the blind students and their leaders, were prominent in many of the popular movements and events in the late eighteenth and early nineteenth centuries, including the risings against the French.

As for the high ulama, it is true that the populace, faced with fiscal oppression and famine, often resorted to them, particularly to the *Shaykh al-Azhar.* The responses of the ulama, however, with few exceptions, were seldom favorable. They were sometimes coerced by potentially violent crowds into leading processions to the Citadel and airing their grievances. Raymond (1999, 432–33) draws a typical scenario: the crowd proceeds to the Grand Mosque, occupies the minarets and calls for resistance, the calls accompanied by the beat of drums. They close the markets and the shops. They assemble in the forecourts and at the gates of the mosque and demand the presence of the shaykhs and their intervention with the authorities regarding their grievances. They proceed in a procession with the ulama at its head "more dead than alive." If a favorable response is obtained from the Citadel, then the ulama are nominated guarantors of its implementation. The people suspect that the ulama are in league with the authorities, and the authorities suspect them of stirring up the people. Naturally, the ulama tried, whenever they could, to distance themselves from this role. Their response was always to try and calm down any potential agitation, and if they failed, to avoid involvement. They naturally shared the attitudes of the authorities and the bourgeoisie, of fear and contempt of the lowly crowds. In addition, many of the higher ulama had close political and economic ties with the princes. When Hasan Pasha arrived in Cairo from Istanbul in 1786 with orders from the Porte to remove the rapacious Mamluks, the attitude of the ulama toward him was reserved, and when the Mamluk beys in question fled to Upper Egypt and Hasan proceeded to sequester their properties and harems, the leading ulama pleaded on their behalf. In these and other ways, it is clear that the interests of the ulama were far removed from the interests or demands of the popular masses. Even in the revolts against the French, in which lower ulama were prominent, the higher ulama largely avoided involvement and tried to calm the situation. Some of the most prominent cooperated with the French, subsequently incurring the wrath of the crowds (Baer 1977, 230–231).

Baer gives many examples of the ulama evading the calls of the masses in situations of intense conflict. For example, in 1805, they cancelled their classes at al-Azhar and retired to their homes until a clear winner emerged in the struggle, at which point they came out to support him. The extensive popular participation in these events, as we have seen, was led by figures from the quarters and the guilds, but also in the early stages by Sayyid 'Umar Makram, whose name is firmly associated with Muhammad 'Ali, as a leader of the crowds. Baer argues that Makram was not an alim, in the sense of a religious rank or any special learning, but a *sayyid* (1977, 236–41). He was a notable, involved in political alliances with Mamluk beys. The popular masses soon lost confidence in him and followed their local leaders. Baer gives examples of two other prominent ulama associated with the popular leadership and argues that they were representing constituencies in which they had material and political interests (1977, 229–30). For example, Shaykh al-Dardir, mentioned above as the defender of al-Husayniyya quarter, was closely associated with the Bayumiyya order centered in that quarter and was in that instance championing a political constituency.

One of the most important religious sentiments that emerged in the course of these events was what was later called "communalism," the sense of solidarity of Muslims against Christians, which came most prominently to the fore during the French occupation. It is exemplified in the sermon preached to the crowds by an al-Azhar student: "O Muslims, the *jihad* is incumbent upon you. How can you free men agree to pay the poll tax (*jizya*) to the unbelievers? Have you no pride? Has the call not reached you?" (Baer 1977, 231).

As has been mentioned, Christian and Jewish communities were sometimes targets of popular unrest. In the first revolt against the French in 1798, the crowds started stealing and looting from the markets, and then turned to the residential quarters of Syrian Christians, not sparing Muslim houses in the vicinity. Women and girls were raped. The second revolt against the French in 1800 started with the looting of the stores of the French army and continued with the plunder of Christian houses. This second revolt "turned into a general massacre of Christians and other minorities" (Baer 1977, 224–26). On that occasion Ottoman representatives rewarded the crowds for capturing Christians and Jews.

It may be argued, as Raymond does (1999, 455), that this hostility to minorities was not "traditional" but a product of their cooperation with the occupiers, and that is largely correct. However, on other occasions of disorder before the French invasion, though looting and pillage were largely indiscriminate, the Christians also tended to be targeted particularly. There were other occasions on which Christians angered the crowds by public religious displays that were felt to breach their inferior status. This occurred in 1749, when a Coptic pilgrimage to Jerusalem, though authorized by a *fatwa*, was judged to be too ostentatious. The pilgrim camp was attacked by al-Azhar students leading a crowd who looted and stoned the camp and a neighboring church, causing many casualties (Baer 1977, 225–26).

As European penetration and domination spread in the region in the course of the nineteenth and twentieth centuries, the religious minorities became more closely associated with the foreigners. Though modern nationalist ideologies generally emphasize national unity across religious and sectarian boundaries, popular sentiment in the nineteenth century sometimes caused hostility to be directed against religious minorities. The communal clashes in Aleppo in 1850, followed by the intercommunal massacres in Syria and Lebanon in 1860, were among the most notable instances in the nineteenth century (Masters 1990; Fawaz 1994; Rafeq 1988a; Rogan 2004).

### Conditions of Political Modernity in Middle East Cities

Over the course of the nineteenth and twentieth centuries Walzer's conditions of political modernity developed at a different pace in different parts of the region. They naturally took their various forms following the peculiarities of history and society. Let us briefly review some of these conditions.

Larger and more inclusive political units developed with increasing state centralization, breaking down local isolation, autonomy, and centers of power. In Egypt, Muhammad 'Ali's gradual assumption of rule, perhaps the earliest and most thorough in this regard, was greatly facilitated by the topography and economy of the country. The Mamluk amirs were liquidated at a famous massacre in 1811, early in Muhammad 'Ali's reign, and their followers absorbed into his entourage. Extensive controls were established over the rural areas and a strict regime of crop allocation and state monopolies established

(Marsot 1984a; Cuno 1988). A conscript army of peasants was established, the first of its kind in the region and indeed in most of the world at that time. The regime incorporated technical methods and imported skilled personnel from Europe to work in a variety of military and economic enterprises. Although unintentionally, Muhammad 'Ali was laying the foundations of what was later to become a nation-state. In other parts of the Ottoman Empire, the local powers of notables, warlords, and tribal aristocracies were very evidently under attack by the middle of the nineteenth century and were slowly whittled down in favor of varying degrees of state centralization; in Iran, this was only achieved in the early decades of the twentieth century by Reza Shah. Modern military technology, transport, and communications were essential conditions for this centralization. However, these same conditions facilitated the organization and mobilization of modern political movements of opposition and rebellion on a national scale.

These processes of centralization proceeded in the general context of increasing European penetration, leading, in some cases, as in Egypt, to direct foreign military and political control. This shaped the structure of modern politics, predominantly urban, in the direction of forms of anticolonial struggle. The models of liberation and of independence were derived from European ideas and ideologies, first liberal and nationalist, and later fascist and socialist. National liberation and nationalism remained a central component of all these ideologies and political movements.

On the social level, processes of economic development and political centralization contributed to the breakdown of primary social units and solidarities, of tribe, village, and urban quarter, although this proceeded unevenly in different places. Egyptian guilds were weakened as they lost their monopoly over labor in their particular crafts and had mostly become redundant by the 1920s (Baer 1968, 142–47; Chalcraft 2004), but their Iranian counterparts retained many of their social and political functions in the bazaars until much later in the century (Floor 1975, 1983). Rural to urban migration, a crucial factor for the shaping of the urban economy, society, and politics, proceeded apace in early-twentieth-century Egypt. The quarters of central Cairo were transformed, the rural influx leading to the departure of the rich and middle classes to the more salubrious suburbs, and the old quarters became slums for the poor. This process also weakened the organization and solidarity of the quarters and their function as corporate units.

The expansion of a modernized state and its associated public sectors, most notably education, spawned a new, largely secular, intelligentsia. This became the ideological class par excellence that absorbed and adapted the new reformist, nationalist, and revolutionary ideas whose goal was the achievement of national independence and strength and the transformation of state and society in accordance with particular ideological blueprints. From these ranks came Walzer's "zealous men" organized for "sustained political activity."

A new political element emerging in the early decades of the twentieth century in Cairo and elsewhere was the modern working class.[9] Industrialization in Egypt was limited to particular sectors, such as textiles, food processing, tobacco, and sugar. In addition, transport and utilities, notably railways and tramways, were significant employers, and the Iranian oil industry became an important employer in the 1930s and 1940s. Workers in these industries were numerically few but politically significant when organized and led by cadres from rival modern political parties and in the context of nationalist struggles. There remained, however, the large majority of the urban popular classes who were not part of this class and did not share its organization. The majority of the urban poor were (and still remain) engaged in the "informal economy," employed in small businesses and workshops, petty trade, casual work in construction, and numerous petty services (Santos 1979). These sectors had, for the most part, lost the traditional organizational forms of villages, guilds, *tariqas*, or quarters and had not acquired new forms of working class organization. The flood of rural migrants into cities persisting to the present day has ensured that these groups are an ever-increasing proportion of the urban poor in most cities. Politically, these groups oscillate between apathy or quietism and militancy in relation to particular grievances. Governments and organized parties and movements have tried to control and mobilize some of these groups with varying degrees of success. There is a prevalent view that they only respond ideologically to Islamic appeals, and it is certainly the case

9. For studies of labor, see the various essays in Lockman 1994 and E. Goldberg 1996. For Iraq, see Farouk-Sluglett and Sluglett 1983b.

that at various points, notably in the Iranian Revolution, Islamic appeals were successful in addressing their grievances and mobilizing them. However, as we shall show, communist and nationalist parties also enjoyed great favor with the urban masses, specially the communists in Iraq and Iran in the middle decades of the twentieth century, and the Nasserists in Egypt. I shall now elaborate on some of these themes in relation to examples drawn from Egypt and Iran.

## Urban Politics in the Modern Period: Egypt

Egyptian agriculture was transformed during the nineteenth century. Increased food and cotton production facilitated population growth, but also created increasing numbers of landless peasants. Rapid industrialization and construction in Cairo in the late nineteenth and early twentieth centuries attracted waves of rural migrants into the city. The British military presence, especially during the two world wars, spawned demands for goods and labor. Successive economic booms in Egypt attracted migration from outside, mainly of Europeans and "Levantines," entrepreneurs, bankers, and traders, but also of craftsmen and skilled workers. The largest communities were Greek and Italian, the richest French and British (Reimer 1991, 1993, 1997).

In the decade after 1917, Cairo absorbed more than 200,000 newcomers, an increase in population from fewer than 800,000 in 1917 to over one million in 1927 and over two million in 1947 (Abu-Lughod 1971, 173–74). Beginning in the nineteenth century the waves of rural migrants were mostly accommodated in the old quarters of medieval Cairo. Population density increased to very high levels in these areas, raising the incidence and frequency of epidemics. The middle class inhabitants of these quarters moved out, and the quarters became increasingly dilapidated. Land speculation and building developments enveloped the city, but had the effect of segregating and isolating classes and ethnic groups. Ilbert characterizes these divisions as a hierarchical division of urban space between the bourgeoisie (of various nationalities) and the workers and employees (Ilbert 1989, 278). These popular classes were divided and ranked by nationality and place of origin: non-Egyptians on top, followed by urban Egyptians, and the rural migrants at the bottom of the pile, each group with its particular neighborhoods and levels of housing.

How did this situation feed into political sentiments, organization, and action? Opposition to foreign domination constituted the overall framework of Egyptian politics. It was the raison d'être for the most important political party, the Wafd, formed in 1919 to press for Egyptian representation at the Paris Peace Conference, which developed into a national liberation rally led by Sa'd Zaghlul. The Muslim Brotherhood, formed in 1928, had national independence, combined with Islamic self-assertion, at the core of its advocacy. The communist movement, which included prominent European and Jewish elements, was often divided, but exercised considerable influence, and the trade unions articulated their ideas of class struggle in the quest for national liberation (Botman 1988). Though experiencing periodic waves of relative prosperity in the interwar period and after World War II, the poorer classes were also exposed to high inflation, great employment insecurity, and poor living conditions. The European elements, both bourgeoisie and workers, occupied a special position in society, and their privileges over the natives were highly visible at an everyday level. Many elements of the urban classes were engaged in servile jobs for the foreign communities. Hence a colonial situation was superimposed on class conflict.

During the first half of the twentieth century, labor organization and activism constituted an important element of Egyptian politics.[10] Textile manufacture was the single largest sector of Egyptian industry, and the largest employer: in 1945 it employed 37 percent of officially enumerated industrial workers in Egypt, mostly in large enterprises employing between 2,000 and 20,000 workers (Beinin 1988, 208). The factories were concentrated in two industrial suburbs of Cairo, Shubra al-Khayma and al-Mahalla al-Kubra. The majority of enterprises in the first were owned by non-Egyptians, Europeans and Levantines, and those in the second were entirely owned by Misr Company, a national Egyptian enterprise. The population of Shubra al-Khayma grew rapidly from several tens of thousands in the early 1930s to 250,000 by the end of that decade (Beinin 1988, 209). Trade union organization started in the early 1930s, first under the patronage of the Wafd Party, which viewed organized labor as part of the national movement, denying the existence of separate class interests. Some members of the leadership of the new unions, however, insisted on the formation of independent unions run by their members that would not

10. This section on the Egyptian labor movement draws on E. Goldberg 1986, Beinin and Lockman 1987, and Beinin 1988. See also Burke 1986.

be dependent on the patronage of notables. This view was to prevail over the following decades, and these unions, forming part of a national federation of trade unions, were to become one of the most militant elements of the national movement and to engage in prolonged and effective strikes.

The communist movement became closely involved in the organization and propaganda of trade unionism and played an important part in establishing the idea of working class interests and of independent unions. The Society of Muslim Brothers, which was also involved in popular organization and mobilization, moved into this area in an attempt to establish its hegemony over workers' organizations. Its outlook, however, was far removed from notions of class struggle, unless the bosses were non-Muslims. Otherwise, like the Wafd, it espoused an organicist view of national (and for the Muslim Brothers, Muslim) solidarity undisturbed by class divisions. Within such ideologies, workers' aspirations were to be guided by principles of overriding national interest, and the idea of autonomous organization and struggle was not favored. Until 1952, Shubra al-Khayma remained a center of militancy backed by strike actions and of much bitter strife. The Misr Company, regarded as a national institution, escaped industrial struggles until 1947 by dealing harshly with any manifestations of militancy (Beinin 1988, 209).

Hence, there was a struggle for the control of the workers' movement between the Wafd, the communists, and the Muslim Brothers. These movements represented different styles of politics with regard to the formation of constituencies of support. We may distinguish two such styles. The first proceeded through networks of patronage and influence as well as straight bargaining for favors, and the second depended on ideological conversion, organization, and a disciplined membership and following. The Wafd, the dominant party in Egyptian political life, followed both styles in different contexts. It maintained an important constituency of support among the intelligentsia and workers, especially in the 1920s and 1930s (although with neither membership nor branch structure) (Owen 1992, 227). At the same time, its electoral success depended on the patronage and influence of its notable leaders and deputies. Landlords were assured of the votes of their peasants and the villages under their patronage. Similarly, urban deputies utilized networks of influence of leading personalities in government offices, urban districts, and business sectors.

The Muslim Brothers relied primarily on ideological conversion and the disciplined and systematic work of members and branch (at one time called "families") organizers. In this respect they were typically "modern" and thus distinct from the Islamic movements of earlier periods. At the same time, however, they tended to find their constituencies in communities where they organized social services, mutual help associations, and businesses which provided employment (including a Muslim Brothers' textile mill in Shubra al-Khayma, founded with the intention of absorbing the unemployed) (Beinin 1988, 224). Such communal foundations of constituencies are to be found in other instances of the politics of the poor, including the Italian Communist Party in more recent times. Numerically weak and fragmented, the communist movement played an important part in the organization of workers, students, and intellectuals. It followed an ideological political style, but its achievements were limited. Neither the Muslim Brothers nor the communists were permitted to participate directly in elections, and were often banned, persecuted, and forced into clandestinity.

The main actors in all these opposition political movements and events were students and members of the modern intelligentsia: teachers, functionaries, professionals, low-ranking army officers, and organized workers. In addition, the Muslim Brothers included some businessmen and members of the urban lower middle classes. There is little evidence of the systematic involvement of the urban poor from the popular quarters in organized politics, although they may have been the object of political agitation and attempts at mobilization. The communists devoted their energies to organized workers. The Wafd and other government parties may have included sectors of these classes in electorally oriented favors, but the Muslim Brothers were the most consistently active at the popular level. However, the poor did not constitute part of their organization, but were rather objects of preaching and propaganda. In the 1940s, the Muslim Brothers held regular political rallies in urban centers, including a series of meetings after the end of World War II that it called a "People's Congress" (Mitchell 1969, 192–93). Some of these gatherings culminated in demonstrations with nationalist, anti-British and anti-Zionist slogans. The social composition of these meetings and demonstrations can only be guessed at, but they were most likely composed of the same elements noted earlier, but perhaps with some participation of the poorer classes.

Descriptions of the riots and uprisings that erupted in Cairo in January 1952 suggest somewhat wider participation, including members of the poor urban classes, whose frustrations and discontents coincided with a period of nationalist ferment against the dominant British and foreign presence. The years 1945–52 were marked by ever more intensive political agitation and struggle, with the object of ending British military occupation of the Canal Zone, but also directed against Egyptian governments, politicians, and the king, all of whom were regarded as pursuing their own, as well as Britain's interests. In 1948–49 the crushing defeat of the Arab forces, including the Egyptian army, in the first Arab-Israeli war, added to the profound sense of national grievance and humiliation. All the political parties were involved in these agitations, jockeying for popular leadership, and guerrilla fighters were dispatched to the Canal Zone to harass the British military. In January 1952, the British military command ordered a detachment of Egyptian auxiliary police to leave their barracks in Isma'iliyya, suspecting them of participation in armed activity. When they refused to go they were attacked with tanks and artillery leading to many deaths and injuries. This caused great national outrage, and the following day there were demonstrations in Cairo led by members of the police force, but with the organized participation of all the opposition parties. Many others joined the demonstrations, which became a violent riot. At the royal palace the king came out to the balcony to acknowledge shouts of "Long live the King," only to be insulted and jeered at by the crowd. It was reported that he then ordered his guards to machine-gun the crowd. (Mostyn 1989, 168). The angry mob proceeded to attack and burn British, European, or Jewish establishments in the city, including the Opera House, the Turf Club, large (Jewish-owned) department stores, various cabarets, and Shepheard's Hotel, a monument of British domination. By the end of that day, much of European Cairo had been destroyed and burned. A few months later, the Free Officers' coup brought about the end of the monarchy, and ultimately the end of pluralist party politics, inaugurating the single party military nationalist state and a very different style of government.

## Transitions to Political Modernity in Iranian Cities

Iran presents patterns of urban sociology and of transitions to modernity very different from those in Egypt, reflecting its very different social and political structure. During the nineteenth century, Iranian cities were controlled by more or less autonomous power elites on whom the Qajar authorities depended for effective rule, in marked contrast to the powerful centralization and control under Muhammad 'Ali and his successors. The urban power elites in Iran consisted of landowners, tribal chiefs, merchants, and ulama. Senior ulama were often themselves landowners or merchants, or at least members of landowning and merchant families. In each city, the bazaar, its guilds and powerful merchants, with close links to the ulama and to the land, dominated the urban economy and the sociopolitical organization of the city. A large sector of the urban popular classes (though not all) were included in the bazaar economy and society through ties of work, guild, religious allegiance, dependence, and charity. Like those in Cairo, the Iranian guilds comprised religious associations (not Sufi orders), hierarchical structures, and had an esprit de corps—some in Isfahan even had their own secret dialects (Abrahamian 1968, 192). Iranian cities had their own toughs, *lutis*, who trained in gymnasia with strong religious affiliations known as *zurkhane* (house of strength). They engaged in interquarter hostilities, but also took sides in factional and political fights following allegiances and rewards.

In the late nineteenth and early twentieth centuries, Iranian cities witnessed a number of protracted disturbances, with demonstrations, strikes, and riots directed against the government. For the most part these events were organized and orchestrated by elements of the urban elite whose interests were threatened by the ruler's involvements with European interests. Unlike Egypt and other parts of the Ottoman Empire in the nineteenth century, the foreign presence in Iran was less pronounced or direct. Nevertheless, the trading privileges and concessions ceded by cash-hungry shahs to British and Russian interests had an adverse effect on the bazaar economy. Goods imported from the various European empires threatened traditional Iranian markets, and the low tariffs enjoyed by foreign merchants gave them a great advantage over their Iranian counterparts.

The two most important episodes were the Tobacco Protest of 1891–92, followed by the Constitutional Revolution of 1905–11.[11] The first was in

---

11. For an analysis of the tobacco episode, see Keddie 1966; on the Constitutional Revolution, see Martin 1989 and Abrahamian 1982. The discussion of popular participation in

response to the grant of a monopoly for the production and trade of tobacco by the Shah to a British company. Protests culminated in a *fatwa* proclaiming a boycott of all tobacco products, which resulted in the deal being reversed. On one level, the Constitutional Revolution was fired by modern political objectives, specifically a constitution to limit the absolute rule of the Qajar monarch, and these demands were put forward by the small group of European-influenced intellectuals. These intellectuals were also backed, however, by important groups of ulama and bazaaris, including sectors of the urban population. The decisive participation of these groups was motivated not so much by their commitment to little-understood modern political concepts as by an increasing sense of frustration and alarm at the *direction* in which the country and the economy seemed to be heading under a shah allied to the very foreigners who were threatening their interests. This movement, then, presents a fascinating combination of traditional organization and allegiances with modern politics and would as such make a good case study of the transition between the two.[12]

The movement started in 1905 with a protest by merchants and money lenders against official tariffs, taxes, and impositions which harmed them, in which they were supported by other guilds and prominent ulama. The protests took the form of bazaar strikes, then marching in a procession to some notable location of sanctuary (*bast*), a favorite being 'Abd al-'Azim, a mosque on the outskirts of Tehran. The protracted crisis led in 1906 to a general strike organized by the Society of Guilds (recently formed to coordinate action), which then led a massive demonstration of some 14,000 people, who took sanctuary in the gardens of the British Legation for a period of three weeks. This was certainly a novel location for *bast*, which usually took place at a religious site. The protesters were mostly craftsmen and traders with their apprentices, but also included "modern" elements in the form of students from the newly established technical colleges.

---

this section draws extensively on Abrahamian's seminal article, "The Crowd in Iranian Politics 1905–1953" (1968). For the "Syrian crowd," see Grehan 2003.

12. "The Constitutional Revolution was a movement of the bazaar. Its rank-and-file came from the guilds, its financial backing from the merchants, its moral support from religious authorities, and its theorizing from a few westernized intellectuals." Abrahamian 1968, 192.

By 1906 the movement had succeeded in forcing the shah to accept a constitution and a parliament, and the first elections were held. However, this was the beginning of protracted struggles leading toward a civil war between the royalists and the constitutionalists that was to continue sporadically till Reza Khan's coup d'état against the Qajar monarchy in 1924, which eventually established his own dynasty. Foreign powers intervened, including a Russian invasion in 1911 which laid siege to parliament. The royalist backlash was supported by many ulama who were tied to the court by their own material interests, but also by some who feared the spread of modern ideas of constitutionalism and its implications for religious legal authority. What is of special interest for this discussion is that the royalist ranks also included large sectors of the urban poor who were mobilized against the predominantly bazaari constitutionalists. The latter were dominated by moneyed and commercial interests, and were not interested in securing cheap bread for the poor. On the contrary, the free market advocacy by these groups in parliament turned the poor against them, and made them receptive to the preaching of the royalist ulama against the new heresies. During this period the poor also staged spontaneous bread riots along traditional lines. In Isfahan, a peaceful procession of women presented a petition for cheaper bread to the governor, which turned into a riot when he gave them an obscene answer. They chased him through the streets and killed him, and then sacked government offices. Another element in the poor royalist crowd was the large numbers of servants, retainers, and dependents of the court. Parliament's newfound control of the royal budget led to many of these people not being paid or losing their jobs. Hence specific material interests played a major role in determining individual allegiances (Abrahamian 1968, 196–98).

During the civil war, Tabriz was geographically divided on class lines between the constitutionalists who were centered in the rich quarters, and the royalists who occupied the slum area (Abrahamian 1968, 199). However, class only determined political stance at a superficial and partial level. The poor of the bazaar, those who were members of guilds and dependent on bazaar personages and associations, followed those allegiances. In both cases the poor, though following their immediate interests and constraints, did so not out of any ideological questioning of the system, but in allegiance to one set or another of traditional patrons and superiors, the court and royalist ulama in the one case, and the bazaar magnates and associations in the other. In Abrahamian's analysis, it was only later in the twentieth century that class began to crystallize more clearly as a basis for political action, when it was also shaped by the ideologies of socialism and nationalism.

### The Period of Political Modernity in Iran

Abrahamian analyzed the transformations in crowd behavior from the events of the Constitutional Revolution to the political struggles surrounding the Mossadegh government in the early 1950s (1968, 201–207). Modern political organizations, both nationalist and socialist, developed and grew during the 1920s. In particular the Tudeh (Communist) Party became an important political force which played a crucial role in subsequent events. As could have been expected, the leadership of the various political parties consisted of educated middle-class professionals, particularly students and teachers, but the parties also attracted elements of the new working classes in the oil refineries, railways, and the few modern factories, as well as some traditional artisans and bazaar workers. The Tudeh Party became dominant in trade union organization and militancy. Until Reza Shah's removal in September 1941 these activities took place clandestinely and were subjected to violent repression. Reza Shah's forced abdication by the Allies (including the Soviet Union) inaugurated a more tolerant though by no means liberal regime, which allowed more open political activity and organization and during which first the Tudeh Party and then the National Front came to prominence. This episode ultimately culminated in the premiership of Mosaddeq, his nationalization of Iranian oil, and his struggle against the monarchy and its allies. Mosaddeq's stormy rule was ended in 1953 by a United States–instigated military coup which returned Mohammad Reza Shah to absolute power and brought back the kind of political repression familiar from the 1930s (Abrahamian 2001).

The Tudeh Party and the trade unions associated with it assumed commanding positions in popular organization and mobilization. In 1945 the Central Council of United Trade Unions had a total membership of 400,000 (Abrahamian 1968, 202). In addition to workers in modern industries, it included the syndicates of teachers, lawyers, engineers, and doctors. One public meeting in 1946 was attended by 15,000 people; on May Day 1946, the union parade in Abadan brought out 81,000 demonstrators. The union pursued militant demands in the oil industry, and the company's attempt to break a strike led to violent riots in Abadan and Ahwaz (Abrahamian 1968, 203).

Mosaddeq had come to national prominence as a radical leader in 1945 and immediately attracted mass support, particularly from the bazaar and the students. The National Front, a coalition of nationalist parties, organized this support, and the Tudeh Party joined in, though the alliance was often uneasy because of serious differences within the Front over communism and the Soviet Union. The ulama were notable for the minor role they played in these events, apart from one prominent cleric, Ayatollah Kashani, who supported Mosaddeq. Although the mullahs may well have continued to have the allegiance of some popular sectors, they were not politically significant at this point. New sectors of the urban population were affiliated to the new politics and set loose from the earlier hegemony and affiliations of bazaar and ulama.

In July 1952, a revolt broke out in Tehran as soon as the news reached the bazaar that Mosaddeq had been forced to resign. Bazaar traders and craftsmen fought the security forces to make their way to parliament. The National Front deputies called for a general strike, and the Tudeh joined in. The bazaar closed down entirely and there were strikes in all the sectors controlled by the Tudeh and the unions. After attempts at violent suppression, the government capitulated. The heaviest fighting took place in the bazaar, in the working class industrial districts and the railway repair shops, on the route between the university and parliament and in Parliament Square. Students, of course, were prominent in these events. The worst slum districts of southern Tehran were quiet. The centers of popular activism had shifted.

There were marked differences between Cairo and the Iranian cities in the first half of the twentieth century. Cairo underwent a basic dislocation of its old structures of quarter organization, guild, and *tariqa*, caused both by mass migration to the city from the countryside and by a significant level of industrialization. In contrast, through bazaar associations and their coordination Iranian cities were able to maintain important sectors of autonomous urban organization. Modern politics and ideologies of nationalism, liberalism, and communism developed and thrived for the most part in the new social spaces of university, school, workshop, and coffeehouse. At the same time they were only effective in urban mass mobilization through articulation with the structures and interests of the bazaar. These, in turn, were transformed by the forces and processes of modernity, but were never entirely displaced as centers of urban autonomy. The bazaar was to be the hub of organization, finance, and coordination in all the political upheavals of the century, perhaps most crucially, for the Islamic Revolution of 1978–79.

Iraqi cities, like their Iranian counterparts, maintained strong elements of quarter identity and solidarity. In the first half of the twentieth century migration to Baghdad was confined to specific areas adjacent to the city. Urban identities in Baghdad were reinforced by its religious and ethnic divisions. The suburb of al-Kadhimayn, for instance, housed the holy shrine and pilgrimage center of the Shi'i Imam al-Kadhim. Across the river was al-'Adhamiyya, named after the shrine of Abu Hanifa (known as al-Imam al-'Adham) which was located there, and as such a Sunni center. Other districts were predominantly Jewish or Kurdish. In the political and ideological struggles of this century, these quarters did not function according to their sectarian identities, but mostly as centers of the various modern political forces. The Iraqi Communist Party organized broad popular constituencies among the intelligentsia and the workers and also had a wide following among the urban poor in the middle decades of the century. Their rivals and antagonists in opposition politics were adherents of various strands of Arab nationalism. In the 1940s and 1950s, the Shi'i and Kurdish quarters of Baghdad were strong bastions of communism, while some of the Sunni quarters were centers of Arabism. Here we have another example of modern political organization and ideology being articulated through urban identities and solidarities.[13]

The second half of the twentieth century saw the recasting of urban politics and popular movements in the Middle East and North Africa, as in other parts of the developing world. The pace of population growth and the enormous volume of rural to urban migration transformed most cities. For the most part the regimes became more monolithic and authoritarian and effectively suppressed modern organized political forces and incorporated or co-opted autonomous social associations such as trade unions. This process was greatly facilitated by the enormous oil wealth accruing to some of the regimes, which also contributed to the transformation of the urban landscape. The newly urbanized poor have been largely cut off from any source of political organization or

13. See Batatu 1978, 709–925; Farouk-Sluglett and Sluglett 2001; see also Zubaida 1991.

mobilization, except, that is, for "Islam," which was generally able to escape repression through the mosque, communal networks, and welfare services. On several occasions the frustration of the poor broke out in riots, some, like the 1977 outbursts in Egyptian cities, clearly "bread riots" like those of the past.

Islamic political forces of various kinds have tried to harness these mass frustrations, with considerable success in some instances. The Islamic Salvation Front in Algeria is one example: its success in popular organization and mobilization culminated in victory in the elections in 1991 and led to the military coup d'état that suppressed it. The Islamic forces in the Iranian Revolution of 1979 utilized the zeal of the crowds as well as bazaar organization and finance. In the early twenty-first century the Islamic Republic has become much less able to manage or contain economic problems and disruptions than its predecessor, and the urban crowds are on the march again expressing their frustrations in demonstrations and riots, suppressed by the might of the Islamic Republic, but also, during the 1997 presidential elections with their landslide vote for Khatami, seen as a relatively liberal reformer, as against the now-entrenched interests of the conservative Islamic establishment. The (manipulated) election of the hard-line populist Mahmud Ahmedinejad as president in 2005 signaled the continuing turbulence of mass sentiments and discontents, so far prevented from organized political expression by increased repression. This turbulence and repression seem to characterize contemporary Middle Eastern political fields, both shaping and inhibiting the political modernity signaled in earlier decades.

GLOSSARY

BIBLIOGRAPHY

INDEX

# Glossary

'abat, 'ubi: woolen cloak

'amma: commoners

agha: military notable

ahl al-kitab: people of the book, monotheists with written scriptures (normally Christians, Jews, Sabaeans, and Zoroastrians)

al-ahya' al-barraniya: outlying suburbs

ajir: apprentice

amir al-hajj: leader of the pilgrimage

'anatiyya: makers of silk robes

'avania, 'awn: extraordinary taxes

'aqd: (apprenticeship) contract

ashraf, sharif: descendant(s) of the Prophet

askari: military class (Arabic)

askeriya: military class (Turkish)

'attar: druggist

awamir sultaniyya: administrative decrees and orders sent out from Istanbul to the provinces

a'yan: notables

bash(i): head, chief

bast: sanctuary (in the sense of protected place)

bay' bi-al-dayn: sale on credit

bazar bashi: chief merchant

bedel-i askeriyya: cash payment in return for exemption from military service

berat: certificate of foreign protection (given by consuls etc. to non-Muslim Ottoman subjects)

**bilad al-makhzan:** rural areas under the control of, or paying taxes to, the central state

**çiftlik:** plantation, estate

**cizye:** Turkish for **jizya**

**dabbagh:** tanner

**dallal:** auctioneer, broker

**dayn:** debt

**dhimmi,** Turkish **zimmi:** non-Muslims in Muslim lands (in practice, Christians, Jews, and Zoroastrians)

**evkaf:** see **waqf**

**diwan:** council (as in city council, provincial council)

**fatwa,** Turkish **fetva:** legal opinion delivered by religious scholar

**fiqh:** jurisprudence

**fuqaha', sing. faqih:** legal or religious scholar

**futuh, sing. fath:** early Islamic conquests

**futuwwa:** street gang

**gedik:** equipment for a workshop

**habus:** see **waqf** (North African equivalent)

**hajji:** one who has made the pilgrimage to Mecca

**hara:** city quarter

**harir:** silk

**hawsh:** house built round central courtyard

**hayy, pl. ahy'a:** city quarter

**hirfa:** guild

**hujja:** certified legal document

**i'ane:** additional taxation to provide money for the army

**iltizam:** tax farming

**imtiyazat [ajnabiyya]:** Capitulations (for foreigners), giving them a special legal status within the Ottoman Empire

**jizya:** canonical tax paid by non-Muslims

**kafil:** (financial) guarantor

**kapudan bashi:** admiral of the fleet

**kasba:** historic or precolonial city

**kahya:** quarter or village head

**khan:** caravanserai

**khatib:** mosque preacher

**khayyat:** tailor

**khilu:** the right to use vacant premises

**khuwwa:** protection money

**madina:** historic/precolonial city

**mahalla:** city quarter

**mahkama, pl. ahakim shar'iyya:** Islamic law court(s)

**makhzan:** central government of Morocco

**maktab:** elementary or Qura'nic school

**malikane:** lifetime tax farm (**iltizam**)

**mastaba:** stone seats on sidewalks between shops and the street

**mawat:** "dead" or uncultivated land

**Mecelle:** Ottoman Civil Code (issued 1869–78)

**mellah:** Jewish quarter (in North Africa cities)

**mi'mar:** builder

**milk, mulk:** freehold propery

**miri:** state land

**mu'arrif:** individual charged with assigning the amount of tax guild members should pay

**mufti:** jurisconsult

**muhami:** lawyer

**muhandis:** engineer

**muhassil:** tax collector

**muhtasib:** market inspector

**multazim:** tax farmer (possessor of iltizam)

**murabaha:** the investment of money at interest

**mutawalli:** manager of an endowment (**waqf**)

**mutasallim:** lieutenant governor of a province

**nahdha:** Arabic literary and linguistic renaissance of the late nineteenth century

**najjar:** carpenter

**naqib al-ashraf:** custodian of the records of the descendants of the Prophet (in a particular city)

**ocak:** Ottoman regiment in Egypt

**qadi, Turkish kadi:** judge

**qanun, pl. qawanin:** civil (i.e., non-Islamic) statute(s) of the Ottoman state

**qanunnamler:** lists of civil statutes

**qard:** loan

**qassab:** butcher

**qassam shar'i:** court official responsible for the canonical division of the property of deceased persons

**qaysariyya:** commercial building, often for storage of manufactured goods

**qism:** division, share

ra'aya: flock, subjects
sabbagh: dyer
sadah, sing. sayyid: descendants of the Prophet Muhammad
salam: contract to purchase crops before the harvest
sani': journeyman
sarraf: money changer
sayyid, pl. sadah: descendant of the Prophet Muhammad
shahbandar: chief merchant
sharaka/shirka: business partnership
shar'i: sanctioned by Islamic law
sharif, pl. ashraf: see ashraf
shartnameh: rules for qualification
shaykh al-balad: city chief
shaykh al-mashayikh: paramount shaykh
sijillat: documents that form the Islamic court records
simsar: broker
sipahi: cavalryman
subashi: city police chief
sukhra: forced labor
suq: covered market (bazaar)
sura: section of the Qur'an
sürgün: forced migration and resettlement
taba': follower
ta'ifat: sect, confessional group, guild, corporation
ta'ifa al-ru'sa: merchant corporation in Algiers
tariqa, pl. turuq: (Sufi) brotherhood
timar: an assignation of rural fiefs
timariot: fief holder
uluf: military rations
'urf: customary (e.g., tribal) law
ustadh, usta: (guild) master
waqf, awqaf; Turkish vakf, evkaf: mortmain properties, endowments in perpetuity
wasta: connections, influence, "networks"
yamak: assistant, subordinate (in the case of mergers between more and less
    powerful guilds)
yerliyya: local janissaries
zabtiyya: irregular troops
zahir: outside (the walls of)

# Bibliography

Abdel Nour, Antoine. 1982a. *Introduction à l'histoire urbaine de la Syrie ottomane.* Beirut: Librarie Orientale.

———. 1982b. "Habitat et structures sociales à Alep aux XVIIe et XVIIIe siècles d'après des sources arabes inédites." In *La Ville arabe dans l'islam,* ed. Abdelwahhab Bouhdiba and Dominique Chevallier. Paris: Éditions du Centre National de la Recherche Scientifique.

Abdel-Fadil, Mahmoud. 1975. *Development, Income Distribution and Social Change in Rural Egypt 1952–1979: A Study in the Political Economy of Agrarian Transition.* Cambridge: Cambridge Univ. Press.

Abdulac, Samir. 1982. "Damas: les années Écochard (1932–1982)." *Les cahiers de la recherche architecturale* 10–11:32–43.

Abdullah, Thabit. 2001. *Merchants, Mamluks and Murder: The Political Economy of Trade in Eighteenth Century Basra.* Albany: State Univ. of New York Press.

Abitbol, Michel, ed. 1980. *Le judaisme d'Afrique du nord aux XIXe–XXe siècles.* Jerusalem: Yad Izhak Ben-Zvi.

Abou-El-Haj, Rifa'at. 1982. "The Social Uses of the Past: Recent Arab Historiography of Ottoman Rule." *International Journal of Middle East Studies* 14:185–201.

———. 1991. *The Formation of the Modern State: The Ottoman Empire.* Albany: State Univ. of New York Press.

Abrahamian, Ervand. 1968. "The Crowd in Iranian Politics 1905–1953." *Past and Present* 41:184–210.

———. 1974. "Oriental Despotism: The Case of Qajar Iran." *International Journal of Middle East Studies* 5:3–31.

———. 1979. "The Causes of the Constitutional Revolution in Iran." *International Journal of Middle East Studies* 19:381–414.

————. 1982. *Iran between Two Revolutions.* Princeton: Princeton Univ. Press.

————. 2001. "The 1953 Coup in Iran." *Science and Society* 65 (2): 182–215.

Abu-Husayn, Abdul-Rahim. 1985. *Provincial Leaderships in Syria, 1575–1650.* Beirut: American Univ. of Beirut Press.

Abu-Lughod, Janet. 1971. *Cairo: 1001 Years of the City Victorious.* Princeton: Princeton Univ. Press.

————. 1980. *Rabat: Urban Apartheid in Morocco.* Princeton: Princeton Univ. Press.

————. 1984. "Culture, 'Modes of Production', the Nature of Cities in the Arab World." In *The City in Cultural Context,* ed. John Agnew, John Mercer, and Davis Sopher, 94–119. Boston: Allen and Unwin.

————. 1987. "The Islamic City: Historic Myth, Islamic Essence and Contemporary relevance." *International Journal of Middle East Studies* 19:155–76.

Abu-Manneh, Butrus. 1990. "Jerusalem in the Tanzimat Period: The New Ottoman Administration and the Notables." *Die Welt des Islams* 39:1–44.

————. 1994. "The Islamic Roots of the Gülhane Rescript." *Die Welt des Islams* 34:173–203.

Abu'l-Sha'r, Hind Ghassan. 1995. *Irbid wa-jiwaruha (nahiyyat Bani 'Ubayd) 1850–1928.* Amman: Jami'a Āl al-Bayt.

Adam, André. 1968. *Histoire de Casablanca, des origines à 1914.* Gap: Éditions Ophrys.

————. 1972. *Casablanca, essai sur la transformation de la société marocaine au contact de l'Occident.* 2nd edition. Paris: Éditions du Centre National de la Recherche Scientifique.

Adle, Chahryar, and Bernard Hourcade, eds. 1992. *Téhéran: capitale bicentenaire.* Paris: Institut français de recherche en Iran; Louvain, Belgium: Peeters.

Afary, Janet. 2002. "From Outcastes to Citizens. Jews in Qajar Iran." In *Esther's Children: A Portrait of Iranian Jews,* ed. Houman Sarshar, 139–74. Beverly Hills: Center for Iranian Oral History; Philadelphia: Jewish Publication Society.

Afshari, M. R. 1983. "The Pishvaran and Merchants in Pre-capitalist Iranian society: An Essay on the Background and Causes of the Constitutional Revolution." *International Journal of Middle East Studies* 15:133–55.

Agmon, Iris. 2006. *Family and Court: Legal Culture and Modernity in Late Ottoman Palestine.* Syracuse: Syracuse Univ. Press.

Ahmad, Feroz. 2000. "Ottoman Perceptions of the Capitulations 1800–1914." *Journal of Islamic Studies* 11:1–20.

Akarlı, Engin. 1985–86. "Gedik: Implements, Mastership, Shop Usufruct and Monopoly among Istanbul Artisans." *Wissenschaftskolleg-Jahrbuch* 1985–1986:223–32.

———. 1993. *The Long Peace, Ottoman Lebanon, 1861–1920.* Berkeley: Univ. of California Press.

Aksan, Virginia. 1998. "Whatever Happened to the Janissaries? Mobilization for the 1768–1774 Russo-Ottoman War." *War in History* 5:23–26.

———. 1999. "Ottoman Military Recruitment Strategies in the Late Eighteenth Century." In *Arming the State: Military Conscription in the Middle East and Central Asia, 1775–1925,* ed. Erik Jan Zürcher, 21–39. London: I. B. Tauris.

Algar, Hamid. 1969. *Religion and State in Iran: 1785–1906.* Berkeley: Univ. of California Press.

Ali, Nadje Sadiq Al-, 2007. *Iraqi Women: Untold Stories from 1948 to the Present.* London: Zed Books.

Alleaume, Ghislaine, and Philippe Fargues. 1998. "Voisinage et frontière: résider au Caire en 1846." In *Urbanité arabe. Hommage à Bernard Lepetit,* ed. Jocelyne Dakhlia and Bernard Lepetit, 77–112. Paris: Sindbad.

Amine, M. 1994. "Moyens et aspects techniques de l'activité commerciale d'Alger." *Revue d'Histoire Maghrébine* 75–76:167–98.

Anastassiadou, Meropi. 1997. *Salonique, 1830–1912. Une ville ottomane à l'âge des réformes.* Leiden: Brill.

Anderson, Benedict. 1991. *Imagined Communities: Reflections on the Origin and Spread of Nationalism.* London: Verso.

Ansari, Bassim al-. 1979. "al-Thawra, Quartier de Bagdad." Doctorat du troisième cycle, Paris, École des hautes études en sciences sociales.

Ansari, Sharaf al-Din Makki al-, ed. 'Adnan Ibrahim. 1991. *Nuzhat al-khatir wa-bahjat al-nazir.* Published version of manuscript no. 7814, Asad National Library, Damascus, fols. 3351–342b, 388b, 2 vols. Damascus: Wizarat al-Thaqafa.

Ansky, Michel. 1950. *Les Juifs d'Algérie du Décret Crémieux à la Libération.* Paris: Centre de documentation juive contemporaine.

Arjomand, Said. 1984. *The Shadow of God and the Hidden Imam: Religion, Political Order, and Societal Change in Iran from the Beginning to 1890.* Chicago: Univ. of Chicago Press.

Arnon, Adar. 1992. "The Quarters of Jerusalem in the Ottoman period." *Middle Eastern Studies* 28:1–65.

Ashraf, Ahmed. 1994. "The Social History of Teheran in the Early 20th Century." *Iranian Studies* 26:411–18.

Atiya, Aziz S. 1968. *A History of Eastern Christianity.* London: Methuen.

Aubin, Eugène [Collard-Descos]. 1904. *Le Maroc d'aujourd'hui.* Paris: A. Colin.

Avery, Peter, Gavin Hambly, and Charles Melville, eds. 1991. *The Cambridge History of Iran*, vol. 7, *From Nadir Shah to the Iranian Revolution*. Cambridge: Cambridge Univ. Press.

Avez, Renaud. 1993. *L'Institut français de Damas au Palais Azem (1922–1946) à travers les Archives*. Damascus: Institut français d'études arabes de Damas.

Awad, M. F. 1987. "Le modèle européen; l'évolution urbaine de 1807 à 1958." *Revue de l'occident musulman et de la Méditerranée* 46:93–109.

Azmeh, A. al-. 1976. "What Is the Islamic City?" *Review of Middle East Studies* 2:1–12.

'Azzawi, Qays Jawad al-. 1994. *al-Dawla al-'Uthmaniyya: qira'a jadida li 'awamil inhitat* (The Ottoman state: A new interpretation of the reasons for decline). Beirut: Arab Scientific Publishers.

Bacqué-Grammont, J. L., and Paul Dumont, eds. 1983. *Économie et sociétés dans l'empire ottoman (fin du XVIIIe–début du XXe siècles)*. Paris: Éditions du Centre National de la Recherche Scientifique.

Badran, 'Abd al-Qadir. 1960. *Munazzamat al-atlal wa-musamarat al-khayal*. Damascus: al-Maktab al-Islami.

Baer, Gabriel. 1968a. "Social Change in Egypt: 1821–1962." In *Political and Social Change in Modern Egypt*, ed. P. M. Holt, 142–47. London: Oxford Univ. Press.

———. 1968b. "The Beginning of Municipal Government in Egypt." *Middle Eastern Studies* 4:118–40.

———. 1969. *Studies in the Social History of Modern Egypt*. Chicago: Chicago Univ. Press.

———. 1977. "Popular Revolt in Ottoman Cairo." *Der Islam* 54:213–42.

———. 1982. *Fellah and Townsman in the Middle East: Studies in Social History*. London: Frank Cass.

———. 1986. "Jerusalem's Families of Notables and the Wakf in the Early 19th Century." In *Palestine in the Late Ottoman Period: Political, Social and Economic Transformation*, ed. David Kushner, 109–22. Jerusalem: Yad Izhak Ben Zvi.

———. 1990. "The Dismemberment of Awqaf in Early 19th Century Jerusalem." In *Ottoman Palestine, 1800–1914: Studies in Economic and Social History*, ed. Gad Gilbar, 299–319. Leiden: Brill.

Bağiş, Ali Ihsan. 1983. *Osmanli Ticaretinde Ġayri Müslimler (1750–1839)*. Ankara: Turhan.

Bahloul, Joelle. 1996. *The Architecture of Memory: A Jewish-Muslim Household in Colonial Algeria 1937–1962*. Cambridge: Cambridge Univ. Press.

Bakhash, Shaul. 1981. "Center-Periphery Relations in 19th Century Iran." *Iranian Studies* 14:29–51.

Bakhit, 'Muhammad 'Adnan al-. 1992. *Buhuth fi ta'rikh Bilad al-Sham fi'l-'asr al-'Uthmani.* Amman: Lajnat Ta'rikh Bilad al-Sham, al-Jam'iyya al-Urduniyya, Jam'iyya al-Yarmuk.

Bakhit, Muhammad 'Adnan al-, et al. 1984. *Kashshaf ihsa'i zamani li-sijillat al-mahakim al-shar'iyya wa al-awqaf al-islamiyya fi Bilad al-Sham.* Amman: al-Jami'a al-Urduniyya, Markaz al-Watha'iq wa-al-Makhtutat.

Barbir, Karl K. 1979–1980. "From Pasha to Efendi: The Assimilation of Ottomans into Damascene Society 1516–1783." *International Journal of Turkish Studies* 1:68–83.

———. 1980. *Ottoman Rule in Damascus, 1708–1758.* Princeton: Princeton Univ. Press.

———. 1996a. "Memory, Heritage, and History: The Ottomans and the Arabs." In *Imperial Legacy: The Ottoman Imprint on the Balkans and the Middle East,* ed. L. Carl Brown, 100–14. New York: Columbia Univ. Press.

———. 1996b. "From Ernest Renan to André Raymond: Changing French Approaches to the Modern History of the Arab World, Maghrib and Mashriq." In *Franco-Arab Encounters: Studies in Memory of David C. Gordon,* ed. L. Carl Brown and Matthew Gordon, 449–59. Beirut: American Univ. of Beirut Press.

Barillari, Diana, and Ezio Godoli. 1996. *Istanbul 1900.* New York: Rizzoli.

Barkan, Ömer Lütfi. 1940. "Türk Toprak Hukuku Tarihinde Tanzimat ve 1274 (1858) Tarihli Arazi Kannunamesi." *Tanzimat* 1:321–421.

Barsoumian, Hagop. 1982. "The Dual Role of the Armenian Amira Class within the Ottoman Government and the Armenian Millet (1750–1850)." In *Christians and Jews in the Ottoman Empire: The Functioning of a Plural Society,* ed. Benjamin Braude and Bernard Lewis, vol. 1, 171–84. New York: Holmes and Meier.

Barth, Fredrik, ed. 1969. *Ethnic Groups and Boundaries: The Social Organization of Culture Difference.* Bergen: Universitets Forlaget; London: Allen and Unwin.

Batatu, Hanna. 1978. *The Old Social Classes and the Revolutionary Movements of Iraq: A Study of Iraq's Old Landed Classes and Its Communists, Ba'thists and Free Officers.* Princeton: Princeton Univ. Press.

———. 1984. *The Egyptian, Syrian, and Iraqi Revolutions: Some Observations on Their Underlying Causes and Social Character.* Washington, D.C.: Georgetown Univ. Press.

———. 1999. *Syria's Peasantry: The Descendants of Its Lesser Rural Notables and Their Politics.* Princeton: Princeton Univ. Press.

Bat Ye'or (pseud.). 1985. *The Dhimmi: Jews and Christians under Islam.* Trans. David Maisel and David Littman. Rutherford, N.J.: Farleigh Dickinson Univ. Press.

Bayly, C. A. 2004. *The Birth of the Modern World 1789–1914: Global Connections and Comparisons.* Oxford: Blackwell.

Behrens-Abouseif, Doris. 1986. "Locations of Non-Muslim Quarters in Medieval Cairo." *Annales Islamologiques* 22:117–32.

Beinin, Joel. 1988. "Islam, Marxism and the Shubra al-Khayma Textile Workers: Muslim Brothers and Communists in the Egyptian Trade Union Movement." In *Islam, Politics and Social Movements,* ed. Edmund Burke III and Ira M. Lapidus, 207–27. Berkeley: Univ. of California Press.

Beinin, Joel, and Zachary Lockman. 1988. *Workers on the Nile: Nationalism, Communism, Islam, and the Egyptian Working Class, 1882–1954.* London: I. B. Tauris.

Ben-Arieh, Yehoshua. 1984. *Jerusalem in the 19th Century: The Old City.* New York: St. Martin's.

———. 1986. *Jerusalem in the 19th century: Emergence of the New City.* New York: St. Martin's.

Benevolo, Leonardo. 1993. *The European City.* Trans. Carl Ipsen. Oxford: Blackwell.

Berchtold, Thomas. 2001. "Organisation und sozioökonomische Strategien von Handwerkern im späten Osmanischen Reich (18.–19.Jht.)." Master's diss., Freie Universität Berlin.

Berque, Jacques. 1958. "Médinas, villes neuves et bidonvilles." *Les Cahiers de Tunisie* 6:5–42.

Bianquis, Anne-Marie. 1980. "Damas et la Ghouta." In *La Syrie d'aujourd'hui,* ed. André Raymond, 359–84. Paris: Éditions du Centre National de la Recherche Scientifique.

Bierman, Irene A., Rifa'at Abou-El-Haj, Donald Preziosi, eds. 1991. *The Ottoman City and Its Parts: Urban Structure and Social Order.* New Rochelle, N.Y.: Aristide D. Caratzas.

Bilici, Faruk, ed. 1994. *Le waqf dans le monde musulman contemporain (XIXe et XXe siècles). Fonctions sociales, économiques et politiques.* Ankara: Institut français d'etudes anatoliennes.

Bishri, Tariq al-. 1980. *al-Muslimun w'al-aqbat fi itar al-jama'a al-wataniyya.* Cairo: al-Hay'a al-misriyya al-'amma lil-kitab.

Bittar, André. 1992. "La Dynamique commerciale des Grecs-Catholiques en Égypte au XVIIIe siècle." *Annales Islamologiques* 26:181–96.

Blake, G. H. 1980. "The Small Town." In *The Changing Middle Eastern City,* ed. G. H. Blake and R. I. Lawless, 209–29. London: Croom Helm.

Blake, G. H., and R. I. Lawless, eds. 1980. *The Changing Middle Eastern City.* London: Croom Helm.

Bobek, Hans. 1974. "Zum Konzept der Rentenkapitalismus." *Tijdschrift voor Economische en Sociale Geografie* 75–78.

Bodman, Herbert L. 1963. *Political Factions in Aleppo, 1760–1826.* Chapel Hill: Univ. of North Carolina Press.

Bonine, Michael E., Eckart Ehlers, Thomas Krafft, and Georg Stöber, eds. 1994. *The Middle Eastern City and Islamic Urbanism: An Annotated Bibliography of Western Literature.* Bonn: Ferd. Dümmlers.

Boogert, Maurits H. van den. 2005. *The Capitulations and the Ottoman Legal System: Qadis, Consuls and Beraths in the 18th Century.* Leiden: Brill.

Bosworth, Edmund, and Carole Hillenbrand, eds. 1983. *Qajar Iran: Political, Social and Cultural Change 1800–1925.* Edinburgh: Edinburgh Univ. Press.

Botman, Selma. 1988. *The Rise of Egyptian Communism, 1939–1970.* Syracuse: Syracuse Univ. Press.

Boubaker, Sadok. 1994. "Le transfert des capitaux entre l'empire ottoman et l'Europe. L'utilisation de la lettre de change; l'exemple de la Société Garavaque et Cusson à Smyrne (1760–1772)." *Revue d'Histoire Maghrébine* 75–76:199–218.

Bouchain, Julie D. 1996. *Juden in Syrien: Aufstieg und Niedergang der Familie Farhi von 1740 bis 1995.* Hamburg: LIT.

Bouhdiba, Abdelwahhab, and Dominique Chevallier, eds. 1982. *La Ville arabe dans l'Islam.* Paris: Éditions du Centre National de la Recherche Scientifique.

Bou-Nacklie, N. E. 1998. "Tumult in Syria's Hama in 1925: The Failure of a Revolt." *Journal of Contemporary History* 33:273–90.

Bourguet, Marie-Noelle. 1995. "Voyage, enquête, statistique: les polytechniciens et la construction de l'espace au début du XIXe siècle." In *La France des X: deux siècles d'histoire,* ed. Bruno Belhoste et al., 215–30. Paris: Economica.

Bowie, Leland. 1976. "An Aspect of Muslim-Jewish Relations in Late Nineteenth-Century Morocco: A European Diplomatic View." *International Journal of Middle East Studies* 7:3–19.

Bowring, Sir John. 1840. *Report on the Commercial Statistics of Syria.* London: W. Clowes for H. M. Stationery Office. Reprint, New York: Arno Press, 1973.

Boyce, Mary. 1991. *Zoroastrians: Their Religious Beliefs and Practices.* London: Routledge and Kegan Paul.

Braude, Benjamin. 1982. "Foundation Myths of the Millet System." In *Christians and Jews in the Ottoman Empire: The Functioning of a Plural Society,* ed. Benjamin Braude and Bernard Lewis, vol. 1, 69–88. New York: Holmes and Meier.

Braude, Benjamin, and Bernard Lewis, eds. 1982. *Christians and Jews in the Ottoman Empire: The Functioning of a Plural Society.* 2 vols. New York: Holmes and Meier.

Braudel, Fernand. 1975. *The Mediterranean and the Mediterranean World in the Age of Philip II*. Trans. Siân Reynolds. London: Fontana/Collins.

Brebner, Philip. 1984. "The Impact of Thomas-Robert Bugéaud and the Decree of 9 June 1844 on the Development of Constantine, Algeria." *Revue de l'occident musulman et de la Méditerranée* 38:5–14.

Brenner, Robert. 1976. "Agrarian Class Structure and Economic Development in Pre-Industrial Europe." *Past and Present* 79:30–75.

————. 1977. "The Origins of Capitalist Development: A Critique of Neo-Smithian Marxism." *New Left Review* 104:25–92.

Brown, Kenneth L. 1976. *People of Salé: Tradition and Change in a Moroccan City, 1830–1930*. Manchester: Manchester Univ. Press, 1976.

————. 1986. "The Uses of a Concept: 'The Muslim City.'" In *Middle Eastern Cities in Comparative Perspective/Points de Vue sur les Villes du Maghreb et du Machrek*, ed. Kenneth L. Brown, Michèle Jolé, Peter Sluglett, and Sami Zubaida, 73–81. London: Ithaca Press.

Brown, Kenneth L., Bernard Hourcade, Michèle Jolé, Claude Liauzu, Peter Sluglett, and Sami Zubaida, eds. 1989. *État, ville et mouvements sociaux au Maghreb et au Moyen Orient/Arab and Muslim Cities: The State, Urban Crisis and Social Movements*. Paris: L'Harmattan.

Brown, Kenneth L., Michèle Jolé, Peter Sluglett, and Sami Zubaida, eds. 1986. *Middle Eastern Cities in Comparative Perspective/Points de Vue sur les Villes du Maghreb et du Machrek*. London: Ithaca Press.

Brown, L. Carl. 1973. *From Madina to Metropolis: Heritage and Change in the Near Eastern City*. Princeton: Princeton Univ. Press.

————. 1974. *The Tunisia of Ahmad Bey, 1837–1855*. Princeton: Princeton Univ. Press.

Brown, Nathan J. 1993. "The Precarious Life and Slow Death of the Mixed Courts of Egypt." *International Journal of Middle East Studies* 25:33–52.

Brunschvig, Robert. 1962. "Métiers vils en Islam." *Studia Islamica* 16:21–50.

Budayri, Ahmad al-. 1959. *Hawadith Dimashq al-yawmiyya, 1154–1175/1741–1762*, ed. Ahmad 'Izzat 'Abd al-Karim. Cairo: Matbu'at lajnat al-bayan al-'Arabi.

Burke, Edmund. 1986. "Understanding Arab Protest Movements." *Arab Studies Quarterly* 8:333–45.

————. 1989. "Towards a History of Urban Collective Action in the Middle East: Continuities and Changes." In *État, ville et mouvements sociaux au Maghreb et au Moyen Orient/Arab and Muslim Cities: The State, Urban Crisis and Social Movements*, ed. Kenneth L. Brown, Bernard Hourcade, Michèle Jolé, Claude Liauzu, Peter Sluglett, and Sami Zubaida, 42–56. Paris: L'Harmattan.

————. 1991. "Changing Patterns of Peasant Protest in the Middle East, 1750–1950." In *Peasants and Politics in the Modern Middle East,* ed. Farhad Kazemi and John Waterbury, 24–37. Miami: Florida International Univ. Press.

Busson de Janssens, G. 1951. "Les Wakfs dans l'Islam contemporain." *Revue des Études Islamiques* 19:1–72.

Cahen, Claude. 1970. "Y a-t-il eu des corporations professionnelles dans le monde musulman classique?" In *The Islamic City,* ed. A. H. Hourani and S. M. Stern, 51–63. Oxford: Cassirer; Philadelphia: Univ. of Pennsylvania Press.

Çanbakal, Hülya. 2006. *Society and Politics in an Ottoman Town: 'Ayntab in the Seventeenth Century.* Leiden: Brill.

Cannon, Byron D. 1987. "Le marché de location des habous en Tunisie: dialectique de développement agricole." In *Terroirs et sociétés au Maghreb et au Moyen Orient,* ed. Byron Cannon, 79–108. Lyon: Maison de l'Orient.

————. 1988. *Politics of Law and the Courts in Nineteenth-Century Egypt.* Salt Lake City: Univ. of Utah Press.

Çelik, Zeynep. 1993. *The Remaking of Istanbul: Portrait of an Ottoman City in the Nineteenth Century.* Seattle: Univ. of Washington Press.

————. 1997. *Urban Forms and Colonial Confrontations: Algiers under French Rule.* Berkeley: Univ. of California Press.

Chabrol de Volvic, Gilbert. 1822. "Essai sur les moeurs des habitants modernes de l'Egypte." In *Description de l'Égypte: État Moderne,* vol. 2, part 2, 361–524.

Chalcraft, John. 2004. *The Striking Cabbies of Cairo and Other Stories: Crafts and Guilds in Egypt, 1863–1914.* Albany: State Univ. of New York Press.

Chamberlain, Michael. 1994. *Knowledge and Social Practice in Medieval Damascus, 1190–1350.* Cambridge: Cambridge Univ. Press.

Chelhod, J. 1978. "Introduction à l'histoire sociale et urbaine de Zabid." *Arabica* 25:48–88.

Chenntouf, Tayeb. 1981. "L'évolution du travail en Algérie au XIXe siècle. La formation du salariat." *Revue de l'occident musulman et de la Méditerranée* 31:85–103.

Chevalier, Louis. 1958. *Classes laborieuses et classes dangereuses à Paris pendant la première moitié du XIXe siècle.* Paris: Plon. [Trans. Frank Jellinek. 1973. *Labouring Classes and Dangerous Classes in Paris during the First Half of the Nineteenth Century.* London: Routledge and Kegan Paul.]

Chevallier, Dominique. 1971. *La société du Mont Liban a l'époque de la révolution industrielle en Europe.* Paris: Geuthner.

————, ed. 1979. *L'Espace social de la ville arabe.* Paris: Maisonneuve et Larose.

———. 1982a. "Les villes arabes depuis le XIXe siècle ; structures, visions, trans-formations." In *Villes et travail en Syrie: du XIXe au XXe siècle,* ed. Dominique Chevallier, 29–40. Paris: Maisonneuve et Larose.

———. 1982b. "Non-Muslim Communities in Arab Cities." In *Christians and Jews in the Ottoman Empire: The Functioning of a Plural Society,* ed. Benjamin Braude and Bernard Lewis, vol. 2, 165–95. New York: Holmes and Meier.

———. 1984 "Legalité de la ville." In *Politiques urbaines dans le Monde Arabe,* vol. 1, ed. Jean Métral and Georges Mutin, 489–94. Lyon: Maison de l'Orient.

———. 1986. "Un titre ambigu pour des normes réelles." In *Middle Eastern Cities in Comparative Perspective/Points de Vue sur les Villes du Maghreb et du Machrek,* ed. Kenneth L. Brown, Michèle Jolé, Peter Sluglett, and Sami Zubaida, 83–89. London, Ithaca Press.

Choksy, Jamsheed K. 1989. *Purity and Pollution in Zoroastrianism: Triumph over Evil.* Austin: Univ. of Texas Press.

Chouraqui, André. 1965. *Cent ans d'histoire: L'Alliance Israélite Universelle et la renais-sance juive contemporaine (1860–1960).* Paris: Presses Universitaires de France.

Cigar, Norman. 1981. "Socio-Economic Structures and the Development of an Urban Bourgeoisie in Pre-Colonial Morocco." *Maghreb Review* 6:55–76.

Çizackça, Murat. 2000. *A History of Philanthropic Foundations: The Islamic World from the Seventh Century to the Present.* Istanbul: Boğaziçi Univ. Press.

Cleveland, William L. 1978. "The Municipal Council of Tunis, 1858–1870: A Study in Urban Institutional Change." *International Journal of Middle East Studies* 9:33–61.

———. 2004. *A History of the Modern Middle East.* Boulder, Colo.: Westview.

Clogg, Richard. 1982. "The Greek Millet in the Ottoman Empire." In *Christians and Jews in the Ottoman Empire: The Functioning of a Plural Society,* ed. Benjamin Braude and Bernard Lewis, vol. 1, 185–208. New York: Holmes and Meier.

Cohen, Amnon. 1973. *Palestine in the Eighteenth Century: Patterns of Government and Administration.* Jerusalem: Magnes Press.

———. 1984. *Jewish Life under Islam: Jerusalem in the Sixteenth Century.* Cambridge, Mass.: Harvard Univ. Press.

———. 2001. *The Guilds of Ottoman Jerusalem.* Leiden: Brill.

Cohen, Hayyim J. 1973. *The Jews of the Middle East, 1860–1972.* Jerusalem: Israel Universities Press.

Cohen, Mark R. 1994. *Under Crescent and Cross: The Jews in the Middle Ages.* Princeton: Princeton Univ. Press.

———. 1999. "What Was the Pact of 'Umar? A Literary-Historical Study." *Jerusalem Studies in Arabic and Islam* 23:100–57.

Cole, Juan. 1985. "Shi'i Clerics in Iraq and Iran, 1722–1780: The Akhbari-Usuli Conflict Reconsidered." *Iranian Studies* 18:3–33.

———. 1986. "Indian Money and the Holy Shrines of Iraq." *Middle Eastern Studies* 22:461–80.

———. 1989. "Of Crowds and Empires: Afro-Asian Riots and European Expansion 1857–1882." *Comparative Studies in Society and History* 31:106–33.

———. 1993. *Colonialism and Revolution in the Middle East: Social and Cultural Origins of Egypt's 'Urabi Revolution.* Princeton: Princeton Univ. Press.

Collins, Jeffrey B. 1984. *The Egyptian Elite under Cromer, 1882–1907.* Berlin: Klaus Schwarz.

Colonna, Fanny. 1974. "Les élites par la culture et les villes en Algérie, de la réforme Ferry (1883) à la veille de la deuxième guerre mondiale." In *Les influences occidentales dans les villes maghrébines à l'époque contemporaine,* ed. CRESM, 97–122. Aix en Provence: Éditions de l'Université d'Aix en Provence.

Cook, M. A. 1972. *Population Pressure in Rural Anatolia, 1450–1600.* London: Oxford Univ. Press.

Coon, Carleton S. 1958. *Caravan: The Story of the Middle East.* Revised edition. New York: Holt, Rinehart and Winston.

Corri, Alan D. 1980. "The Algiers Riot, January 1898." *Maghreb Review* 5:74–80.

Courbage, Youssef, and Fargues, Philippe. 1997. *Christians and Jews under Islam.* London: I. B. Tauris.

Crecelius, Daniel. 1981. *The Roots of Modern Egypt: A Study of the Regimes of Ali Bey al-Kabir and Muhammad Bey Abu al-Dhahab, 1760–1775.* Minneapolis: Bibliotheca Islamica.

———. 1986. "Incidences of Waqf Cases in Three Cairo Courts, 1640–1802." *Journal of the Economic and Social History of the Orient* 29:176–89.

———. 1991. "The Waqf of Muhammad Bey Abu al-Dhahab in Historical Perspective." *International Journal of Middle East Studies* 23:57–81.

Cromer, Earl of (Lord Cromer). 1908. *Modern Egypt.* 2 vols. London: Macmillan.

Crouch, Dora P., Daniel J. Garr, and Axel I. Mundigo, eds. 1982. *Spanish City Planning in North America.* Cambridge, Mass.: MIT Press.

Cuno, Kenneth M. 1988. "Commercial Relations between Towns and Villages in Eighteenth and Early Nineteenth Century Egypt." *Annales Islamologiques* 24:111–35.

———. 1992. *The Pasha's Peasants: Land, Society and Economy in Lower Egypt, 1740–1858.* Cambridge: Cambridge Univ. Press.

*Dalil Suriyya wa Misr al-tijari.* 1908. Cairo: n.p.

Darling, Linda T. 1995. "Capitulations." In *The Oxford Encyclopedia of the Modern Islamic World*, ed. John Esposito, vol. 1, 257–61. Oxford: Oxford Univ. Press.

David, Jean-Claude. 1975. "Alep; dégradation et tentatives actuelles de l'adaptation des structures urbaines traditionnelles." *Bulletin d'Études Orientales* 27:19–50.

———. 1979a. "Alep." In *La Syrie d'aujourd'hui*, ed. André Raymond, 385–406. Paris: Éditions du Centre National de la Recherche Scientifique.

———. 1979b. "Les quartiers anciens dans la croissance de la ville moderne d'Alep." In *L'Espace sociale de la ville arabe*, ed. Dominique Chevallier, 135–44. Paris: Maisonneuve et Larose.

———. 1982a. "Évolution et déplacement des fonctions centrales à Alep au XIXe et XXe siècles." In *La Ville arabe dans l'Islam*, ed. Abdelwahhab Bouhdiba and Dominique Chevallier, 247–58. Paris: Éditions du Centre National de la Recherche Scientifique.

———. 1982b. *Le Waqf d'Ipshir Pasha à Alep (1063/1653?): Étude d'urbanisme historique*. Damascus: Institut français d'études arabes de Damas.

———. 1990. "L'espace des chrétiens à Alep: ségrégation et mixité stratégies communautaires (1750–1950)." *Revue des monde musulman et de la Méditerranée* 55–56:152–70.

———. 1997. "Les territoires de groupes à Alep à l'époque ottomane." *Revue des mondes musulmans et de la Méditerranée* 79–80:225–54.

———. 1998. *La Suwayqat 'Ali à Alep*. Damascus: Institut français d'études arabes de Damas.

David, Jean-Claude, and Thierry Grandin. 1994. "L'habitat permanent des grands commerçants dans les khans à Alep à l'époque ottomane." In *Les villes dans l'Empire Ottoman: activites et sociétés*, vol. 2, ed. Daniel Panzac, 85–124. Paris: Éditions du Centre National de la Recherche Scientifique.

David, Jean-Claude, and Mahmoud Hreitani. 1984. "Souks traditionnels et centre moderne; espaces et pratiques à Alep (1930–1980)." *Bulletin d'Études Orientales* 36:1–78.

Davie, May. 1993. "Les Orthodoxes entre Beyrouth et Damas: une millet chrétienne dans deux villes ottomanes." In *State and Society in Syria and Lebanon*, ed. Youssef M. Choueiri, 32–45. Exeter: Exeter Univ. Press.

———. 1996. *Beirut et ses Faubourgs (1840–1940): Une intégration inachevée*. Beirut: Centre d'Études et de Recherches sur le Moyen-Orient Contemporain.

———. 2005. "Au Prisme de l'Alterité: les Orthodoxes de Beyrouth au Début du XIXe siècle." *Revue des mondes musulmans et de la Méditerranée* 109–119: 161–82.

Davison, Roderic H. 1953–1954. "Turkish Attitudes Concerning Christian-Muslim Equality in the 19th Century." *American Historical Review* 59:844–64.

———. 1963. *Reform in the Ottoman Empire, 1856–1876.* Princeton: Princeton Univ. Press.

———. 1982. "The Millets as Agents of Change in the Nineteenth-Century Ottoman Empire." In *Christians and Jews in the Ottoman Empire. The Functioning of a Plural Society,* ed. Benjamin Braude and Bernard Lewis, vol. 1, 319–37. New York: Holmes and Meir.

Debbas, Fouad. 1986. *Beirut: An Illustrated Tour in the Old City from 1880 to 1930.* Beirut: C. Debbas.

———. 2001. *Des Photographes à Beyrouth 1840–1918.* Paris: Marval.

Deeb, Marius. 1976. "Bank Misr and the Emergence of the Local Bourgeoisie in Egypt." *Middle Eastern Studies* 12:69–86.

———. 1978. "The Socio-economic Role of the Local Foreign Minorities in Modern Egypt, 1805–1961." *International Journal of Middle East Studies* 9:11–22.

Degeorge, Gérard. 1994. *Damas des Ottomans à nos jours.* Paris: L'Harmattan.

Deguilhem, Randi. 1994. "Waqf Documents as a Socio-economic Source for Ottoman History." In *CIÉPO: Osmanlı Öncesi ve Osmanlı Araştırmaları Uluslararası Komitesi: VII. Sempozyumu bildirileri, Peç, 7–11 Eylül 1986/yayına hazırlayanlar,* ed. Jean-Louis Bacqué-Grammont, İlber Ortaylı, and E. J. van Donzel, 35–41. Ankara: Türk Kurumu Basımevi.

———. ed. 1995. *Le waqf dans l'espace islamique: outil de pouvoir socio-politique.* Damascus: Institut français d'études arabes de Damas.

———. 1997. "La gestion des biens communautaires chrétiens en Syrie au XIXe siècle: politique ottomane et ingérence." *Revue des mondes musulmans et de la Méditerranée* 78–79:215–24.

———. 1998. "State Civil Education in Late Ottoman Damascus: A Unifying or a Separating Force?" In *The Syrian Land: Processes of Integration and Fragmentation,* ed. Thomas Philipp and Birgit Schaebler, 221–50. Stuttgart: Franz Steiner.

Denoix, Sylvie. 1992. *Décrire le Caire: Fustat-Misr d'après Ibn Duqmaq et Maqrizi.* Cairo: Institut français d'archéologie orientale.

Deshen, Shlomo. 1989. *The Mellah Society: Jewish Community Life in Sherifian Morocco.* Revised edition. Chicago: Univ. of Chicago Press.

———. 1994. "La communauté juive de Bagdad à la fin de l'époque ottomane; émergence de classes sociales et de la sécularisation." *Annales, Histoire, Sciences Sociales* 49:681–703.

————. 1996. "Community Life in Nineteenth-Century Moroccan Jewry." In *Jews among Muslims: Communities in the Pre-colonial Middle East*, ed. Shlomo Deshen and Walter P. Zenner, 98–108. Basingstoke, U.K.: Macmillan.

Deshen, Shlomo, and Walter P. Zenner, eds. 1982. *Jewish Societies in the Middle East: Community, Culture and Authority*. Washington, D.C.: Univ. Press of America.

————, eds. 1996. *Jews among Muslims: Communities in the Precolonial Middle East*. Basingstoke, U.K.: Macmillan.

Dettmann, Klaus. 1969. *Damaskus. Eine orientalische Stadt zwischen Tradition und Moderne*. Erlangen: Selbstverlag der Fränkischen Geographischen Gesellschaft in Kommission bei Palm und Enke.

Deverdun, Gaston. 1959. *Marrakech, des origines à 1912*. 2 vols. Rabat: Editions Techniques Nord Africaines.

Dimashqi, Mikha'il al-. 1912. *Tarikh hawadith al-Sham wa Lubnan, 1197–1257/1782–1842*, ed. Luwis Ma'luf. Beirut: al-Matba'a al-Kathulikiyya.

Doumani, Bishara. 1995. *Rediscovering Palestine: Merchants and Peasants in Jabal Nablus, 1700–1900*. Berkeley: Univ. of California Press.

Duben, Alan, and Cem Behar. 1991. *Istanbul Households: Marriage, Family, and Fertility, 1880–1940*. Cambridge: Cambridge Univ. Press.

Dumont, Paul. 1982. "Jewish Communities in Turkey during the Last Decades of the Nineteenth Century in the Light of the Archives of the Alliance Israélite Universelle." In *Christians and Jews in the Ottoman Empire: The Functioning of a Plural Society*, ed. Benjamin Braude and Bernard Lewis, vol. 1, 209–42. New York: Holmes and Meier.

————. 1992. "Les Juifs, les Arabes et le choléra. Les relations inter-communautaires à Baghdad à la fin du XIXe siècle." In *Villes ottomanes à la fin de l'Empire*, ed. Paul Dumont and François Georgeon, 153–70. Paris: L'Harmattan.

————. 1994. "Jews, Muslims and Cholera: Inter-communal Relations in Baghdad at the End of the 19th Century." In *The Jews of the Ottoman Empire*, ed. Avigdor Levy, 353–72. Princeton: Darwin Press.

Dumont, Paul, and François Georgeon, eds. 1992. *Villes ottomanes à la fin de l'Empire*. Paris: L'Harmattan.

Dyos, H. J. 1961. *Victorian Suburb: A Study of the Growth of Camberwell*. Leicester: Leicester Univ. Press.

Ehlers, Eckart. 1992. "The City of the Islamic Middle East." In *Modelling the City: Cross-Cultural Perspectives*, ed. Eckart Ehlers, 89–107. Bonn: F. Dümmlers.

Ehlers, Eckart, and Willem Floor. 1993–94. "Urban Change in Iran 1920–1941." *Iranian Studies* 26:251–75.

Eickelman, Dale. 1974. "Is There an Islamic City? The Making of a Quarter in a Moroccan Town." *International Journal of Middle East Studies* 5:274–94.

Eldem, Edhem. 1991. "Structure et acteurs du commerce international d'Istanbul au XVIIIe siècle." In *Les Villes dans l'Empire ottoman: activités et sociétés*, ed. Daniel Panzac, vol. 1, 243–71. Paris: Centre National de la Recherche Scientifique.

———. 1999. *French Trade in Istanbul in the Eighteenth Century*. Leiden: Brill.

Eldem, Edhem, Daniel Goffman, and Bruce Masters. 1999. *The Ottoman City between East and West: Aleppo, Izmir and Istanbul*. Cambridge: Cambridge Univ. Press.

Elisséeff, Nikita. 1965. "Dimashk." *Encyclopedia of Islam*. 2nd edition, vol. 2, 277–91. Leiden: Brill.

———. 1970. "Damas à la lumière des théories de Jean Sauvaget." In *The Islamic City*, ed. A. H. Hourani and S. M. Stern, 157–78. Oxford: Cassirer; Philadelphia: Univ. of Pennsylvania Press.

Engeli, Christian, and Horst Matzerath, eds. 1989. *Modern Urban History Research in Europe, the USA and Japan*. Oxford: Berg.

English, Paul Ward. 1966. "Culture Change and the Structure of a Persian City." *Texas Quarterly* 9:158–70.

Ergene, Boğaç. 2003. *Court, Provincial Society and Justice in the Ottoman Empire: Legal Practice and Dispute Resolution in Çankırı and Kastamonu (1652–1744)*. Leiden: Brill.

Erim, Nese. 1991. "Trade, Traders and the State in Eighteenth-Century Erzurum." *New Perspectives on Turkey* 5–6:123–49.

Escher, Anton, and Eugen Wirth. 1992. *Die Medina von Fes: Geographische Beiträge zu Persistenz und Dynamik, Verfall und Erneuerung einer traditionellen islamischen Stadt in handlungstheoretischer Sicht*. Erlangen: Erlanger geographische Arbeiten.

Establet, Colette, and Jean-Paul Pascual. 1994. *Familles et fortunes à Damas: 450 foyers damascains en 1700*. Damascus: Institut français d'études arabes de Damas.

Ettahadieh, Mansoureh. 1983. "Patterns in Urban Development: The Growth of Teheran 1852–1903." In *Qajar Iran: Political Social and Cultural Change 1800–1925*, ed. Edmund Bosworth and Carole Hillenbrand, 199–212. Edinburgh: Edinburgh Univ. Press.

Fahmy, Khaled. 1997. *All the Pasha's Men: Mehmed Ali, His Army and the Making of Modern Egypt*. Cambridge: Cambridge Univ. Press.

Faradi, Yass al-. n.d. Kitab nusrat al-mutagharribin 'an al-awtan 'ala al-zalama w'ahl al-'udwan. Manuscript, Asad National Library, Damascus, no. 6879.

Farah, Caesar E. 1986. "Protestantism and Politics: The 19th Century Dimension in Syria." In *Palestine in the Late Ottoman Period*, ed. David Kushner, 320–40. Jerusalem: Yad Izhak Ben-Zvi; Leiden: Brill.

Faroqhi, Suraiya. 1984. *Men of Modest Substance: House Owners and House Property in Seventeenth-Century Ankara and Kayseri.* Cambridge: Cambridge Univ. Press.

———. 1987. *Towns and Townsmen of Ottoman Anatolia: Trade, Crafts, and Food Production in an Urban Setting, 1520–1650.* Cambridge: Cambridge Univ. Press.

———. 1989. "Agriculture and Rural Life in the Ottoman Empire (ca. 1500–1878)." *New Perspectives on Turkey* 1:3–34.

———. 1994. *Pilgrims and Sultans: The Hajj under the Ottomans.* London: I. B. Tauris.

Faroqhi, Suraiya, and Deguilhem, Randi, eds. 2005. *Crafts and Craftsmen in the Middle East: Fashioning the Individual in the Muslim Mediterranean.* London: I. B. Tauris.

Farouk-Sluglett, Marion, and Peter Sluglett. 1983a. "The Transformation of Land Tenure and Rural Social Structure in Central and Southern Iraq, 1870–1958." *International Journal of Middle East Studies* 15:491–505.

———. 1983b. "Labour and National Liberation: The Trade Union Movement in Iraq, 1920–1958." *Arab Studies Quarterly* 5:139–54.

———. 2001. *Iraq since 1958: From Revolution to Dictatorship.* 3rd edition. London: I. B. Tauris.

Fattah, Hala. 1991. "The Politics of the Grain Trade in Iraq, c. 1840–1917." *New Perspectives on Turkey* 5–6:151–65.

———. 1997. *The Politics of Regional Trade in Iraq, Arabia and the Gulf, 1745–1900.* Albany: State Univ. of New York Press.

Fattal, Antoine. 1958. *Le Statut légal des non-musulmans en pays d'Islam.* Beirut: Imprimerie Catholique.

Fawaz, Leila Tarazi. 1983. *Merchants and Migrants in Nineteenth Century Beirut.* Cambridge, Mass.: Harvard Univ. Press.

———. 1990. "The Changing Balance of Forces between Beirut and Damascus in the Nineteenth and Twentieth Centuries." *Revue des mondes musulmans et de la Méditerranée* 55/56:208–14.

———. 1994. *An Occasion for War: Civil Conflict in Lebanon and Damascus in 1860.* Berkeley: Univ. of California Press.

Fawaz, Leila Tarazi, and C. A. Bayly, eds. 2002. *Modernity and Culture from the Mediterranean to the Indian Ocean.* New York: Columbia Univ. Press.

Findley, Carter V. 1982. "The Acid Test of Ottomanism: The Acceptance of Non-Muslims in the Late Ottoman Bureaucracy." In *Christians and Jews in the Ottoman Empire: The Functioning of a Plural Society,* vol. 1, ed. Benjamin Braude and Bernard Lewis, 339–68. New York: Holmes and Meier.

Floor, Willem. 1975. "The Guilds in Iran: An Overview from the Earliest Beginnings till 1972." *Zeitschrift der Deutschen Morgenländischen Gesellschaft* 125:99–116.

―――. 1976. "The Merchants (tujjar) of Qajar Iran." *Zeitschrift der Deutschen Morgenländischen Gesellschaft* 126:101–35.

―――. 1979. "The Bankers (sarraf) in Qajar Iran." *Zeitschrift der Deutschen Morgenländischen Gesellschaft* 129:263–81.

―――. 1983. "Change and Development in the Judicial System of Qajar Iran (1800–1925)." In *Qajar Iran: Political, Social and Cultural Change 1800–1925,* ed. Edmund Bosworth and Carole Hillenbrand, 113–47. Edinburgh: Edinburgh Univ. Press.

―――. 2003. *Traditional Crafts in Qajar Iran, 1800–1925.* Costa Mesa, Calif.: Mazda.

Fortna, Benjamin. 2002. *Imperial Classroom: Islam, the State and Education in the Late Ottoman Empire.* Oxford: Oxford Univ. Press.

Frangakis-Syrett, Elena. 1991a. "British Economic Activities in Izmir in the Second Half of the Nineteenth and Early Twentieth Centuries." *New Perspectives on Turkey* 5–6:191–222.

―――. 1991b. "The Trade in Cotton and Cloth in Izmir: From the Second Half of the Eighteenth Century to the Early Nineteenth Century." In *Landholding and Commercial Agriculture in the Middle East,* ed. Çağlar Keyder and Faruk Tabak, 97–112. Albany: State Univ. of New York Press.

―――. 2002. "Networks of Friendship, Networks of Kinship: Eighteenth-Century Levant Merchants." *Eurasian Studies* 1:183–205.

Frankel, Jonathan. 1997. *The Damascus Affair: "Ritual Murder," Politics and the Jews in 1840.* Cambridge: Cambridge Univ. Press.

Frazee, Charles A. 1983. *Catholics and Sultans: the Church and the Ottoman Empire, 1453–1923.* Cambridge: Cambridge Univ. Press.

Friedman, Isaiah. 1986. "The System of Capitulations and Its Effects on Turco-Jewish Relations in Palestine, 1856–1897." In *Palestine in the Late Ottoman Period,* ed. David Kushner, 280–93. Jerusalem: Yad Izhak Ben-Zvi; Leiden: Brill.

Friedmann, Yohanan. 2003. *Tolerance and Coercion in Islam. Interfaith Relations in the Muslim Tradition.* Cambridge: Cambridge Univ. Press.

Fuccaro, Nelida. 2000. "Understanding the Urban History of Bahrain." *Critique* 17:49–81.

―――. 2003. "Ethnicity and the City: The Kurdish Quarter of Damascus Between Ottoman and French Rule, c. 1714–1946." *Urban History* 30:206–24.

Fukusawa, K. 1987. *Toilerie et commerce du Levant au XVIIIe siècle: d'Alep à Marseille.* Paris: Éditions du Centre National de la Recherche Scientifique.

Fustel de Coulanges, Numa Denis. 1864. *La cité antique: étude sur le culte, le droit, les institutions de la Grèce et de Rome*. Paris: Hachette. [Translated as *The Ancient City: A Study on the Religions, Laws and Institutions of Greece and Rome*. Garden City, N.Y.: Doubleday, 1956.]

Gabriel, Alfons. 1971. *Religionsgeographie von Persien*. Vienna: Kommissionsverlag Gebrüder Hollinek.

Gaillard, Henri. 1905. *Une ville d'Islam: Fès*. Paris: J. André.

Ganiage, Jean. 1994. *Histoire contemporaine du Maghreb de 1830 à nos jours*. Paris: Fayard.

García-Arenal, Mercedes, ed. 200a. *Conversions islamiques: identités religieuses en Islam méditerranéen/Islamic Conversions: Religious Identities in Mediterranean Islam*. Paris: Maisonneuve et Larose.

Gaube, Heinz, and Eugen Wirth. 1984. *Aleppo: Historische and geographische Beiträge zur baulichen Gestaltung, zur sozialen Organisation und zur wirtschaftlichen Dynamik einer vorderasiatischen Fernhandelsmetropole*. Wiesbaden: Ludwig Reichert.

Gauvain, Richard. 2005. "Ritual Rewards: A Consideration of Three Recent Approaches to Sunni Purity Laws." *Islamic Law and Society* 12:333–93.

Geertz, Clifford, Hildred Geertz, and Lawrence Rosen. 1979. *Meaning and Order in Moroccan Society: Three Essays in Cultural Analysis*. Cambridge: Cambridge Univ. Press.

Gellner, Ernest. 1983. *Muslim Society*. Cambridge: Cambridge Univ. Press.

Genç, Mehmet. 1976. "A Comparative Study of the Life Tax-farming Data and the Volume of Industrial Activities in the Ottoman Empire in the Second Half of the Eighteenth Century." *La Revolution industrielle dans le Sud-Est européen au XIXe siècle: rapports presentés au colloque international de la Commission de l'AIESEE sur l'histoire sociale et économique, Hamburg, 23–26 mars 1976*. Sofia: Institut d'Etudes Balkaniques.

Georgelin, Hervé. 2005. *La fin de Smyrne. Du cosmopolitisme aux nationalismes*. Paris: Centre National de la Recherche Scientifique.

Georgeon, François, and Paul Dumont, eds. 1997. *Vivre dans l'Empire ottoman: sociabilités et relations intercommunautaires (XVIIe–XXe siècles)* Paris: L'Harmattan.

Gerber, Haim. 1976. "Guilds in Seventeenth Century Anatolian Bursa." *Asian and African Studies* 11:59–86.

———. 1979. "The Population of Syria and Palestine in the 19th Century." *Asian and African Studies* 13:58–80.

———. 1985. *Ottoman Rule in Jerusalem, 1890–1914*. Berlin: Klaus Schwarz.

————. 1988. *Economy and Society in an Ottoman City: Bursa, 1600–1700.* Jerusalem: Institute of Asian and African Studies, Hebrew Univ. of Jerusalem.

Gervers, Michael, and Ramzi Jibran Bikhazi, eds. 1990. *Conversion and Continuity: Indigenous Christian Communities in Islamic Lands. Eighth to Eighteenth Centuries.* Toronto: Pontifical Institute of Medieval Studies.

Ghazaleh, Pascale. 1995. "The Guilds: Between Tradition and Modernity." In *The State and Its Servants: Administration in Egypt from Ottoman Times to the Present,* ed. Nelly Hanna, 60–74. Cairo: American Univ. in Cairo Press.

————. 1999. *Masters of the Trade: Crafts and Craftspeople in Cairo, 1750–1850.* Cairo: American Univ. in Cairo Press.

Ghazzal, Zouhair. 1993. *L'économie politique de Damas durant le XIXe siècle: Structures traditionelles et capitalisme.* Damascus: Institut français d'études arabes de Damas.

Ghazzi, Kamil al-. 1926. *Nahr al-Dhahab fi Tarikh Halab.* 3 vols. Aleppo: al-Matba'a al-Maruniyya.

Ghazzi, Najm al-Din al-. 1979. *al-Kawakib al-sa'ira bi-a'yan al-mi'a al-'ashira,* ed. Jibra'il Jabbur. 3 vols. 2nd impression. Beirut: Dar al-Afaq al-Jadida.

————. 1981–82. *Lutf al-samar wa-qatf al-thamar,* ed. Mahmud al-Shaykh. 2 vols. Damascus: Wizarat al-Thaqafa.

Gibb, Hamilton, and Harold Bowen. 1969. *Islamic Society and the West: A Study of the Impact of Western Civilization in the Near East.* 2 vols., 2nd edition. London: Oxford Univ. Press.

Gilbar, Gad G. 1976. "Demographic Developments in Late Qajar Persia, 1870–1907." *Asian and African Studies* 11:125–56.

Gilbert, Martin. 1976. *The Jews of Arab Lands: Their History in Maps.* London: Board of Deputies of British Jews.

Girard, P. S. 1812. "Mémoire sur l'agriculture, l'industrie et le commerce de l'Égypte." *Description de l'Égypte: État Moderne,* vol. 2, part 1, 491–714.

Goffman, Daniel. 1990. *Izmir and the Levantine World, 1550–1650.* Seattle: Univ. of Washington Press.

Goitein, S. D. 1971. *A Mediterranean Society,* vol. 2. Berkeley: Univ. of California Press.

Golany, Gideon S. 1994. *ha-Bayit veha-rova' ha-Yehudi be-Bagdad: arkhitektura u-sevivat hayim* [Vernacular house design and the Jewish quarter in Baghdad]. Or-Yehuda, Israel: Merkaz moreshet Yehude Bavel, no. 754.

Goldberg, Ellis. 1986. *Tinker, Tailor, Textile Worker: Class and Politics in Egypt, 1930–1952.* Berkeley: Univ. of California Press.

————. 1991. "Was There an Islamic City?" In *Cities in the World System*, ed. Reşat Kasaba, 3–16. Westport, Conn.: Greenwood.

————, ed. 1996. *The Social History of Labor in the Middle East*. Boulder: Westview Press.

Goldberg, Harvey E. 1990. *Jewish Life in Muslim Libya: Rivals and Relatives*. Chicago: Univ. of Chicago Press.

————, ed. 1996. *Sephardi and Middle Eastern Jewries: History and Culture in the Modern Era*. Bloomington: Indiana Univ. Press.

Gottreich, Emily. 2007. *The Mellah of Marrakesh: Jewish and Muslim Space in Morocco's Red City*. Bloomington: Indiana Univ. Press.

Gran, Peter. 1987. "Late-Eighteenth–Early-Nineteenth-Century Egypt: Merchant Capitalism or Modern Capitalism?" In *The Ottoman Empire and the World-Economy*, ed. Huri İslamoğlu-İnan, 27–41. Cambridge: Cambridge Univ. Press.

————. 1994. Review of Kenneth M. Cuno, *The Pasha's Peasants: Land, Society and Economy in Lower Egypt, 1740–1858*. Cambridge: Cambridge Univ. Press, 1992, in *International Journal of Middle East Studies* 26:289–91.

Grangaud, Isabelle. 2002. *La ville imprenable: une histoire sociale de Constantine au XVIII siècle*. Paris: École des Hautes Études en Sciences Sociales.

Great Britain. 1919. *Administration Report for the Vilayet of Mosul, 1919*.

Great Britain, Naval Intelligence Division. 1917–18. *A Handbook of Mesopotamia*. London: Naval Staff, Intelligence Department.

Greene, Molly. 2000. *A Shared World: Christians and Muslims in the Early Modern Mediterranean*. Princeton: Princeton Univ. Press.

Greenshields, T. H. 1980. "'Quarters' and Ethnicity." In *The Changing Middle Eastern City*, ed. G. H. Blake and R. I. Lawless, 120–40. London: Croom Helm.

Gregorian, Vartan. 1974. "Minorities in Isfahan: The Armenian Community of Isfahan, 1587–1722." *Iranian Studies* 1:652–80.

Grehan, James. 2003. "Street Violence and Social Imagination in Late Mamluk and Ottoman Damascus (ca. 1500–1800)." *International Journal of Middle East Studies* 35:215–36.

————. 2007. *Everyday Life and Consumer Culture in Eighteenth Century Damascus*. Seattle: Univ. of Washington Press.

Gunn, Simon. 2002. "Knowledge, Power and the City since 1700." *Social History* 27:59–63.

Gurney, J. D. 1983. "A Qajar Household and Its Estates." *Iranian Studies* 16:137–76.

Hacker, Joseph. 1992. "The Sürgün System and Jewish Society in the Ottoman Empire during the Fifteenth to the Seventeenth Centuries." In *Ottoman and Turkish*

*Jewry: Community and Leadership,* ed. Aron Rodrigue, 1–65. Bloomington: Indiana Univ. Turkish Studies.

———. 1994. "Jewish Autonomy in the Ottoman Empire: Its Scope and Limits. Jewish Courts from the Sixteenth to the Eighteenth Centuries." In *The Jews of the Ottoman Empire,* ed. Avigdor Levy, 153–202. Princeton: Darwin Press.

Haddad, Robert M. 1970. *Syrian Christians in Muslim Society: An Interpretation.* Princeton: Princeton Univ. Press.

Hajjar, Joseph N. 1962. *Les chrétiens uniates du Proche-Orient.* Paris: Éditions du Seuil.

Halliday, Fred. 1992. "The Millet of Manchester: Arab Merchants and the Cotton Trade." *British Journal of Middle Eastern Studies* 19:159–76.

Hanna, 'Abdallah. 1985. *Harakat al-'ammiyya al-dimashqiyya fi l-qarnayn al-thamin 'ashar wa al-tasi 'ashar.* Beirut: Dar Ibn Khaldun.

———. 2004. "The Attitude of the French Mandatory Authorities towards Landownership in Syria." In *The British and French Mandates in Comparative Perspectives/Les mandats français et anglais dans une perspective comparative,* ed. Nadine Méouchy and Peter Sluglett, 457–76. Leiden: Brill.

Hanna, Nelly. 1983. *An Urban History of Bulaq in the Mamluk and Ottoman Periods.* Cairo: Institut français d'archéologie orientale.

———. 1991. *Habiter au Caire. La Maison moyenne et ses habitants aux XVIIe et XVIIIe siècles.* Cairo: Institut français d'archéologie orientale.

———. 2003. *In Praise of Books: A Cultural History of Cairo's Middle Class, Sixteenth to the Eighteenth Century.* Syracuse: Syracuse Univ. Press.

Hanna, Nelly, and Raouf Abbas, eds. 2005. *Society and Economy in Egypt and the Eastern Mediterranean 1600–1900: Essays in Honor of André Raymond.* Cairo: American Univ. in Cairo Press.

Hannoyer, Jean, and Seteny Chami, eds. 1996. *Amman: ville et société: the city and its society.* Beirut: Centre d'Études et de Recherches sur le Moyen-Orient Contemporain.

Hansen, Bent. 1981. "An Economic Model for Ottoman Egypt: The Economics of Collective Tax Responsibility." In *The Islamic Middle East East, 700–1900: Studies in Economic and Social History,* ed. Avram L. Udovitch, 473–519. Princeton: Darwin Press.

Hanssen, Jens. 2005. *Fin de Siècle Beirut: The Making of an Ottoman Provincial Capital.* Oxford: Oxford Univ. Press.

Hanssen, Jens, Thomas Philipp, and Stefan Weber, eds. 2002. *The Empire in the City: Arab Provincial Capitals in the Late Ottoman Empire.* Beirut: Orient-Institut; Würzburg: Ergon.

Harbi, Mohamed. 1989. "Appartenance sociale et dynamique politique: Skikda 1937–1955." In *État, ville et mouvements sociaux au Maghreb et au Moyen Orient/Arab and Muslim Cities: The State, Urban Crisis and Social Movements,* ed. Kenneth L. Brown, Bernard Hourcade, Michèle Jolé, Claude Liauzu, Peter Sluglett, Sami Zubaida, 103–14. Paris: L'Harmattan.

Harel, Yaron. 1998. "Jewish-Christian Relations in Aleppo as a Background for the Jewish Response to the Events of October 1850." *International Journal of Middle East Studies* 30:77–96.

Hartmann, Klaus-Peter. 1980. *Untersuchungen zur Sozialgeographie christlicher Minderheiten im Vorderen Orient.* Wiesbaden: Ludwig Reichert.

Hathaway, Jane. 1997. *The Politics of Households in Ottoman Egypt: The Rise of the Qazdağlis.* Cambridge: Cambridge Univ. Press.

Helfgott, Leonard M. 1994. *Ties That Bind: A Social History of the Iranian Carpet.* Washington: Smithsonian Institution Press.

Hénia, Abdelhamid. 1995. "Pratique habous, mobilité sociale et conjoncture économique à Tunis à l'époque moderne, XVIIe et XIXe siècles." In *Le waqf dans l'espace islamique: outil de pouvoir socio-politique,* ed. Randi Deguilhem, 70–100. Damascus: Institut français d'études arabes de Damas.

———. 2000. *Villes et territoires au Maghreb: itinéraire d'une recherche.* Tunis: Institut de la Recherche sur le Maghreb Contemporain.

Henneberg, Krystyna von. 1996. "The Construction of Fascist Libya: Modern Colonial Architecture and Urban Planning in Italian North Africa 1922–1943." Ph.D. diss., Univ. of California at Berkeley.

Hess, Andrew C. 1978. *The Forgotten Frontier: A History of the Sixteenth Century Ibero-African Frontier.* Chicago: Univ. of Chicago Press.

Heyberger, Bernard. 1994. *Les chrétiens du Proche-orient au temps de la réforme catholique.* Rome: École française de Rome.

———, ed. 2003. *Chrétiens du monde arabe: un archipel en terre d'Islam.* Paris: Éditions Autrement.

Hoexter, Miriam. 1983. "Effects of the Transition from the Turkish to the French regime in Algiers: The Case of the Mzabi Talaba (Tolba)." *Asian and African Studies* 17:121–37.

Hohenberg, Paul, and Lynn Hollen Lees. 1995. *The Making of Urban Europe 1000–1994.* 2nd edition. Cambridge, Mass.: Harvard Univ. Press.

Hoisington, William A. 1978. "Cities in Revolt: The Berber Dahir (1930) and France's Urban Strategy in Morocco." *Journal of Contemporary History* 13:443–48.

Homsy, Basile. 1956. *Les capitulations et la protection des Chrétiens du Proche Orient au XVIe, XVIIe et XVIIIe siècles.* Harissa, Lebanon.

Hopwood, Derek. 1969. *The Russian Presence in Syria and Palestine, 1843–1914.* Oxford: Clarendon Press.

Hourani, Albert. 1947. *Minorities in the Arab World.* London: Oxford Univ. Press.

———. 1957. "The Changing Face of the Fertile Crescent in the Eighteenth Century." *Studia Islamica* 8:89–122.

———. 1968. "Ottoman Reform and the Politics of Notables." In *Beginnings of Modernization in the Middle East: The Nineteenth Century,* ed. William R. Polk and Richard L. Chambers, 41–68. Chicago: Univ. of Chicago Press.

———. 1981. "The Islamic City." In *The Emergence of the Modern Middle East,* ed. Albert Hourani, 19–35. Berkeley: Univ. of California Press.

———. 1983. *Arabic Thought in the Liberal Age, 1798–1939.* Cambridge: Cambridge Univ. Press.

———. 1990. "L'oeuvre d'André Raymond." *Revue du monde musulman et de la Méditerranée* 55–56:18–27.

———. 1991. "How Should We Write the History of the Middle East?" *International Journal of Middle East Studies* 23:125–136.

Hourcade, Bernard. 1989. "Vaqf et modernité en Iran. Les agro-business de l'Astân-e Qods de Mashhad." In *Entre l'Iran et l'Occident,* ed. Yann Richard, 117–41. Paris: Maison des Sciences de l'Homme.

Hudson, Leila. 2006. "Late Ottoman Damascus: Investments in Public Space and the Emergence of Popular Sovereignty." *Critique: Critical Middle Eastern Studies* 15:151–69.

———. Forthcoming. *Transforming Damascus: Space and Modernities in an Islamic City.* London: I. B. Tauris.

Humphreys, R. Stephen. 1991. *Islamic History: A Framework for Inquiry.* Revised edition. London: I. B. Tauris.

Ibrahim, Samir 'Amru. 1992. *al-Hayat al-ijtima'iyya fi madinat al-Qahira khilal al-nisf al-awwal min al-qarn al-tasi' 'ashar.* Cairo: al-Hay'a al-misriyya al-'amma lil-kitab.

Ihsanoğlu, Ekmeleddin. 2001. *Egypt: As Viewed in the 19th Century.* Istanbul: Research Centre for Islamic History, Art and Culture.

Ilbert, Robert. 1981. *Héliopolis: Le Caire, 1905–1922, genèse d'une ville.* Paris: Éditions du Centre National de la Recherche Scientifique.

———. 1982. "La ville islamique: realité et abstraction." *Cahiers de la Recherche Architecturale* 10–11:6–13.

———. 1987. "L'exclusion du voisin: pouvoirs et relations intercommunautaires, 1870–1900." *Revue de l'occident musulman et de la Méditerranée* 46:177–86.

———. 1989. "Égypte 1900, habitat populaire, société coloniale." In *État, ville et mouvements sociaux au Maghreb et au Moyen Orient/Arab and Muslim Cities: The State, Urban Crisis and Social Movements,* ed. Kenneth L. Brown, Bernard Hourcade, Michèle Jolé, Claude Liauzu, Peter Sluglett, and Sami Zubaida, 262–82. Paris: L'Harmattan.

———. 1992. "Alexandrie, cosmopolite?" In *Villes ottomanes à la fin de l'Empire,* ed. François Georgeon and Paul Dumont, 171–85. Paris: L'Harmattan.

———. 1994. "L'invention du marché : Alexandrie 1850–1920." In *Les villes dans L'Empire Ottomane: activités et sociétés,* ed. Daniel Panzac, vol. 2, 357–76. Paris: Éditions du Centre National de la Recherche Scientifique.

———. 1996. *Alexandrie 1830–1930: Histoire d'une communauté citadine.* 2 vols. Cairo: Institut français d'archéologie orientale.

İnalcik, Halil. 1973a. "The Application of the Tanzimat and Its Social Effects." *Archivum Ottomanicum* 5:97–127.

———. 1973b. *The Ottoman Empire: The Classical Age 1300–1600.* Trans. Norman Itzkowitz and Colin Imber. London: Weidenfeld and Nicolson

———. 1979. "Harir." *Encyclopedia of Islam.* 2nd edition, vol. 3, 211–18. Leiden, Brill.

———. 1991. "The Emergence of Big Farms, Çiftliks: State, Landlords and Tenants." In *Landholding and Commercial Agriculture in the Middle East,* ed. Çağlar Keyder and Faruk Tabak, 17–34. Albany: State Univ. of New York Press.

İnalcik, Halil, and Donald Quataert, eds. 1994. *An Economic and Social History of the Ottoman Empire 1300–1914.* Cambridge: Cambridge Univ. Press.

İslamoğlu-İnan, Huri, ed. 1987. *The Ottoman Empire and the World-Economy.* Cambridge: Cambridge Univ. Press.

Isma'il, Sayf al-Din 'Abd al-Fattah. 1992. "al-Mujtama'al-madani wa al-dawla fi'l-fikr wa al-mumarasa al-islamiyya al-mu'asira" [Civil society and the state in contemporary Islamic thought and practice]. In *al-Mujtama' al-Madani fi'l-Watan al-'Arabi wa-Dawruhu fi Tahqiq al-Dimuqratiyya* [Civil society in the Arab homeland and its role in assuring democracy], ed. Sa'id Bin Sa'id al-'Alawi et al. Beirut: Markaz Dirasat al-Wahda al-'Arabiyya.

Issawi, Charles. 1966. *The Economic History of the Middle East 1800–1914.* Chicago: Univ. of Chicago Press.

———. 1969. "Economic Change and Urbanization in the Middle East." In *Middle Eastern Cities: A Symposium on Contemporary Middle Eastern Urbanization,* ed. Ira M. Lapidus, 102–21. Berkeley: Univ. of California Press.

————. 1977. "British Trade and the Rise of Beirut 1830–1860." *International Journal of Middle East Studies* 8:91–101

————. 1980. *The Economic History of Turkey.* Chicago: Univ. of Chicago Press.

————. 1982. "The Transformation of the Economic Position of the Millets in the Nineteenth century." In *Christians and Jews in the Ottoman Empire: The Functioning of a Plural Society,* ed. Benjamin Braude and Bernard Lewis, vol. 1, 261–86. New York: Holmes and Meier.

————. 1988. *The Fertile Crescent, 1800–1914: A Documentary Economic History.* New York: Oxford Univ. Press.

Jabarti, 'Abd al-Rahman al-. n.d. *Ta'rikh 'Aja'ib al-Athar fi'l-Tarajim wa al-Akhbar.* 3 vols. Beirut: Dar al-Jil.

Janabi, Hashim Khudayyir al-. 1981. *al-Tarkib al-Dakhili li-Madinat al-Mawsil al-Qadima.* Mosul: Univ. of Mosul.

Jennings, Ronald C. 1973. "Loans and Credit in Early 17th Century Ottoman Judicial Records: The Sharia Court of Anatolian Kayseri." *Journal of the Economic and Social History of the Orient* 16:168–207.

————. 1999. *Studies on Ottoman Social History in the Sixteenth and Seventeenth Centuries: Women, Zimmis and Shari'a Courts in Kayseri, Cyprus and Trabzon.* Istanbul, Isis Press.

Johansen, Baber. 1981a. "The All-Embracing Town and Its Mosques: al-misr al-gami'." *Revue de l'occident musulman et de la Méditerranée* 32:139–61.

————. 1981b. "The Servants of the Mosques." *Maghreb Review* 7:23–31.

————. 1990. "Urban Structures in the View of Muslim Jurists: The Case of Damascus in the Early 19th Century." *Revue des mondes musulmans et de la Méditerranée* 55–56:94–100.

Jomard, E. F. 1822. "Description de la ville et de la citadelle du Kaire accompagnée de l'explication des plans de cette ville et de ses environs, et de renseignements sur sa distribution, ses monumens [sic], sa population, son commerce et son industrie." *Description de l'Égypte: État Moderne,* vol. 2, part 1, 579–764.

Joseph, John. 1961. *The Nestorians and Their Muslim Neighbors: A Study of Western Influences on Their Relationship.* Princeton: Princeton Univ. Press.

————. 1983. *Muslim-Christian Relations and Inter-Christian Rivalries in the Middle East: The Case of the Jacobites in an Age of Transition.* Albany: State Univ. of New York Press.

Joseph, Suad. 1997. "Gender and Civil Society." In *Political Islam,* ed. Joel Beinin and Joe Stork, 64–71. Berkeley: Univ. of California Press.

Joudah, Ahmad. 1987. *Revolt in Palestine in the Eighteenth Century: The Era of Shaykh Zahir al-Umar.* Princeton: Kingston Press.

Julien, Charles-André. 1970. *History of North Africa: Tunisia, Algeria, Morocco. From the Arab Conquest to 1830*. Trans. John Petrie. London: Routledge and Kegan Paul.

Jwaideh, Albertine. 1984. "Aspects of Land Tenure and Social Change in Lower Iraq during Late Ottoman Times." In *Land Tenure and Social Transformation in the Middle East,* ed. Tarif Khalidi, 333–56. Beirut: American Univ. of Beirut Press.

Kark, Ruth. 1980. "The Jerusalem Municipality at the End of Ottoman Rule." *Asian and African Studies* 14:117–41.

———. 1981. "The Traditional Middle Eastern City: The Cases of Jerusalem and Jaffa during the 19th Century." *Zeitschrift des Deutschen Palästina Vereins* 97:94–108.

———. 1990. "The Rise and Decline of Coastal Towns in Palestine." In *Ottoman Palestine 1800–1914: Studies in Economic and Social History,* ed. Gad G. Gilbar, 127–77. Leiden: Brill.

Karmi, Ilan. 1984. *The Jewish Community of Istanbul in the Nineteenth Century: Social, Legal and Administrative Transformations*. Istanbul: Isis Press.

Karpat, Kemal H. 1978. "Ottoman Population Records and the Census of 1881/82–1883." *International Journal of Middle East Studies* 9:237–74.

———. 1985. *Ottoman Population 1830–1914: Demographic and Social Characteristics*. Madison: Univ. of Wisconsin Press.

Kasaba, Reşat. 1988. *The Ottoman Empire and the World Economy: The Nineteenth Century*. Albany: State Univ. of New York Press.

———. 1993. "Izmir." *Review* [State Univ. of New York, Binghamton] 16:387–410.

Kasaba, Reşat, Çağlar Keyder, and Faruk Tabak. 1986. "Eastern Mediterranean Port Cities and Their Bourgeoisies: Merchants, Political Prospects and Nation States." *Review* [State Univ. of New York, Binghamton] 10:121–35.

Kateb, Kamel. 2001. *Européens, "indigènes" et juifs en Algérie (1830–1962): Représentations et réalités des populations*. Paris: Éditions de l'Institut National d'Études Démographiques.

Katz, Kimberly. 2005. *Jordanian Jerusalem: Holy Places and National Spaces*. Gainesville: Univ. Press of Florida.

Kawtharani, Wajih. 1988. *al-Sulta wa al-Mujtama' wa al-'Amal al-Siyasi, min Tarikh al-Wilaya al-'Uthmaniyya fi Bilad al-Sham* [Power, society and political praxis: The history of Ottoman rule in Syria.] Beirut: Markaz Dirasat al-Wahda al-'Arabiyya.

———. 1990. *al-Faqih wa al-Sultan fi Tajrubatayn Tarikhiyyatayn: al-Tajruba al-'Uthmaniyya wa al-Tajruba al-Safawiyya al-Qajariyya* [The legal scholar and the sultan in two historical experiences: The Ottoman experience and the Safavid/Qajar experience]. Beirut: Dar al-Rashid Press.

Kayalı, Hasan. 1997. *Arabs and Young Turks: Ottomanism, Arabism, and Islamism in the Ottoman Empire, 1908–1918*. Berkeley: Univ. of California Press.

Keddie, Nikki R. 1966. *Religion and Rebellion in Iran: The Tobacco Protest of 1891–1892*. London: Frank Cass.

Kedourie, Elie. 1971a. "The Jews of Baghdad in 1910." *Middle Eastern Studies* 7:355–61.

———. 1971b. "Vice Consul H. Wilkie Young, Mosul, Mosul, to Sir Gerard Lowther, Constantinople, 28 January 1909." *Middle Eastern Studies* 7:229–35.

Kenbib, Muhammad. 1985. "Les relations entre musulmans et juifs au Maroc, 1859–1945." *Hespéris Tamuda* 23:83–104.

Keyder, Çağlar, and Faruk Tabak, eds. 1991. *Landholding and Commercial Agriculture in the Middle East*. Binghamton: State Univ. of New York Press.

Keyder, Çağlar, Y. Özveren, and Donald Quataert. 1993. "Port Cities in the Ottoman Empire: Some Historical and Theoretical Perspectives." *Review* [State Univ. of New York, Binghamton] 16:519–58.

Keyvani, Mehdi. 1982. *Artisans and Guild Life in the later Safavid Period*. Berlin: Klaus Schwarz.

Khalaf, Samir, and Philip S. Khoury, eds. 1993. *Recovering Beirut*. Leiden: Brill.

Khalidi, Rashid, Lisa Anderson, Muhammad Muslih, and Reeva S. Simon, eds. 1991. *The Origins of Arab Nationalism*. New York: Columbia Univ. Press.

Khater, Akram. 2001. *Inventing Home: Emigration, Gender, and the Middle Class in Lebanon, 1870–1920*. Berkeley: Univ. of California Press.

Khoury, Adel T. 1994. *Christen unterm Halbmond. Religiöse Minderheiten unter der Herrschaft des Islams*. Freiburg: Herder.

Khoury, Dina Rizk. 1991. "Merchants and Trade in Early Modern Iraq." *New Perspectives on Turkey* 5–6:53–86.

———. 1997a. *State and Provincial Society in the Ottoman Empire, Mosul 1540–1834*. Cambridge: Cambridge Univ. Press.

———. 1997b. "Slippers at the Entrance or Behind Closed Doors: Domestic and Public Spaces of Mosuli Women." In *Women in the Ottoman Empire: Middle Eastern Women in the Early Modern Era*, ed. Madeline C. Zilfi, 105–27. Leiden: Brill.

———. 2008. "Violence and Spatial Politics between the Local and the Imperial: Baghdad 1778–1810." In *Cities: Space, Society and History*, ed. Gyan Prakash and Kevin Kruze, 181–213. Princeton: Princeton Univ. Press.

Khoury, Philip S. 1983. *Urban Notables and Arab Nationalism: The Politics of Damascus 1860–1920*. Cambridge: Cambridge Univ. Press.

———. 1984. "Syrian Urban Politics in Transition: The Quarters of Damascus during the French Mandate." *International Journal of Middle East Studies* 16:507–40.

———. 1987. *Syria and the French Mandate: The Politics of Arab Nationalism, 1920–1945*. London: I. B. Tauris.

———. 1990. "The Urban Notables Paradigm Revisited." *Revue des mondes musulmans et de la Méditerranée* 55–56:215–28.

Khuri, Fuad I. 1975. *From Village to Suburb: Order and Change in Greater Beirut*. Chicago: Univ. of Chicago Press.

———. 1990. *Imams and Emirs: State, Religion and Sects in Islam*. London: Saqi Books.

Kitroeff, Alexander. 1989. *The Greeks in Egypt, 1919–1937: Ethnicity and Class*. London: Ithaca Press.

Klein-Franke, Aviva. 1997. "Zum Rechtsstatus der Juden im Jemen." *Die Welt des Islams* 37:178–209.

Kopp, Horst, and Eugen Wirth. 1990. *Beiträge zur Stadtgeographie von Sanaa'*. Wiesbaden: Ludwig Reichert.

Kortepeter, C. Max. 1994. "Jew and Turk in Algiers in 1800." In *The Jews of the Ottoman Empire*, ed. Avigdor Levy, 327–53. Princeton: Darwin Press.

Krämer, Gudrun. 1989. *The Jews in Modern Egypt, 1914–1952*. London: I. B. Tauris.

Krikorian, Mesrov K. 1977. *Armenians in the Service of the Ottoman Empire, 1860–1908*. London: Routledge and Kegan Paul.

Kuhnke, LaVerne. 1990. *Lives at Risk: Public Health in Nineteenth-Century Egypt*. Berkeley: Univ. of California Press.

Kunt, Metin. 1982. "The Transformation of Zimmi into Askeri." In *Christians and Jews in the Ottoman Empire: The Functioning of a Plural Society*, ed. Benjamin Braude and Bernard Lewis, vol. 1, 55–67. New York: Holmes and Meier.

———. 1983. *The Sultan's Servants: The Transformation of Ottoman Provincial Government, 1550–1650*. New York: Columbia Univ. Press.

Kuroki, Hidemitsu. 1993. "The Orthodox-Catholic Clash in Aleppo in 1818." *Orient* (Tokyo) 29:1–18.

———. 1998. "Zimmis in Mid-Nineteenth-Century Aleppo: An Analysis of Cizye Defteris." In *Essays in Ottoman Civilization: Proceedings of the XIIth Congress of CIEPO. Archiv Orientální*(Prague), supplement 8:204–50.

Kushner, David. 1987. "The Place of the Ulema of the Ottoman Empire during the Age of Reform." *Turcica* 19:51–74.

Labaki, Boutros. 1984. *Introduction a l'histoire économique du Liban: soie et commerce extérieur à la fin de la période ottomane*. Beirut: Université Libanaise.

———. 1988. *Éducation et mobilité sociale dans la société multi-communautaire du Liban: approche socio-historique*. Frankfurt: Deutsches Institut für internationale pädagogische Forschung.

————. 1994. "The Commercial Network of Beirut in the Last Twenty-five Years of Ottoman Rule." In *Decision Making and Change in the Ottoman Empire,* ed. Caesar E. Farah, 243–62. Kirksville, Mo.: Thomas Jefferson Univ. Press.

Lafi, Nora. 2002. *Une ville du Maghreb entre ancien régime et réformes ottomanes: Genèse des institutions municipales à Tripoli de Barbarie (1795–1911).* Paris: L'Harmattan.

————, ed. 2005. *Municipalités méditerranénnes: Les réformes urbaines ottomanes au miroir d'une historie comparée (Moyen-Orient, Maghreb, Europe méridionale.)* Berlin: Klaus Schwarz.

Lambton, A. K. S. 1953. *Landlord and Peasant in Persia: A Study of Land Tenure and Land Revenue Administration.* Oxford: Oxford Univ. Press.

————. 1987. *Qajar Persia.* London: I. B. Tauris.

Landau, Jacob M. 1973. "Ritual Murder Accusations in Nineteenth-Century Egypt." In *Middle Eastern Themes: Papers in History and Politics,* ed. Jacob M. Landau, 99–142. London: Frank Cass.

Lapidus, Ira. 1967. *Muslim Cities in the Later Middle Ages.* Cambridge: Harvard Univ. Press. Reprint, Cambridge: Harvard Univ. Press, 1984.

————. 1973. "The Evolution of Muslim Urban Society." *Comparative Studies in Society and History* 15:21–50.

Larguèche, Abdelhamid. 2000. *Les ombres de Tunis, pauvres et minorités aux XVIIIe et XIXe siècles.* Paris: Arcantères.

Laskier, Michael M. 1983. *The Alliance Israélite Universelle and the Jewish Community of Morocco, 1862–1962.* Albany: State Univ. of New York Press.

Le Tourneau, Roger. 1949. *Fès avant le protectorat: Étude économique et sociale d'une ville de l'occident musulman.* Casablanca: Société marocaine de librarie et d'édition.

————. 1957. *Les villes musulmanes de l'Afrique du Nord.* Alger: La Maison des Livres.

Leeuwen, Richard van. 1999. *Waqfs and Urban Structures: The Case of Ottoman Damascus.* Leiden: Brill.

Levy, Avigdor, ed. 1994. *The Jews of the Ottoman Empire.* Princeton: Darwin Press.

Lewis, Bernard. 1979. *The Emergence of Modern Turkey.* London: Oxford Univ. Press.

————. 1984. *The Jews of Islam.* London: Routledge and Kegan Paul.

Lewis, Norman. 1987. *Nomads and Settlers in Syria and Jordan, 1800–1980.* Cambridge: Cambridge Univ. Press.

Liauzu, Claude. 1986. "Sociétés urbaines et mouvements sociaux: état de recherches en langue anglaise sur le 'Middle East.'" *Maghreb/Machrek* 111:24–56.

————. 1989. "Crises urbaines, crise de l'état, mouvements sociaux. " In *État, Ville et Mouvements Sociaux au Maghreb et au Moyen Orient/Arab and Muslim Cities: The State, Urban Crisis and Social Movements,* ed. Kenneth L. Brown, Bernard

Hourcade, Michèle Jolé, Claude Liauzu, Peter Sluglett, and Sami Zubaida, 23–41. Paris: L'Harmattan.

Lier, Thomas. 2004. *Haushalte und Haushaltspolitik in Bagdad 1704–1831.* Beirut: Orient-Institut: Würzburg: Ergon.

Lingenau, Walter. 1994. "Al-Qāʻ al-Yahūd. The Former Jewish Quarter of Sanʻa." *Daedalos* 54:102–111.

Lockman, Zachary, ed. 1994. *Workers and Working Classes in the Middle East: Struggles, Histories, Historiographies.* Albany: State Univ. of New York Press.

Loeb, Laurence D. 1996. "Dhimmi Status and Jewish Roles in Iranian Society." In *Jews Among Muslims. Communities in the Precolonial Middle East,* ed. Shlomo Deshen and Walter P. Zenner, 247–60. Basingstoke, U.K.: Macmillan.

Longrigg, S. H. 1925. *Four Centuries of Modern Iraq.* London: Oxford Univ. Press.

Maghen, Ze'ev. 1999. "Much Ado About Wudu'." *Der Islam* 76:205–52.

Mahfuz, Najib. 1977. *Malhamat al-Harafish.* Cairo: Maktabat Misr. [Trans. Catherine Cobham. 1994. *The Harafish.* New York: Doubleday.]

Makdisi, Usama. 2000. *The Culture of Sectarianism. Community, History and Violence in Nineteenth-Century Lebanon.* Berkeley: Univ. of California Press.

Mandaville, Jon E. 1979. "Usurious Piety: The Cash Waqf Controversy in the Ottoman Empire." *International Journal of Middle East Studies* 10:289–308.

Mantran, Robert. 1962. *Istanbul dans la seconde moitié du XVIIe siècle; essai d'histoire institutionelle, économique et sociale.* Paris: Maisonneuve.

———. 1970. "North Africa in the Sixteenth and Seventeenth Centuries." In *The Cambridge History of Islam,* vol. 2A. Cambridge: Cambridge Univ. Press.

———. ed. 1989. *Histoire de l'empire ottoman.* Paris: Fayard.

Maʻoz, Moshe. 1968. *Ottoman Reform in Syria and Palestine, 1840–1861: The Impact of the Tanzimat on Politics and Society.* Oxford: Clarendon Press.

———. 1982. "Communal Conflicts in Ottoman Syria during the Reform Era: The Role of Political and Economic Factors." In *Christians and Jews in the Ottoman Empire: The Functioning of a Plural Society,* ed. Benjamin Braude and Bernard Lewis, vol. 2, 91–106. New York: Holmes and Meier.

Marçais, Georges. 1954. "La conception des villes dans l'Islam." *Revue d'Alger* 2:517–33.

Marçais, William. 1928. "L'Islamisme et vie urbaine." *Comptes-Rendus de l'Académie des Inscriptions et Belles Lettres* 7:86–100.

Marcus, Abraham. 1983. "Men, Women and Property: Dealers in Real Estate in Eighteenth Century Aleppo." *Journal of the Economic and Social History of the Orient* 26:137–63.

————. 1989. *The Middle East on the Eve of Modernity: Aleppo in the Eighteenth Century.* New York: Columbia Univ. Press.

Mardin, Şerif. 1995. "Tanzimat." In *The Oxford Encyclopedia of the Modern Islamic World,* ed. John L. Esposito, vol. 4, 183–86. Oxford: Oxford Univ. Press.

Marino, Brigitte. 1997. *Le Faubourg du Mīdān à Damas à l'époque ottomane; espace urbain, société et habitat (1742–1830).* Damascus: Institut français d'études arabes de Damas.

Marmorstein, Emile. 1969. *Heaven at Bay: The Jewish Kulturkampf in the Holy Land.* Oxford Univ. Press.

Marsot, Afaf Lutfi al-Sayyid. 1984a. "Religion or Opposition? Urban Protest Movements in Cairo." *International Journal of Middle East Studies* 16:541–52.

————. 1984b. *Egypt in the Reign of Muhammad Ali.* Cambridge: Cambridge Univ. Press.

Martin, Vanessa. 1989. *Islam and Modernism: The Iranian Revolution of 1906.* London: I. B. Tauris.

Masqueray, Émile. 1886. *La Formation des cités chez les populations sédentaires de l'Algérie (Kabyles du Djuradjura–Chaouias de l'Aurès Beni Mzab).* Paris: E. Leroux.

Massignon, Louis. 1920. "Les corps de métiers et la cité islamique." *Revue Internationale de Sociologie* 28:473–89.

————. 1924 "Enquête sur les corporations musulmanes d'artisans et de commerçants au Maroc." *Revue du monde musulman* 43:1–250.

Masters, Bruce. 1988. *The Origins of Western Economic Dominance in the Middle East; Mercantilism and the Islamic Economy in Aleppo, 1600–1750.* Albany: State Univ. of New York Press.

————. 1990. "The 1850 Events in Aleppo: An Aftershock of Syria's Incorporation into the World Capitalist System." *International Journal of Middle East Studies* 22:3–20.

————. 1991. "Power and Society in Aleppo in the Eighteenth and Nineteenth Centuries." *Revue des mondes musulmans et de la Méditerranée* 62–64:151–58.

————. 1992. "The Sultan's Entrepreneurs: The Avrupa Tüccaris and the Hayriye Tüccaris in Syria." *International Journal of Middle East Studies* 24:579–97.

————. 2001. *Christians and Jews in the Ottoman Arab World: The Roots of Sectarianism.* Cambridge: Cambridge Univ. Press.

Maury, Bernard, André Raymond, Jacques Revault, M. Zakariya. 1982–83. *Palais et maisons du Caire: Vol II, Époque ottomane, XVIe–XVIIIe siècles.* Paris: Éditions du Centre National de la Recherche Scientifique.

Mazières, Nathalie de. 1985. "Homage [to Michel Écochard]." *Environmental Design: Journal of the Islamic Environmental Design Research Centre* 1:22–25.

Mazower, Mark. 2004. *Salonica, City of Ghosts: Christians, Muslims, and Jews, 1430–1950*. New York: Vintage Books.

McAuliffe, Jane Dammen. 1991. *Qur'anic Christians: An Analysis of Classical and Modern Exegesis*. Cambridge: Cambridge Univ. Press.

McCabe, Ina Baghdiantz. 1999. *The Shah's Silk for Europe's Silver: The Eurasian Trade of the Julfa Armenians in Safavid Iran and India (1530–1750)*. Atlanta: Scholars Press.

McCarthy, Justin. 1981. "The Population of Ottoman Syria and Iraq, 1878–1914." *Asian and African Studies* 15:3–44.

———. 1983. *Muslims and Minorities: The Population of Ottoman Anatolia at the End of the Empire*. New York: New York Univ. Press.

———. 1989. *The Population of Palestine. Population Statistics of the Late Ottoman Period and the Mandate*. New York: Columbia Univ. Press.

McGowan, Bruce. 1994. "The Age of the Ayan, 1699–1812." In *An Economic and Social History of the Ottoman Empire 1300–1914*, ed. Halil İnalcik and Donald Quataert, 637–758. Cambridge: Cambridge Univ. Press.

Meier, Astrid. 2004. "Perceptions of a New Era? Historical Writing in Early Ottoman Damascus." *Arabica* 51:419–34.

Meriwether, Margaret L. 1987. "Urban Notables and Rural Resources in Aleppo 1770–1830." *International Journal of Turkish Studies* 4:55–73.

———. 1993. "Women and Economic Change in Nineteenth Century Syria: The Case of Aleppo." In *Arab Women: Old Boundaries, New Frontiers*, ed. Judith Tucker, 65–83. Bloomington: Indiana Univ. Press.

———. 1999. *The Kin Who Count: Family and Society in Ottoman Aleppo, 1770–1840*. Austin: Univ. of Texas Press.

Mermier, Franck. 1993. "La 'Commune' de San'a; pouvoir citadin et légitimité réligieuse au XIXe siècle." In *Studies in Oriental Culture and History: Festschrift for Walter Dostal*, ed. André Gingrich et al., 242–52. Frankfurt: Peter Lang.

———. 1996. *Le Sheykh de la Nuit*. Paris: Sindbad.

Merriman, John M. 1991. *The Margins of City Life: Explorations of the French Urban Frontier, 1815–1851*. New York: Oxford Univ. Press.

Métral, Jean. 2004. "Robert Montagne et les études ethnographiques françaises dans la Syrie sous mandat." In *The British and French Mandates in Comparative Perspectives/Les mandats français et anglais dans une perspective comparative*, ed. Nadine Méouchy and Peter Sluglett, 217–34. Leiden: Brill.

Métral, Jean, and Georges Mutin, eds. 1984. *Politiques urbaines dans le monde Arabe.* Lyon: Maison de l'Orient.

Miège, Jean-Louis. 1993. "Entre désert et océan: l'espace économique d'Essaouira au XIXe siècle." *Revue Maroc-Europe* 4:45–60.

Migeod, Heinz-Georg. 1990. *Die persische Gesellschaft unter Nasiru'd-Din Šah (1848–1896).* Berlin: Klaus Schwarz.

Miller, Susan Gilson. 1991. "Crisis and Community: The People of Tangier and the French Bombardment of 1844." *Middle Eastern Studies* 27:583–96.

Mitchell, Richard P. 1969. *The Society of the Muslim Brothers.* Oxford: Oxford Univ. Press.

Montagne, Robert. 1952. *Naissance du prolétariat marocain: Enquête collective exécutée de 1948 à 1950.* Paris: Peyronnet.

Moreen, Vera B. 1981. "The Persecution of Iranian Jews under Shah 'Abbas II (1642–1666)." *Hebrew Union College Annual* 52:275–303.

———. 1994. "Risala-yi Sawa'iq al-Yahud [The Treatise of Lightning Bolts Against the Jews] by Muhammad Baqir b. Muhammad Taqi al-Majlisi (d. 1699)." *Die Welt des Islams* 32:177–95.

Moreh, Shmuel, ed. and trans. 1993. *Napoleon in Egypt: al-Jabarti's Chronicle of the First Seven Months of the French Occupation, 1798.* Princeton: Markus Weiner.

Moriconi-Ebrard, François. 1993a. *Géopolis: pour comparer les villes du monde.* Paris: Anthropos.

———. 1993b. *L'urbanisation du monde depuis 1950.* Paris: Anthropos.

Morineau, M. 1976. "Naissance d'une domination: Marchands européens et marchands et marches du Levant aux XVIIIe et XIXe siècles." In *Commerce de gros, commerce de détail dans les pays méditerranéens (XVIe–XIXe siècles).* Nice: Centre de la Méditerranée moderne et contemporaine, 145–84.

Mostyn, Trevor. 1989. *Egypt's Belle Epoque: Cairo 1869–1952.* London: Quartet Books.

Motzki, Harald. 1979. *Dimma und Égalité: Die nichtmuslimischen Minderheiten Ägyptens in der zweiten Hälfte des 18. Jahrhunderts und die Expedition Bonapartes (1798–1801).* Bonn: Selbstverlag des Orientalischen Seminars.

Muhibbi, Muhammad al-. 1869. *Khulasat al-athar fi a'yan al-qarn al-hadi 'ashar.* 4 vols. Cairo: Bulaq.

Murphey, Rhoades. 1990. "Conditions of Trade in the Eastern Mediterranean: An Appraisal of 18th Century Ottoman Documents from Aleppo." *Journal of the Economic and Social History of the Orient* 33:35–50.

Nabulsi, 'Abd al-Ghani al-. 1924. *al-Sulh bayna al-ikhwan fi hukm ibahat al-dukhkhan,* ed. Muhammad Ahmad Dahman. Damascus: al-Maktaba al-Salafiyya.

————. 1987–88. "Takhyir al-ʿibad fi sukna al-bilad." Ed. and trans. Bakri Aladdin, "Le libre choix des hommes d'habiter dans toutes les contrées." In "Deux fatwa-s du Šayh ʿAbd al-Ġani al-Nabulusi." *Bulletin d'Etudes Orientales* 39–40:7–37.

Naff, Alixa. 1972. "A Social History of Zahle, the Principal Market Town in Nineteenth-Century Lebanon." Ph.D. diss., Univ. of California, Los Angeles.

Nahum, Henri. 1997. *Juifs de Smyrne. XIXe–XXe siècle.* Paris: Aubier.

Nashat, Guity. 1981. "From Bazaar to Market: Foreign Trade and Economic Development in Nineteenth-Century Iran." *Iranian Studies* 14:53–86.

Nieuwenhuis, Tom. 1981. *Politics and Society in Early Modern Iraq: Mamluk Pashas, Tribal Shaikhs and Local Rule between 1802 and 1831.* The Hague: Martinus Nijhoff.

Niewöhner-Eberhard, Elke. 1985. *Saʿda. Bauten und Bewohner einer traditionellen islamischen Stadt.* Wiesbaden: Ludwig Reichert.

Nikbakht, Faryar. 2002. "As With Moses in Egypt." In *Esther's Children: A Portrait of Iranian Jews,* ed. Houman Sarshar, 199–212. Beverly Hills: Center for Iranian Oral History; Philadelphia: Jewish Publication Society.

Noth, Albrecht. 1987. "Abgrenzungsprobleme zwischen Muslimen und Nicht-Muslimen: Die 'Bedingungen 'Umars' (aš-šurūt al-ʿumariyya) unter einem anderem Aspekt gelesen." *Jerusalem Studies in Arabic and Islam* 9:290–315.

Nowshirvani, V. F. 1981. "The Beginnings of Commercialized Agriculture in Iran." In *The Islamic Middle East East, 700–1900: Studies in Economic and Social History,* ed. Avram L. Udovitch, 547–91. Princeton: Darwin Press.

Ochsenwald, William. 1984. *Religion, Society and the State in Arabia: The Hijaz under Ottoman Control, 1840–1908.* Columbus: Ohio State Univ. Press.

Olson, Robert W. 1974. "The Esnaf and the Patrona Halil Rebellion of 1730: A Realignment in Ottoman Politics." *Journal of the Economic and Social History of the Orient* 17: 329–44.

————. 1977. "Jews, Janissaries, Esnaf and the Revolt of 1740 in Istanbul." *Journal of the Economic and Social History of the Orient* 20:185–207.

Owen, Roger. 1981a. *The Middle East in the World Economy 1800–1914.* London: Methuen.

————. 1981b. "The Development of Agricultural Production in Nineteenth-Century Egypt: Capitalism of What Type?" In *The Islamic Middle East East, 700–1900: Studies in Economic and Social History,* ed. Avram L. Udovitch, 521–46. Princeton: Darwin Press.

————. 1992. *State, Power and Politics in the Making of the Modern Middle East.* London: Routledge.

————. 1993. *The Middle East in the World Economy 1800–1914.* 2nd rev. ed. London: I. B. Tauris.

Özbaran, Saleh. 1972. "The Ottoman Turks and the Portuguese in the Persian Gulf, 1534–1581." *Journal of Asian History* 6:48–87.

Palmowski, Jan. 1999. *Urban Liberalism in Imperial Germany: Frankfurt am Main, 1866–1914.* Oxford: Oxford Univ. Press.

Pamuk, Şevket. 1987. *The Ottoman Empire and European Capitalism, 1820–1913: Trade, Investment and Production.* Cambridge: Cambridge Univ. Press.

Panerai, Philippe. 1989. "Sur la notion de la ville islamique." *Peuples Méditerranéens* 46:193–202.

Panzac, Daniel 1979. "Alexandrie: évolution d'une ville cosmopolite au XIXe siècle." *Annales Islamologiques* 14:195–215.

————. 1985. *La peste dans l'Empire Ottoman 1700–1850.* Leuven: Peeters.

————. 1987. "The Population of Egypt in the 19th Century." *Asian and African Studies* 21:11–32.

————, ed. 1991. *Les villes dans l'Empire ottoman: activités et sociétés.* 2 vols. Paris: Éditions du Centre National de la Recherche Scientifique.

Paris, R. 1957. *Histoire du commerce de Marseille, Vol V, 1660–1789: Le Levant.* Paris: Plon.

Parker, David. S. 1998. *The Idea of the Middle Class: White-Collar Workers and Peruvian Society, 1900–1950.* University Park: Pennsylvania State Univ. Press.

Pascual, Jean-Paul. 1990. "Approches de la ville du Levant. Continuités et renouvellements." *Revue de l'occident musulman et de la Méditerranée* 55–56: 9–17.

————. 1998. *Ultime voyage pour la Mecque: les inventaires après décès de pèlerins morts à Damas vers 1700.* Damascus: Institut français d'études arabes de Damas.

Pauty, Edmond. 1951. "Villes spontanées et villes crées en Islam." *Annales de l'Institut d'Études Orientales* 9:52–75.

Peirce, Leslie. 2003. *Morality Tales: Law and Gender in the Ottoman Court of Aintab.* Berkeley: Univ. of California Press.

Peri, Oded. 1983. "Waqf as an Instrument to Increase and Consolidate Political Power: The Case of Khasseki Sultan Waqf in Late 18th Century Jerusalem." *Asian and African Studies* 17:47–62.

Perry, J. R. 1975. "Forced Migration in Iran during the Seventeenth and Eighteenth Centuries." *Iranian Studies* 8:199–215.

Peters, Rudolph, and Gert J. J. de Vries. 1976–1977. "Apostasy from Islam." *Die Welt des Islams* 17:1–25.

Petit, Marianne. 1994. "La plume, la canne à pèche et le lutrin: une sociabilité de quartiers à Alep au XIXe siècle." In *Du privé au public; espaces et valeurs du politique au Proche-Orient,* 27–48. Beirut: Centre d'Études et Recherches sur le Moyen Orient.

Philipp, Thomas. 1984a. "The Farhi Family and the Changing Position of the Jews in Syria, 1750–1860." *Middle Eastern Studies* 20:37–52.

———. 1984b. "Isfahan 1881–1891: A Close-up View of Guilds and Production." *Iranian Studies* 17:391–409.

———. 1985. *The Syrians in Egypt, 1725–1975.* Stuttgart: Franz Steiner.

———, ed. 1992. *The Syrian Land in the 18th and 19th Century: The Common and the Specific in the Historical Experience.* Stuttgart: Franz Steiner.

———. 1994. "French Merchants and Jews in the Ottoman Empire during the Eighteenth Century." In *The Jews of the Ottoman Empire,* ed. Avigdor Levy, 315–25. Princeton: Darwin Press.

———. 2001. *Acre: The Rise and Fall of a Palestinian City, 1730–1831.* New York: Columbia Univ. Press.

Philipp, Thomas, and Birgit Schaebler, eds. 1998. *The Syrian Land: Processes of Integration and Fragmentation.* Stuttgart: Franz Steiner.

Philipp, Thomas, and Christoph Schumann, eds. 2004. *From the Syrian Land to the States of Syria and Lebanon.* Beirut: Orient-Institut; Würzburg: Ergon.

Pinson, Mark. 1975. "Ottoman Bulgaria in the First Tanzimat Period: The Revolts in Niš (1841) and Vidin (1850)." *International Journal of Middle East Studies* 11:103–46.

Planhol, Xavier de. 1993. *Les nations du Prophète: Manuel géographique de politique musulmane.* Paris: Fayard.

———. 1997. *Minorités en Islam. Géographie politique et sociale.* Paris: Flammarion.

Preziosi, Donald. 1991. "The Mechanism of Urban Meaning." In *The Ottoman City and Its Parts: Urban Structure and Social Order,* ed. Irene Bierman, Rifa'at Abou-El-Haj, and Donald Preziosi, 3–12. New Rochelle, N.Y.: Aristide D. Caratzas.

Prochaska, David. 1990. *Making Algeria French: Colonialism in Bône, 1870–1920.* Cambridge: Cambridge Univ. Press.

Provence, Michael. 2005. *The Great Syrian Revolt and the Rise of Arab Nationalism.* Austin: Univ. of Texas Press.

Qasatli, Nu'man al-. 1879. *al-Rawda al-ghanna' fi Dimashq al-Fayha'.* Beirut: n.p.

Qasim, Qasim'Abduh. 1987. *al-Yahud fi Misr min al-fath al-'Arabi hatta al-ghazw al-'Uthmani.* Cairo: Dar al-Fikr li'l-Dirasat wa al-Nashr wa al-Tawzi'.

Qasimi, Zafir al-, ed. 1960. *Qamus al-sina'at al-Shamiyya.* Vol. 1 ed. Muhammad al-Qasimi and Muhammad Sa'id; vol. 2 ed. Jamal al-Din al-Qasimi and Khalil al-'Azm. Paris: Mouton.

Qattan, Najwa Al-. 1992. "The Damascene Jewish Community in the Latter Decades of the Eighteenth Century: Aspects of Socio-Economic Life Based on the Registers of the Shari'a Courts." In *The Syrian Land in the 18th and 19th Century: The Common and the Specific in the Historical Experience,* ed. Thomas Philipp, 197–216. Stuttgart: Franz Steiner.

———. 1999. "Dhimmis in the Muslim Court: Legal Autonomy and Religious Discrimination." *International Journal of Middle East Studies* 31:429–44.

———. 2002. "Litigants and Neighbors: The Communal Topography of Ottoman Damascus." *Comparative Studies in Society and History* 44:511–33.

———. 2003. "The Sijills of Beirut al-Mahrousa." *Bulletin of the Middle East Studies Association* 37:58–66.

Quataert, Donald. 1973. "Ottoman Reform and Agriculture in Anatolia." Ph.D. diss., Univ. of California, Los Angeles.

———. 1980. "Agriculture in Anatolia, 1800–1914." Paper presented at the International Conference on the Economic History of the Middle East, 1800–1914: A Comparative Approach, Haifa.

———. 1983. *Social Disintegration and Popular Resistance in the Ottoman Empire 1881–1908: Reactions to European Economic Penetration.* New York: New York Univ. Press.

———. 1991. "Rural Unrest in the Ottoman Empire 1830–1914." In *Peasants and Politics in the Modern Middle East,* ed. Farhad Kazemi and John Waterbury, 38–49. Miami: Florida International Univ. Press.

———. 1993a. *Ottoman Manufacturing in the Age of the Industrial Revolution.* Cambridge: Cambridge Univ. Press.

———. 1993b. "Labor Policies and Politics in the Ottoman Empire: Porters and the Sublime Porte, 1826–1896." In *Humanist and Scholar: Essays in Honor of Andreas Tietze,* ed. Heath Lowry and Donald Quataert, 59–69. Istanbul: Isis Press; Washington, D.C.: Institute of Turkish Studies.

———. 1996. "The Social History of Labor in the Ottoman Empire: 1800–1914." In *The Social History of Labor in the Middle East,* ed. Ellis Jay Goldberg, 19–36. Boulder, Colo.: Westview.

———. 1997. "Clothing Laws, State, and Society in the Ottoman Empire, 1720–1829." *International Journal of Middle East Studies* 29:403–25.

————. 2003. "Ottoman History Writing and Changing Attitudes towards the Notion of 'Decline.'" *History Compass* 1:1–11.

Qudsi, Ilyas 'Abduh. 1885. "Nubdha ta'rikhiyya fi'l-hiraf al-Dimashqiyya." In *Actes du VIe Congrès des orientalistes*, ed. Carlo Landberg, vol. 2, 7–34. Leiden: Brill.

Raafat, Samir W. 1994. *Maadi 1904–1962: Society and History in a Cairo Suburb.* Cairo: Palm Press.

Rafeq, Abdul-Karim. 1962–63. "The Province of Damascus from 1723 to 1783, with Special Reference to the 'Azm pashas." Ph.D. diss., School of Oriental and African Studies, London University.

————. 1970. *The Province of Damascus, 1723–1783.* Beirut: Khayats.

————. 1974/1993. *al-'Arab wa al-'Uthmaniyun, 1516–1916.* Damascus: Maktabat Atlas.

————. 1975. "The Local Forces in Syria in the Seventeenth and Eighteenth Centuries." In *War, Technology and Society in the Middle East,* ed. V. J. Parry and M. E. Yapp, 277–307. London: Oxford Univ. Press.

————. 1977. "Changes in the Relationship between the Ottoman Central Administration and the Syrian Provinces from the Sixteenth to the Eighteenth Centuries." In *Studies in Eighteenth Century Islamic History,* ed. Thomas Naff and Roger Owen, 53–73. Carbondale: Southern Illinois Univ. Press.

————. 1980. *Ghazza: dirasa 'umraniyya wa-ijtima'iyya wa-iqtisadiyya min khilal al-watha'iq al-shar'iyya, 1273–1277/1857–1861.* Damascus: n.p.

————. 1981a. "Qafilat al-hajj al-Shami wa ahammiyatuha fi 'ahd al-'uthmaniyya." *Dirasat ta'rikhiyya* 2:5–28.

————. 1981b. "Economic Relations between Damascus and the Dependent Countryside, 1743–1771." In *The Islamic Middle East East, 700–1900: Studies in Economic and Social History,* ed. Avram L. Udovitch, 653–85. Princeton: Darwin Press.

————. 1983. "The Impact of Europe on a Traditional Economy: The Case of Damascus, 1840–1870." In *Économie et société dans l'empire ottomane (fin du XVIIIe–debut du XXe siècles): Actes du Colloque de Strasbourg (1980),* ed. Jean-Louis Bacqué-Grammont and Paul Dumont, 419–32. Paris: Éditions du Centre National de la Recherche Scientifique.

————. 1984a. "Land Tenure Problems and Their Social Impact in Syria around the Middle of the Nineteenth Century." In *Land Tenure and Social Transformation in the Middle East,* ed. Tarif Khalidi, 371–96. Beirut: American Univ. of Beirut Press.

————. 1984b. "al-Iqtisad al-Dimashqi fi muwajahat al-iqtisad al-Awrubbi fi'l-qarn al-tasi"ashar." *Dirasat Ta'rikhiyya* 17–18:115–59.

———. 1987a. "New Light on the Transportation of the Damascene Pilgrimage during the Ottoman Period." In *Islamic and Middle Eastern Societies: A Festschrift in Honor of Professor Wadie Jwaideh,* ed. Robert Olson, 127–36. Brattleboro, Vt.: Amana Books.

———. 1987b. "Aspects of Land Tenure in Syria in the Early 1580s." In *Les Provinces Arabes à l'Époque Ottomane,* ed. Abdeljelil Temim, 153–63. Zaghwan, Tunisia: Centre d'études et de recherches ottomanes, morisques, de documentation et d'information.

———. 1988a. "New Light on the 1860 Riots in Ottoman Damascus." *Die Welt des Islams* 28:412–30.

———. 1988b. "The Social and Economic Structure of Bab al-Musalli (al-Midan), Damascus, 1825–1875." In *Arab Civilisation: Challenges and Responses. Studies in Honor of Constantine K. Zurayk,* ed. George N. Atiyeh and Ibrahim M. Oweiss, 272–311. Albany: State Univ. of New York Press.

———. 1991. "Craft Organisation, Work Ethics and the Strains of Change in Ottoman Syria." *Journal of the American Oriental Society* 111:495–511.

———. 1992a. "City and Countryside in a Traditional Setting: The Case of Damascus in the First Quarter of the Eighteenth Century." In *The Syrian Land in the 18th and 19th Century: The Common and the Specific in the Historical Experience,* ed. Thomas Philipp, 295–332. Stuttgart: Franz Steiner.

———. 1992b. "al-'Alaqat al-zira'iyya fi Bilad al-Sham bayna al-madhahib al-fiqhiyya wa al-waqi'." *Dirasat Ta'rikhiyya* 43–44:120–39.

———. 1993a. "Arabism, Society and Economy in Syria, 1918–1920." In *State and Society in Syria and Lebanon,* ed. Youssef Choueiri, 1–31. Exeter: Exeter Univ. Press.

———. 1993b. "Craft Organization and Religious Communities in Ottoman Syria (XVI–XIX centuries)." In *La Shi'a Nell'Impero Ottomano,* 25–56. Rome: Accademia Nazionale dei Lincei, Fondazione Leone Caetani.

———. 1994a. "Registers of Succession (Mukhallafat) and Their Importance for Socio-economic History: Two Samples from Damascus and Aleppo 1277/1861." In *CIEPO: Osmanli Öncesi ve Osmanli Arastirmalari Ulusararasi Komitesi: VII. Sempozyumu bildirileri. Peç: 7–11 Eylül 1986,* ed. Jean-Louis Bacqué-Grammont, İlber Ortaylı, and E. J. van Donzel, 479–91. Ankara: Türk Kurumu Basımevi.

———. 1994b. "The Syrian 'Ulama, Ottoman Law and Islamic Shari'a." *Turcica* 26:9–32.

———. 1998. Préface to *La Ville Arabe, Alep, à l'époque Ottomane (XVIe–XVIIIe siècles),* by André Raymond. Damascus: Institut français d'études arabes de Damas, 9–10.

———. 1999. "Injustice and Complaint (Zulm wa Shikayat) in Mid-Nineteenth-Century Syria (The Case of the I'ana Tax)." In *Acta Viennensia Ottomanica*, ed. Markus Köhbach, Gisela Procházka-Eisl, and Claudia Römer, 293–301. Vienna: im Selbstverlag des Instituts für Orientalistik.

———. 2001. "The Socioeconomic and Political Implications of the Introduction of Coffee into Syria, 16th–18th Centuries." In *Le commerce du café avant l'ère des plantations coloniales: espaces, réseaux, sociétés (XVe–XIXe siècle)*, ed. Michel Tuchscherer. *Cahiers des Annales Islamologiques* 20:127–42. Cairo: Institut français d'archéologie orientale.

———. 2002a. "Damascus and the Pilgrim Caravan." In *Modernity and Culture from the Mediterranean to the Indian Ocean*, ed. Leila Tarazi Fawaz and C. A. Bayly, 13–43. New York: Columbia Univ. Press.

———. 2002b. "Making a Living or Making a Fortune in Ottoman Syria." In *Money, Land and Trade: An Economic History of the Muslim Mediterranean*, ed. Nelly Hanna, 101–23. London: I. B. Tauris.

———. 2003a. "Kingship, Caliphate or Sultanate: Why Syria Chose Kingship in 1920." In *Courtiers and Warriors: Comparative Historical Perspectives on Ruling Authority and Civilization*, ed. Kazuhiko Kasaya, 445–55. Kyoto: Kokusai Nihon Bunka Kenkyū Sentā.

———. 2003b. "Coexistence and Integration among the Religious Communities in Ottoman Syria." In *Islam in Middle Eastern Studies: Muslims and Minorities*, ed. Akira Usuki and Hiroshi Kato, JCAS Symposium Series 7, 97–131. Osaka: Japan Center for Area Studies, National Museum of Ethnology.

———. 2004. "al-Ta'ayush Bayna al-Tawa'if fi Bilad al-Sham 'ibra Sijillat al-Mahakim al-Shar'iyya." In *Les relations entre musulmans et chrétiens dans le Bilad al-Cham à l'époque ottomane aux XVIIe–XIXe siècles. Apport des archives des tribunaux religieux des villes: Alep, Beyrouth, Damas, Tripoli*, ed. Louis Boisset, Floréal Sanagustin, and Souad Slim, 75–119. Damascus: Institut français du Proche Orient; Beirut: Université de Balamand, Université Saint-Joseph.

———. 2005. "The Integration of the Religious Communities in the Workplace in Ottoman Syria and During Their Stay in Egypt." In *Society and Economy in Egypt and the Eastern Mediterranean, 1600–1900: Essays in Honor of André Raymond*, ed. Nelly Hanna and Raouf Abbas, 99–116. Cairo: American Univ. of Cairo Press.

———. 2006. "The Application of Islamic Law in the Ottoman Courts in Damascus: The Case of the Rental of Waqf Land." In *Dispensing Justice in Islam: Qadis and their Judgments*, ed. Muhammad Khalid Masud, Rudolph Peters, and David S. Powers, 411–25. Leiden: Brill.

Raymond, André. 1953. "British Policy towards Tunis 1830–1881." D.Phil. diss., Oxford University.

———. 1968. "Quartiers et mouvements populaires au Caire au XVIIIème siècle." In *Political and Social Change in Modern Egypt,* ed. P. M. Holt, 104–16. London: Oxford Univ. Press.

———. 1970. "North Africa in the Pre-Colonial Period." In *The Cambridge History of Islam,* vol. 2A. Cambridge: Cambridge Univ. Press.

———. 1973–74. *Artisans et commerçants au Caire au XVIIIe siècle,* 2 vols. Damascus: Institut français d'études arabes de Damas. Reprint, Cairo: Institut français d'Archéologie Orientale, 1999.

———. 1974. "Signes urbains et études de la population des grandes villes arabes à l'époque ottomane." *Bulletin des Études Orientales* 27:183–93.

———. 1977a. "The Sources of Urban Wealth in 18th Century Cairo." In *Studies in Eighteenth Century Islamic History,* ed. Thomas Naff and Roger Owen, 184–204. Carbondale: Southern Illinois Univ. Press.

———. 1977b. "Le Déplacement des tanneries à Alep, au Caire et à Tunis." *Revue d'Histoire Maghrebine* 7–8:192–200.

———. 1979. "La conquête ottomane et le développement des grandes villes arabes; le cas du Caire, de Damas et d'Alep." *Revue de l'occident musulman et de la Méditerranée* 27:115–34.

———. 1979–80. "The Ottoman Conquest and the Development of the Great Arab Towns." *International Journal of Turkish Studies* 1:84–101.

———. 1980. "Les grands waqfs et l'organisation de l'espace urbain à Alep et au Caire à l'époque ottomane (XVIe–XVIIe siècles)." *Bullétin d'Études Orientales* 31:113–28.

———. 1984. *The Great Arab Cities in the 16th–18th Centuries: An Introduction.* New York: New York Univ. Press.

———. 1985. *Les grandes villes arabes à l'époque ottomane.* Paris: Sindbad.

———. 1987. "Les caractéristiques d'une ville arabe moyenne au XVIIIe siècle. Le cas de Constantine." *Revue de l'occident musulmane et de la Méditerranée* 44:134–47.

———. 1989. "Espaces publics et espaces privés dans les villes arabes traditionnelles." *Maghreb-Machrek* 123:194–201.

———. 1991. "Soldiers in Trade: The Case of Ottoman Cairo." *Bulletin of the British Society for Middle Eastern Studies* 18:16–37.

———. 1992. "Groupes Sociaux et Géographie Urbaine à Alep au XVIIIe Siècle." In *The Syrian Land in the 18th and 19th Century: The Common and the Specific in the Historical Experience,* ed. Thomas Philipp, 147–63. Stuttgart: Franz Steiner.

————. 1993. *Le Caire.* Paris: Fayard. [Trans. Willard Wood. 2000. *Cairo.* Cambridge, Mass.: Harvard Univ. Press.]

————. 1994a. "Le Caire traditionnel: une ville administrée par ses communautés?" *Maghreb/Machreq* 143:9–16.

————. 1994b. "Islamic City, Arab City: Orientalist Myths and Recent Views." *British Journal of Middle Eastern Studies* 21:3–18.

————. 1995. "The Role of the Communities (Tawa'if) in the Administration of Cairo in the Ottoman Period." In *The State and Its Servants: Administration in Egypt from Ottoman Times to the Present,* ed. Nelly Hanna, 32–43. Cairo: American Univ. in Cairo Press.

————. 1995. *Le Caire des Janissaires: L'Apogée de la Ville Ottomane sous 'Abd al-Rahman Kathuda.* Paris: Éditions du Centre National de la Recherche Scientifique, Patrimoine de la Méditerranée.

————. 1998. *La Ville Arabe, Alep, à l'époque Ottomane (XVIe–XVIIIe siècles).* Damascus: Institut français d'études arabes de Damas.

————. 2002. *Arab Cities in the Ottoman Period: Cairo, Syria, and the Maghreb.* Aldershot, Great Britain; Burlington, Vt.: Ashgate/ Variorum.

Raymond, André, and Gaston Wiet. 1979. *Les Marchés du Caire, Traduction Annotée de texte de Maqrizi.* Cairo: Institut français d'archéologie orientale.

Reeder, David. 1979. "H. J. Dyos; an Appreciation." *Urban History Yearbook* 4–10.

Reid, Donald. 1970. "Syrian Christians, the Rags-to-Riches Story, and Free Enterprise." *International Journal of Middle East Studies* 1:358–67.

Reilly, James A. 1989. "Status Groups and Property Holding in the Damascus Hinterland 1828–1880." *International Journal of Middle East Studies* 21:517–39.

————. 1992a. "Property, Status and Class in Ottoman Damascus: Case Studies from the 19th Century." *Journal of the American Oriental Society* 112:9–21.

————. 1992b. "Damascus Merchants and Trade in the Transition to Capitalism." *Canadian Journal of History* 27:1–27.

————. 1993. "From Workshops to Sweatshops: Damascus Textiles and the World-Economy in the Last Ottoman Century." *Review* [State Univ. of New York, Binghamton] 16:199–213.

————. 1996. "Inter-Confessional Relations in Nineteenth-Century Syria: Damascus, Homs and Hama compared." *Islam and Christian-Muslim Relations* 7:213–24.

————. 2002. *A Small Town in Syria: Ottoman Hama in the Eighteenth and Nineteenth Centuries.* Oxford: Peter Lang.

————. 2007. "Recent Lebanese Histories of Ottoman Saida." Unpublished paper, Middle East Studies Association, Montréal.

Reimer, Michael J. 1991. "Ottoman Arab Seaports in the 19th Century: Social Change in Alexandria, Beirut and Tunis." In *Cities in the World System,* ed. Reşat Kasaba, 135–56. Westport, Conn.: Greenwood.

————. 1993. "Reorganizing Alexandria: The Origins and History of the Conseil de l'Ornato." *Journal of Urban History* 19:55–83.

————. 1994. "Ottoman Alexandria: The Paradox of Decline and the Reconfiguration of Power in Eighteenth Century Arab Provinces." *Journal of the Economic and Social History of the Orient* 37, 107–46.

————. 1997. *Colonial Bridgehead: Government and Society in Alexandria, 1807–1882.* Boulder, Colo.: Westview.

————. 2005. "Becoming Urban: Town Administrations in Transjordan." *International Journal of Middle East Studies* 37:189–211.

Reiss, Wolfram. 1998. *Erneuerung in der Koptisch-Orthodoxen Kirche.* Hamburg: LIT.

René-Leclerc, Charles. 1905. "Le commerce et l'industrie à Fès." *Renseignements Coloniaux,* supplement to *Afrique Française:* 229–53, 295–321, 337–50.

*Revue des mondes musulmans et de la Méditerranée.* 1990. *Villes au Levant. Hommage à André Raymond* 55–56.

*Revue des mondes musulmans et de la Méditerranée.* 1994. *Figures de l'orientalisme en architecture* 73–74.

Riis, Thomas. 1982. "Affaires et vie quotidienne à Alep (1870–1920): la maison Giustiniani e Nipoti, puis Vincenzo Marcopoli et Cie. Les sources orientales; un bilan provisoire." *Bulletin d'Études Orientales* 34:141–52.

————. 1999. "Observations sur la Population d'Alep au XIXe siècle." *Bulletin d'Études Orientales* 51:279–78.

Roberts, Bryan. 1978. *Cities of Peasants: The Political Economy of Urbanization in the Third World.* London: Edward Arnold.

Roded, Ruth. 1984. "Ottoman Service as a Vehicle for the Rise of New Upstarts among the Urban Elite Families of Syria in the Last Decades of Ottoman Rule." In *Studies in Islamic Society: Contributions in Memory of Gabriel Baer,* ed. Gabriel R. Warburg and Gad C. Gilbar, 63–94. Leiden: Brill.

————. 1986. "Social Patterns among the Urban Elite of Syria during the Late Ottoman Period 1876–1918." In *Palestine in the Late Ottoman Period: Political, Social and Economic Transformation,* ed. David Kushner, 146–71. Leiden: Brill.

——. 1988. "The Waqf and the Social Elite of Aleppo in the 18th and 19th centuries." *Turcica* 20:71–91.

——. 1990. "Great Mosques, Zawiyas and Neighborhood Mosques: Popular Beneficiaries of Waqf Endowments in 18th and 19th Century Aleppo." *Journal of the American Oriental Society* 110:33–38.

Rodrigue, Aron. 1990. *French Jews, Turkish Jews: The Alliance Israélite Universelle and the Politics of Jewish Schooling in Turkey, 1860–1925.* Bloomington: Indiana Univ. Press.

——, ed. 1992. *Ottoman and Turkish Jewry: Community and Leadership.* Bloomington: Indiana Univ. Turkish Studies.

Rogan, Eugene. 1992. "Moneylending and Capital Flows from Nablus, Damascus and Jerusalem to Qada' al-Salt in the Last Decades of Ottoman Rule." In *The Syrian Land in the 18th and 19th century: The Common and Specific in the Historical Experience,* ed. Thomas Philipp, 239–60. Stuttgart: Franz Steiner.

——. 2004. "Sectarianism and Social Conflict in Damascus: The 1860 Events Reconsidered." *Arabica* 51:493–511.

Rogers, J. M. 1976–77. "Waqfiyya and Waqf-Registers: New Primary Sources for Islamic Architecture." *Kunst des Orients* 11:182–96.

Rosen-Ayalon, Myriam, ed. 1977. *Studies in Memory of Gaston Wiet.* Jerusalem: Institute of Asian and African Studies, Hebrew Univ. of Jerusalem.

Rosenthal, Steven T. 1980a. *The Politics of Dependency: Urban Reform in Istanbul.* Westport, Conn.: Greenwood, 1980.

——. 1980b. "Urban Elites and the Foundation of Municipalities in Alexandria and Istanbul." *Middle Eastern Studies* 16:125–33.

——. 1982. "The Function of a Plural Society: Minorities and Municipal Reform in Istanbul 1850–1870." In *Christians and Jews in the Ottoman Empire: The Functioning of a Plural Society,* ed. Benjamin Braude and Bernard Lewis, vol. 1, 369–85. New York: Holmes and Meier.

Russell Pasha, Sir Thomas. 1949. *Egyptian Service, 1902–1946.* London: Murray.

Saad El-Din, Morsi. 1993. *Alexandria: The Site and the History.* New York: New York Univ. Press.

Sack, Dorothée. 1989. *Damaskus: Entwicklung und Struktur einer orientalisch-islamischen Stadt.* Mainz: Philipp von Zabern.

Sadowski, Yahya. 1997. "The New Orientalism and the Democracy Debate." In *Political Islam,* ed. Joel Beinin and Joe Stork, 33–50. Berkeley: Univ. of California Press.

Salt, Jeremy. 1985–86. "A Precarious Symbiosis: Ottoman Christians and Foreign Missionaries in the Nineteenth Century." *International Journal of Turkish Studies* 3:53–67.

Salzmann, Ariel. 1993. "An Ancien Régime Revisited: Privatization and Political Economy in the Eighteenth Century Ottoman Empire." *Politics and Society* 21:393–424.

———. 1995. "Measures of Empire: Tax-farmers and the Ancien Régime, 1695–1807." Ph.D. diss., Columbia University, 1995.

———. 2004. *Tocqueville in the Ottoman Empire: Rival Paths to the Modern State.* Leiden: Brill, 2004.

Sanasarian, Eliz. 2000. *Religious Minorities in Iran.* Cambridge: Cambridge Univ. Press.

Sanjian, Avedis K. 1965. *The Armenian Communities in Syria under Ottoman Dominion.* Cambridge, Mass.: Harvard Univ. Press.

Santelli, Serge. 1995. *Le Creuset méditerranéen: Tunis.* Paris: Éditions du Demi-Cercle et du Centre National de la Recherche Scientifique.

Santos, Milton. 1979. *The Shared Space: The Two Circuits of the Urban Economy in Underdeveloped Countries.* Trans. Chris Gerry. London: Methuen.

Sarshar, Houman, ed. 2002. *Esther's Children. A Portrait of Iranian Jews.* Beverly Hills: Center for Iranian Oral History; Philadelphia: Jewish Publication Society.

Sauvaget, Jean. 1934. "Esquisse d'une histoire de la ville de Damas." *Revue des Études Islamiques* 8:421–80.

———. 1941. *Alep: essai sur le développement d'une grande ville syrienne, des origines au milieu du XIXe siècle.* 2 vols. Paris: Geuthner.

Sayyid, Ayman Fu'ad. 1998. *La capitale de l'Égypte jusqu'à l'époque fatimide: al-Qahira et al-Fustat.* Stuttgart: Franz Steiner.

Scharabi, Mohamed. 1989. *Kairo. Stadt und Architektur im Zeitalter des europäischen Kolonialismus.* Tübingen: Ernst Wasmuth.

Schatkowski Schilcher, Linda. 1985. *Families in Politics: Damascene Factions and Estates of the 18th and 19th Centuries.* Stuttgart: Franz Steiner.

———. 1991a. "The Great Depression (1873–1896) and the Rise of Syrian Arab Nationalism." *New Perspectives on Turkey* 5–6:167–90.

———. 1991b. "Violence in Rural Syria in the 1880s and 1890s: State Centralization, Rural Integration, and the World Market." In *Peasants and Politics in the Modern Middle East*, ed. Farhad Kazemi and John Waterbury, 50–84. Miami: Florida International University Press.

Scheben, Thomas. 1991. *Verwaltungsreformen der frühen Tanzimatzeit: Gesetze, Maßnahmen, Auswirkungen.* Frankfurt: Peter Lang.

Schlicht, Alfred. 1981. *Frankreich und die syrischen Christen 1799–1861: Minoritäten und europäischer Imperialismus im Vorderen Orient.* Berlin: Klaus Schwarz.

Schmelz, Uziel O. 1994. "The Population of Jerusalem's Urban Neighborhoods according to the Ottoman Census of 1905." In *Aspects of Ottoman History: Papers from CIEPO IX, Jerusalem*, ed. Amy Singer and Amnon Cohen. *Scripta Hierosolymitana* 35:93–113. Jerusalem: Magnes Press.

Schneider, Robert A. 1995. *The Ceremonial City: Toulouse Observed, 1738–1780*. New York: Oxford Univ. Press.

Schölch, Alexander. 1972. *Ägypten den Ägyptern! Die politische und gesellschaftliche Krise der Jahre 1878–1882 in Ägypten*. Zürich: Atlantis.

Schroeter, Daniel. 1988. *Merchants of Essaouira: Urban Society and Imperialism in South Western Morocco, 1844–1886*. Cambridge: Cambridge Univ. Press.

———. 1994. "Jewish Quarters in the Arab-Islamic Cities of the Ottoman Empire." In *The Jews of the Ottoman Empire*, ed. Avigdor Levy, 287–300. Princeton: Darwin Press.

———. 2002. *The Sultan's Jew: Morocco and the Sephardi World*. Stanford: Stanford Univ. Press.

Schwartz, Richard Merrill. 1985. *The Structure of Christian-Muslim Relations in Contemporary Iran*. Halifax, Nova Scotia: Department of Anthropology, St. Mary's University.

Scott, James C. 1985. *Weapons of the Weak: Everyday Forms of Peasant Resistance*. New Haven: Yale Univ. Press.

Seikaly, May. 1995. *Haifa: Transformation of a Palestinian Arab Society 1918–1939*. London: I.B. Tauris.

Sekaly, Achille. 1929 "Le problème des wakfs en Égypte." *Revue des Études Islamiques* 3:75–126, 227–338, 395–454, 601–59.

Seni, Nora. 1994. "The Camondos and Their Imprint on 19th Century Istanbul." *International Journal of Middle East Studies* 26:663–75.

Serjeant, R. B., and Ronald Lewcock, eds. 1983. *San'a'. An Arabian Islamic City*. London: The World of Islam Festival Trust.

Shaham, Ron. 1991. "Christian and Jewish Waqf in Palestine during the Late Ottoman Period." *Bulletin of the School of Oriental and African Studies* 54:460–72.

Shaked, H. M. 1971. "The Biographies of 'ulama in Mubarak's *Khitat* as a Source for the History of the 'ulama in 19th Century Egypt." *Asian and African Studies* 7:41–76.

Shalabi, Hilmi Ahmad. 1993. *al-Aqalliyyat al-'irqiyya fi misr fi l-qarn al-tasi' 'ashar*. Cairo: Maktabat al-nahda al-misriyya.

Shalit, Yoram. 1996. *Nicht-Muslime und Fremde in Aleppo und Damaskus im 18. und in der ersten Hälfte des 19. Jahrhunderts*. Berlin: Klaus Schwarz.

Shamir, Shimon, ed. 1987. *The Jews of Egypt: A Mediterranean Society in Modern Times.* Boulder, Colo.: Westview.

Shaw, Stanford. 1975. "The Nineteenth Century Tax Reforms and Revenue System." *International Journal of Middle East Studies* 6:421–59.

———. 1991. *The Jews of the Ottoman Empire and the Turkish Republic.* Basingstoke, U.K.: Macmillan.

Shaw, Stanford, and Ezel Kural Shaw. 1976–77. *History of the Ottoman Empire and Modern Turkey.* 2 vols. Cambridge: Cambridge Univ. Press.

Shepherd, Naomi. 1999. *Ploughing Sand: British Rule in Palestine 1917–1948.* London: John Murray.

Shields, Sarah. 1991. "Regional Trade and 19th Century Mosul: Revising the Role of Europe in the Middle East Economy." *International Journal of Middle East Studies* 23:19–37.

———. 1992. "Sheep, Nomads, and Merchants in Nineteenth-Century Mosul: Creating Transformations in an Ottoman Society." *Journal of Social History* 25:773–89.

———. 2000. *Mosul before Iraq, Like Bees Making Five-Sided Cells.* Albany: State Univ. of New York Press.

Shinnawi, 'Abd al-'Aziz al-. 1980–83. *al-Dawla al-'Uthmaniyya dawla Islamiyya muftara 'alayha* [The Ottoman State is an unjustifiably vilified Islamic state]. 3 vols. Cairo: Anglo-Egyptian Press.

Shkodra, Zija. 1973. *Esnafet shqiptare: shekujt XV–XX* (with French summary). Tirana: Akademia e Shencave e R.P. te Shqipërisë. Instituti i Historisë.

———. 1975. "Les Esnaf ou corporations dans la vie urbaine Balkanique des XVII–XVIIIe siècle." *Studia Albanica* 2:47–76.

Shuman, Mohsen. 1995. "The Beginnings of Urban *Iltizam* in Egypt." In *The State and Its Servants: Administration in Egypt from Ottoman Times to the Present,* ed. Nelly Hanna, 17–31. Cairo: American Univ. in Cairo Press.

Shuval, Tal. 1998. *La ville d'Alger vers la fin du XVIII siècle: population et cadre urbain.* Paris: Éditions du Centre National de la Recherche Scientifique.

———. 2000. "The Ottoman Algerian Elite and Its Ideology." *International Journal of Middle East Studies* 32:323–44.

Simon, Rachel. 1993. "Jewish Itinerant Peddlers in Ottoman Libya: Economic, Social, and Cultural Aspects." In *Decision Making and Change in the Ottoman Empire,* ed. Caesar E. Farah, 293–304. Kirksville, Mo.: Thomas Jefferson Univ. Press.

———. 1994. "Jewish Participation in the Reform in Libya during the Second Ottoman Period, 1835–1911." In *The Jews of the Ottoman Empire,* ed. Avigdor Levy, 485–506. Princeton: Darwin Press.

Singer, Amy. 1994. *Palestinian Peasants and Ottoman Officials: Rural Administration around Sixteenth Century Jerusalem.* Cambridge: Cambridge Univ. Press.

Singerman, Diane. 1995. *Avenues of Participation: Family, Politics, and Networks in Urban Quarters of Cairo.* Princeton: Princeton Univ. Press.

Sluglett, Peter. 1989. "Urban Dissidence in Mandatory Syria: Aleppo 1918–1936." In *État, Ville et Mouvements Sociaux au Maghreb et au Moyen Orient/Arab and Muslim Cities: The State, Urban Crisis and Social Movements,* ed. Kenneth L. Brown, Bernard Hourcade, Michèle Jolé, Claude Liauzu, Peter Sluglett, and Sami Zubaida, 310–16. Paris: L'Harmattan.

———. 2002. "Aspects of Economy and Society in the Syrian Provinces: Aleppo in Transition, 1880–1925." In *Modernity and Culture from the Mediterranean to the Indian Ocean,* ed. Leila Tarazi Fawaz and C. A. Bayly, 144–57. New York: Columbia Univ. Press.

———, ed. Forthcoming. *Recent Research on Bilad al-Sham under Ottoman Rule: Essays in Honour of Abdul-Karim Rafeq.* Leiden: Brill.

Sluglett, Peter, and Marion Farouk-Sluglett. 1984. "The Application of the 1858 Land Code in Greater Syria: Some Preliminary Observations." In *Land Tenure and Social Transformation in the Middle East,* ed. Tarif al-Khalidi, 409–24. Beirut: American Univ. of Beirut Press.

Smilianskaya, Irene M. 1972. *al-Haraka al-fallahiyya fi Lubnan.* Ed. Salim Yusuf, trans. ʿAdnan Jammus. Beirut: Dar al-Farabi.

Somel, Selçuk Akşin. 2001. *The Modernization of Public Education in the Ottoman Empire 1839–1908. Islamization, Autocracy and Discipline.* Leiden: Brill.

Sourati, B. 1986. "La ville contre l'état. Evolution politique d'une métropole arabe: Tripoli-Liban 1900–1950." *Bulletin de la Société Languédocienne de Géographie* 20:223–39.

Sourdel-Thomine, Janine. 1954. *Mémorial Jean Sauvaget.* 2 vols. Damascus: Institut français de Damas.

Sousa, Nasim. 1933. *The Capitulatory Régime of Turkey: Its History, Origin, and Nature.* Baltimore: Johns Hopkins Press.

Stambouli, F., and A. Zghal. 1976. "Urban Life in Pre-Colonial North Africa." *British Journal of Sociology* 27:1–20.

Starkey, Janet. 2002. "No Myopic Image: Alexander and Patrick Russell in Aleppo." *History and Anthropology* 13:257–73.

Stillman, Norman A. 1991. *The Jews of Arab Lands in Modern Times.* Philadelphia: Jewish Publication Society.

Stillman, Yedida K. 2003. *Arab Dress: From the Dawn of Islam to Modern Times.* Ed. Norman A. Stillman. Leiden: Brill.

Stoianovich, Trajan. 1980. "Family and Household in the Western Balkans 1500–1870." In *Mémorial Omer Lutfi Barkan*, 189–203. Paris: Adrien Maisonneuve.

Stümpel-Hatami, Isabel. 1996. *Das Christentum aus der Sicht zeitgenössischer iranischer Autoren*. Berlin: Schwarz.

Sulayman, Hatim. 2001. "al-Aqalliyyat ghayr al-islamiyya fi Tarablus min khilal sijillat al-mahkama al-shar'iyya." In *Minorités et nationalités dans l'Empire ottoman/ al-aqalliyyat wa al-qawmiyyat fi'l-saltana al-'uthmaniyya ba' da 1516, par un groupe de chercheurs/majmu'at bahithin*, 439–87. Beirut: al-Fanar.

Sussnitzki, A. J. 1966. "Ethnic Division of Labor." In *The Economic History of the Middle East, 1800–1914*, ed. Charles Issawi, 114–25. Chicago: Univ. of Chicago Press.

Tabak, Faruk. 1988. "Local Merchants in Peripheral Areas of the Empire: The Fertile Crescent during the Long Nineteenth Century." In *Review* [State Univ. of New York, Binghamton] 11:179–214.

Tekeli, Ilhan. 1975. "On Institutionalised External Relations of Cities in the Ottoman Empire." *Études Balkaniques* 8:46–72.

Temimi, Abdeljelil. 1994. *Dirasat fi'l-ta'rikh al-'Arabi al-'Uthmani, 1453–1918*. Zaghouan, Tunisia: Centre d'études et de recherches ottomanes, morisques, de documentation et d'information.

Ter Minassian, Anahide. 1995. "Une famille d'amiras arméniens: les Dadian." In *Histoire économique et sociale de l'Empire ottoman et de la Turquie (1326–1960)*, ed. Daniel Panzac, 505–19. Louvain: Peeters.

Thieck, Jean-Pierre. 1985. "Décentralisation ottomane et affirmation urbaine à Alep à la fin du XVIIIe siècle." In *Mouvements Communautaires et Espaces Urbains au Machreq*, 117–68. Beirut: Centre d'Études et de Recherches sur le Moyen-Orient Contemporain.

Thompson, Elizabeth. 1993. "Ottoman Political Reform in the Provinces: The Damascus Advisory Council in 1844–45." *International Journal of Middle East Studies* 25:457–75.

————. 2000. *Colonial Citizens: Republican Rights, Paternal Privilege, and Gender in French Syria and Lebanon*. New York: Columbia Univ. Press.

Tibawi, A. L. 1966. *American Interests in Syria, 1800–1901: A Study of Educational, Literary and Religious Work*. Oxford: Clarendon Press.

Tignor, Robert. 1980. "The Economic Activities of Foreigners in Egypt, 1920–1950: From Millet to Haute Bourgeoisie." *Comparative Studies in Society and History* 22:416–49.

Tilly, Charles, and Wim Blockmans, eds. 1994. *Cities and the Rise of States in Europe, A.D. 1000–1800*. Boulder, Colo.: Westview Press.

Tilly, Louise A. 1992. *Politics and Class in Milan, 1881–1901.* New York: Oxford Univ. Press.

Todorov, Nikolai. 1983. *The Balkan City 1400–1900.* Seattle: Univ. of Washington Press.

Toledano, Ehud. 1985. "Mehmet Ali Pasa or Muhammad Ali Basha? A Historiographical Appraisal in the Wake of a Recent Book." *Middle Eastern Studies,* 141–59.

———. 1990. *State and Society in Mid-Nineteenth-Century Egypt.* Cambridge: Cambridge Univ. Press.

———. 1993. "Shemsigul: A Circassian Slave in Mid-Nineteenth Century Cairo." In *Struggle and Survival in the Modern Middle East,* ed. Edmund Burke III, 59–74. London: I. B. Tauris.

———. 1997. "The Emergence of Ottoman-Local Elites (1700–1900): A Framework for Research." In *Middle Eastern Politics and Ideas: A History from Within,* ed. Ilan Pappé and Moshe Maoz, 145–62. London: I. B. Tauris.

Traboulsi, Fawwaz. 2007. *A History of Modern Lebanon.* London: Pluto Press.

Trégan, François-Xavier. 2004. "Approche des savoirs de l'Institut français de Damas: à la recherche d'un temps mandataire." In *The British and French Mandates in Comparative Perspectives/Les mandats français et anglais dans une perspective comparative,* ed. Nadine Méouchy and Peter Sluglett, 235–58. Leiden: Brill.

Tsadik, Daniel. 2003. "The Legal Status of Religious Minorities: Imami Shi'i Law and Iran's Constitutional Revolution." *Islamic Law and Society* 10:376–408.

Tucker, Judith. 1985. *Women in Nineteenth-Century Egypt.* Cambridge: Cambridge Univ. Press.

Turgay, A. 1993. "Trabzon." *Review* [State Univ. of New York, Binghamton] 16:435–65.

Udovitch, Abraham L., and Lucette Valensi. 1984. *The Last Arab Jews: The Community of Jerba, Tunisia.* Chur: Harwood Academic Publishers.

Valensi, Lucette. 1977. *On the Eve of Colonialism: North Africa before the French Conquest.* New York: Africana.

———. 1985. *Tunisian Peasants in the Eighteenth and Nineteenth Centuries.* Cambridge: Cambridge Univ. Press.

———. 1986. "La Tour de Babel: Groupes et relations ethniques au Moyen Orient et en Afrique du Nord." *Annales* 41:817–38.

———. 1997. "Inter-Communal Relations and Changes in Religious Affiliation in the Middle East (Seventeenth to Nineteenth Centuries)." *Comparative Studies in Society and History* 39:251–69.

Vashitz, Joseph. 1984. "Dhawat and 'Isamiyyun: Two Groups of Arab Community Leaders in Haifa during the British Mandate." In *Studies in Islamic Society: Contributions in Memory of Gabriel Baer,* ed. Gabriel R. Warburg and Gad G. Gilbar, 95–120. Leiden: Brill.

Veinstein, Gilles. 1976. "Ayan de la Région d'Izmire et la commerce du Levant dans la deuxième moitié du XVIIIe siècle." *Études Balkaniques,* 71–83.

———. 1991. "On the Çiftlik Debate." In *Landholding and Commercial Agriculture in the Ottoman Empire,* ed. Çaglar Keyder and Faruk Tabak, 35–53. Albany: State Univ. of New York Press.

Visser, Reidar. 2005. *Basra, the Failed Gulf State: Separatism and Nationalism in Southern Iraq.* Münster: LIT.

Volait, Mercedes. 2005. *Architectes et architectures de l'Égypte moderne (1830–1950): genèse et essor d'une expertise locale.* Paris: Maisonneuve et Larose.

Volney [Chasseboeuf], Constantin-François. 1787. *Voyage en Egypte et en Syrie.* 2 vols. Paris: Volland et Desenne.

Walz, Terence. 1978. *Trade Between Egypt and Bilad as-Sudan, 1700–1820.* Cairo: Institut français d'Archéologie Orientale.

Walzer, Michael. 1966. *The Revolution of the Saints: A Study in the Origins of Radical Politics.* London: Weidenfeld and Nicolson.

Warburg, Gabriel, and Gad Gilbar, eds. 1984. *Studies in Islamic Society: Contributions in Memory of Gabriel Baer.* Haifa: Haifa Univ. Press.

Watenpaugh, Keith. 2005. "Cleansing the Cosmopolitan City: Historicism, Journalism and the Arab Nation in the Post-Ottoman Eastern Mediterranean." *Social History* 30:1–24.

———. 2006. *Being Modern in the Middle East: Revolution, Nationalism and the Arab Middle Class.* Princeton: Princeton Univ. Press.

Waterfield, Robin E. 1973. *Christians in Persia: Assyrians, Armenians, Roman Catholics and Protestants.* London: Allen and Unwin.

Weiker, Walter F. 1992. *Ottomans, Turks and the Jewish Polity: A History of the Jews of Turkey.* Lanham, Mass.: Univ. Press of America.

Weismann, Itzchak. 2001. *Taste of Modernity: Sufism, Salafism and Arabism in Late Ottoman Damascus.* Brill: Leiden.

Weulersse, Jacques. 1934. "Antioche: essai de géographie urbaine." *Bulletin d'Études Orientales* 4:27–79.

Wikan, Unni. 1980. *Life among the Poor in Cairo.* Trans Ann Henning. London: Tavistock.

Wirth, Eugen. 1971. *Syrien. Eine geographische Landeskunde.* Darmstadt: Wissenschaftliche Buchgesellschaft.

———. 1993. "Esquisse d'une conception de la ville islamique; vie privée dans l'Orient islamique par opposition . . . la vie publique dans l'Antiquité et l'Occident." *Géographie et Cultures* 5:71–90.

———. 2000. *Die orientalische Stadt im islamischen Vorderasien und Nordafrika.* 2 vols. Mainz: Philipp von Zabern.

Wright, Gwendolyn. 1991. *The Politics of Design in French Colonial Urbanism.* Chicago: Univ. of Chicago Press.

Wulff, Hans E. 1966. *The Traditional Crafts of Persia.* Cambridge, Mass.: MIT Press.

Yazbak, Mahmoud. 1994. "Jewish-Muslim Social and Economic Relations in Haifa (1870–1914) according to Sijill Registers." In *Aspects of Ottoman History: Papers from CIEPO IX, Jerusalem,* ed. Amy Singer and Amnon Cohen. *Scripta Hierosolymitana* 35:114–25. Jerusalem: Magnes Press, Hebrew University.

———. 1998. *Haifa in the Late Ottoman Period, 1864–1914: A Muslim Town in Transition.* Leiden: Brill.

Yi, Eunjeong. 2004. *Guild Dynamics in Seventeenth-Century Istanbul, Fluidity and Leverage.* Leiden: E. J. Brill.

Young, George. 1905–6. *Corps de droit ottoman : recueil des codes, lois, règlements, ordonnances et actes les plus importants du droit intérieur, et d'études sur le droit cotumier de l'Empire ottoman.* 7 vols. Oxford: Clarendon Press.

Zabbal, F. 1989. "Des rebelles aux nationalistes: la Syrie au début du XXe siècle." *Maghreb/Machrek* 123:81–87.

Zaki, 'Abd al-Rahman. 1964. *A Bibliography of the Literature of the City of Cairo.* Cairo: Société de géographie d'Égypte.

Zarcone, Thierry, ed. 1993. *Les Iraniens d'Istanbul.* Paris: Institut français de Recherche en Iran.

Zaydan, 'Abd al-Karim. 1988. *Ahkam al-dhimmiyyin w'al-musta'minin fi dar al-islam.* Beirut: Mu'assasat al-risala.

Ze'evi, Dror. 1996. *An Ottoman Century: The District of Jerusalem in the 1600s.* Albany: State Univ. of New York Press.

Zubaida, Sami. 1986. "The City and Its 'Other' in Islamic Political Movements." In *Middle Eastern Cities in Comparative Perspective/Points de Vue sur les Villes du Maghreb et du Machrek,* ed. Kenneth L. Brown, Michèle Jolé, Peter Sluglett, and Sami Zubaida, 327–41. London: Ithaca Press.

———. 1989. "Class and Community in Urban Politics." In *État, ville et mouvements sociaux au Maghreb et au Moyen Orient/Arab and Muslim Cities: The State,*

*Urban Crisis and Social Movements,* ed. Kenneth L. Brown, Bernard Hourcade, Michèle Jolé, Claude Liauzu, Peter Sluglett, and Sami Zubaida, 57–71. Paris: L'Harmattan.

———. 1991. "Community, Class and Minorities in Iraqi Politics." In *The Iraqi Revolution of 1958: The Old Social Classes Revisited,* ed. Robert Fernea and Wm. Roger Louis, 197–210. London: I. B. Tauris.

———. 1995. "Is There a Muslim Society? Ernest Gellner's Sociology of Islam." *Economy and Society* 24:151–88.

Zürcher, Erik Jan. 1999. "The Ottoman Conscription System in Theory and Practice, 1844–1918." In *Arming the State: Military Conscription in the Middle East and Central Asia, 1775–1925,* ed. Erik J. Zürcher, 79–84. London, I. B. Tauris.

# Index

Napoleon Bonaparte, 18, 20, 40, 46, 91, 95, 137, 151, 154, 173, 230

Nasreddin/Nasir al-Din (shah of Iran), 164, 173, 217

Nasser, Gamal (Jamal 'Abd al-Nasir) (president of Egypt), 152, 242

nationalism, 61, 141, 148, 150, 240, 250–52

nomads, 58, 59, 60, 63, 64, 66, 116

non-Muslims, 36, 37, 38, 39, 40, 93, 118, 136, 177, 178, 182–223, 244. *See also dhimmis*

notables *(a'yan)* in urban politics, 6, 7, 10, 17, 23, 25, 31–34, 40, 48, 53, 55–57, 60–62, 67, 69, 74, 81, 82, 84–89, 95, 97, 99, 102, 132–33, 139, 143, 146, 149, 151, 153, 179, 211, 213, 221, 222, 225–29, 233, 238–40, 244, 248, 251; Hourani's "politics of notables" (1968), 7, 25, 86–87, 146, 226, 229

*ocaks,* 91, 96, 225, 230

oil: mineral, 155, 160, 164, 166, 169, 170, 179, 180, 241, 250–52; olive, 46, 52, 65, 94, 121, 231

Oran, 17, 159, 162, 165, 178

Palestine, 23, 72, 87, 94, 147, 148, 156, 174, 203, 216

Pact of 'Umar, 187, 192, 201

Paris, 8, 14, 16, 20, 23, 24, 26, 33, 35, 63, 130, 131, 148, 149, 154, 155, 159, 164, 173, 177, 200, 217, 243

peasants: in Middle East, 28, 29, 30, 40, 43–55, 60–65, 119, 122–28, 130, 131, 137, 139, 145, 166, 240, 242, 244

Persia, 100, 134, 162, 164

Persian Gulf, 92, 98, 100, 101, 196

plague, 5, 162, 196, 205

Poche family (Aleppo), 204

Police/policing: in France, 14; in Middle East, 32, 71, 73, 79–81, 85, 97, 172, 205, 231, 246

ports/port cities, 24, 32, 33, 71, 91–101, 106, 134, 162, 179, 183, 206, 209

Port Said, 157, 166

Portugal/Portuguese, 5, 9, 98

Prost, Henri, 175

protégés (of European powers), 30, 38, 105, 136, 144, 203–5, 218, 222

provisioning, 31, 32, 40, 71–73, 77–82, 90, 152, 226, 228, 232, 234

*qadi,* 27, 29, 30, 105, 108, 128, 130, 202, 217, 227, 228

Qajar dynasty, 41, 70, 77, 164, 190, 199, 209, 247–49

*qanun,* 31, 71. *See also* law, Ottoman

quarters (of cities), 13, 37–38, 39, 40, 81, 84, 86, 93, 97, 108, 118, 136–38, 145, 148, 170–80, 194–97, 206, 212, 215–18, 220, 221, 226–28, 231, 233, 234, 238, 240, 241, 242, 245, 247, 249, 251, 252

Qur'an, 118, 186, 187, 188

Rabat, 23, 24, 36, 155, 167, 171, 175, 177, 178, 216

revolution(s): French, 13, 16, 20, 105, 134; Iranian Constitutional (1905–11), 41, 164, 247, 248; Iranian Islamic (1979), 42, 152, 242, 252, Industrial, 11, 105, 134, 154, 157; in Middle East, 2, 36, 152, 153, Turkish (1908), 55, 105

Reza Shah (ruler of Iran), 36, 41, 176, 200, 249, 250

rice, 50, 51, 52

Riyadh, 154, 157, 169, 180